Emerson

A Modern Anthology

Emerson
A Modern Anthology

Edited by Alfred Kazin
and Daniel Aaron

Houghton Mifflin Company, Boston
The Riverside Press, Cambridge

Third Printing R

Copyright © 1958 by
Alfred Kazin and Daniel Aaron
All rights reserved including the right to
reproduce this book or parts thereof in any form
Library of Congress Catalog Card Number: 59-8374

The Riverside Press
Cambridge, Massachusetts
Printed in the U.S.A.

CONTENTS

Introduction

All over this country today there are people for whom Emerson's star has never gone out, who read him with intensely personal reactions of gratitude and delight. For them Emerson is not an antiquarian subject for academic specialists, not a ready source of quotations for after-dinner speakers, not an assignment in schoolbooks to be read with adolescent indifference, but a writer who helps them to live, who encourages and rejoices them because he starts as a matter of course from a point of view about the world which they instinctively share, but which they feel they no longer have a right to believe in. And equally, there are many people who refuse to take Emerson on trust, who very properly see in him a profound and continuing influence on American literature which they deeply dislike; but however they may disapprove of Emerson, they take him very seriously, read him with meticulous disapproval, and pay him the enormous compliment of regarding him as alive and dangerous.

It is these intensely personal reactions to Emerson that explain the kind of writer he is. He is a writer who lives entirely by ideas, but who really *lives* them—he is not a philosopher, not a maker of systems or a prover of systems or a justifier of them. He starts from a conviction about man's central importance in the world which he never really elaborates, but which he accepts as necessary and evident and profoundly human—he could almost have said, the *only* human account of the world in modern, "scientific" times. The reader who instinctively agrees with him finds himself surprised and refreshed by Emerson's observations; while the reader who does not agree, who may insist not so much on proofs as on a clearer articulation of Emerson's point of view, finds himself, while generally alive to Emerson's brilliance and grave wit, irritated and frustrated by a writer who, living by ideas, simply sails off into the world on them as if he were on a personal journey, as if everything he describes had come to him first as a daily experience.

This intensely personal side to Emerson's ideas, this air of having picked up his ideas as the natural human necessities of an American and a New Englander at a certain period— this is exactly Emerson's genius and the reason why, without being a systematic philosopher, without being in the least able to prove his theories, he has affected and persuaded so many people that even today he remains, in Matthew Arnold's tribute, "the friend of those who would live in the spirit." For while Emerson is just the reverse of a systematic philosopher or a formal analyst of ideas, the very foundation of his work is the overwhelming personal importance of a point of view about the world. What makes Emerson so valuable is what keeps alive all genuine religious thinking, despite the erosion of so many ancient myths by science: it gives man a sense of his necessity and importance in the universe. As against the chaos and meaninglessness of mere unreflected experience; as against the inevitable moments of doubt and sadness and even of terror before the imponderables of man's existence, Emerson provides us with what is a *sine qua non* even to those who don't know that they have it or who think that they don't need it: a point of view, an essential attitude, a picture of man's lot, that will justify his instinctive striving, his ineradicable hope for himself in the universe.

Emerson is, in fact, essentially a religious and even mystical thinker, and it is his fundamental insistence on a "personal" religion, on man's ability to sustain a wholly individual relation to the divine, that is the basis of his appeal in modern times—especially in a country like America— and thus of the profound irritation which he inspires in traditionalists. But just as his religion consists entirely in the depth of his unsupported individual experience, so he can record it only in personal accounts, in essays and journals, through which Emerson still is able to make his readers feel that he had reached to the heart of the matter.

Emerson inspires intensely personal reactions in his readers because he interprets all experience as personal. For him literature is essentially a truthful account of a man's private thinking, a transcript of his mind. It is a record—faithful, immediate, exact, intuitive, moment by moment—of man's mysterious and moving life in a world alive with divinity, a world in which the common and homely objects can rightly be seen as beautiful, for they are pieces of the divine. Not by abstract doctrine, then; not by any effort to give formal expression to it, does Emerson convey the full significance of his inmost experience, but by the delicate and instinctive rightness with which he reports "the height of every living hour." The burden of proof falls not on logic but on Emerson's literary gift; not on the ability to argue his position but on his personal *tone;* not on ideas as ideas, but on the power and exactness with which he reports those moments which represent real life to him, and which are strung together to make the structure of his books.

Hence, although Emerson's mind is essentially religious, he operates entirely as a literary artist. It was as a writer that Emerson presented his beliefs to a great American audience, and it is as a wholly original and still astonishing writer that Emerson finds his audience now. What kind of a writer shall we call him? He is not, of course, a novelist or a dramatist—in fact, he could hardly read novels or wholly enjoy great plays for their own sake. Although he was a remarkable and inventive poet, no one can claim that poetry is the major side of his work. As we have said, he is not a philosopher—not even a philosopher like Nietzsche, who so much admired him. And though one falls back on the term "essayist," the term hardly explains why the essay form, as Emerson developed it, attains a free form that is profoundly musical and fugal, a series of variations starting from a set theme. His essays obviously have one source in the sermons which Emerson used to preach as a Unitarian minister, and some of them even retain the old-fashioned apparatus of numbered arguments, but traditional marks in Emerson's essays are quite external, for Emerson being Emerson, he follows every new turn and fancy of his mind.

The fact is that Emerson's literary genius cannot be named by any *form* which he developed; it lies in his use of traditional, even nonliterary instruments like the daily journal and the sermon. The way to understand his remarkable literary achievement is to recognize that for him everything starts not merely from the record of inner experience, from the "I" faithfully and even doggedly capturing every spiritual adventure, but from his response to those "moments," to those mystical flights, even to those special passages and "lustres" of light in other people's books, which for him were the height of all being and the reason for it. Just as for many of us, not just for the mystic, life does come down to certain moments, to certain passages in a book, to fragments of understanding, to moments of experience or parts of a landscape, that are raised above the normal flatness as illuminations and justifications of our lives, so to Emerson the really valuable and significant side of personal experience did come down to a passage in a book, a line of poetry, an anecdote out of a great man's life, a phrase, a saying, a moment. He thought in mottoes, in epigrams, in flashes of wit, in *aperçus,* in proverbs—almost in ready-made quotations. And the overwhelming importance of these "lustres," these "flashes," these glimpses, lay, of course, in their power to transfigure human experience, which Emerson regarded not dramatically, for its own sake, as most writers do today, but as that height to which everything turns, on which everything is justified.

It may be that all real spiritual experience is conveyed. only in short flights, in definitions and epigrams and "wise sayings" which give definite names to things and so convince us of their reality; they lay down a pattern of stepping-stones across what would otherwise be the terror of an utterly alien world. But it is true in general that wisdom is brief; that the intelligence works in moments which cut like a sword across the silence. Emerson's pithiness and compressiveness are by no means restricted to his spiritual vision of the world. He is, above all else, an observer and a recorder, a genius at catching life's quickness, a man who knows how to seize whatever occurs to him as a reflection of the circumambient reality in which man is placed. He is a genius of contemplativeness, and as his disciple Walt Whitman said, greatest as "a critic and diagnoser." We may complain that the contemplative mind is too stationary, that it lacks the sense of life as process, that the trouble with an almost purely reflective mind like Emerson's is that whatever it cannot *hold* in contemplation is dismissed. And one could go on to say that a purely observant kind of genius, like Emerson's, leads one to the delusion of Godlike powers, as in the modern detective hero invented by Edgar Allan Poe, and hence to the denial of man's essential frailty and humanness. True, all true: but there are times when we have to forgive a writer what it is not in his power to give us, and then we can enjoy all the more that distinct power in him which no one else has to the same degree.

The truth is that Emerson is one of the supreme examples of a kind of literary genius which is nearer the actual life of the mind, nearer to what really goes on inside of us all day long, as thinking, than to what is forcibly created, by an act of will, in dramas or novels. "Life," as Emerson says, "consists of what a man is thinking of all day." And while this thinking is not as obvious as the doing that we observe in a novel, the thinking is, in the actual process of life, what we are nearest to; it is the first screen on which life is reflected—our own minds. In an age which has turned away from external realism in all the arts, which recognizes the prime importance to human affairs of symbol and myth, of the unconscious residue in us of forces which speak to us through the mind and nowhere else, Emerson's conception of man as constantly knowing, seeking, perceptive, inward-dwelling, is particularly recognizable and illuminating. He believes that life *is* thought, that man is a reflective, noticing, seizing creature; for above all, he believes in welcoming the thoughts that rise up to our minds, no matter how odd, disturbing and unexpected they may seem.

It is because of this that Emerson called himself, in the largest and most generic sense, a "Poet"—by which he meant a type of the original man who was once entirely alive to the universe, mystically open to the now unimagined span of the full creation. By the "poet" Emerson meant the full force of that which we dimly recognize in ourselves, that other self who somehow contains in himself a deeper closeness to life. The "poet" has only to read his own mind, to be alive to the promptings of his unconscious, to trust the symbols which his mind presents to him of the outward world. Such a man is the largest possible type of the observer; he is above all the man who *knows,* for whom life comes down to those moments that contain the secret of earth. And this knowledge came swiftly to Emerson, in phrases and sentences, in bare notations that he entered first in his "savings-bank," his Journal. From this he would "quarry" sentences for his lectures, and from these prepare his essays for publication. Fundamentally, the unit of all Emerson's thought is in these Journal notes, and the remarkable thing about him as a writer is that although he had professionally to deliver lectures and to write essays, he always trusted to the spontaneous epigram, the dry reflection, the original entry, in which he met life with the greatest possible directness.

Everyone knows Emerson's genius for phrases that hit the mark and stay in the mind. He is not only one of the most quoted authors in the English language, but, like Bacon and Montaigne, Franklin and Lincoln, he is the very type of gnomic wisdom, of the pithy phrase and the keen sentence. He used this side of himself so consciously that, as he said, he "Boswellized himself." But too often, this side of Emerson, which is so obvious in his Journals, is obscured in his essays and more general works. It is in an effort to present this epigrammatic side of him, to display Emerson's genius for miniature, that this anthology has been made. We have no delusion that this is a substitute for Emerson's works. But we do feel that this anthology, drawn from the whole range of his published works, his published journals, his poems and his letters, and from that entertaining literature on him which reveals his gift for inspiring others to write about him as brilliantly (and pithily) as he did about the world, represents the essential range and unexpected width of Emerson's gift far better than those commonplace books of selections from his work which regularly feature the same well-known essays and poems, and which suggest neither the surprises in his thought nor his genius for the essential.

No, this anthology is not a substitute for Emerson's work; it is, we hope, an introduction to Emerson, in the form that is most congenial to his admirers and most characteristic of his mind. We have assembled these "nuggets," these "lustres," these prisms and facets of light, into chapters which present his daily life, his faith in human independence, his sense of the infinite symbolism lying at hand in the universe, his attitude toward his age, his belief in the hero or great man, his deep concern with art, his opinions of America, his pungent portraits of others—and of himself. We close with a revelation of Emerson the realist, on "the way things are," and on Emerson the aphorist, the maker of apothogms and sayings, the writer whose words are sometimes as swift and as keen as the felt passage of a thought through the mind itself. In this way we hope to leave an impression of Emerson's range, in the form that is the essence of his genius and in the highly compressed style with which, for him, all writing truly began.

Kinsmen, Friends and Neighbors

ALCOTT, Amos Bronson (1799-1888): reformer, educator; father of Louisa May Alcott; an intimate of Emerson and Thoreau, celebrated for his conversations and for his very yeasty brand of Transcendentalism.

ALLSTON, Washington (1779-1843): painter and writer, born in South Carolina, but after a sojourn in England and the continent, a familiar figure in Boston.

BARRON, Nancy: madwoman who was one of the inmates of the Concord poor farm. Emerson could hear her screams from his study window.

CHANNING, William Ellery (1780-1842): "Dr. Channing," as Emerson refers to him, one of the leaders of the Unitarian revolt against Calvinism, forerunner of Transcendentalism, and a leader in cultural and reform movements of his day.

CHANNING, William Ellery (1818-1901): nephew of Dr. Channing, the "Ellery" of the Journals, friend and neighbor of Emerson, Thoreau, brother-in-law of Margaret Fuller, and poet and biographer.

EMERSON, Lydia Jackson: "Lidian" in the Journals, whom Emerson married after the death of his first wife, Ellen.

EMERSON, Mary Moody: Emerson's aunt, strong-minded, intelligent, bookish, who assisted his mother in bringing up the family after the death of his father in 1811. Her influence can be detected in his style if not in his religious opinions, for he rejected her religious orthodoxy.

EMERSON, Waldo: Emerson's beloved son who died in his fifth year of scarlatina.

EMERSON, William: R. W. Emerson's oldest brother who became a successful if not a distinguished lawyer. Emerson's two younger and more promising brothers died while still in their youth.

EVERETT, Edward (1794-1865): Unitarian minister, Harvard professor of Greek, editor of the *North American Review*, Congressman, and Governor of Massachusetts. When Emerson was at Harvard, he idolized Everett and memorized his speeches. His mature opinion was somewhat cooler.

FULLER, (Sarah) Margaret (1810-1850): literary critic and social commentator, feminist, and leading figure among the women Transcendentalists. While in Italy, became supporter of Mazzini and married the Marquis Angelo Ossoli. Returning to America with her child and husband, her ship was wrecked near New York and all three perished.

GREENOUGH, Horatio (1805-1852): Emerson first met this Boston-born sculptor in Italy; "grandest of democrats," he shared Emerson's ideas on the relation between beauty and function.

HAWTHORNE, Nathaniel (1804-1864): friend (although never a close one) of his neighbor, Emerson. Hawthorne was both drawn to and repelled by Emerson's doctrines and implicitly condemned certain aspects of Transcendentalism in some of his plots and characters.

PALMER, Edward: an occasional guest at the Emerson house, an enthusiast who advocated the renunciation of money, editor of the *Herald of Holiness,* and a gentle crackpot.

PEABODY, Elizabeth Palmer (1804-1894): reformer, teacher, the sister-in-law of Hawthorne and Horace Mann; her bookshop a meeting place for the Transcendentalists in Boston; she was the friend of Emerson, Margaret Fuller, and Alcott.

PILLSBURY, Parker (1809-1898): Abolitionist and leader in woman suffrage movement.

RIPLEY, Ezra: Concord clergyman and Emerson's step-grandfather whom the young Emerson used to visit.

RIPLEY, George (1802-1880): minister and reformer, defender of Emerson's Transcendental views, one of founders of the *Dial* and of the Brook Farm community, book-reviewer and critic.

RIPLEY, Samuel (1783-1847): son of Ezra Ripley and Emerson's half-uncle.

RIPLEY, Sophia: wife of George Ripley.

STURGIS, Caroline: wife of William A. Tappan, introduced into Concord circle by Margaret Fuller.

THOREAU, Henry David (1817-1862): a neighbor and almost a member of the Emerson family, a disciple who lived some of Emerson's injunctions and developed some of Emerson's ideas beyond the scope and power of the originator.

VERY, Jones (1813-1862): poet and mystic whose poems Emerson admired and helped to edit. Very spent some time in an asylum for the insane, but Emerson said Very was "profoundly sane."

WARE, Henry, Jr., (1794-1843): conservative Unitarian who challenged the implications of Emerson's "Divinity School Address."

WEBSTER, Daniel (1782-1852): the idol of Emerson's youth whom Emerson regretfully abandoned after Webster's defense of the Fugitive Slave Law.

WHITMAN, Walt (1819-1892): the second of Emerson's original disciples whose *Leaves of Grass* owed much to the "Concord seer" although Whitman later denied such influence. But in his more candid moments, he confessed that "I was simmering, simmering, and Emerson brought me to a boil."

Symbols Used in References

Roman numerals refer to volume numbers; Arabic numerals, to page numbers.

W: The Complete Works of Ralph Waldo Emerson. 12 volumes. Boston: Houghton, Mifflin and Company, 1903–1904.

J: The Journals of Ralph Waldo Emerson. 10 volumes. Boston: Houghton, Mifflin and Company, 1909–1914.

L: The Letters of Ralph Waldo Emerson, edited by Ralph L. Rusk. New York: Columbia University Press, 1939.

E–C: The Correspondence of Thomas Carlyle and Ralph Waldo Emerson, 1834–1872, edited by Charles Eliot Norton. Boston: James R. Osgood and Company, 1883.

E–G: Correspondence Between Ralph Waldo Emerson and Hermann Grimm, edited by F. W. Holls. Boston: Houghton, Mifflin and Company, 1903.

U: Uncollected Writings by Ralph Waldo Emerson. The Lamb Publishing Company, 1912.

Chapter One

Morning, Noon and Night

The natural unit of Emerson's writing was a day. As a Transcendentalist, he believed that the most ordinary and commonplace daily experiences had their equivalent "correspondence" in the spiritual world. Life, even at its most unconscious and humdrum, could be transfigured whenever one recognized the symbolic extent of the ordinary event. As a writer, he was always at his best when he was lightest and easiest—when he casually put down, in the course of a day, his fleeting glimpse of what lay behind the actual and eventful flow of things. For him, as for all the great modern artists of personal experience, from Goethe to Proust, the cosmic—which was all his love— finally, like a sea crashing into foam on a rock, came down to a morning, to an afternoon, to rest and sleep and waking. For a day alone represented the unit of time that one could actually follow. A day, with its cycle out of darkness into life and back into darkness, represented, as Goethe had said, life in little.

Thus both as a writer philosophically concerned with the human transfiguration of time, and as a writer whose material was always the daily experience, Emerson saw in a day not merely the tangible wrested from the dark abysm and wreck of time, but a prism. Each day was full of light and ennui, of sun and shade, of brightness and danger. Each was as many colored as the iridescence of the foam which the day had caught from the sea of time. It is these contrasts in Emerson's attentive response to the many colors of the day that we have tried to illuminate in this section. Beginning with Emerson's identification of time with thought, we see him moving through the different significances of a single day. We see him thinking about the meaning of a day, recording some of his days for us, getting down the actual tang of his life and the occasional bitterness of it. Emerson is shown capturing the actual flow of a single day, then several days, in Concord. But when everything has finally been said about how a man spends his day and what a day is for, we end this section with Emerson's much misunderstood "optimism," which is not ignorance of evil but awareness of its place in the cosmic scale. So a day appears for him as the most precious gift, fraught with importance. He has the sense that "the day" supports more in our minds than we can actually stage. Above all, a day flows, it moves, it runs. In this image of time running, of the day moving on swift feet, is the image of the eternal "dance of life" that is one of Emerson's most profound—and modern—concepts.

Look sharply after your thoughts. They come unlooked for, like a new bird seen on your trees, and, if you turn to your usual task, disappear; and you shall never find that perception again; never, I say—but perhaps years, ages, and I know not what events and worlds may lie between you and its return! [J, X, 365]

You must treat the days respectfully, you must be a day yourself, and not interrogate it like a college professor. The world is enigmatical—everything said, and everything known or done—and must not be taken literally, but genially. We must be at the top of our condition to understand anything rightly. You must hear the bird's song without attempting to render it into nouns and verbs. Cannot we be a little abstemious and obedient? Cannot we let the morning be? [W, VII, 180]

The problem which life has to solve is, how to exist in harmonious relation to a certain number of perceptions, such as hunger, thirst, cold, society, self, God—it is the problem of three bodies. [J, IV, 22]

I dreamed that I floated at will in the great Ether, and I saw this world floating also not far off, but diminished to the size of an apple. Then an angel took it in his hand and brought it to me and said, "This must thou eat." And I ate the world. [J, V, 485]

DAYS

Daughters of Time, the hypocritic Days,
Muffled and dumb like barefoot dervishes,
And marching single in an endless file,
Bring diadems and fagots in their hands.
To each they offer gifts after his will,
Bread, kingdoms, stars, and sky that holds them all.
I, in my pleached garden, watched the pomp,
Forgot my morning wishes, hastily
Took a few herbs and apples, and the Day
Turned and departed silent. I, too late,
Under her solemn fillet saw the scorn.

[W, IX, 228]

To go into solitude, a man needs to retire as much from his chamber as from society. I am not solitary whilst I read and write, though nobody is with me. But if a man would be alone, let him look at the stars. The rays that come from those heavenly worlds will separate between him and what he touches. One might think the atmosphere was made transparent with this design, to give man, in the heavenly bodies, the perpetual presence of the sublime. Seen in the streets of cities, how great they are! If the stars should appear one night in a thousand years, how would men believe and adore; and preserve for many generations the remembrance of the city of God which had been shown! But every night come out these envoys of beauty, and light the universe with their admonishing smile.

The stars awaken a certain reverence, because though

always present, they are inaccessible; but all natural objects make a kindred impression, when the mind is open to their influence. Nature never wears a mean appearance. Neither does the wisest man extort her secret, and lose his curiosity by finding out all her perfection. Nature never became a toy to a wise spirit. The flowers, the animals, the mountains, reflected the wisdom of his best hour, as much as they had delighted the simplicity of his childhood.

When we speak of nature in this manner, we have a distinct but most poetical sense in the mind. We mean the integrity of impression made by manifold natural objects. It is this which distinguishes the stick of timber of the wood-cutter from the tree of the poet. The charming landscape which I saw this morning is indubitably made up of some twenty or thirty farms. Miller owns this field, Locke that, and Manning the woodland beyond. But none of them owns the landscape. There is a property in the horizon which no man has but he whose eye can integrate all the parts, that is, the poet. This is the best part of these men's farms, yet to this their warranty-deeds give no title.

To speak truly, few adult persons can see nature. Most persons do not see the sun. At least they have a very superficial seeing. The sun illuminates only the eye of the man, but shines into the eye and the heart of the child. The lover of nature is he whose inward and outward senses are still truly adjusted to each other; who has retained the spirit of infancy even into the era of manhood. His intercourse with heaven and earth becomes part of his daily food. In the presence of nature a wild delight runs through the man, in spite of real sorrows. Nature says—he is my creature, and maugre all his impertinent griefs, he shall be glad with me. Not the sun or the summer alone, but every hour and season yields its tribute of delight; for every hour and change corresponds to and authorizes a different state of the mind, from breathless noon to grimmest midnight. Nature is a setting that fits equally well a comic or a mourning piece. In good health, the air is a cordial of incredible virtue. Crossing a bare common, in snow puddles, at twilight, under a clouded sky, without having in my thoughts any occurrence of special good fortune, I have enjoyed a perfect exhilaration. I am glad to the brink of fear. In the woods, too, a man casts off his years, as the snake his slough, and at what period soever of life is always a child. In the woods is perpetual youth. Within these plantations of God, a decorum and sanctity reign, a perennial festival is dressed, and the guest sees not how he should tire of them in a thousand years. In the woods we return to reason and faith. There I feel that nothing can befall me in life— no disgrace, no calamity (leaving me my eyes), which nature cannot repair. Standing on the bare ground—my head bathed by the blithe air, and uplifted into infinite space— all mean egotism vanishes. I become a transparent eyeball; I am nothing; I see all; the currents of the Universal Being circulate through me; I am part or parcel of God.

[W, I, 7–10]

I have no hostility to nature, but a child's love to it. I expand and live in the warm day like corn and melons. Let us speak her fair. I do not wish to fling stones at my beautiful mother, nor soil my gentle nest. I only wish to indicate the true position of nature in regard to man, wherein to establish man all right education tends; as the ground which to attain is the object of human life, that is, of man's connection with nature.   [W, I, 59]

From the miracle of a day and the holiness of spontaneous thought, Emerson passes to the revelations that await the "attentive eye," the trees and leaves, refulgent summer nights and snowflakes. He conveys the mystery of landscape as he studies the "face of the earth." He celebrates carrots and turnips, the art of walking.

We want all the elements of our being. High culture cannot spare one. We want the Exact and the Vast; we want our Dreams, and our Mathematics; we want our Folly and Guilt.   [J, V, 237]

Only so much do I know, as I have lived. Instantly we know whose words are loaded with life, and whose not.

The world—this shadow of the soul, or *other me*—lies wide around. Its attractions are the keys which unlock my thoughts and make me acquainted with myself. I run eagerly into this resounding tumult. I grasp the hands of those next me, and take my place in the ring to suffer and to work, taught by an instinct that so shall the dumb abyss be vocal with speech. I pierce its order; I dissipate its fear; I dispose of it within the circuit of my expanding life. So much only of life as I know by experience, so much of the wilderness have I vanquished and planted, or so far have I extended my being, my dominion. I do not see how any man can afford, for the sake of his nerves and his nap, to spare any action in which he can partake. It is pearls and rubies to his discourse. Drudgery, calamity, exasperation, want, are instructors in eloquence and wisdom. The true scholar grudges every opportunity of action past by, as a loss of power. It is the raw material out of which the intellect moulds her splendid products. A strange process too, this by which experience is converted into thought, as a mulberry leaf is converted into satin. The manufacture goes forward at all hours.

The actions and events of our childhood and youth are now matters of calmest observation. They lie like fair pictures in the air. Not so with our recent actions—with the business which we now have in hand. On this we are quite unable to speculate. Our affections as yet circulate through it. We no more feel or know it than we feel the feet, or the hand, or the brain of our body. The new deed is yet a part of life—remains for a time immersed in our unconscious life. In some contemplative hour it detaches itself from the life like a ripe fruit, to become a thought of the mind. Instantly it is raised, transfigured; the corruptible has put on incorruption. Henceforth it is an object of beauty, however base its origin and neighborhood. Observe too the impossibility of antedating this act. In its grub state, it cannot fly, it cannot shine, it is a dull grub. But suddenly, without observation, the selfsame thing unfurls beautiful wings, and is an angel of wisdom. So is there no fact, no event, in our private history, which shall not, sooner or later, lose its adhesive, inert form, and astonish us by soaring from our body into the empyrean. Cradle and infancy, school and playground, the fear of boys, and dogs, and ferules, the love of little maids and berries, and many another fact that once filled the whole sky, are gone already; friend and relative, profession and party, town and country, nation and world, must also soar and sing.

Of course, he who has put forth his total strength in fit actions has the richest return of wisdom. I will not shut myself out of this globe of action, and transplant an oak into a flowerpot, there to hunger and pine; nor trust the revenue of some single faculty, and exhaust one vein of thought, much like those Savoyards, who, getting their livelihood by carving shepherds, shepherdesses, and smoking Dutchmen, for all Europe, went out one day to the mountain to find stock, and discovered that they had whittled up the last of their pine trees. Authors we have, in numbers, who have written out their vein, and who, moved by a commendable prudence, sail for Greece or Palestine, follow the trapper into the prairie, or ramble round Algiers, to replenish their merchantable stock.

If it were only for a vocabulary, the scholar would be covetous of action. Life is our dictionary. Years are well spent in country labors; in town; in the insight into trades and manufactures; in frank intercourse with many men and women; in science; in art; to the one end of mastering in all their facts a language by which to illustrate and embody our perceptions. I learn immediately from any speaker how much he has already lived, through the poverty or the splendor of his speech. Life lies behind us as the quarry from whence we get tiles and copestones for the masonry of today. This is the way to learn grammar. Colleges and books only copy the language which the field and the workyard made. [W, I, 95–98]

I talked yesterday with a pair of philosophers; I endeavored to show my good men that I liked everything by turns and nothing long; that I loved the centre, but doted on the superficies; that I loved man, if men seemed to me mice and rats; that I revered saints, but woke up glad that the old pagan world stood its ground and died hard; that I was

glad of men of every gift and nobility, but would not live
in their arms. Could they but once understand that I loved
to know that they existed, and heartily wished them God-
speed, yet, out of my poverty of life and thought, had no
word or welcome for them when they came to see me, and
could well consent to their living in Oregon for any claim
I felt on them—it would be a great satisfaction.

[W, III, 248]

The ancient Greeks called the world κόσμος, beauty.
Such is the constitution of all things, or such the plastic
power of the human eye, that the primary forms, as the
sky, the mountain, the tree, the animal, give us a delight
in and for themselves; a pleasure arising from outline, color,
motion, and grouping. This seems partly owing to the eye
itself. The eye is the best of artists. By the mutual action
of its structure and of the laws of light, perspective is produced, which integrates every mass of objects, of what
character soever, into a well colored and shaded globe, so
that where the particular objects are mean and unaffecting,
the landscape which they compose is round and symmetrical. And as the eye is the best composer, so light is the first
of painters. There is no object so foul that intense light
will not make beautiful. And the stimulus it affords to the
sense, and a sort of infinitude which it hath, like space and
time, make all matter gay. Even the corpse has its own
beauty. But besides this general grace diffused over nature,
almost all the individual forms are agreeable to the eye,
as is proved by our endless imitations of some of them, as
the acorn, the grape, the pine-cone, the wheat-ear, the egg,
the wings and forms of most birds, the lion's claw, the ser-
pent, the butterfly, sea-shells, flames, clouds, buds, leaves,
and the forms of many trees, as the palm.
    . . . The simple perception of natural forms is a delight.
The influence of the forms and actions in nature is so needful to man that, in its lowest functions, it seems to lie on the
confines of commodity and beauty. To the body and mind
which have been cramped by noxious work or company,
nature is medicinal and restores their tone. The tradesman,
the attorney comes out of the din and craft of the street

and sees the sky and the woods, and is a man again. In their eternal calm, he finds himself. The health of the eye seems to demand a horizon. We are never tired, so long as we can see far enough.

But in other hours, nature satisfies by its loveliness, and without any mixture of corporeal benefit. I see the spectacle of morning from the hilltop over against my house, from daybreak to sunrise, with emotions which an angel might share. The long slender bars of cloud float like fishes in the sea of crimson light. From the earth, as a shore, I look out into that silent sea. I seem to partake its rapid transformations; the active enchantment reaches my dust, and I dilate and conspire with the morning wind. How does nature deify us with a few and cheap elements! Give me health and a day, and I will make the pomp of emperors ridiculous. The dawn is my Assyria; the sunset and moonrise my Paphos, and unimaginable realms of faerie; broad noon shall be my England of the senses and the understanding; the night shall be my Germany of mystic philosophy and dreams.

Not less excellent, except for our less susceptibility in the afternoon, was the charm, last evening, of a January sunset. The western clouds divided and subdivided themselves into pink flakes modulated with tints of unspeakable softness, and the air had so much life and sweetness that it was a pain to come within doors. What was it that nature would say? Was there no meaning in the live repose of the valley behind the mill, and which Homer or Shakespeare could not re-form for me in words? The leafless trees become spires of flame in the sunset, with the blue east for their background, and the stars of the dead calices of flowers, and every withered stem and stubble rimed with frost, contribute something to the mute music.

The inhabitants of cities suppose that the country landscape is pleasant only half the year. I please myself with the graces of the winter scenery, and believe that we are as much touched by it as by the genial influences of summer. To the attentive eye, each moment of the year has its own beauty, and in the same field, it beholds, every hour, a picture which was never seen before and which shall never be seen again. The heavens change every moment, and reflect their glory or gloom on the plains beneath. The state of the crop in the surrounding farms alters the expression of the earth from week to week. The succession of native plants in the pastures and roadsides, which make the silent clock by which time tells the summer hours, will make even the divisions of the day sensible to a keen observer. The tribes of birds and insects, like the plants punctual to their time, follow each other, and the year has room for all. By watercourses, the variety is greater. In July, the blue Pontederia or pickerel-weed blooms in large beds in the shallow parts of our pleasant river, and swarms with yellow butterflies in continual motion. Art cannot rival this pomp of purple and gold. Indeed the river is a perpetual gala, and boasts each month a new ornament.

[W, I, 15–19]

TWO RIVERS

Thy summer voice, Musketaquit,
Repeats the music of the rain;
But sweeter rivers pulsing flit
Through thee, as thou through Concord Plain.

Thou in thy narrow banks art pent:
The stream I love unbounded goes
Through flood and sea and firmament;
Through light, through life, it forward flows.

I see the inundation sweet,
I hear the spending of the stream
Through years, through men, through nature fleet,
Through love and thought, through power and dream.

Musketaquit, a goblin strong,
Of shard and flint makes jewels gay;
They lose their grief who hear his song,
And where he winds is the day of day.

So forth and brighter fares my stream,
Who drink it shall not thirst again;

No darkness stains its equal gleam,
And ages drop in it like rain.

[W, IX, 248]

I beheld him and he turned his eyes on me, his great serious eyes. Then a current of spiritual power ran through me, and I looked farther and wider than I was wont, and the visages of all men were altered and the semblances of things. The men seemed to me as mountains, and their faces seamed with thought, and great gulfs between them, and their tops reached high into the air. And when I came out of his sight, it seemed to me as if his eyes were a great river, like the Ohio or the Danube, which was always pouring a torrent of strong, sad light on some men, wherever he went, and tingeing them with the quality of his soul.

[J, V, 537]

. . . so much lecturing, and now a little printing, has bronzed me, and I am growing very dogmatic and I mean to insist that whatsoever elements of humanity have been the subjects of my studies constitute the indisputable core of Modern History—to such lengths of madness trot we, when we have not the fear of criticism before our eyes, and the literary man in this country has no critic.

[J, IV, 123–124]

I went by him in the night. Who can tell the moment when the pine outgrew the whortleberry that shaded its first sprout. It went by in the night.   [J, III, 460]

Went yesterday to Cambridge and spent most of the day at Mount Auburn; got my luncheon at Fresh Pond, and went back again to the woods. After much wandering and seeing many things, four snakes gliding up and down a hollow for no purpose that I could see—not to eat, not for love, but only gliding; then a whole bed of *Hepatica triloba,* cousins of the Anemone, all blue and beautiful, but constrained by niggard nature to wear their last year's faded jacket of leaves; then a black-capped titmouse, who came upon a tree, and when I would know his name, sang *chick-a-dee-dee;* then a far-off tree full of clamorous birds, I know not what, but you might hear them half a mile. I forsook the tombs, and found a sunny hollow where the east wind would not blow, and lay down against the side of a tree to most happy beholdings. At least I opened my eyes and let what would pass through them into the soul. I saw no more my relation, how near and petty, to Cambridge or Boston; I heeded no more what minute or hour our Massachusetts clocks might indicate—I saw only the noble earth on which I was born, with the great Star which warms and enlightens it. I saw the clouds that hang their significant drapery over us. It was Day—that was all Heaven said. The pines glittered with their innumerable green needles in the light, and seemed to challenge me to read their riddle. The drab oak-leaves of the last year turned their little somersets and lay still again. And the wind bustled high overhead in the forest top. This gay and grand architecture, from the vault to the moss and lichen on which I lay—who shall explain to me the laws of its proportions and adornments?

See the perpetual generation of good sense: nothing wholly false, fantastic, can take possession of men who, to live and move, must plough the ground, sail the sea, have orchards, hear the robin sing, and see the swallow fly.

Today I found in Roxbury the *Saxifraga vernalis.*

[J, III, 270–271]

An enchanting night of south wind and clouds; mercury at 73°; all the trees are wind-harps; blessed be light and darkness; ebb and flow, cold and heat; these restless pulsations of nature which by and by will throb no more.

[J, IV, 261]

Last night the moon rose behind four distinct pine-tree tops in the distant woods and the night at ten was so bright that I walked abroad. But the sublime light of night is unsatisfying, provoking; it astonishes but explains not. Its charm floats, dances, disappears, comes and goes, but palls in five minutes after you have left the house. Come out of your warm, angular house, resounding with few voices, into the chill, grand, instantaneous night, with such a Presence as a full moon in the clouds, and you are struck with poetic wonder. In the instant you leave far behind all human relations, wife, mother and child, and live only with the savages—water, air, light, carbon, lime, and granite. I think of Kuhleborn. I become a moist, cold element. "Nature grows over me." Frogs pipe; waters far off tinkle; dry leaves hiss; grass bends and rustles, and I have died out of the human world and come to feel a strange, cold, aqueous, terraqueous, aerial, ethereal sympathy and existence. I sow the sun and moon for seeds. [J, IV, 450–451]

In the Indian summers, of which we have eight or ten every year, you can almost see the Indians under the trees in the wood. These are the reconciling days which come to graduate the autumn into winter, and to comfort us after the first attacks of the cold. Soothsayers, prediction as well as memory, they look over December and January into the crepuscular light of March and April. [J, VI, 281]

In this finest of all Indian summer days it seems sad that each of us can only spend it once. We sigh for the thousand heads and thousand bodies of the Indian gods, that we might celebrate its immense beauty in many ways and places, and absorb all its good. [J, VII, 122]

The moon and Jupiter side by side last night stemmed the sea of clouds and plied their voyage in convoy through the sublime Deep as I walked the old and dusty road. The snow and the enchantment of the moonlight make all landscapes alike, and the road that is so tedious and homely that I never take it by day—by night is Italy or Palmyra. In these divine pleasures permitted to me of walks in the June night under moon and stars, I can put my life as a fact before me and stand aloof from its honor and shame.

[J, IV, 499]

'Tis the coldest November I have ever known. This morning the mercury is at 26. Yesterday afternoon cold, fine

ride with Ellery to Sudbury Inn, and mounted the side of
Nobscot. Finest picture through wintry air of the russet
Massachusetts. The landscape is democratic, not gathered
into one city or baronial castle, but equally scattered into
these white steeples, round which a town clusters in every
place where six roads meet, or where a river branches or
falls, or where the pan of soil is a little deeper. The horizon
line marched by hills tossing like waves in a storm: firm
indigo line. 'Tis a pretty revolution which is effected in
the landscape by simply turning your head upside down, or,
looking through your legs: an infinite softness and loveliness is added to the picture. It changes the landscape at
once from November to June, or, as Ellery declared, makes
Campagna of it at once; so, he said, Massachusetts is Italy
upside down.   [J, VII, 555–556]

Every day shows a new thing to veteran walkers. Yesterday reflections of trees in the ice: snowflakes, perfect
rowels, on the ice; beautiful groups of icicles all along
the eastern shore of Flint's Pond, in which, especially
where encrusting the bough of a tree, you have the union
of the most flowing with the most fixed.   [J, VIII, 72]

A thaw for more than a week and three days of heavenly
weather, bringing all mythology on their breezy dawns.
Down falls the water from the steeps; up shoots the northern light after sunset from the horizon. But Nature seems
a dissipated hussy. She seduces us from all work; listen
to her rustling leaves—to the invitations which each blue
peak and rolling river and fork of woodland road offers—
and we should never wield the shovel or the trowel.

[J, VII, 6]

Oct. 30, 1841. On this wonderful day when Heaven and
earth seem to glow with magnificence, and all the wealth
of all the elements is put under contribution to make the
world fine, as if Nature would indulge her offspring, it
seemed ungrateful to hide in the house. Are there not dull
days enough in the year for you to write and read in, that
you should waste this glittering season when Florida and

Cuba seem to have left their seats and come to visit us with all their shining hours, and almost we expect to see the jasmine and cactus burst from the ground instead of these last gentians and asters which have loitered to attend this latter glory of the year? All insects are out, all birds come forth, the very cattle that lie on the ground seem to have great thoughts, and Egypt and India look from their eyes.

[W, III, 329; J, VI, 113–114]

Among fossil remains, the willow and the pine appear with the ferns. They bend all day to every wind; the cart-wheel in the road may crush them; every passenger may strike off a twig with his cane; every boy cuts them for a whistle; the cow, the rabbit, the insect, bite the sweet and tender bark; yet, in spite of accident and enemy, their gentle persistency lives when the oak is shattered by storm, and grows in the night and snow and cold. When I see in these brave plants this vigor and immortality in weakness, I find a sudden relief and pleasure in observing the mighty law of vegetation, and I think it more grateful and health-giving than any news I am likely to find of man in the journals, and better than Washington politics.   [W, VIII, 152–153]

One long disgust is the sea. No personal bribe would hire one who loves the present moment. Who am I to be treated in this ignominious manner, tipped up, shoved against the side of the house, rolled over, suffocated with bilge mephitis and stewing-oil? These lack-lustre days go whistling over us and are those intercalaries I have often asked for, and am cursed now with—the worthless granting of my prayer.   [J, VII, 494]

The first care of a man settling in the country should be to open the face of the earth to himself by a little knowledge of Nature, or a great deal, if he can; of birds, plants, rocks, astronomy; in short, the art of taking a walk. This will draw the sting out of frost, dreariness out of November and March, and the drowsiness out of August.

[W, VIII, 151]

Pope and Johnson and Addison write as if they had never seen the face of the country, but had only read of trees and rivers in books. The striped fly that eats our squash and melon vines, the rosebug, the corn worm, the red old leaf of the vines that entices the eye to new search for the lurking strawberry, the thicket and little bowers of the pea-vine, the signs of ripeness and all the hints of the garden, these grave city writers never knew. The towers of white blossoms which the chestnut tree uplifts in the landscape in July, the angle of strength (almost a right angle), at which the oak puts out its iron arms; the botany of the meadows and water sides—what had Queen Anne's wits to do with these creatures? Did they ever prick their fingers with a thorn of a gooseberry? Did they ever hear the squeak of a bat or see his flitting? [J, IV, 259–260]

A man must have aunts and cousins, must buy carrots and turnips, must have barn and woodshed, must go to market and to the blacksmith's shop, must saunter and sleep and be inferior and silly. [J, IV, 465]

"It is as easy as falling."—In nature nothing is done but in the cheapest way. When the fruit is ripe, it *falls*. When the fruit is despatched, the leaf *falls*. The circuit of the waters is mere falling; the walking of man and all animals is a falling forward. All our manual labor and works of strength, as prying, splitting, digging, rowing, etc., are done by dint of continual falling; and the globe and the globes, earth, moon, sun, comet, star, fall forever and ever. Nature works by short ways. [J, V, 163]

The hurts of the husbandmen are many. As soon as the heat bursts his vine-seed and the cotyledons open, the striped yellow bugs and the stupid squash-bug, smelling like a decomposing pear, sting the little plants to death and destroy the hope of melons. And as soon as the grass is well cut and spread on the ground, the thunderclouds, which are the bugs of the haymakers, come growling down the heaven and make tea of his hay. [J, VI, 388]

I too have a new plaything, the best I ever had—a wood-lot. Last fall I bought a piece of more than forty acres, on the border of a little lake half a mile wide and more, called Walden Pond—a place to which my feet have for years been accustomed to bring me once or twice a week at all seasons. My lot to be sure is on the farther side of the water, not so familiar to me as the nearer shore. Some of the wood is an old growth, but most of it has been cut off within twenty years and is growing thriftily. In these May days, when maples, poplars, oaks, birches, walnut, and pine are in their spring glory, I go thither every afternoon, and cut with my hatchet an Indian path through the thicket all along the bold shore, and open the finest pictures.

My two little girls know the road now, though it is nearly two miles from my house, and find their way to the spring at the foot of a pine grove, and with some awe to the ruins of a village of shanties, all overgrown with mullein, which the Irish who built the railroad left behind them. At a good distance in from the shore the land rises to a rocky head, perhaps sixty feet above the water. Thereon I think to place a hut; perhaps it will have two stories and be a petty tower, looking out to Monadnoc and other New Hampshire mountains. There I hope to go with book and pen when good hours come. [E–C, II, 101–102]

I have found my advantage in going in summer to a country inn, in winter to a city hotel, with a task which would not prosper at home. I thus secured a more absolute seclusion; for it is almost impossible for a housekeeper who is in the country a small farmer, to exclude interruptions and even necessary orders, though I bar out by system all I can, and resolutely omit, to my constant damage, all that can be omitted. At home, the day is cut into short strips. In the hotel, I have no hours to keep, no visits to make or receive, and I command an astronomic leisure. I forget rain, wind, cold and heat. At home, I remember in my library the wants of the farm, and have all too much sympathy. I envy the abstraction of some scholars I have known, who could sit on a curbstone in State Street, put up their back, and solve their problem. I have more womanly eyes. All the conditions must be right for my success, slight as that is. What untunes is as bad as what cripples or stuns me. Novelty, surprise, change of scene, refresh the artist—"break up the tiresome old roof of heaven into new forms," as Hafiz said. The seashore and the taste of two metals in contact, and our enlarged powers in the presence, or rather at the approach and at the departure of a friend, and the mixture of lie in truth, and the experience of poetic creativeness which is not found in staying at home nor yet in travelling, but in transitions from one to the other, which must therefore be adroitly managed to present as much transitional surface as possible—these are the types or conditions of this power.

[W, VIII, 288–289]

Few men know how to take a walk. The qualifications of a professor are endurance, plain clothes, old shoes, an eye for Nature, good humor, vast curiosity, good speech, good silence and nothing too much. If a man tells me that he has an intense love of Nature, I know, of course, that he has none. Good observers have the manners of trees and animals, their patient good sense, and if they add words, 'tis only when words are better than silence. But a loud singer, or a story-teller, or a vain talker profanes the river and the forest, and is nothing like so good company as a dog.

[W, XII, 142]

. . . go into the forest, you shall find all new and undescribed. The honking of the wild geese flying by night; the thin note of the companionable titmouse in the winter day; the fall of swarms of flies, in autumn, from combats high in the air, pattering down on the leaves like rain; the angry hiss of the wood-birds; the pine throwing out its pollen for the benefit of the next century; the turpentine exuding from the tree—and indeed any vegetation, any animation, any and all, are alike unattempted. The man who stands on the seashore, or who rambles in the woods, seems to be the first man that ever stood on the shore, or entered a grove, his sensations and his world are so novel and strange. Whilst I read the poets, I think that nothing new can be said about morning and evening. But when I see the daybreak I am not reminded of these Homeric, or Shakespearean, or Miltonic, or Chaucerian pictures. No, but I feel perhaps the pain of an alien world; a world not yet subdued by the thought; or I am cheered by the moist, warm, glittering, budding, melodious hour, that takes down the narrow walls of my soul, and extends its life and pulsation to the very horizon. *That* is morning, to cease for a bright hour to be a prisoner of this sickly body, and to become as large as nature.

The noonday darkness of the American forest, the deep, echoing, aboriginal woods, where the living columns of the oak and fir tower up from the ruins of the trees of the last millenium; where, from year to year, the eagle and the crow see no intruder; the pines, bearded with savage moss, yet touched with grace by the violets at their feet; the broad, cold lowland which forms its coat of vapor with the stillness of subterranean crystallization; and where the traveller, amid the repulsive plants that are native in the swamp, thinks with pleasing terror of the distant town; this beauty, haggard and desert beauty, which the sun and the moon, the snow and the rain, repaint and vary, has never been recorded by art, yet is not indifferent to any passenger.

[W, I, 168–169]

I went into the woods. I found myself not wholly present there. If I looked at a pine-tree or an aster, *that* did not seem to be Nature. Nature was still elsewhere: this, or this was but outskirt and far-off reflection and echo of the triumph that had passed by and was now at its glancing splendor and heyday—perchance in the neighboring fields, or, if I stood in the field, then in the adjacent woods. Always the present object gave me this sense of the stillness that follows a pageant that has just gone by. [J, V, 455–456]

In this refulgent summer, it has been a luxury to draw the breath of life. The grass grows, the buds burst, the meadow is spotted with fire and gold in the tint of flowers. The air is full of birds, and sweet with the breath of the pine, the balm-of-Gilead, and the new hay. Night brings no gloom to the heart with its welcome shade. Through the transparent darkness the stars pour their almost spiritual rays. Man under them seems a young child, and his huge globe a toy. The cool night bathes the world as with a river, and prepares his eyes again for the crimson dawn. The mystery of nature was never displayed more happily. The corn and the wine have been freely dealt to all creatures, and the never-broken silence with which the old bounty goes forward has not yielded yet one word of explanation. One is constrained to respect the perfection of this world in which our senses converse. How wide; how rich; what invitation from every property it gives to every faculty of man! In its fruitful soils; in its navigable sea; in its mountains of metal and stone; in its forests of all woods; in its animals; in its chemical ingredients; in the powers and path of light, heat, attraction and life, it is well worth the pith and heart of great men to subdue and enjoy it. The planters, the mechanics, the inventors, the astronomers, the builders of cities, and the captains, history delights to honor.

But when the mind opens and reveals the laws which traverse the universe and make things what they are, then shrinks the great world at once into a mere illustration and fable of this mind. What am I? and What is? asks the human spirit with a curiosity new-kindled, but never to be quenched. Behold these outrunning laws, which our imperfect apprehension can see tend this way and that, but not come full circle. Behold these infinite relations, so like, so unlike; many, yet one. I would study, I would know, I would admire forever. These works of thought have been the entertainments of the human spirit in all ages.

A more secret, sweet, and overpowering beauty appears to man when his heart and mind open to the sentiment of virtue. Then he is instructed in what is above him. He learns that his being is without bound; that to the good, to the perfect, he is born, low as he now lies in evil and weakness. That which he venerates is still his own, though he has not realized it yet. *He ought.* He knows the sense of that grand word, though his analysis fails to render account of it. When in innocency or when by intellectual perception he attains to say, "I love the Right; Truth is beautiful within and without for evermore. Virtue, I am thine; save me; use me; thee will I serve, day and night, in great, in small, that I may be not virtuous, but virtue;"—then is the end of the creation answered, and God is well pleased.

[W, I, 119–121]

The sky is the daily bread of the eyes. What sculpture in these hard clouds; what expression of immense amplitude in this dotted and rippled rack, here firm and continental, there vanishing into plumes and auroral gleams. No crowding; boundless, cheerful, and strong. [J, VI, 410]

If nature is "boundless, cheerful, and strong," it is also rough and ferocious, and man himself is filled with the black Earth Spirit. But the cataclysms of nature are less to be feared than man-made tyrannies and the risks of self-imprisonment.

It is curious to see how a creature so feeble and vulnerable as a man, who, unarmed, is no match for the wild beasts, tiger, or crocodile, none for the frost, none for the sea, none for fog or a damp air, or the feeble fork of a poor worm— each of a thousand petty accidents puts him to death every day—is yet able to subdue to his will these terrific forces, and more than these. His whole frame is responsive to the world, part for part, every sense, every pore to a new element, so that he seems to have as many talents as there are qualities in Nature. No force but is his force. He does not possess them, he is a pipe through which their currents flow. If a straw be held still in the direction of the ocean-current, the sea will pour through it as through Gibraltar. If he should measure strength with them, if he should fight the sea and the whirlwind with his ship, he would snap his spars, tear his sails, and swamp his bark; but by cunningly dividing the force, tapping the tempest for a little side-wind, he uses the monsters, and they carry him where he would go.

[W, X, 73–74]

The mid-world is best. Nature, as we know her, is no saint. The lights of the church, the ascetics, Gentoos and corn-eaters, she does not distinguish by any favor. She comes eating and drinking and sinning. Her darlings, the great, the strong, the beautiful, are not children of our law; do not come out of the Sunday School, nor weigh their food, nor punctually keep the commandments. If we will be strong with her strength we must not harbor such disconsolate consciences, borrowed too from the consciences of other nations. We must set up the strong present tense against all the rumors of wrath, past or to come.

[W, III, 64]

The terrible aristocracy that is in Nature. Real people dwelling with the real, face to face, undaunted: then, far down, people of taste, people dwelling in a relation, or rumor, or influence of good and fair, entertained by it, superficially touched, yet charmed by these shadows—and, far below these, gross and thoughtless, the animal man, billows of chaos, down to the dancing and menial organizations.   [W, X, 33]

I know how steep the contrast of condition looks; such excess here and such destitution there; like entire chance, like the freaks of the wind, heaping the snow-drift in gorges, stripping the plain; such despotism of wealth and comfort in banquet-halls, whilst death is in the pots of the wretched —that it behooves a good man to walk with tenderness and heed amidst so much suffering.   [W, X, 46]

Earth Spirit, living, a black river like that swarthy stream which rushes through the human body is thy nature, demoniacal, warm, fruitful, sad, nocturnal.   [J, VI, 347]

I please myself with getting my nail-box set in the snuggest corner of the barn-chamber and well filled with nails, and gimlet, pincers, screwdriver and chisel. Herein I find an old joy of youth, of childhood, which perhaps all domestic children share—the catlike love of garrets, barns and corn-chambers, and of the conveniences of long housekeeping. It is quite genuine. When it occurs today, I ask, Have others the same? Once I should not have thought of such a question. What I loved, I supposed all children loved and knew, and therefore I did not name them. We were at accord. But much conversation, much comparison, apprises us of difference. The first effect of this new learning is to incline to hide our tastes. As they differ, we must be wrong. Afterwards some person comes and wins *éclat* by simply describing this old but concealed fancy of ours. Then we immediately learn to value all the parts of our nature, to rely on them as self-authorized and that to publish them is to please others. So now the nail-box figures for its value in my Journal.

We are indeed discriminated from each other by very slight inequalities which, by their accumulation, constitute at last broad contrasts. Genius surprises us with every word. It does not surprise itself. It is moving by the selfsame law as you obey in your daily cogitation, and one day you will tread without wonder the same steps.

[J, IV, 283–284]

. . . life takes its color and quality not from the days, but the dawns. The lucid intervals are like drowning men's moments, equivalent to the foregoing years. Besides, Nature *uses* us. We live but little for ourselves, a good deal for our children, and strangers. Each man is one more lump of clay to hold the world together.　[E–C, II, 244]

My life is a May game, I will live as I like. I defy your strait-laced, weary, social ways and modes. Blue is the sky, green the fields and groves, fresh the springs, glad the rivers, and hospitable the splendor of sun and star. I will play my game out. And if any shall say me nay, shall come out with swords and staves against me to prick me to death for their foolish laws—come and welcome. I will not look grave for such a fool's matter. I cannot lose my cheer for such trumpery. Life is a May game still.　[J, V, 215–216]

. . . Nature is no sentimentalist—does not cosset or pamper us. We must see that the world is rough and surly, and will not mind drowning a man or a woman, but swallows your ship like a grain of dust. The cold, inconsiderate of persons, tingles your blood, benumbs your feet, freezes a man like an apple. The diseases, the elements, fortune, gravity, lightning, respect no persons. The way of Providence is a little rude. The habit of snake and spider, the snap of the tiger and other leapers and bloody jumpers, the crackle of the bones of his prey in the coil of the anaconda—these are in the system, and our habits are like theirs. You have just dined, and however scrupulously the slaughter-house is concealed in the graceful distance of miles, there is complicity, expensive races—race living at the expense of race. The planet is liable to shocks from comets, perturbations from planets, rendings from earthquake and volcano, alterations of climate, precessions of equinoxes. Rivers dry up by opening of the forest. The sea changes its bed. Towns and counties fall into it. At Lisbon an earthquake killed men like flies. At Naples three years ago ten thousand persons were crushed in a few minutes. The scurvy at sea, the sword of the climate in the west of Africa, at Cayenne, at Panama, at New Orleans, cut off men like a massacre. Our western prairie shakes with fever and ague. The cholera, the smallpox, have proved as mortal to some tribes as a frost to the crickets, which, having filled the summer with noise, are silenced by a fall of the temperature of one night. Without uncovering what does not concern us, or counting how many species of parasites hang on a bombyx, or groping after intestinal parasites or infusory biters, or the obscurities of alternate generation—the forms of the shark, the *labrus*, the jaw of the sea-wolf paved with crushing teeth, the weapons of the grampus, and other warriors hidden in the sea, are hints of ferocity in the interiors of nature. Let us not deny it up and down. Providence has a wild, rough, incalculable road to its end, and it is of no use to try to whitewash its huge, mixed instrumentalities, or to dress up that terrific benefactor in a clean shirt and white neckcloth of a student in divinity.

Will you say, the disasters which threaten mankind are exceptional, and one need not lay his account for cataclysms every day? Aye, but what happens once may happen again, and so long as these strokes are not to be parried by us they must be feared.

But these shocks and ruins are less destructive to us than the stealthy power of other laws which act on us daily. An expense of ends to means is fate—organization tyrannizing over character. The menagerie, or forms and powers of the spine, is a book of fate; the bill of the bird, the skull of the snake, determines tyrannically its limits. So is the scale of races, of temperaments; so is sex; so is climate; so is the reaction of talents imprisoning the vital power in certain directions. Every spirit makes its house; but afterwards the house confines the spirit. [W, VI, 6–9]

Emerson sits in "a dark corner." He hears the cries of a madwoman and is afraid in his solitude; he lives with death, is humiliated in his dreams, and broods over the insults that nature visits upon decrepit men. Yet he refuses to read his private miseries into the cosmos. "Look, look, old mole! there, straight up before you, is the magnificent sun."

Yesterday I went to the Athenaeum and looked through journals and books—for wit, for excitement, to wake in me the muse. In vain, and in vain. And am I yet to learn that the God dwells within? That books are but crutches, the resorts of the feeble and lame, which, if used by the strong, weaken the muscular power, and become necessary aids. I return home. Nature still solicits me. Overhead the sanctities of the stars shine forevermore, and to me also, pouring satire on the pompous business of the day which they close, and making the generations of men show slight and evanescent. A man is but a bug, the earth but a boat, a cockle, drifting under their old light. [J, IV, 258]

Now for near five years I have been indulged by the gracious Heaven in my long holiday in this goodly house of mine, entertaining and entertained by so many worthy and gifted friends, and all this time poor Nancy Barron, the mad-woman, has been screaming herself hoarse at the Poorhouse across the brook and I still hear her whenever I open my window. [J, V, 422–423]

I cannot . . . travel with parties of pleasure or with parties of business. The frivolous make me lonely. Neither can
I well go to see those whom I esteem, unless they also
esteem me, for I can bestow my time well at home. I have
thus found that I cannot visit anyone with advantage for a
longer time than one or two hours.   [J, V, 445]

Here I am in a dark corner again. We have no one example of the poetic life realized, therefore all we say seems
bloated. If life is sad and do not content us, if the heavens
are brass, and rain no sweet thoughts on us, and especially
we have nothing to say to shipwrecked and self-tormenting
and young-old people, let us hold our tongues. . . . And if
to my soul the day does not seem dark, nor the cause lost,
why should I use such ruinous courtesy as to concede that
God has failed, because the plain colors or the storm-suit
of grey clouds in which the day is drest, do not please the
rash fancy of my companions? Patience and truth, patience
with our own frosts and negations, and few words must
serve. . . . If our sleeps are long, if our flights are short, if
we are not plumed and painted like orioles and Birds of
Paradise, but like sparrows and plebeian birds, if our taste
and training are earthen, let that fact be humbly and happily
borne with. The wise God beholds that also with compla-
cency. Wine and honey are good, but so are rice and meal.
Perhaps all that is not performance is preparation, or performance that shall be.   [J, VI, 80–81]

Our philosophy is to *wait*. We have retreated on Patience,
transferring our oft-shattered hope now to larger and eternal
good. We meant well, but our uncle was crazy and must be
restrained from waking the house. The roof leaked, we were
out of wood, our sisters were unmarried and must be maintained; there were taxes to pay, and notes, and, alas, a tomb
to build: we were obliged continually to postpone our best
action, and that which was life to do could only be smug-
gled in to odd moments of the month and year. Then we
say, Dear God, but the life of man is not by man, it is
consentaneous and far-related, it came with the sun and
Nature, it is crescive and vegetative, and it is with it as
with the sun and the grass.   [J, VII, 520–521]

Solitude is fearsome and heavy-hearted. I have never known a man who had so much good accumulated upon him as I have. Reason, health, wife, child, friends, competence, reputation, the power to inspire, and the power to please; yet, leave me alone a few days, and I creep about as if in expectation of a calamity. My mother, my brother, are at New York. A little farther, across the sea, is my friend Thomas Carlyle. In the Islands I have another friend, it seems. I will love you all and be happy in your love. My gentle wife has an angel's heart, and for my boy, his grief is more beautiful than other people's joy.

Carlyle, too: ah, my friend! I thought, as I looked at your book today, which all the brilliant so admire, that you have spoiled it for me. Why, I say, should I read this book? The man himself is mine: he can sit under trees of Paradise and tell me a hundred histories deeper, truer, dearer than this, all the eternal days of God. I shall not tire, I shall not shame him: we shall be children in heart and men in counsel and in act. The pages which to others look so rich and alluring, to me have a frigid and marrowless air, for the warm hand and heart I have an estate in, and the living eye of which I can almost discern across the sea some sparkles. I think my affection to that man really incapacitates me from reading his book. In the windy night, in the sordid day, out of banks and bargains and disagreeable business, I espy you; and run to my pleasant thoughts. [J, IV, 398–399]

Yesterday night, at fifteen minutes after eight, my little Waldo ended his life.

What he looked upon is better; what he looked not upon is insignificant. The morning of Friday, I woke at three o'clock, and every cock in every barnyard was shrilling with the most unnecessary noise. The sun went up the morning sky with all his light, but the landscape was dishonored by this loss. For this boy, in whose remembrance I have both slept and awaked so oft, decorated for me the morning star, the evening cloud, how much more all the particulars of daily economy; for he had touched with his lively curiosity every trivial fact and circumstance in the household, the hard coal and the soft coal which I put into my stove; the

wood, of which he brought his little quota for grand-
mother's fire; the hammer, the pincers and file he was so
eager to use; the microscope, the magnet, the little globe,
and every trinket and instrument in the study; the loads of
gravel on the meadow, the nests in the hen-house, and many
and many a little visit to the dog-house and to the barn.
For everything he had his own name and way of thinking,
his own pronunciation and manner. And every word came
mended from that tongue. A boy of early wisdom, of a
grave and even majestic deportment, of a perfect gentleness.

Every tramper that ever tramped is abroad, but the little
feet are still.

He gave up his little innocent breath like a bird.

[J, VI, 150–151]

What for the visions of the night? Our life is so safe and
regular that we hardly know the emotion of terror. Neither
public nor private violence, neither natural catastrophes, as
earthquake, volcano, or deluge; nor the expectation of
supernatural agents in the form of ghosts, or of purgatory
and devils and hell fire, disturb the sleepy circulations of
our blood in these calm, well-spoken days. And yet dreams
acquaint us with what the day omits. Eat a hearty supper,
tuck up your bed tightly, put an additional bedspread over
your three blankets, and lie on your back, and you may, in
the course of an hour or two, have this neglected part of
your education in some measure supplied. Let me consider:
I found myself in a garret disturbed by the noise of someone
sawing wood. On walking towards the sound, I saw lying in
a crib an insane person whom I very well knew, and the
noise instantly stopped: there was no saw, a mere stirring
among several trumpery matters, fur muffs and empty
baskets that lay on the floor. As I tried to approach, the
muffs swelled themselves a little, as with wind, and whirled
off into a corner of the garret, as if alive, and a kind of animation appeared in all the objects in that corner. Seeing this,
and instantly aware that here was Witchcraft, that here was
a devilish Will which signified itself plainly enough in the
stir and the sound of the wind, I was unable to move; my
limbs were frozen with fear; I was bold and would go for-

ward, but my limbs I could not move; I mowed the defiance I could not articulate, and woke with the ugly sound I made. After I woke and recalled the impressions, my brain tingled with repeated vibrations of terror; and yet was the sensation pleasing, as it was a sort of rehearsal of a Tragedy. [J, VI, 178–180]

What games sleep plays with us! We wake indignant that we have been so played upon, and should have lent ourselves to such mountains of nonsense. All night I was scarifying with my wrath some conjuring miscreant, but unhappily I had an old age in my toothless gums, I was as old as Priam, could not articulate, and the edge of all my taunts and sarcasms, it is to be feared, was quite lost. Yet, spite of my dumb palsy, I defied and roared after him, and rattled in my throat, until life waked me up. Then I bit my lips. So one day we shall wake up from this longer confusion, and be not less mortified that we had lent ourselves to such rigmarole. [J, VII, 458]

Dreams. I owe real knowledge and even alarming hints to dreams, and wonder to see people extracting emptiness from mahogany tables, when there is vaticination in their dreams. For the soul in dreams has a subtle synthetic power which it will not exert under the sharp eyes of day. It does not like to be watched or looked upon, and flies to real twilights, as the rappers do in their wretched mummeries. If in dreams you see loose and luxurious pictures, an inevitable tie drags in the sequel of cruelty and malignity. If you swallow the devil's bait, you will have a horizon full of dragons shortly.

When I higgled for my dime and half-dime in the dream, and lost, the parrots on the chimney tops, and church pinnacles scoffed at me, Ho! ho! [J, IX, 120–121]

I cannot afford to be irritable and captious, nor to waste all my time in attacks. If I should go out of church whenever I hear a false sentiment I could never stay there five minutes. But why come out? the street is as false as the church, and when I get to my house, or to my manners, or to my speech, I have not got away from the lie. When we see an eager assailant of one of these wrongs, a special reformer, we feel like asking him, What right have you, sir, to your one virtue? Is virtue piecemeal? This is a jewel amidst the rags of a beggar. [W, III, 262–263]

Sad is this continual postponement of life. I refuse sympathy and intimacy with people, as if in view of some better sympathy and intimacy to come. But whence and when? I am already thirty-four years old. Already my friends and fellow workers are dying from me. Scarcely can I say that I see any new men or women approaching me; I am too old to regard fashion; too old to expect patronage of any greater or more powerful. Let me suck the sweetness of those affections and consuetudes that grow near me—that the Divine Providence offers me. These old shoes are easy to the feet. But no, not for mine, if they have an ill savor. I was made a hermit, and am content with my lot. I pluck golden fruit from rare meetings with wise men. I can well abide alone in the intervals, and the fruit of my own tree shall have a better flavor. [J, IV, 229]

'Tis strange that it is not in vogue to commit hari-kari, as the Japanese do at sixty. Nature is so insulting in her hints and notices; does not pull you by the sleeve, but pulls out your teeth, tears off your hair in patches, steals your eyesight, twists your face into an ugly mask; in short, puts all contumelies upon you, without in the least abating your zeal to make a good appearance; and all this at the same time that she is moulding the new figures around you into wonderful beauty, which, of course, is only making your plight worse. [J, IX, 536]

Let me never fall into the vulgar mistake of dreaming that I am persecuted whenever I am contradicted. No man, I think, had ever a greater well-being with a less desert than I. I can very well afford to be accounted bad or foolish by a few dozen or a few hundred persons—I who see myself greeted by the good expectation of so many friends far beyond any power of thought or communication of thought residing in me. Besides, I own, I am often inclined to take part with those who say I am bad or foolish, for I fear I am both. I believe and know there must be a perfect compensation. I know too well my own dark spots. Not having myself attained, not satisfied myself, far from a holy obedience—how can I expect to satisfy others, to command their love? A few sour faces, a few biting paragraphs—is but a cheap expiation for all these short-comings of mine.

[J, V, 123]

Life wears to me a visionary face. Hardest roughest action is visionary also. It is but a choice between soft and turbulent dreams. People disparage knowing and the intellectual life, and urge doing. I am very content with knowing, if only I could know. That is an august entertainment, and would suffice me a great while. To know a little would be worth the expense of this world. I hear always the law of Adrastia, "that every soul which had acquired any truth, should be safe from harm until another period."

I know that the world I converse with in the city and in the farms, is not the world I *think*. I observe that difference, and shall observe it. One day I shall know the value and law of this discrepance. But I have not found that much was gained by manipular attempts to realize the world of thought. Many eager persons successively make an experiment in this way, and make themselves ridiculous. They acquire democratic manners, they foam at the mouth, they hate and deny. Worse, I observe that in the history of mankind there is never a solitary example of success—taking their own tests of success. I say this polemically, or in reply to the inquiry, Why not realize your world? But far be from me the despair which prejudices the law by a paltry empiricism—since there never was a right endeavor but it succeeded. Patience and patience, we shall win at the last. We must be very suspicious of the deceptions of the element of time. It takes a good deal of time to eat or to sleep, or to earn a hundred dollars, and a very little time to entertain a hope and an insight which becomes the light of our life. We dress our garden, eat our dinners, discuss the household with our wives, and these things make no impression, are forgotten next week; but, in the solitude to which every man is always returning, he has a sanity and revelations which in his passage into new worlds he will carry with him. Never mind the ridicule, never mind the defeat; up again, old heart!—it seems to say, there is victory yet for all justice; and the true romance which the world exists to realize will be the transformation of genius into practical power.

[W, III, 84–86]

Perhaps I am not made obnoxious to much suffering, but I have had happy hours enough in gazing from afar at the splendors of the Intellectual Law, to overpay me for any pains I know. Existence may go on to be better, and, if it have such insights, it can never be bad. You sometimes charge me with I know not what sky-blue, sky-void idealism. As far as it is a partiality, I fear I may be more deeply infected than you think me. I have very joyful dreams which I cannot bring to paper, much less to any approach to practice, and I blame myself not at all for my reveries, but that they have not yet got possession of my house and barn.

[E–C, II, 59]

I live a good while and acquire as much skill in literature as an old carpenter does in wood. It occurs, then, what pity! that now, when you know something, have at least learned so much good omission, your organs should fail you; your eyes, health, fire, and zeal of work, should decay daily. Then I remember that it is the mind of the world which is the good carpenter, the good scholar, sailor, or blacksmith, thousand-handed, versatile, all-applicable, in all these indifferent channels entering with wild vigor, excited by novelty in that untried channel confined by dikes of pedantry. . . . In you, this rich soul has peeped, despite your horny, muddy eyes, at books and poetry. Well, it took you up, and showed you something to the purpose; that there was something there. Look, look, old mole! there, straight up before you, is the magnificent Sun. If only for the instant, you see it. Well, in this way it educates the youth of the universe; in this way warms, suns, refines every particle; then it drops the little channel or canal, through which the Life rolled

beatific, like a fossil to the ground, thus touched and educated, by a moment of sunshine, to be the fairer material
for future channels and canals, through which the old Glory
shall dart again, in new directions, until the Universe shall
have been shot through and through, *tilled* with light.

[J, VIII, 303–305]

*Grief is finally illusion and old age a harbinger of com-
plete and final alleviation. We break the chains of "physical
necessity" through the intervention of heart and head—although the "dear old Devil" is never far away. "Every hour
has its morning, noon, and night."*

What opium is instilled into all disaster! It shows fore-
midable as we approach it, but there is at last no rough rasp-
ing friction, but the most slippery sliding surfaces; we fall
soft on a thought; *Ate Dea* is gentle,

> "Over men's heads walking aloft,
> With tender feet treading so soft."

People grieve and bemoan themselves, but it is not half so
bad with them as they say. There are moods in which we
court suffering, in the hope that here at least we shall find
reality, sharp peaks and edges of truth. But it turns out to be
scene-painting and counterfeit. The only thing grief has
taught me is to know how shallow it is. That, like all the
rest, plays about the surface, and never introduces me into
the reality, for contact with which we would even pay the
costly price of sons and lovers. Was it Boscovich who found
out that bodies never come in contact? Well, souls never
touch their objects. An innavigable sea washes with silent
waves between us and the things we aim at and converse
with. Grief too will make us idealists. In the death of my
son, now more than two years ago, I seem to have lost a
beautiful estate—no more. I cannot get it nearer to me. If
tomorrow I should be informed of the bankruptcy of my
principal debtors, the loss of my property would be a great
inconvenience to me, perhaps, for many years; but it would

leave me as it found me—neither better nor worse. So is it
with this calamity; it does not touch me; something which
I fancied was a part of me, which could not be torn away
without tearing me nor enlarged without enriching me,
falls off from me and leaves no scar. It was caducous. I
grieve that grief can teach me nothing, nor carry me one
step into real nature. The Indian who was laid under a
curse that the wind should not blow on him, nor water flow
to him, nor fire burn him, is a type of us all. The dearest
events are summer-rain, and we the Para coats that shed
every drop. Nothing is left us now but death. We look to
that with a grim satisfaction, saying, There at least is reality
that will not dodge us.

I take this evanescence and lubricity of all objects, which
lets them slip through our fingers then when we clutch hardest, to be the most unhandsome part of our condition. Nature does not like to be observed, and likes that we should
be her fools and playmates. We may have the sphere for
our cricket-ball, but not a berry for our philosophy. Direct
strokes she never gave us power to make; all our blows
glance, all our hits are accidents. Our relations to each
other are oblique and casual.

Dream delivers us to dream, and there is no end to illusion. Life is a train of moods like a string of beads, and as
we pass through them they prove to be many-colored lenses
which paint the world their own hue, and each shows only
what lies in its focus. From the mountain you see the mountain. We animate what we can, and we see only what we
animate. Nature and books belong to the eyes that see them.
It depends on the mood of the man whether he shall see
the sunset or the fine poem. There are always sunsets, and
there is always genius; but only a few hours so serene that
we can relish nature or criticism. The more or less depends
on structure or temperament. Temperament is the iron wire
on which the beads are strung. Of what use is fortune or
talent to a cold and defective nature? Who cares what sensibility or discrimination a man has at some time shown, if
he falls asleep in his chair? or if he laugh and giggle? or if
he apologize? or is infected with egotism? or thinks of his
dollar? or cannot go by food? or has gotten a child in his

boyhood? Of what use is genius, if the organ is too convex or too concave and cannot find a focal distance within the actual horizon of human life? Of what use, if the brain is too cold or too hot, and the man does not care enough for results to stimulate him to experiment, and hold him up in it? or if the web is too finely woven, too irritable by pleasure and pain, so that life stagnates from too much reception without due outlet? Of what use to make heroic vows of amendment, if the same old law-breaker is to keep them? What cheer can the religious sentiment yield, when that is suspected to be secretly dependent on the seasons of the year and the state of the blood? I knew a witty physician who found the creed in the biliary duct, and used to affirm that if there was disease in the liver, the man became a Calvinist, and if that organ was sound, he became a Unitarian. Very mortifying is the reluctant experience that some unfriendly excess or imbecility neutralizes the promise of genius. We see young men who owe us a new world, so readily and lavishly they promise, but they never acquit the debt; they die young and dodge the account; or if they live they lose themselves in the crowd.

Temperament also enters fully into the system of illusions and shuts us in a prison of glass which we cannot see. There is an optical illusion about every person we meet. In truth they are all creatures of given temperament, which will appear in a given character, whose boundaries they will never pass; but we look at them, they seem alive, and we presume there is impulse in them. In the moment it seems impulse; in the year, in the lifetime, it turns out to be a certain uniform tune which the revolving barrel of the music-box must play. Men resist the conclusion in the morning, but adopt it as the evening wears on, that temper prevails over everything of time, place and condition, and is inconsumable in the flames of religion. Some modifications the moral sentiment avails to impose, but the individual texture holds its dominion, if not to bias the moral judgments, yet to fix the measure of activity and of enjoyment.

I thus express the law as it is read from the platform of ordinary life, but must not leave it without noticing the capital exception. For temperament is a power which no man willingly hears anyone praise but himself. On the platform of physics we cannot resist the contracting influences of so-called science. Temperament puts all divinity to rout. I know the mental proclivity of physicians. I hear the chuckle of the phrenologists. Theoretic kidnappers and slave-drivers, they esteem each man the victim of another, who winds him round his finger by knowing the law of his being; and, by such cheap signboards as the color of his beard or the slope of his occiput, reads the inventory of his fortunes and character. The grossest ignorance does not disgust like this impudent knowingness. The physicians say they are not materialists; but they are—Spirit is matter reduced to an extreme thinness: O *so* thin!—But the definition of *spiritual* should be, *that which is its own evidence*. What notions do they attach to love! what to religion! One would not willingly pronounce these words in their hearing, and give them the occasion to profane them. I saw a gracious gentleman who adapts his conversation to the form of the head of the man he talks with! I had fancied that the value of life lay in its inscrutable possibilities; in the fact that I never know, in addressing myself to a new individual, what may befall me. I carry the keys of my castle in my hand, ready to throw them at the feet of my lord, whenever and in what disguise soever he shall appear. I know he is in the neighborhood, hidden among vagabonds. Shall I preclude my future by taking a high seat and kindly adapting my conversation to the shape of heads? When I come to that, the doctors shall buy me for a cent.—"But, sir, medical history; the report to the Institute; the proven facts!"—I distrust the facts and the inferences. Temperament is the veto or limitation-power in the constitution, very justly applied to restrain an opposite excess in the constitution, but absurdly offered as a bar to original equity. When virtue is in presence, all subordinate powers sleep. On its own level, or in view of nature, temperament is final. I see not, if one be once caught in this trap of so-called sciences, any escape for the man from the links of the chain of physical necessity. Given such an embryo, such a history must follow. On this platform one lives in a sty of sensualism, and would soon come to suicide. But it is impossible that the creative power should exclude itself. Into every intelligence there is a door which is never closed, through which the creator passes. The intellect, seeker of absolute truth, or the heart, lover of absolute good, intervenes for our succor, and at one whisper of these high powers we awake from ineffectual struggles with this nightmare. We hurl it into its own hell, and cannot again contract ourselves to so base a state.

[W, III, 48–55]

Old Age. The world wears well. These autumn afternoons and well-marbled landscapes of green and gold and russet, and steel-blue river, and smoke-blue New Hampshire mountains, are and remain as bright and perfect pencilling as ever.   [J, VIII, 140]

Old age brings along with its ugliness the comfort that you will soon be out of it—which ought to be a substantial relief to such discontented pendulums as we are. To be out of the war, out of debt, out of the drouth, out of the blues, out of the dentist's hands, out of the second thoughts, mortifications, and remorses that inflict such twinges and shooting pains—out of the next winter, and the high prices, and company below your ambition—surely these are soothing hints. And, harbinger of this, what an alleviator is sleep, which muzzles all these dogs for me every day? Old age— 'tis proposed to call an indignation meeting.   [J, X, 51]

I woke up and found the dear old world, wife, babe and mother, Concord and Boston, the dear old spiritual world, and even the dear old Devil not far off.   [J, VI, 246]

Every hour has its morning, noon, and night.

[J, V, 461]

Chapter Two

An Original Relation
to the Universe

*Nothing of Emerson's is so well-known as his insistence on
"self-reliance" and "nonconformity"—terms whose literary
use he virtually discovered. Yet Emerson does not mean by
these hack phrases what we now mean by them, and the
vulgar habit of ascribing to Emerson's doctrine of self-
reliance nothing but the "good old Yankee virtues" is actually a perversion of Emerson.*

*For Emerson the individual was not someone to defend
from "mass culture" and the unthinking majority; the individual was the actual stage on which life was lived out.
Whatever happened, happened first to a person, and the way
it happened was determined by the capacity of this person.
History was not full of violent impersonal tendencies, as it
seemed; it was full of persons—some of whom did think of
themselves as members of the masses, as types of the
"common man," and it was precisely these who made for
the tragedy of life. "The cheapness of man is every day's
tragedy" is one of his key thoughts; another (which profoundly irritated Herman Melville, who thought Emerson a
hypocrite for not admitting this more often) was "the calamity is the masses."*

*Emerson's insistence on the prime importance of the
individual is essentially Christian. He is concerned with the
profound mystery of the person, and with the spiritual
power that a sense of his own freedom confers upon the
individual. But in addition to this permanently Christian*

side of his thought, Emerson's regard for the individual as the real battleground of life is in the revolutionary spirit of the emergent middle class of the nineteenth century. For Emerson the individual is not only a supreme value, but the only real agent of historical action. As a free citizen, the individual who embodies so much that is valuable in American history, he can achieve perfectibility; his perceptions of God constitute to him a religion; he is in these same free perceptions wiser than the scholar or traditionalist; he can withstand (or should) the tyranny of conventional opinion; above all, he has bearing, he has dignity. Even the "common man," as history has previously considered him, becomes the free individual and history the epic of the individual soul.

Emerson summed up all these evaluations into a single value: the individual counts because only the individual thinks. For Emerson it is thought that moves the world, that fills up life itself. The individual is the creator of human history as well as the only real embodiment of history (races and nations being his tools). For Emerson, it is precisely the open, dramatic and provisional quality of life that gives the individual back to himself; and in the last analysis, he believed in the individual as poets and dramatists and novelists do, because literature must deal with the self. It is the individual who makes life dramatic; and equally, it is the individual who gives meaning to life by imposing on brute existence that claim to know, that belief that man can know, which is the specific touch that makes all history human history.

We are bound hand and foot with our decorums and superstitions. England has achieved respectability at what a cost! America with a valet's eyes admires and copies in vain.

[J, VII, 33]

The timidity of our public opinion is our disease, or, shall I say, the publicness of opinion, the absence of private opinion. Good nature is plentiful, but we want justice, with heart of steel, to fight down the proud. The private mind

has the access to the totality of goodness and truth that it
may be a balance to a corrupt society; and to stand for the
private verdict against popular clamor is the office of the
noble. If a humane measure is propounded in behalf of the
slave, or of the Irishman, or the Catholic, or for the succor
of the poor; that sentiment, that project, will have the
homage of the hero. [W, I, 389–390]

It is true, the public mind wants self-respect. We are full
of vanity, of which the most signal proof is our sensitiveness
to foreign and especially English censure. One cause of this
is our immense reading, and that reading chiefly confined to
the productions of the English press. It is also true that to
imaginative persons in this country there is somewhat bare
and bald in our short history and unsettled wilderness. They
ask, who would live in a new country that can live in an old?
and it is not strange that our youths and maidens should
burn to see the picturesque extremes of an antiquated
country. But it is one thing to visit the Pyramids, and another to wish to live there. Would they like tithes to the
clergy, and sevenths to the government, and Horse-Guards,
and licensed press, and grief when a child is born, and
threatening, starved weavers, and a pauperism now consti-
tuting one thirteenth of the population? Instead of the open
future expanding here before the eye of every boy to vast-
ness, would they like the closing in of the future to a narrow
slit of sky, and that fast contracting to be no future? One
thing for instance, the beauties of aristocracy, we commend
to the study of the travelling American. The English, the
most conservative people this side of India, are not sensible
of the restraint, but an American would seriously resent it.
The aristocracy, incorporated by law and education, de-
grades life for the unprivileged classes. It is a questionable
compensation to the embittered feeling of a proud com-
moner, the reflection that a fop, who, by the magic of title,
paralyzes his arm and plucks from him half the graces and
rights of a man, is himself also an aspirant excluded with
the same ruthlessness from higher circles, since there is no
end to the wheels within wheels of this spiral heaven. Something may be pardoned to the spirit of loyalty when it be-

comes fantastic; and something to the imagination, for the baldest life is symbolic. Philip II. of Spain rated his ambassador for neglecting serious affairs in Italy, whilst he debated some point of honor with the French ambassador; "You have left a business of importance for a ceremony." The ambassador replied, "Your Majesty's self is but a ceremony." In the East, where the religious sentiment comes in to the support of the aristocracy, and in the Romish church also, there is a grain of sweetness in the tyranny; but in England, the fact seems to me intolerable, what is commonly affirmed, that such is the transcendent honor accorded to wealth and birth, that no man of letters, be his eminence what it may, is received into the best society, except as a lion and a show. The English have many virtues, many advantages, and the proudest history of the world; but they need all and more than all the resources of the past to indemnify a heroic gentleman in that country for the mortifications prepared for him by the system of society, and which seem to impose the alternative to resist or to avoid it. That there are mitigations and practical alleviations to this rigor, is not an excuse for the rule. Commanding worth and personal power must sit crowned in all companies, nor will extraordinary persons be slighted or affronted in any company of civilized men. But the system is an invasion of the sentiment of justice and the native rights of men, which however decorated, must lessen the value of English citizenship. It is for Englishmen to consider, not for us; we only say, Let us live in America, too thankful for our want of feudal institutions. Our houses and towns are like mosses and lichens, so slight and new; but youth is a fault of which we shall daily mend. This land too is as old as the Flood, and wants no ornament or privilege which nature could bestow. Here stars, here woods, here hills, here animals, here men abound, and the vast tendencies concur of a new order. If only the men are employed in conspiring with the designs of the Spirit who led us hither and is leading us still, we shall quickly enough advance out of all hearing of others' censures, out of all regrets of our own, into a new and more excellent social state than history has recorded.

[W, I, 392–395]

Our age is bewailed as the age of Introversion. Must that needs be evil? We, it seems, are critical; we are embarrassed with second thoughts; we cannot enjoy any thing for hankering to know whereof the pleasures consists; we are lined with eyes; we see with our feet; the time is infected with Hamlet's unhappiness,

"Sicklied o'er with the pale cast of thought."

It is so bad then? Sight is the last thing to be pitied. Would we be blind? Do we fear lest we should outsee nature and God, and drink truth dry? I look upon the discontent of the literary class as a mere announcement of the fact that they find themselves not in the state of mind of their fathers, and regret the coming state as untried; as a boy dreads the water before he has learned that he can swim. If there is any period one would desire to be born in, is it not the age of Revolution; when the old and the new stand side by side and admit of being compared; when the energies of all men are searched by fear and by hope; when the historic glories of the old can be compensated by the rich possibilities of the new era? This time, like all times, is a very good one, if we but know what to do with it.

I read with some joy of the auspicious signs of the coming days, as they glimmer already through poetry and art, through philosophy and science, through church and state.

One of these signs is the fact that the same movement which effected the elevation of what was called the lowest class in the state, assumed in literature a very marked and as benign an aspect. Instead of the sublime and beautiful, the near, the low, the common, was explored and poetized. That which had been negligently trodden under foot by those who were harnessing and provisioning themselves for long journeys into far countries, is suddenly found to be richer than all foreign parts. The literature of the poor, the feelings of the child, the philosophy of the street, the meaning of the household life, are the topics of the time. It is a great stride. It is a sign—is it not?—of new vigor when the extremities are made active, when currents of warm life run into the hands and the feet. I ask not for the great, the remote, the romantic; what is doing in Italy or Arabia; what is

Greek art, or Provençal minstrelsy; I embrace the common, I explore and sit at the feet of the familiar, the low. Give me insight into today, and you may have the antique and future worlds. What would we really know the meaning of? The meal in the firkin; the milk in the pan; the ballad in the street; the news of the boat; the glance of the eye; the form and the gait of the body—show me the ultimate reason of these matters; show me the sublime presence of the highest spiritual cause lurking, as always it does lurk, in these suburbs and extremities of nature; let me see every trifle bristling with the polarity that ranges it instantly on an eternal law; and the shop, the plough, and the ledger referred to the like cause by which light undulates and poets sing—and the world lies no longer a dull miscellany and lumber-room, but has form and order; there is no trifle, there is no puzzle, but one design unites and animates the farthest pinnacle and the lowest trench.

This idea has inspired the genius of Goldsmith, Burns, Cowper, and, in a newer time, of Goethe, Wordsworth, and Carlyle. This idea they have differently followed and with various success. In contrast with their writing, the style of Pope, of Johnson, of Gibbon, looks cold and pedantic. This writing is blood-warm. Man is surprised to find that things near are not less beautiful and wondrous than things remote. The near explains the far. The drop is a small ocean. A man is related to all nature. This perception of the worth of the vulgar is fruitful in discoveries. Goethe, in this very thing the most modern of the moderns, has shown us, as none ever did, the genius of the ancients.

There is one man of genius who has done much for this philosophy of life, whose literary value has never yet been rightly estimated—I mean Emanuel Swedenborg. The most imaginative of men, yet writing with the precision of a mathematician, he endeavored to engraft a purely philosophical Ethics on the popular Christianity of his time. Such an attempt of course must have difficulty which no genius could surmount. But he saw and showed the connection between nature and the affections of the soul. He pierced the emblematic or spiritual character of the visible, audible, tangible world. Especially did his shade-loving muse hover over and interpret the lower parts of nature; he showed the mysterious bond that allies moral evil to the foul material forms, and has given in epical parables a theory of insanity, of beasts, of unclean and fearful things.

Another sign of our times, also marked by an analogous political movement, is the new importance given to the single person. Every thing that tends to insulate the individual—to surround him with barriers of natural respect, so that each man shall feel the world is his, and man shall treat with man as a sovereign state with a sovereign state—tends to true union as well as greatness. "I learned," said the melancholy Pestalozzi, "that no man in God's wide earth is either willing or able to help any other man." Help must come from the bosom alone. The scholar is that man who must take up into himself all the ability of the time, all the contributions of the past, all the hopes of the future. He must be an university of knowledges. If there be one lesson more than another which should pierce his ear, it is, The world is nothing, the man is all; in yourself is the law of all nature, and you know not yet how a globule of sap ascends; in yourself slumbers the whole of Reason; it is for you to know all; it is for you to dare all. . . . this confidence in the unsearched might of man belongs, by all motives, by all prophecy, by all preparation, to the American Scholar. We have listened too long to the courtly muses of Europe. The spirit of the American freeman is already suspected to be timid, imitative, tame. Public and private avarice make the air we breathe thick and fat. The scholar is decent, indolent, complaisant. See already the tragic consequence. The mind of this country, taught to aim at low objects, eats upon itself. There is no work for any but the decorous and the complaisant. Young men of the fairest promise, who begin life upon our shores, inflated by the mountain winds, shined upon by all the stars of God, find the earth below not in unison with these, but are hindered from action by the disgust which the principles on which business is managed inspire, and turn drudges, or die of disgust, some of them suicides. What is the remedy? They did not yet see, and thousands of young men as hopeful now crowding to the barriers for the career do not yet see, that if the single man plant himself indomitably on his instincts, and there abide, the huge world will come round to him. Patience— patience; with the shades of all the good and great for company; and for solace the perspective of your own infinite life; and for work the study and the communication of principles, the making those instincts prevalent, the conversion of the world. Is it not the chief disgrace in the world, not to be an unit—not to be reckoned one character —not to yield that peculiar fruit which each man was created to bear, but to be reckoned in the gross, in the hundred, or the thousand, of the party, the section, to which we belong; and our opinion predicted geographically, as the north, or the south? Not so, brothers and friends— please God, ours shall not be so. We will walk on our own feet; we will work with our own hands; we will speak our own minds. The study of letters shall be no longer a name for pity, for doubt, and for sensual indulgence. The dread of man and the love of man shall be a wall of defence and a wreath of joy around all. A nation of men will for the first time exist, because each believes himself inspired by the Divine Soul which also inspires all men.

[W, I, 109–115]

Our age is retrospective. It builds the sepulchres of the fathers. It writes biographies, histories, and criticism. The foregoing generations beheld God and nature face to face; we, through their eyes. Why should not we also enjoy an original relation to the universe? Why should not we have a poetry and philosophy of insight and not of tradition, and a religion by revelation to us, and not the history of theirs? Embosomed for a season in nature, whose floods of life stream around and through us, and invite us by the powers they supply, to action proportioned to nature, why should we grope among the dry bones of the past, or put the living generation into masquerade out of its faded wardrobe? The sun shines today also. There is more wool and flax in the fields. There are new lands, new men, new thoughts. Let us demand our own works and laws and worship.

Undoubtedly we have no questions to ask which are unanswerable. We must trust the perfection of the creation so far as to believe that whatever curiosity the order of things has awakened in our minds, the order of things can satisfy. Every man's condition is a solution in hieroglyphic to those inquiries he would put. He acts it as life, before he apprehends it as truth. In like manner, nature is already, in its forms and tendencies, describing its own design. Let us interrogate the great apparition that shines so peacefully around us. Let us inquire, to what end is nature?

All science has one aim, namely, to find a theory of nature. We have theories of races and of functions, but scarcely yet a remote approach to an idea of creation. We are now so far from the road to truth, that religious teachers dispute and hate each other, and speculative men are esteemed unsound and frivolous. But to a sound judgment, the most abstract truth is the most practical. Whenever a true theory appears, it will be its own evidence. Its test is, that it will explain all phenomena. Now many are thought not only unexplained but inexplicable; as language, sleep, madness, dreams, beasts, sex. [W, I, 3–4]

It is not the office of a man to receive gifts. How dare you give them? We wish to be self-sustained. We do not quite forgive a giver. The hand that feeds us is in some danger of being bitten. We can receive anything from love, for that is a way of receiving it from ourselves; but not from anyone who assumes to bestow. We sometimes hate the meat which we eat, because there seems something of degrading dependence in living by it. [W, III, 162]

Originality. The great majority of men are not original, for they are not primary, have not assumed their own vows, but are secondaries—grow up and grow old in seeming and following; and when they die they occupy themselves to the last with what others will think, and whether Mr. A and Mr. B will go to their funeral. [J, VI, 123–124]

We all give way to superstitions. The house in which we were born is not quite mere timber and stone; is still haunted by parents and progenitors. The creeds into which we were initiated in childhood and youth no longer hold their old place in the minds of thoughtful men, but they are not nothing to us, and we hate to have them treated with contempt. There is so much that we do not know, that we give to these suggestions the benefit of the doubt.

[W, X, 201]

But now we are a mob. Man does not stand in awe of man, nor is his genius admonished to stay at home, to put itself in communication with the internal ocean, but it goes abroad to beg a cup of water of the urns of other men. We must go alone. I like the silent church before the service begins, better than any preaching. How far off, how cool, how chaste the persons look, begirt each one with a precinct or sanctuary! So let us always sit. Why should we assume the faults of our friend, or wife, or father, or child, because they sit around our hearth, or are said to have the same blood? All men have my blood and I all men's. Not for that will I adopt their petulance or folly, even to the extent of being ashamed of it. But your isolation must not be mechanical, but spiritual, that is, must be elevation. At times the whole world seems to be in conspiracy to importune you with emphatic trifles. Friend, client, child, sickness, fear, want, charity, all knock at once at thy closet door and say, "Come out unto us." But keep thy state; come not into their confusion. The power men possess to annoy me I give them by a weak curiosity. No man can come near me but through my act. "What we love that we have, but by desire we bereave ourselves of the love."

[W, II, 71–72]

We accept the religions and politics into which we fall, and it is only a few delicate spirits who are sufficient to see that the whole web of convention is the imbecility of those whom it entangles—that the mind suffers no religion and no empire but its own.   [W, VIII, 248]

Having affirmed one of his favorite themes, the enslavement of men to creeds and categories, Emerson invites his readers to put aside their affectations and their masquerades. Society invariably detects the fraud, and character is unconcealable.

As to what we call the masses, and common men,—there are no common men. All men are at last of a size; and true art is only possible on the conviction that every talent has its apotheosis somewhere. [W, IV, 31]

The poverty of the saint, of the rapt philosopher, of the naked Indian, is not comic. The lie is in the surrender of the man to his appearance; as if a man should neglect himself and treat his shadow on the wall with marks of infinite respect. It affects us oddly, as to see things turned upside down, or to see a man in a high wind run after his hat, which is always droll. The relation of the parties is inverted—hat being for the moment master, the bystanders cheering the hat. [W, VIII, 169]

A classification or nomenclature used by the scholar only as a memorandum of his last lesson in the laws of Nature, and confessedly a makeshift, a bivouac for a night, and implying a march and a conquest tomorrow—becomes through indolence a barrack and a prison, in which the man sits down immovably, and wishes to detain others.
[W, VIII, 166–167]

Men in all ways are better than they seem. They like flattery for the moment, but they know the truth for their own. It is a foolish cowardice which keeps us from trusting them and speaking to them rude truth. They resent your honesty for an instant, they will thank you for it always. What is it we heartily wish of each other? Is it to be pleased and flattered? No, but to be convicted and exposed, to be shamed out of our nonsense of all kinds, and made men of, instead of ghosts and phantoms. We are weary of gliding ghostlike through the world, which is itself so slight and unreal. We crave a sense of reality, though it comes in strokes of pain. [W, III, 273–274]

We are always coming up with the emphatic facts of history in our private experience and verifying them here. All history becomes subjective; in other words there is properly no history, only biography. Every mind must know the whole lesson for itself—must go over the whole ground. What it does not see, what it does not live, it will not know. . . . The better for him. [W, II, 9–10]

Man is not order of nature, sack and sack, belly and members, link in a chain, nor any ignominious baggage; but a stupendous antagonism, a dragging together of the poles of the Universe. He betrays his relation to what is below him —thick-skulled, small-brained, fishy, quadrumanous, quadruped ill-disguised, hardly escaped into biped—and has paid for the new powers by loss of some of the old ones. But the lightning which explodes and fashions planets, maker of planets and suns, is in him. On one side elemental order, sandstone and granite, rock-ledges, peat-bog, forest, sea and shore; and on the other part thought, the spirit which composes and decomposes nature—here they are, side by side, god and devil, mind and matter, king and conspirator, belt and spasm, riding peacefully together in the eye and brain of every man.

Nor can he blink the freewill. To hazard the contradiction—freedom is necessary. If you please to plant yourself on the side of Fate, and say, Fate is all; then we say, a part of Fate is the freedom of man. Forever wells up the impulse of choosing and acting in the soul. Intellect annuls Fate. So far as a man thinks, he is free. And though nothing is more disgusting than the crowing about liberty by slaves, as most men are, and the flippant mistaking for freedom of some paper preamble like a Declaration of Independence or the statute right to vote, by those who have never dared to think or to act—yet it is wholesome to man to look not at Fate, but the other way: the practical view is the other. His sound relation to these facts is to use and command, not to cringe to them. [W, VI, 22–23]

Nature created a police of many ranks. God has delegated himself to a million deputies. . . .

You cannot hide any secret. If the artist succor his flagging spirits by opium or wine, his work will characterize itself as the effect of opium or wine. If you make a picture or a statue, it sets the beholder in that state of mind you had when you made it. If you spend for show, on building or gardening or on pictures or on equipages, it will so appear. We are all physiognomists and penetrators of character, and things themselves are detective. If you follow the suburban fashion in building a sumptuous-looking house for a little money, it will appear to all eyes as a cheap dear house. There is no privacy that cannot be penetrated. No secret can be kept in the civilized world. Society is a masked ball, where everyone hides his real character, and reveals it by hiding. If a man wish to conceal anything he carries, those whom he meets know that he conceals somewhat, and usually know what he conceals. Is it otherwise if there be some belief or some purpose he would bury in his breast? 'Tis as hard to hide as fire. He is a strong man who can hold down his opinion. A man cannot utter two or three sentences without disclosing to intelligent ears precisely where he stands in life and thought, namely, whether in the kingdom of the senses and the understanding, or in that of ideas and imagination, in the realm of intuitions and duty. People seem not to see that their opinion of the world is also a confession of character. [W, VI, 223–224]

Speak with the vulgar, think with the wise. See how Plato managed it, with an imagination so gorgeous, and a taste so patrician, that Jove, if he descended, was to speak in his style. Into the exquisite refinement of his Academy, he introduces the low-born Socrates, relieving the purple diction by his perverse talk, his gallipots, and cook, and trencher, and cart-wheels—and steadily kept this coarseness to flavor a dish else too luscious. Everybody knows the points in which the mob has the advantage of the Academy, and all able men have known how to import the petulance of the street into correct discourse. I heard, when a great bank president was expounding the virtues of his party and of the government to a silent circle of bank pensioners, a grave Methodist exclaimed "Fiddlesticks!" The whole party were surprised and cheered, except the bank president, though it would be difficult to explain the propriety of the expression, as no music or fiddle was so much as thought of.

[W, XII, 286–287]

Hell is better than Heaven, if the man in Hell knows his place, and the man in Heaven does not. It is in vain you pretend that you are not responsible for the evil law because you are not a magistrate, or a party to a civil process, or do not vote. You eat the law in a crust of bread, you wear it in your hat and shoes. The Man—it is his attitude: the attitude makes the man.   [J, VI, 168]

EXPERIENCE

> The lords of life, the lords of life—
> I saw them pass
> In their own guise,
> Like and unlike,
> Portly and grim—
> Use and Surprise,
> Surface and Dream,
> Succession swift and spectral Wrong,
> Temperament without a tongue,
> And the inventor of the game
> Omnipresent without name;
> Some to see, some to be guessed,
> They marched from east to west:
> Little man, least of all,
> Among the legs of his guardians tall,
> Walked about with puzzled look.
> Him by the hand dear Nature took,
> Dearest Nature, strong and kind,
> Whispered, "Darling, never mind!
> Tomorrow they will wear another face,
> The founder thou; these are thy race!"
>   [W, IX, 269]

. . . we hate snivelling. I do not wish you to surpass others in any narrow or professional or monkish way. We like the natural greatness of health and wild power. I confess that I am as much taken by it in boys, and sometimes in people not normal, nor educated, nor presentable, nor church-members—even in persons open to the suspicion of irregular and immoral living, in Bohemians—as in more orderly examples. For we must remember that in the lives of soldiers, sailors and men of large adventure, many of the stays and guards of our household life are wanting, and yet the opportunities and incentives to sublime daring and performance are often close at hand. We must have some charity for the sense of the people, which admires natural power, and will elect it over virtuous men who have less. [W, VIII, 316]

Our churches are dismal phantasms, and the formalists who usurp the pulpit are insulated from the Real. We are pagans still, superstitiously worshiping old idols. We are waiting for the new Adam who can make every day a Sabbath.

The test of a religion or philosophy is the number of things it can explain: so true is it. But the religion of our churches explains neither art nor society nor history, but itself needs explanation. [J, V, 151]

If Jesus came now into the world, he would say, You, YOU! He said to his age, I. [J, IV, 277]

Whenever the pulpit is usurped by a formalist, then is the worshipper defrauded and disconsolate. We shrink as soon as the prayers begin, which do not uplift, but smite and offend us. We are fain to wrap our cloaks about us, and secure, as best we can, a solitude that hears not. I once heard a preacher who sorely tempted me to say I would go to church no more. Men go, thought I, where they are wont to go, else had no soul entered the temple in the afternoon. A snow-storm was falling around us. The snow-storm was real, the preacher merely spectral, and the eye felt the sad contrast in looking at him, and then out of the window behind him into the beautiful meteor of the snow.

[W, I, 137]

The clergy are as like as peas. I cannot tell them apart. It was said: They have bronchitis because they read from their papers sermons with a near voice, and then, looking at the congregation, they try to speak with their far voice, and the shock is noxious. I think they do this, or the converse of this, with their thought. They look into Plato, or into the mind, and then try to make parish mince-meat of the amplitudes and eternities, and the shock is noxious. It is the old story again: once we had wooden chalices and golden priests, now we have golden chalices and wooden priests.   [W, X, 229]

We say the old forms of religion decay, and that a skepticism devastates the community. I do not think it can be cured or stayed by any modification of theologic creeds, much less by theologic discipline. The cure for false theology is mother-wit. Forget your books and traditions, and obey your moral perceptions at this hour. That which is signified by the words "moral" and "spiritual," is a lasting essence, and, with whatever illusions we have loaded them, will certainly bring back the words, age after age, to their ancient meaning. I know no words that mean so much. In our definitions we grope after the *spiritual* by describing it as invisible. The true meaning of *spiritual* is *real;* that law which executes itself, which works without means, and which cannot be conceived as not existing. Men talk of "mere morality"—which is much if one should say, "Poor God, with nobody to help him."   [W, VI, 214–215]

George Sand is a great genius, and yet owes to her birth in France her entire freedom from the cant and snuffle of our dead Christianity.   [J, VII, 503–504]

Our ancestors spoke continually of angels and archangels with the same good faith as they would have spoken of their own parents or their late minister. Now the words pale, and rhetoric, and all credence is gone. Our horizon is not far, say one generation, or thirty years: we all see so much. The older see two generations, or sixty years. But what has been running on through three horizons, or ninety years, looks to all the world like a law of Nature, and 'tis an impiety to doubt. Thus, 'tis incredible to us, if we look into the religious books of our grandfathers, how they held themselves in such a pinfold. But why not? As far as they could see, through two or three horizons, nothing but ministers and ministers. Calvinism was one and the same thing in Geneva, in Scotland, in Old and New England. If there was a wedding, they had a sermon; if a funeral, then a sermon; if a war, or small-pox, or a comet, or canker-worms, or a deacon died—still a sermon: Nature was a pulpit; the church-warden or tithing-man was a petty persecutor; the presbytery a tyrant; and in many a house in country places the poor children found seven sabbaths in a week. Fifty or a hundred years ago, prayers were said, morning and evening, in all families; grace was said at table; an exact observance of the Sunday was kept in the houses of laymen as of clergymen. And one sees with some pain the disuse of rites so charged with humanity and aspiration. But it by no means follows, because those offices are much disused, that the men and women are irreligious; certainly not that they have less integrity or sentiment, but only, let us hope, that they see that they can omit the form without loss of real ground; perhaps that they find some violence, some cramping of their freedom of thought, in the constant recurrence of the form.   [W, X, 106–107]

Mankind at large always resemble frivolous children: they are impatient of thought, and wish to be amused. Truth is too simple for us; we do not like those who unmask our illusions. Fontenelle said: "If the Deity should lay bare to the eyes of men the secret system of Nature, the causes by which all the astronomic results are affected, and they finding no magic, no mystic numbers, no fatalities, but the greatest simplicity, I am persuaded they would not be able to suppress a feeling of mortification, and would exclaim, with disappointment, 'Is that all?' " And so we paint over

the bareness of ethics with the quaint grotesques of theology.

We boast the triumph of Christianity over Paganism,
meaning the victory of the spirit over the senses; but Paganism hides itself in the uniform of the Church. Paganism
has only taken the oath of allegiance, taken the cross, but
is Paganism still, outvotes the true men by millions of majority, carries the bag, spends the treasure, writes the tracts,
elects the minister, and persecutes the true believer.

[W, X, 109–110]

Jesus has immense claims on the gratitude of mankind, and
knew how to guard the integrity of his brother's soul from
himself also; but, in his disciples, admiration of him runs
away with their reverence for the human soul, and they
hamper us with limitations of person and text. Every exaggeration of these is a violation of the soul's right, and
inclines the manly reader to lay down the New Testament,
to take up the Pagan philosophers. It is not that the Upani-
shads or the Maxims of Antoninus are better, but that they
do not invade his freedom; because they are only suggestions, whilst the other adds the inadmissible claim of positive authority—of an external command, where command
cannot be. This is the secret of the mischievous result that,
in every period of intellectual expansion, the Church ceases
to draw into its clergy those who best belong there, the
largest and freest minds, and that in its most liberal forms,
when such minds enter it, they are coldly received, and
find themselves out of place. This charm in the Pagan mor-
alists, of suggestion, the charm of poetry, of mere truth
(easily disengaged from their historical accidents which nobody wishes to force on us), the New Testament loses by
its connection with a church. Mankind cannot long suffer
this loss, and the office of this age is to put all these writings
on the eternal footing of equality of origin in the instincts
of the human mind.   [W, X, 115–116]

*The scholar, a "divine pilgrim in nature," is kinsman to
the great discoverers of the past and bridges the centuries.
The recognition of truth dissolves time, obliterates epochs*

and nationalities and literary classifications. Solitude, cour-
age, energy, self-trust are the requirements for the man of
letters; vulgar prosperity, despair, conformity destroy him.

I call our system a system of despair, and I find all the
correction, all the revolution that is needed and that the
best spirits of this age promise, in one word, in Hope. Nature, when she sends a new mind into the world, fills it
beforehand with a desire for that which she wishes it to
know and do. Let us wait and see what is this new creation,
of what new organ the great Spirit had need when it in-
carnated this new Will. A new Adam in the garden, he is to
name all the beasts in the field, all the gods in the sky. And
jealous provision seems to have been made in his constitution that you shall not invade and contaminate him with
the worn weeds of your language and opinions.

[W, X, 136–137]

Our admiration of the antique is not admiration of the old,
but of the natural. The Greeks are not reflective, but perfect in their senses and in their health, with the finest physical organization in the world. Adults acted with the simplicity and grace of children. They made vases, tragedies
and statues, such as healthy senses should—that is, in good
taste. Such things have continued to be made in all ages,
and are now, wherever a healthy physique exists; but, as a
class, from their superior organization, they have surpassed
all. They combine the energy of manhood with the engaging
unconsciousness of childhood. The attraction of these manners is that they belong to man, and are known to every
man in virtue of his being once a child; besides that there
are always individuals who retain these characteristics. A
person of child-like genius and inborn energy is still a Greek,
and revives our love of the Muse of Hellas. I admire the
love of nature in the Philoctetes. In reading those fine apos-
trophes to sleep, to the stars, rocks, mountains and waves, I
feel time passing away as an ebbing sea. I feel the eternity
of man, the identity of his thought. The Greek had, it seems,
the same fellow-beings as I. The sun and moon, water and

and that never gets acquainted with himself, but is always as its muse. We get news daily of the world within, as well and the world outside, and not less of the central than of surface facts. A new thought is awaiting him every morn-   [J, X, 264–265]

When a man, through stubbornness, insists to do this or that, something absurd or whimsical, only because he will, he is weak; he blows with his lips against the tempest, he dams the incoming ocean with his cane. It were an unspeakable calamity if anyone should think he had the right to impose a private will on others. That is the part of a striker, an assassin. All violence,' all that is dreary and repels, is not power but the absence of power.   [W, X, 92]

. . . if we explore the literature of Heroism we shall quickly come to Plutarch, who is its Doctor and historian. To him we owe the Brasidas, the Dion, the Epaminondas, the Scipio of old, and I must think we are more deeply indebted to him than to all the ancient writers. Each of his "Lives" is a refutation to the despondency and cowardice of our religious and political theorists. A wild courage, a Stoicism not of the schools but of the blood, shines in every anecdote, and has given that book its immense fame.

We need books of this tart cathartic virtue more than books of political science or of private economy. Life is a festival only to the wise. Seen from the nook and chimney-side of prudence, it wears a ragged and dangerous front. The violations of the laws of nature by our predecessors and our contemporaries are punished in us also. The disease and deformity around us certify the infraction of natural, intellectual and moral laws, and often violation on violation to breed such compound misery. A lockjaw that bends a man's head back to his heels; hydrophobia that makes him bark at his wife and babes; insanity that makes him eat grass; war, plague, cholera, famine, indicate a certain ferocity in nature, which, as it had its inlet by human crime, must have its outlet by human suffering. Unhappily no man exists who has not in his own person become to some amount a stockholder in the sin, and so made himself liable to a share in the expiation.

Our culture therefore must not omit the arming of the man. Let him hear in season that he is born into the state of war, and that the commonwealth and his own well-being require that he should not go dancing in the weeds of peace, but warned, self-collected and neither defying nor dreading the thunder, let him take both reputation and life in his hand, and with perfect urbanity dare the gibbet and the mob by the absolute truth of his speech and the rectitude of his behavior.   [W, II, 248–250]

Yesterday at ΦBK anniversary. Steady, steady. I am convinced that if a man will be a true scholar, he shall have perfect freedom. The young people and the mature hint at odium, and aversion of faces to be presently encountered in society. I say, No: I fear it not. No scholar need fear it. For if it be true that he is merely an observer, a dispassionate reporter, no partisan, a singer merely for the love of music, his is a position of perfect immunity: to him no disgusts can attach: he is invulnerable. The vulgar think he would found a sect, and would be installed and made much of. He knows better, and much prefers his melons and his woods. Society has no bribe for me, neither in politics, nor church, nor college, nor city. My resources are far from exhausted. If they will not hear me lecture, I shall have leisure for my book which wants me. Besides it is an universal maxim worthy of all acceptation that a man may have that allowance which he takes. Take the place and attitude to which you see your unquestionable right, and all men acquiesce.

Who are these murmurers, these haters, these revilers? Men of no knowledge, and therefore no stability. The scholar, on the contrary, is sure of his point, is fast-rooted, and can securely predict the hour when all this roaring multitude shall roar for him. Analyze the chiding opposition, and it is made up of such timidities, uncertainties and no opinions, that it is not worth dispersing.   [J, V, 30–31]

The scholar blunders along on his own path for a time, assured by the surprise and joy of those to whom he first communicates his results; then new solitudes, new marches; but after a time, on looking up he finds the sympathy gone

or changed, he fancies himself accused by all the bystanders; the faces of his friends are shaded by grief; and yet
no tongue ever speaks of the cause. There is some indict-
ment out against him, on which he is arraigned in many
courts, and he cannot learn the charge. A prodigious power
we have of begetting false expectations. These are the mistakes of others' subjectiveness. The true scholar will not
heed them. Jump into another bush, and scratch your eyes
in again. He passes on to acquit himself of their charges
by developments as surprising as was his first word; by in-
directions and wonderful *alibis* which dissipate the whole
crimination.   [J, VII, 113]

A man must consider what a blind-man's-buff is this game
of conformity. If I know your sect I anticipate your argument. I hear a preacher announce for his text and topic the
expediency of one of the institutions of his church. Do I
not know beforehand that not possibly can he say a new
and spontaneous word? Do I not know that with all this
ostentation of examining the grounds of the institution he
will do no such thing? Do I not know that he is pledged to
himself not to look but at one side, the permitted side, not
as a man, but as a parish minister? He is a retained attorney,
and these airs of the bench are the emptiest affectation.
Well, most men have bound their eyes with one or another
handkerchief, and attached themselves to some one of these
communities of opinion. This conformity makes them not
false in a few particulars, authors of a few lies, but false
in all particulars. Their every truth is not quite true. Their
two is not the real two, their four not the real four; so that
every word they say chagrins us and we know not where
to begin to set them right. Meantime nature is not slow to
equip us in the prison-uniform of the party to which we
adhere. We come to wear one cut of face and figure, and
acquire by degrees the gentlest asinine expression. There is
a mortifying experience in particular, which does not fail
to wreak itself also in the general history; I mean "the foolish face of praise," the forced smile which we put on in
company where we do not feel at ease, in answer to conversation which does not interest us. The muscles, not spon-

taneously moved but moved by a low usurping wilfulness, grow tight about the outline of the face, with the most disagreeable sensation.

For nonconformity the world whips you with its displeasure. And therefore a man must know how to estimate a sour face. The by-standers look askance on him in the public street or in the friend's parlor. If this aversion had its origin in contempt and resistance like his own he might well go home with a sad countenance; but the sour faces of the multitude, like their sweet faces, have no deep cause, but are put on and off as the wind blows and a newspaper directs. Yet is the discontent of the multitude more formidable than that of the senate and the college. It is easy enough for a firm man who knows the world to brook the rage of the cultivated classes. Their rage is decorous and prudent, for they are timid, as being very vulnerable themselves. But when to their feminine rage the indignation of the people is added, when the ignorant and the poor are aroused, when the unintelligent brute force that lies at the bottom of society is made to growl and mow, it needs the habit of magnanimity and religion to treat it godlike as a trifle of no concernment. [W, II, 54–56]

It requires great courage in a man of letters to handle the contemporary practical questions; not because he then has all men for his rivals, but because of the infinite entanglements of the problem, and the waste of strength in gathering unripe fruits. The task is superhuman; and the poet knows well that a little time will do more than the most puissant genius. Time stills the loud noise of opinions, sinks the small, raises the great, so that the true emerges without effort and in perfect harmony to all eyes; but the truth of the present hour, except in particulars and single relations, is unattainable. Each man can very well know his own part of duty, if he will; but to bring out the truth for beauty, and as literature, surmounts the powers of art. The most elaborate history of today will have the oddest dislocated look in the next generation. The historian of today is yet three ages off. The poet cannot descend into the turbid present without injury to his rarest gifts. Hence that

necessity of isolation which genius has always felt. He must stand on his glass tripod, if he would keep his electricity.
[W, XII, 383]

I cannot forgive a scholar his homeless despondency. He represents intellectual or spiritual force. I wish him to rely on the spiritual arm; to live by his strength, not by his weakness. A scholar defending the cause of slavery, of arbitrary government, of monopoly, of the oppressor, is a traitor to his profession. He has ceased to be a scholar. He is not company for clean people.   [W, X, 247]

Here you are set down, scholars and idealists, as in a barbarous age; amidst insanity, to calm and guide it; amidst fools and blind, to see the right done; among violent proprietors, to check self-interest, stone-blind and stone-deaf, by considerations of humanity to the workman and to his child; amongst angry politicians swelling with self-esteem, pledged to parties, pledged to clients, you are to make valid the large considerations of equity and good sense; under bad governments to force on them, by your persistence, good laws. Around that immovable persistency of yours, statesmen, legislatures, must resolve, denying you, but not less forced to obey.   [W, VIII, 230–231]

Difficulties exist to be surmounted. The great heart will no more complain of the obstructions that make success hard, than of the iron walls of the gun which hinder the shot from scattering. It was walled round with iron tube with that purpose, to give it irresistible force in one direction. A strenuous soul hates cheap successes. It is the ardor of the assailant that makes the vigor of the defender. The great are not tender at being obscure, despised, insulted. Such only feel themselves in adverse fortune. Strong men greet war, tempest, hard times, which search till they find resistance and bottom. They wish, as Pindar said, "to tread the floors of hell, with necessities as hard as iron."   [W, VIII, 231–232]

Why should I hasten to solve every riddle which life offers me? I am well assured that the Questioner who brings me so many problems will bring the answers also in due time. Very rich, very potent, very cheerful Giver that he is, he shall have it all his own way, for me. Why should I give up my thought, because I cannot answer an objection to it? Consider only whether it remains in my life the same it was. [W, VI, 230]

Emerson knows how hard it is for the self to preserve its freedom, appreciates the despotism of popular opinion, yet self-reliance is sanity and the mob is deranged. The scholar must often choose between repose and truth. By his deeds he reminds the man in the street that he, too, need not skulk through the world.

We need not much mind what people please to say, but what they must say; what their natures say, though their busy, artful, Yankee understandings try to hold back and choke that word, and to articulate something different. If we will sit quietly, what they ought to say is said, with their will or against their will. We do not care for you, let us pretend what we may—we are always looking through you to the dim dictator behind you. [W, VI, 228–229]

We know who is benevolent, by quite other means than the amount of subscription to soup-societies. It is only low merits that can be enumerated. Fear, when your friends say to you what you have done well, and say it through; but when they stand with uncertain timid looks of respect and half-dislike, and must suspend their judgment for years to come, you may begin to hope. Those who live to the future must always appear selfish to those who live to the present.
[W, III, 103]

No sane man at last distrusts himself. His existence is a perfect answer to all sentimental cavils. If he is, he is wanted, and has the precise properties that are required. That we are here, is proof we ought to be here. [W, VI, 252]

The moment a man says, "Give up your rights, here is money," there is tyranny. It comes masquerading in monks' cowls and in citizens' coats; comes savagely or comes politely. But it is tyranny. [J, VIII, 242–243]

The mass are animal, in pupilage, and near chimpanzee. But the units whereof this mass is composed, are neuters, every one of which may be grown to a queen-bee. The rule is, we are used as brute atoms until we think: then we use all the rest. [W, VI, 251–252]

The history of persecution is a history of endeavors to cheat nature, to make water run up hill, to twist a rope of sand. It makes no difference whether the actors be many or one, a tyrant or a mob. A mob is a society of bodies voluntarily bereaving themselves of reason and traversing its work. The mob is man voluntarily descending to the nature of the beast. Its fit hour of activity is night. Its actions are insane, like its whole constitution. It persecutes a principle; it would whip a right; it would tar and feather justice, by inflicting fire and outrage upon the houses and persons of those who have these. It resembles the prank of boys, who run with fire-engines to put out the ruddy aurora streaming to the stars. The inviolate spirit turns their spite against the wrongdoers. The martyr cannot be dishonored. Every lash inflicted is a tongue of fame; every prison a more illustrious abode; every burned book or house enlightens the world; every suppressed or expunged word reverberates through the earth from side to side. Hours of sanity and consideration are always arriving to communities, as to individuals, when the truth is seen and the martyrs are justified. [W, II, 119–120]

God offers to every mind its choice between truth and repose. Take which you please—you can never have both. Between these, as a pendulum, man oscillates. He in whom the love of repose predominates will accept the first creed, the first philosophy, the first political party he meets—most likely his father's. He gets rest, commodity and reputation; but he shuts the door of truth. He in whom the love of truth predominates will keep himself aloof from all moorings, and afloat. He will abstain from dogmatism, and recognize all the opposite negations between which, as walls, his being is swung. He submits to the inconvenience of suspense and imperfect opinion. . . .   [W, II, 341–342]

What have I gained, that I no longer immolate a bull to Jove or to Neptune, or a mouse to Hecate; that I do not tremble before the Eumenides, or the Catholic Purgatory, or the Calvinistic Judgment-day—if I quake at opinion, the public opinion as we call it; or at the threat of assault, or contumely, or bad neighbors, or poverty, or mutilation, or at the rumor of revolution, or of murder? If I quake, what matters it what I quake at? Our proper vice takes form in one or another shape, according to the sex, age, or temperament of the person, and, if we are capable of fear, will readily find terrors.   [W, III, 98]

I hear with pleasure that a young girl in the midst of rich, decorous Unitarian friends in Boston is well-nigh persuaded to join the Roman Catholic Church. Her friends, who are also my friends, lamented to me the growth of this inclination. But I told them that I think she is to be greatly congratulated on the event. She has lived in great poverty of events. In form and years a woman, she is still a child, having had no experiences, and although of a fine, liberal, susceptible, expanding nature, has never yet found any worthy object of attention; has not been in love, nor been called out by any taste, except lately by music, and sadly wants adequate objects. In this church, perhaps, she shall find what she needs, in a power to call out the slumbering religious sentiment. It is unfortunate that the guide who has led her into this path is a young girl of a lively, forcible, but quite external character, who teaches her the historical argument for the Catholic faith. I told A. that I hoped she would not be misled by attaching any importance to that. If the offices of the church attracted her, if its beautiful forms and humane spirit draw her, if St. Augustine and St. Bernard, Jesus and Madonna, cathedral music and masses, then go, for thy dear heart's sake, but do not go out of this icehouse of Unitarianism, all external, into an icehouse again of external. At all events, I charged her to pay no regard to dissenters, but to suck that orange thoroughly.   [J, VI, 217–218]

If I were a preacher, I should carry straight to church the remark Lidian made today, that "she had been more troubled by piety in her help than with any other fault. The girls that are not pious, she finds kind and sensible, but the church members are scorpions, too religious to do their duties, and full of wrath and horror at her if she does them." [J, V, 569]

That idea which I approach and am magnetized by—is my Country.

How we love to be magnetized! Ah, ye strong iron currents, take me in also! We are so apologetic, such waifs and straws, ducking and imitating, and then the mighty thought comes sailing on a silent wind and fills us also with its virtue, and we stand like Atlas on our legs and uphold the world. [J, VI, 489]

This feeling I have respecting Homer and Greek, that in this great, empty continent of ours, stretching enormous almost from pole to pole, with thousands of long rivers and thousands of ranges of mountains, the rare scholar, who, under a farmhouse roof, reads Homer and the Tragedies, adorns the land. He begins to fill it with wit, to counterbalance the enormous disproportion of the unquickened earth. He who first reads Homer in America is its Cadmus and Numa, and a subtle but unlimited benefactor.

[J, VI, 281]

We have our culture, like Allston, from Europe, and are Europeans. Perhaps we must be content with this and thank God for Europe for a while yet, and there shall be no great Yankee, until, in the unfolding of our population and power, England kicks the beam, and English authors write to America; which must happen ere long. [J, VI, 264–265]

Why are the masses, from the dawn of history down, food for knives and powder? The idea dignifies a few leaders, who have sentiment, opinion, love, self-devotion; and they make war and death sacred—but what for the wretches whom they hire and kill? The cheapness of man is every day's tragedy. It is as real a loss that others should be low as that we should be low; for we must have society.

[W, IV, 30–31]

Let a man then know his worth, and keep things under his feet. Let him not peep or steal, or skulk up and down with the air of a charity-boy, a bastard, or an interloper in the world which exists for him. But the man in the street, finding no worth in himself which corresponds to the force which built a tower or sculptured a marble god, feels poor when he looks on these. To him a palace, a statue, or a costly book have an alien and forbidding air, much like a gay equipage, and seem to say like that, "Who are you, Sir?" Yet they all are his, suitors for his notice, petitioners to his faculties that they will come out and take possession. The picture waits for my verdict; it is not to command me, but I am to settle its claims to praise. That popular fable of the sot who was picked up dead-drunk in the street, carried to the duke's house, washed and dressed and laid in the duke's bed, and, on his waking, treated with all obsequious ceremony like the duke, and assured that he had been insane, owes its popularity to the fact that it symbolizes so well the state of man, who is in the world a sort of sot, but now and then wakes up, exercises his reason and finds himself a true prince.   [W, I, 61–62]

Man is imprisoned by history, books, institutions, by the "ponderous machinery" of what has been done and said before. The fresh and plastic idea hardens into dogma. What once redeemed, later enslaves, and we drag around the corpse of our memories. Live for yourself and let others live for themselves. Trust your private heart.

We are full of mechanical actions. We must needs intermeddle and have things in our own way, until the sacrifices and virtues of society are odious. Love should make joy; but our benevolence is unhappy. Our Sunday-schools and churches and pauper-societies are yokes to the neck. We pain ourselves to please nobody. There are natural ways of arriving at the same ends at which these aim, but do not arrive. Why should all virtue work in one and the same way? Why should all give dollars? It is very inconvenient to us country folk, and we do not think any good will come of it. We have not dollars, merchants have; let them give them. . . . And why drag this dead weight of a Sunday-school over the whole Christendom? It is natural and beautiful that childhood should inquire and maturity should teach; but it is time enough to answer questions when they are asked. Do not shut up the young people against their will in a pew and force the children to ask them questions for an hour against their will.

If we look wider, things are all alike; laws and letters and creeds and modes of living seem a travesty of truth. Our society is encumbered by ponderous machinery, which resembles the endless aqueducts which the Romans built over hill and dale and which are superseded by the discovery of the law that water rises to the level of its source. It is a Chinese wall which any nimble Tartar can leap over. . . .

Let us draw a lesson from nature, which always works by short ways. When the fruit is ripe, it falls. When the fruit is despatched, the leaf falls. The circuit of the waters is mere falling. The walking of man and all animals is a falling forward. All our manual labor and works of strength, as prying, splitting, digging, rowing and so forth, are done by dint of continual falling, and the globe, earth, moon, comet, sun, star, fall for ever and ever.   [W, II, 135–137]

There is less intention in history than we ascribe to it. We impute deep-laid far-sighted plans to Cæsar and Napoleon; but the best of their power was in nature, not in them. Men of an extraordinary success, in their honest moments, have always sung "Not unto us, not unto us." According to the faith of their times they have built altars to Fortune, or to Destiny, or to St. Julian. Their success lay in their parallelism to the course of thought, which found in them an unobstructed channel; and the wonders of which they were the visible conductors seemed to the eye their deed. Did the wires generate the galvanism? It is even true that there was less in them on which they could reflect than in another;

as the virtue of a pipe is to be smooth and hollow. That which externally seemed will and immovableness was willingness and self-annihilation. Could Shakespeare give a theory of Shakespeare? Could ever a man of prodigious mathematical genius convey to others any insight into his methods? If he could communicate that secret it would instantly lose its exaggerated value, blending with the daylight and the vital energy the power to stand and to go.

The lesson is forcibly taught by these observations that our life might be much easier and simpler than we make it; that the world might be a happier place than it is; that there is no need of struggles, convulsions, and despairs, of the wringing of the hands and the gnashing of the teeth; that we miscreate our own evils. We interfere with the optimism of nature; for whenever we get this vantage-ground of the past, or of a wiser mind in the present, we are able to discern that we are begirt with laws which execute themselves.

The face of external nature teaches the same lesson. Nature will not have us fret and fume. She does not like our benevolence or our learning much better than she likes our frauds and wars. When we come out of the caucus, or the bank, or the Abolition-convention, or the Temperance-meeting, or the Transcendental club into the fields and woods, she says to us, "So hot? my little Sir."

[W, II, 134–135]

Truth is our element of life, yet if a man fasten his attention on a single aspect of truth and apply himself to that alone for a long time, the truth becomes distorted and not itself but falsehood; herein resembling the air, which is our natural element and the breath of our nostrils, but if a stream of the same be directed on the body for a time, it causes cold, fever, and even death. How wearisome the grammarian, the phrenologist, the political or religious fanatic, or indeed any possessed mortal whose balance is lost by the exaggeration of a single topic. It is incipient insanity. Every thought is a prison also. I cannot see what you see, because I am caught up by a strong wind and blown so far in one direction that I am out of the hoop of your horizon. [W, II, 339]

Each age, it is found, must write its own books; or rather, each generation for the next succeeding. The books of an older period will not fit this.

Yet hence arises a grave mischief. The sacredness which attaches to the act of creation, the act of thought, is transferred to the record. The poet chanting was felt to be a divine man: henceforth the chant is divine also. The writer was a just and wise spirit: henceforward it is settled the book is perfect; as love of the hero corrupts into worship of his statue. Instantly the book becomes noxious; the guide is a tyrant. The sluggish and perverted mind of the multitude, slow to open to the incursions of Reason, having once so opened, having once received this book, stands upon it, and makes an outcry if it is disparaged. Colleges are built on it. Books are written on it by thinkers, not by Man Thinking; by men of talent, that is, who start wrong, who set out from accepted dogmas, not from their own sight of principles. Meek young men grow up in libraries, believing it their duty to accept the views which Cicero, which Locke, which Bacon, have given; forgetful that Cicero, Locke, and Bacon were only young men in libraries when they wrote these books.

Hence, instead of Man Thinking, we have the bookworm. Hence the book-learned class, who value books, as such; not as related to nature and the human constitution, but as making a sort of Third Estate with the world and the soul. Hence the restorers of readings, the emendators, the bibliomaniacs of all degrees.

Books are the best of things, well used; abused, among the worst. What is the right use? What is the one end which all means go to effect? They are for nothing but to inspire. I had better never see a book than to be warped by its attraction clean out of my own orbit, and made a satellite instead of a system. The one thing in the world, of value, is the active soul. This every man is entitled to; this every man contains within him, although in almost all men obstructed and as yet unborn. The soul active sees absolute truth and utters truth, or creates. In this action it is genius; not the privilege of here and there a favorite, but the sound estate of every man. In its essence it is progressive. The book, the college, the school of art, the institution of any kind, stop with some past utterance of genius. This is good, say they—let us hold by this. They pin me down. They look backward and not forward. But genius looks forward: the eyes of man are set in his forehead, not in his hind-head: man hopes: genius creates. Whatever talents may be, if the man create not, the pure efflux of the Deity is not his —cinders and smoke there may be, but not yet flame. There are creative manners, there are creative actions, and creative words; manners, actions, words, that is, indicative of no custom or authority, but springing spontaneous from the mind's own sense of good and fair.

On the other part, instead of being its own seer, let it receive from another mind its truth, though it were in torrents of light, without periods of solitude, inquest, and self-recovery, and a fatal disservice is done. Genius is always sufficiently the enemy of genius by over-influence. The literature of every nation bears me witness. The English dramatic poets have Shakespearized now for two hundred years.

Undoubtedly there is a right way of reading, so it be sternly subordinated. Man Thinking must not be subdued by his instruments. Books are for the scholar's idle times. When he can read God directly, the hour is too precious to be wasted in other men's transcripts of their readings. But when the intervals of darkness come, as come they must—when the sun is hid and the stars withdraw their shining—we repair to the lamps which were kindled by their ray, to guide our steps to the East again, where the dawn is. We hear, that we may speak. The Arabian proverb says, "A fig tree, looking on a fig tree, becometh fruitful."

It is remarkable, the character of the pleasure we derive from the best books. They impress us with the conviction that one nature wrote and the same reads. We read the verses of one of the great English poets, of Chaucer, of Marvell, of Dryden, with the most modern joy—with a pleasure, I mean, which is in great part caused by the abstraction of all *time* from their verses. There is some awe mixed with the joy of our surprise, when this poet, who lived in some past world, two or three hundred years ago, says that which lies close to my own soul, that which I also

had well-nigh thought and said. But for the evidence thence
afforded to the philosophical doctrine of the identity of all
minds, we should suppose some preëstablished harmony,
some foresight of souls that were to be, and some preparation of stores for their future wants, like the fact observed
in insects, who lay up food before death for the young
grub they shall never see.   [W, I, 88–92]

I console myself in the poverty of my thoughts, in the
paucity of great men, in the malignity and dullness of the
nations, by falling back on these sublime recollections, and
seeing what the prolific soul could beget on actual nature—
seeing that Plato was, and Shakespeare, and Milton—three
irrefragable facts. Then I dare; I also will essay to be.
The humblest, the most hopeless, in view of these radiant
facts, may now theorize and hope. In spite of all the rue-
ful abortions that squeak and gibber in the street, in spite
of slumber and guilt, in spite of the army, the bar-room,
and the jail, *have been* these glorious manifestations of the
mind; and I will thank my great brothers so truly for the
admonition of their being, as to endeavor also to be just
and brave, to aspire and to speak. Plotinus too, and Spinoza,
and the immortal bards of philosophy—that which they
have written out with patient courage, makes me bold. No
more will I dismiss, with haste, the visions which flash and
sparkle across my sky; but observe them, approach them,
domesticate them, brood on them, and draw out of the
past, genuine life for the present hour.
  To feel the full value of these lives, as occasions of hope
and provocation, you must come to know that each admirable genius is but a successful diver in that sea whose floor
of pearls is all your own. The impoverishing philosophy
of ages has laid stress on the distinctions of the individual,
and not on the universal attributes of man. The youth, in-
toxicated with his admiration of a hero, fails to see that it
is only a projection of his own soul which he admires. . . .
  The difference of circumstance is merely costume. I am
tasting the self-same life—its sweetness, its greatness, its
pain, which I so admire in other men. Do not foolishly ask
of the inscrutable, obliterated past, what it cannot tell—the

details of that nature, of that day, called Byron, or Burke
—but ask it of the enveloping Now; the more quaintly you
inspect its evanescent beauties, its wonderful details, its
spiritual causes, its astounding whole—so much the more
you master the biography of this hero, and that, and every
hero. Be lord of a day, through wisdom and justice, and
you can put up your history books. [W, I, 161–163]

Fear disenchants life and the world. If I have not my
own respect I am an impostor, not entitled to other men's,
and had better creep into my grave. I admire the sentiment
of Thoreau, who said, "Nothing is so much to be feared
as fear; God himself likes atheism better." For the world is
a battle-ground; every principle is a war-note, and the most
quiet and protected life is at any moment exposed to inci-
dents which test your firmness. The illusion that strikes me
as the masterpiece in that ring of illusions which our life
is, is the timidity with which we assert our moral sentiment.
We are made of it, the world is built by it, things endure
as they share it; all beauty, all health, all intelligence exist
by it; yet we shrink to speak of it or to range ourselves by
its side. Nay, we presume strength of him or them who
deny it. Cities go against it; the college goes against it, the
courts snatch at any precedent, at any vicious form of law
to rule it out; legislatures listen with appetite to declama-
tions against it, and vote it down. Every new asserter of the
right surprises us, like a man joining the church, and we
hardly dare believe he is in earnest. [W, X, 87–88]

But why should you keep your head over your shoulder?
Why drag about this corpse of your memory, lest you contradict somewhat you have stated in this or that public
place? Suppose you should contradict yourself; what then?
It seems to be a rule of wisdom never to rely on your memory alone, scarcely even in acts of pure memory, but to
bring the past for judgment into the thousand-eyed present,
and live ever in a new day. In your metaphysics you have
denied personality to the Deity, yet when the devout motions of the soul come, yield to them heart and life, though
they should clothe God with shape and color. Leave your
theory, as Joseph his coat in the hand of the harlot, and flee.

A foolish consistency is the hobgoblin of little minds, adored by little statesmen and philosophers and divines. With consistency a great soul has simply nothing to do. He may as well concern himself with his shadow on the wall. Speak what you think now in hard words and tomorrow speak what tomorrow thinks in hard words again, though it contradict everything you said today.—"Ah, so you shall be sure to be misunderstood."—Is it so bad then to be misunderstood? Pythagoras was misunderstood, and Socrates, and Jesus, and Luther, and Copernicus, and Galileo, and Newton, and every pure and wise spirit that ever took flesh. To be great is to be misunderstood.

I suppose no man can violate his nature. All the sallies of his will are rounded in by the law of his being, as the inequalities of Andes and Himmaleh are insignificant in the curve of the sphere. Nor does it matter how you gauge and try him. A character is like an acrostic or Alexandrian stanza—read it forward, backward, or across, it still spells the same thing. In this pleasing contrite wood-life which God allows me, let me record day by day my honest thought without prospect or retrospect, and, I cannot doubt, it will be found symmetrical, though I mean it not and see it not. My book should smell of pines and resound with the hum of insects. The swallow over my window should interweave that thread or straw he carries in his bill into my web also. We pass for what we are. Character teaches above our wills. Men imagine that they communicate their virtue or vice only by overt actions, and do not see that virtue or vice emit a breath every moment.   [W, II, 57–58]

Manners impress as they indicate real power. A man who is sure of his point, carries a broad and contented expression, which everybody reads. And you cannot rightly train one to an air and manner, except by making him the kind of man of whom that manner is the natural expression. Nature forever puts a premium on reality. What is done for effect is seen to be done for effect; what is done for love is felt to be done for love. A man inspires affection and honor because he was not lying in wait for these. The things of a man for which we visit him were done in the dark and cold.

A little integrity is better than any career. So deep are the sources of this surface-action that even the size of your companion seems to vary with his freedom of thought. Not only is he larger, when at ease and his thoughts generous, but everything around him becomes variable with expression. [W, VI, 188–189]

The charm of life is this variety of genius, these contrasts and flavors by which Heaven has modulated the identity of truth, and there is a perpetual hankering to violate this individuality, to warp his ways of thinking and behavior to resemble or reflect your thinking and behavior. A low self-love in the parent desires that his child should repeat his character and fortune; an expectation which the child, if justice is done him, will nobly disappoint. By working on the theory that this resemblance exists, we shall do what in us lies to defeat his proper promise and produce the ordinary and mediocre. I suffer whenever I see that common sight of a parent or senior imposing his opinion and way of thinking and being on a young soul to which they are totally unfit. Cannot we let people be themselves, and enjoy life in their own way? You are trying to make that man another *you*. One's enough. [W, X, 137–138]

One man, you say, dreads erysipelas—show him that this dread is evil: or, one dreads hell—show him that *dread* is evil. He who loves goodness, harbors angels, reveres reverence and lives with God. The less we have to do with our sins the better. No man can afford to waste his moments in compunctions. [W, IV, 137–138]

I call you to a confidence which surmounts this painful experience. You are to have a self-support which maintains you not only against all others, but against your own skepticism. Pain, indolence, sterility, endless ennui have also their lesson for you, if you are great.

The Saharas must be crossed as well as the Nile. It is easy to live for others; everybody does. I call on you to live for yourselves, so shall you find in this penury and absence of thought a purer splendor than ever clothed the exhibitions of wit. [J, VII, 46]

To believe your own thought, to believe that what is true for you in your private heart is true for all men—that is genius. Speak your latent conviction, and it shall be the universal sense; for the inmost in due time becomes the outmost, and our first thought is rendered back to us by the trumpets of the Last Judgment. Familiar as the voice of the mind is to each, the highest merit we ascribe to Moses, Plato and Milton is that they set at naught books and traditions, and spoke not what men, but what *they* thought. A man should learn to detect and watch that gleam of light which flashes across his mind from within, more than the lustre of the firmament of bards and sages. Yet he dismisses without notice his thought, because it is his. In every work of genius we recognize our own rejected thoughts; they come back to us with a certain alienated majesty. Great works of art have no more affecting lesson for us than this. They teach us to abide by our spontaneous impression with good-humored inflexibility then most when the whole cry of voices is on the other side. Else tomorrow a stranger will say with masterly good sense precisely what we have thought and felt all the time, and we shall be forced to take with shame our own opinion from another.

There is a time in every man's education when he arrives at the conviction that envy is ignorance; that imitation is suicide; that he must take himself for better or worse as his portion; that though the wide universe is full of good, no kernel of nourishing corn can come to him but through his toil bestowed on that plot of ground which is given to him to till. The power which resides in him is new in nature, and none but he knows what that is which he can do, nor does he know until he has tried. Not for nothing one face, one character, one fact, makes much impression on him, and another none. This sculpture in the memory is not without preëstablished harmony. The eye was placed where one ray should fall, that it might testify of that particular ray. We but half express ourselves, and are ashamed of that divine idea which each of us represents. It may be safely trusted as proportionate and of good issues, so it be faithfully imparted, but God will not have his work made manifest by cowards. A man is relieved and gay when he has put his heart into his work and done his best; but what he has said or done otherwise shall give him no peace. It is a deliverance which does not deliver. In the attempt his genius deserts him; no muse befriends; no invention, no hope.

Trust thyself: every heart vibrates to that iron string. Accept the place the divine providence has found for you, the society of your contemporaries, the connection of events. Great men have always done so, and confided themselves childlike to the genius of their age, betraying their perception that the absolutely trustworthy was seated at their heart, working through their hands, predominating in all their being. And we are now men, and must accept in the highest mind the same transcendent destiny; and not minors and invalids in a protected corner, not cowards fleeing before a revolution, but guides, redeemers and benefactors, obeying the Almighty effort and advancing on Chaos and the Dark.

What pretty oracles nature yields us on this text in the face and behavior of children, babes, and even brutes! That divided and rebel mind, that distrust of a sentiment because our arithmetic has computed the strength and means opposed to our purpose, these have not. Their mind being whole, their eye is as yet unconquered, and when we look in their faces we are disconcerted. Infancy conforms to nobody; all conform to it; so that one babe commonly makes four or five out of the adults who prattle and play to it. So God has armed youth and puberty and manhood no less with its own piquancy and charm, and made it enviable and gracious and its claims not to be put by, if it will stand by itself. Do not think the youth has no force, because he cannot speak to you and me. Hark! in the next room his voice is sufficiently clear and emphatic. It seems he knows how to speak to his contemporaries. Bashful or bold then, he will know how to make us seniors very unnecessary.

The nonchalance of boys who are sure of a dinner, and would disdain as much as a lord or do or say aught to conciliate one, is the healthy attitude for human nature. A boy is in the parlor what the pit is in the playhouse; independent, irresponsible, looking out from his corner on such people and facts as pass by, he tries and sentences them on their merits, in the swift, summary way of boys, as good, bad, interesting, silly, eloquent, troublesome. He cumbers himself never about consequences, about interests; he gives an independent, genuine verdict. You must court him; he does not court you. But the man is as it were clapped into jail by his consciousness. As soon as he has once acted or spoken with *éclat* he is a committed person, watched by the sympathy or the hatred of hundreds, whose affections must now enter into his account. There is no Lethe for this. Ah, that he could pass again into his neutrality! Who can thus avoid all pledges and, having observed, observe again from the same unaffected, unbiased, unbribable, unaffrighted innocence—must always be formidable. He would utter opinions on all passing affairs, which being seen to be not private but necessary, would sink like darts into the ear of men and put them in fear.

These are the voices which we hear in solitude, but they grow faint and inaudible as we enter into the world. Society everywhere is in conspiracy against the manhood of every one of its members. Society is a joint-stock company, in which the members agree, for the better securing of his bread to each shareholder, to surrender the liberty and culture of the eater. The virtue in most request is conformity. Self-reliance is its aversion. It loves not realities and creators, but names and customs.

Whoso would be a man, must be a nonconformist. He who would gather mortal palms must not be hindered by the name of goodness, but must explore if it be goodness. Nothing is at last sacred but the integrity of your own mind. Absolve you to yourself, and you shall have the suffrage of the world. I remember an answer which when quite young I was prompted to make to a valued adviser who was wont to importune me with the dear old doctrines of the church. On my saying, "What have I to do with the sacredness of traditions, if I live wholly from within?" my friend suggested, "But these impulses may be from below, not from above." I replied, "They do not seem to me to be such; but if I am the Devil's child, I will live then from the Devil." No law can be sacred to me but that of my nature. Good and bad are but names very readily transferable to that or this; the

only right is what is after my constitution; the only wrong
what is against it. A man is to carry himself in the presence
of all opposition as if everything were titular and ephemeral
but he. I am ashamed to think how easily we capitulate to
badges and names, to large societies and dead institutions.
Every decent and well-spoken individual affects and sways
me more than is right. I ought to go upright and vital, and
speak the rude truth in all ways. If malice and vanity were
the coat of philanthropy, shall that pass? If an angry bigot
assumes this bountiful cause of Abolition, and comes to me
with his last news from Barbadoes, why should I not say to
him, "Go love thy infant; love thy wood-chopper; be good-
natured and modest; have that grace; and never varnish
your hard, uncharitable ambition with this incredible
tenderness for black folk a thousand miles off. Thy love
afar is spite at home." Rough and graceless would be such
greeting, but truth is handsomer than the affectation of love.
Your goodness must have some edge to it—else it is none.
The doctrine of hatred must be preached, as the counteraction of the doctrine of love, when that pules and whines.
I shun father and mother and wife and brother when my
genius calls me. I would write on the lintels of the door-post,
Whim. I hope it is somewhat better than whim at last, but
we cannot spend the day in explanation. Expect me not to
show cause why I seek or why I exclude company. Then
again, do not tell me, as a good man did today, of my obligation to put all poor men in good situations. Are they *my*
poor? I tell thee, thou foolish philanthropist, that I grudge
the dollar, the dime, the cent I give to such men as do not
belong to me and to whom I do not belong. There is a class
of persons to whom by all spiritual affinity I am bought and
sold; for them I will go to prison if need be; but your miscel-
laneous popular charities; the education at college of fools;
the building of meetinghouses to the vain end to which
many now stand; alms to sots, and the thousand-fold Relief
Societies—though I confess with shame I sometimes suc-
cumb and give the dollar, it is a wicked dollar, which by and
by I shall have the manhood to withhold.   [W, II, 45–52]

Chapter Three

A Thread Runs through
All Things

*Contemporary writers and artists have learned that Emer-
son is one of their ancestors. Just as nothing is more characteristic of twentieth-century art than its sense that the
essence of reality lies within, in the symbol rather than
through any effort to duplicate external reality, so to Emerson the symbol is, properly speaking, the only tool by
which man can apprehend reality at all. Emerson is in the
deepest sense a symbol-user, a believer in symbols and a
maker of symbols, a writer whose approach to reality is
always delicate, light, on the wing, and full of intellectual
wit. We think of Paul Klee when Emerson observes that
Nature "is no literalist. Everything must be taken genially,"
and of William Butler Yeats when Emerson says that "There
is a joy in perceiving the representative or symbolic character of a fact, which no bare fact or event can ever give."*

*Yet Emerson's belief in the symbol as the central tool of
knowledge—the only bridge open to man, as it were—goes
deeper than the practice of most twentieth-century writers
and artists. Emerson's belief is much more committed,
much more fully expressed than is the case with those
writers who have turned to symbolism as a protest against
the heavy and naïve realism of the nineteenth century. For
Emerson's faith in the symbol is consciously metaphysical;
to him the symbol is not merely the vehicle of art but the
essence of man's individual worship. The transmutation of*

ordinary experience into the passionate perception of the world, the deepening of "fancy" into "imagination," of the mere "understanding" into the higher "reason"—all this double work man must accomplish every day in the world is made possible only by the right perception of symbols. "All things are symbolical," he says here, "and what we call results are beginnings."

The symbol is, ultimately, only a mark of the thread that runs through all things. Standing on this shore, man perceives that his whole life is a symbol and a metaphor of what lies beyond him and all about him. Yet in Emerson's thought, all symbols are accidental and fugitive; he does not look upon them, as the modern artist does, with a gratified sensuousness. Emerson is in some respects more a "Platonist" than Plato himself—he is more abstract, more devoted to the symbol as an intellectual thing than as a piece of the divine. But unlike Plato, he manages at the same time, with breathtaking consistency, to make the "symbol" the vehicle of a mystical private dominion.

The symbol, for Emerson, has its ultimate importance as a sacrament of daily existence. With the symbol, man makes language; he makes art; he becomes a "poet." But for Emerson, "a God-intoxicated man" if ever there was one, the ultimate reach and function of these matters is that through uses of the symbol, man enters into a profoundly fraught "correspondence" with the invisible powers, with the world of spirit. Through the symbol, man is connected with the truth of what is symbolized. So the symbol is not only man's speech and man's art and man's religion, but the symbol is man's freedom. With it, man goes forth anew every day to take possession of his world.

We learn nothing rightly until we learn the symbolical character of life. Day creeps after day, each full of facts, dull, strange, despised things, that we cannot enough despise—call heavy, prosaic and desert. The time we seek to kill: the attention it is elegant to divert from things around us. And presently the aroused intellect finds cold and gems in one of these scorned facts—then finds that the day of facts is a rock of diamonds; that a fact is an Epiphany of God.   [W, X, 132]

Possession, the soul of God poured through the thoughts of men.   [J, IX, 489]

We are far from having exhausted the significance of the few symbols we use. We can come to use them yet with a terrible simplicity. It does not need that a poem should be long. Every word was once a poem. Every new relation is a new word. Also we use defects and deformities to a sacred purpose, so expressing our sense that the evils of the world are such only to the evil eye. In the old mythology, mythologists observe, defects are ascribed to divine natures, as lameness to Vulcan, blindness to Cupid, and the like—to signify exuberances.

For as it is dislocation and detachment from the life of God that makes things ugly, the poet, who re-attaches things to nature and the Whole—re-attaching even artificial things and violation of nature, to nature, by a deeper insight— disposes very easily of the most disagreeable facts.

[W, III, 18–19]

Philosophically considered, the universe is composed of Nature and the Soul. Strictly speaking, therefore, all that is separate from us, all which Philosophy distinguishes as the NOT ME, that is, both nature and art, all other men and my own body, must be ranked under this name, NATURE. In enumerating the values of nature and casting up their sum, I shall use the word in both senses—in its common and in its philosophical import. In inquiries so general as our present one, the inaccuracy is not material; no confusion of thought will occur. *Nature,* in the common sense, refers to essences unchanged by man; space, the air, the river, the leaf. *Art* is applied to the mixture of his will with the same things, as in a house, a canal, a statue, a picture. But his operations taken together are so insignificant, a little chipping, baking, patching, and washing, that in an impression so grand as that of the world on the human mind, they do not vary the result.   [W, I, 4–5]

. . . along with the civil and metaphysical history of man, another history goes daily forward—that of the external world—in which he is not less strictly implicated. . . . His power consists in the multitude of his affinities, in the fact that his life is intertwined with the whole chain of organic and inorganic being. In old Rome the public roads beginning at the Forum proceeded north, south, east, west, to the centre of every province of the empire, making each market-town of Persia, Spain and Britain pervious to the soldiers of the capital: so out of the human heart go as it were highways to the heart of every object in nature, to reduce it under the dominion of man. A man is a bundle of relations, a knot of roots, whose flower and fruitage is the world. His faculties refer to natures out of him and predict the world he is to inhabit, as the fins of the fish foreshow that water exists, or the wings of an eagle in the egg presuppose air. He cannot live without a world. Put Napoleon in an island prison, let his faculties find no men to act on, no Alps to climb, no stake to play for, and he would beat the air, and appear stupid.   [W, II, 35–36]

Language is a . . . use which Nature subserves to man. Nature is the vehicle of thought, and in a simple, double, and three-fold degree.

1. Words are signs of natural facts.
2. Particular natural facts are symbols of particular spiritual facts.
3. Nature is the symbol of spirit.

1. Words are signs of natural facts. The use of natural history is to give us aid in supernatural history; the use of the outer creation, to give us language for the beings and changes of the inward creation. Every word which is used to express a moral or intellectual fact, if traced to its root, is found to be borrowed from some material appearance. *Right* means *straight; wrong* means *twisted; Spirit* primarily means *wind; transgression,* the *crossing of a line; supercilious,* the *raising of the eyebrow.* We say the *heart* to express emotion, the *head* to denote thought; and *thought* and *emotion* are words borrowed from sensible things, and now

appropriated to spiritual nature. Most of the process by which this transformation is made, is hidden from us in the remote time when language was framed; but the same tendency may be daily observed in children. Children and savages use only nouns or names of things, which they convert into verbs, and apply to analogous mental acts.

2. But this origin of all words that convey a spiritual import—so conspicuous a fact in the history of language—is our least debt to nature. It is not words only that are emblematic; it is things which are emblematic. Every natural fact is a symbol of some spiritual fact. Every appearance in nature corresponds to some state of the mind, and that state of the mind can only be described by presenting that natural appearance as its picture. An enraged man is a lion, a cunning man is a fox, a firm man is a rock, a learned man is a torch. A lamb is innocence; a snake is subtle spite; flowers express to us the delicate affections. Light and darkness are our familiar expression for knowledge and ignorance; and heat for love. Visible distance behind and before us, is respectively our image of memory and hope.

Who looks upon a river in a meditative hour and is not reminded of the flux of all things? Throw a stone into the stream, and the circles that propagate themselves are the beautiful type of all influence. Man is conscious of a universal soul within or behind his individual life, wherein, as in a firmament, the natures of Justice, Truth, Love, Freedom, arise and shine. This universal soul he calls Reason: it is not mine, or thine, or his, but we are its; we are its property and men. And the blue sky in which the private earth is buried, the sky with its eternal calm, and full of everlasting orbs, is the type of Reason. That which intellectually considered we call Reason, considered in relation to nature, we call Spirit. Spirit is the Creator. Spirit hath life in itself. And man in all ages and countries embodies it in his language as the FATHER.

It is easily seen that there is nothing lucky or capricious in these analogies, but that they are constant, and pervade nature. These are not the dreams of a few poets, here and there, but man is an analogist, and studies relations in all objects. He is placed in the centre of beings, and a ray of relation passes from every other being to him. And neither can man be understood without these objects, nor these objects without man. All the facts in natural history taken by themselves, have no value, but are barren, like a single sex. But marry it to human history, and it is full of life. Whole floras, all Linnæus' and Buffon's volumes, are dry catalogues of facts; but the most trivial of these facts, the habit of a plant, the organs, or work, or noise of an insect, applied to the illustration of a fact in intellectual philosophy, or in any way associated to human nature, affects us in the most lively and agreeable manner. The seed of a plant—to what affecting analogies in the nature of man is that little fruit made use of, in all discourse, up to the voice of Paul, who calls the human corpse a seed—"It is sown a natural body; it is raised a spiritual body." The motion of the earth round its axis and round the sun, makes the day and the year. These are certain amounts of brute light and heat. But is there no intent of an analogy between man's life and the seasons? And do the seasons gain no grandeur or pathos from that analogy? The instincts of the ant are very unimportant considered as the ant's; but the moment a ray of relation is seen to extend from it to man, and the little drudge is seen to be a monitor, a little body with a mighty heart, then all its habits, even that said to be recently observed, that it never sleeps, become sublime.

Because of this radical correspondence between visible things and human thoughts, savages, who have only what is necessary, converse in figures. As we go back in history, language becomes more picturesque, until its infancy, when it is all poetry; or all spiritual facts are represented by natural symbols. The same symbols are found to make the original elements of all languages. It has moreover been observed, that the idioms of all languages approach each other in passages of the greatest eloquence and power. And as this is the first language, so is it the last. This immediate dependence of language upon nature, this conversion of an outward phenomenon into a type of somewhat in human life, never loses its power to affect us. It is this which gives that piquancy to the conversation of a strong-natured farmer or backwoodsman, which all men relish.

A man's power to connect his thought with its proper symbol, and so to utter it, depends on the simplicity of his character, that is, upon his love of truth and his desire to communicate it without loss. The corruption of man is followed by the corruption of language. When simplicity of character and the sovereignty of ideas is broken up by the prevalence of secondary desires—the desire of riches, of pleasure, of power, and of praise—and duplicity and falsehood take place of simplicity and truth, the power over nature as an interpreter of the will is in a degree lost; new imagery ceases to be created, and old words are perverted to stand for things which are not; a paper currency is employed, when there is no bullion in the vaults. In due time the fraud is manifest, and words lose all power to stimulate the understanding or the affections. Hundreds of writers may be found in every long-civilized nation who for a short time believe and make others believe that they see and utter truths, who do not of themselves clothe one thought in its natural garment, but who feed unconsciously on the language created by the primary writers of the country, those, namely, who hold primarily on nature.

But wise men pierce this rotten diction and fasten words again to visible things; so that picturesque language is at once a commanding certificate that he who employs it is a man in alliance with truth and God. The moment our discourse rises above the ground line of familiar facts and is inflamed with passion or exalted by thought, it clothes itself in images. A man conversing in earnest, if he watch his intellectual processes, will find that a material image more or less luminous arises in his mind, contemporaneous with every thought, which furnishes the vestment of the thought. Hence, good writing and brilliant discourse are perpetual allegories. This imagery is spontaneous. It is the blending of experience with the present action of the mind. It is proper creation. It is the working of the Original Cause through the instruments he has already made.

These facts may suggest the advantage which the country-life possesses, for a powerful mind, over the artificial and curtailed life of cities. We know more from nature than we can at will communicate. Its light flows into the mind ever-

more, and we forget its presence. The poet, the orator, bred
in the woods, whose senses have been nourished by their
fair and appeasing changes, year after year, without design
and without heed—shall not lose their lesson altogether, in
the roar of cities or the broil of politics. Long hereafter,
amidst agitation and terror in national councils—in the hour
of revolution—these solemn images shall reappear in their
morning lustre, as fit symbols and words of the thoughts
which the passing events shall awaken. At the call of a noble
sentiment, again the woods wave, the pines murmur, the
river rolls and shines, and the cattle low upon the mountains, as he saw and heard them in his infancy. And with
these forms, the spells of persuasion, the keys of power are
put into his hands.

3. We are thus assisted by natural objects in the expression of particular meanings. But how great a language to
convey such pepper-corn informations! Did it need such
noble races of creatures; this profusion of forms, this host
of orbs in heaven, to furnish man with the dictionary and
grammar of his municipal speech? Whilst we use this grand
cipher to expedite the affairs of our pot and kettle, we feel
that we have not yet put it to its use, neither are able. We
are like travellers using the cinders of a volcano to roast
their eggs. Whilst we see that it always stands ready to
clothe what we would say, we cannot avoid the question
whether the characters are not significant of themselves.
Have mountains, and waves, and skies, no significance but
what we consciously give them when we employ them as
emblems of our thoughts? The world is emblematic. Parts
of speech are metaphors, because the whole of nature is a
metaphor of the human mind. The laws of moral nature
answer to those of matter as face to face in a glass. "The
visible world and the relation of its parts, is the dial plate
of the invisible." The axioms of physics translate the laws
of ethics. Thus, "the whole is greater than its part"; "reaction is equal to action"; "the smallest weight may be made
to lift the greatest, the difference of weight being compensated by time"; and many the like propositions, which have
an ethical as well as physical sense. These propositions have

a much more extensive and universal sense when applied to human life, than when confined to technical use.

In like manner, the memorable words of history and the proverbs of nations consist usually of a natural fact, selected as a picture or parable of a moral truth. Thus: A rolling stone gathers no moss; A bird in the hand is worth two in the bush; A cripple in the right way will beat a racer in the wrong; Make hay while the sun shines; 'Tis hard to carry a full cup even; Vinegar is the son of wine; The last ounce broke the camel's back; Long-lived trees make roots first— and the like. In their primary sense these are trivial facts, but we repeat them for the value of their analogical import. What is true of proverbs, is true of all fables, parables, and allegories.

This relation between the mind and matter is not fancied by some poet, but stands in the will of God, and so is free to be known by all men. It appears to men, or it does not appear. When in fortunate hours we ponder this miracle, the wise man doubts if at all other times he is not blind and deaf;

> "Can such things be,
> And overcome us like a summer's cloud,
> Without our special wonder?"

for the universe becomes transparent, and the light of higher laws than its own shines through it. It is the standing problem which has exercised the wonder and the study of every fine genius since the world began; from the era of the Egyptians and the Brahmins to that of Pythagoras, of Plato, of Bacon, of Leibnitz, of Swedenborg. There sits the Sphinx at the road-side, and from age to age, as each prophet comes by, he tries his fortune at reading her riddle. There seems to be a necessity in spirit to manifest itself in material forms; and day and night, river and storm, beast and bird, acid and alkali, preëxist in necessary Ideas in the mind of God, and are what they are by virtue of preceding affections in the world of spirit. A Fact is the end or last issue of spirit. The visible creation is the terminus or the circumference of the invisible world. "Material objects," said a French philosopher, "are necessarily kinds of *scoriæ* of the substantial thoughts of the Creator, which must always preserve an exact relation to their first origin; in other words, visible nature must have a spiritual and moral side."

This doctrine is abstruse, and though the images of "garment," "scoriæ," "mirror," etc., may stimulate the fancy, we must summon the aid of subtler and more vital expositors to make it plain. "Every scripture is to be interpreted by the same spirit which gave it forth," is the fundamental law of criticism. A life in harmony with Nature, the love of truth and of virtue, will purge the eyes to understand her text. By degrees we may come to know the primitive sense of the permanent objects of nature, so that the world shall be to us an open book, and every form significant of its hidden life and final cause.

A new interest surprises us, whilst, under the view now suggested, we contemplate the fearful extent and multitude of objects; since "every object rightly seen, unlocks a new faculty of the soul." That which was unconscious truth, becomes, when interpreted and defined in an object, a part of the domain of knowledge—a new weapon in the magazine of power.   [W, I, 25–35]

EACH AND ALL

Little thinks, in the field, yon red-cloaked clown
Of thee from the hill-top looking down;
The heifer that lows in the upland farm,
Far-heard, lows not thine ear to charm;
The sexton, tolling his bell at noon,
Deems not that great Napoleon
Stops his horse, and lists with delight,
Whilst his files sweep round yon Alpine height;
Nor knowest thou what argument
Thy life to thy neighbor's creed has lent.
All are needed by each one;
Nothing is fair or good alone.
I thought the sparrow's note from heaven,
Singing at dawn on the alder bough;

I brought him home, in his nest, at even;
He sings the song, but it cheers not now,
For I did not bring home the river and sky;
He sang to my ear—they sang to my eye.
The delicate shells lay on the shore;
The bubbles of the latest wave
Fresh pearls to their enamel gave,
And the bellowing of the savage sea
Greeted their safe escape to me.
I wiped away the weeds and foam,
I fetched my sea-born treasures home;
But the poor, unsightly, noisome things
Had left their beauty on the shore
With the sun and the sand and the wild uproar.

The lover watched his graceful maid,
As 'mid the virgin train she strayed,
Nor knew her beauty's best attire
Was woven still by the snow-white choir.
At last she came to his hermitage,
Like the bird from the woodlands to the cage;
The gay enchantment was undone,
A gentle wife, but fairy none.
Then I said, "I covet truth;
Beauty is unripe childhood's cheat;
I leave it behind with the games of youth":
As I spoke, beneath my feet
The ground-pine curled its pretty wreath,
Running over the club-moss burrs;
I inhaled the violet's breath;
Around me stood the oaks and firs;
Pine-cones and acorns lay on the ground;
Over me soared the eternal sky,
Full of light and of deity;
Again I saw, again I heard,
The rolling river, the morning bird;
Beauty through my senses stole;
I yielded myself to the perfect whole.

[W, IX, 4–6]

In view of the significance of nature, we arrive at once at a new fact, that nature is a discipline. This use of the world includes the preceding uses, as parts of itself.

Space, time, society, labor, climate, food, locomotion, the animals, the mechanical forces, give us sincerest lessons, day by day, whose meaning is unlimited. They educate both the Understanding and the Reason. Every property of matter is a school for the understanding—its solidity or resistance, its inertia, its extension, its figure, its divisibility. The understanding adds, divides, combines, measures, and finds nutriment and room for its activity in this worthy scene. Meantime, Reason transfers all these lessons into its own world of thought, by perceiving the analogy that marries Matter and Mind.

1. Nature is a discipline of the understanding in intellectual truths. Our dealing with sensible objects is a constant exercise in the necessary lessons of difference, of likeness, of order, of being and seeming, of progressive arrangement; of ascent from particular to general; of combination to one end of manifold forces. Proportioned to the importance of the organ to be formed, is the extreme care with which its tuition is provided—a care pretermitted in no single case. What tedious training, day after day, year after year, never ending, to form the common sense; what continual reproduction of annoyances, inconveniences, dilemmas; what rejoicing over us of little men; what disputing of prices, what reckonings of interest—and all to form the Hand of the mind—to instruct us that "good thoughts are no better than good dreams, unless they be executed!"

The same good office is performed by Property and its filial systems of debt and credit. Debt, grinding debt, whose iron face the widow, the orphan, and the sons of genius fear and hate—debt, which consumes so much time, which so cripples and disheartens a great spirit with cares that seem so base, is a preceptor whose lessons cannot be foregone, and is needed most by those who suffer from it most. Moreover, property, which has been well compared to snow—"if it fall level today, it will be blown into drifts tomorrow," is the surface action of internal machinery, like the index on the face of a clock. Whilst now it is the gymnastics of the understanding, it is hiving, in the foresight of the spirit, experience in profounder laws.

The whole character and fortune of the individual are affected by the least inequalities in the culture of the understanding; for example, in the perception of differences. Therefore is Space, and therefore Time, that man may know that things are not huddled and lumped, but sundered and individual. A bell and a plough have each their use, and neither can do the office of the other. Water is good to drink, coal to burn, wool to wear; but wool cannot be drunk, nor water spun, nor coal eaten. The wise man shows his wisdom in separation, in gradation, and his scale of creatures and of merits is as wide as nature. The foolish have no range in their scale, but suppose every man is as every other man. What is not good they call the worst, and what is not hateful, they call the best.

In like manner, what good heed Nature forms in us! She pardons no mistakes. Her yea is yea, and her nay, nay.

The first steps in Agriculture, Astronomy, Zoölogy (those first steps which the farmer, the hunter, and the sailor take), teach that Nature's dice are always loaded; that in her heaps and rubbish are concealed sure and useful results.

How calmly and genially the mind apprehends one after another the laws of physics! What noble emotions dilate the mortal as he enters into the councils of the creation, and feels by knowledge the privilege to BE! His insight refines him. The beauty of nature shines in his own breast. Man is greater that he can see this, and the universe less, because Time and Space relations vanish as laws are known.

Here again we are impressed and even daunted by the immense Universe to be explored. "What we know is a point to what we do not know." Open any recent journal of science, and weigh the problems suggested concerning Light, Heat, Electricity, Magnetism, Physiology, Geology, and judge whether the interest of natural science is likely to be soon exhausted.

Passing by many particulars of the discipline of nature, we must not omit to specify two.

The exercise of the Will, or the lesson of power, is taught in every event. From the child's successive possession of his several senses up to the hour when he saith, "Thy will be done!" he is learning the secret that he can reduce under his will not only particular events but great classes, nay, the whole series of events, and so conform all facts to his character. Nature is thoroughly mediate. It is made to serve. It receives the dominion of man as meekly as the ass on which the Saviour rode. It offers all its kingdoms to man as the raw material which he may mould into what is useful. Man is never weary of working it up. He forges the subtile and delicate air into wise and melodious words, and gives them wing as angels of persuasion and command. One after another his victorious thought comes up with and reduces all things, until the world becomes at last only a realized will— the double of the man.

2. Sensible objects conform to the premonitions of Reason and reflect the conscience. All things are moral; and in their boundless changes have an unceasing reference to spiritual nature. Therefore is nature glorious with form, color, and motion; that every globe in the remotest heaven, every chemical change from the rudest crystal up to the laws of life, every change of vegetation from the first principle of growth in the eye of a leaf, to the tropical forest and antediluvian coal-mine, every animal function from the sponge up to Hercules, shall hint or thunder to man the laws of right and wrong, and echo the Ten Commandments. Therefore is Nature ever the ally of Religion: lends all her pomp and riches to the religious sentiment. Prophet and priest, David, Isaiah, Jesus, have drawn deeply from this source. This ethical character so penetrates the bone and marrow of nature, as to seem the end for which it was made. Whatever private purpose is answered by any member or part, this is its public and universal function, and is never omitted. Nothing in nature is exhausted in its first use. When a thing has served an end to the uttermost, it is wholly new for an ulterior service. In God, every end is converted into a new means. Thus the use of commodity, regarded by itself, is mean and squalid. But it is to the mind an education in the doctrine of Use, namely, that a thing is good only so far as it serves; that a conspiring of parts and efforts to the production of an end is essential to any being. The first and

gross manifestation of this truth is our inevitable and hated
training in values and wants, in corn and meat.

It has already been illustrated, that every natural process
is a version of a moral sentence. The moral law lies at the
centre of nature and radiates to the circumference. It is the
pith and marrow of every substance, every relation, and
every process. All things with which we deal, preach to us.
What is a farm but a mute gospel? The chaff and the wheat,
weeds and plants, blight, rain, insects, sun—it is a sacred
emblem from the first furrow of spring to the last stack
which the snow of winter overtakes in the fields. But the
sailor, the shepherd, the miner, the merchant, in their several resorts, have each an experience precisely parallel, and
leading to the same conclusion: because all organizations
are radically alike. Nor can it be doubted that this moral
sentiment which thus scents the air, grows in the grain, and
impregnates the waters of the world, is caught by man and
sinks into his soul. The moral influence of nature upon
every individual is that amount of truth which it illustrates
to him. Who can estimate this? Who can guess how much
firmness the sea-beaten rock has taught the fisherman? How
much tranquillity has been reflected to man from the azure
sky, over whose unspotted deeps the winds forevermore
drive flocks of stormy clouds, and leave no wrinkle or stain?
How much industry and providence and affection we have
caught from the pantomime of brutes? What a searching
preacher of self-command is the varying phenomena of
Health!

Herein is especially apprehended the unity of Nature—
the unity in variety—which meets us everywhere. All the
endless variety of things make an identical impression.
Xenophanes complained in his old age, that, look where he
would, all things hastened back to Unity. He was weary of
seeing the same entity in the tedious variety of forms. The
fable of Proteus has a cordial truth. A leaf, a drop, a crystal,
a moment of time, is related to the whole, and partakes of
the perfection of the whole. Each particle is a microcosm,
and faithfully renders the likeness of the world.

Not only resemblances exist in things whose analogy is
obvious, as when we detect the type of the human hand in

the flipper of the fossil saurus, but also in objects wherein
there is great superficial unlikeness. Thus architecture is
called "frozen music," by De Staël and Goethe. Vitruvius
thought an architect should be a musician. "A Gothic
church," said Coleridge, "is a petrified religion." Michael
Angelo maintained, that, to an architect, a knowledge of
anatomy is essential. In Haydn's oratorios, the notes present
to the imagination not only motions, as of the snake, the
stag, and the elephant, but colors also; as the green grass.
The law of harmonic sounds reappears in the harmonic
colors. The granite is differenced in its laws only by the
more or less of heat from the river that wears it away. The
river, as it flows, resembles the air that flows over it; the
air resembles the light which traverses it with more subtile
currents; the light resembles the heat which rides with it
through Space. Each creature is only a modification of the
other; the likeness in them is more than the difference, and
their radical law is one and the same. A rule of one art, or
a law of one organization, holds true throughout nature. So
intimate is this Unity, that, it is easily seen, it lies under the
undermost garment of Nature, and betrays its source in
Universal Spirit. For it pervades Thought also. Every universal truth which we express in words, implies or supposes
every other truth. *Omne verum vero consonat.* It is like a
great circle on a sphere, comprising it in like manner. Every
such truth is the absolute Ens seen from one side. But it has
innumerable sides.

The central Unity is still more conspicuous in actions.
Words are finite organs of the infinite mind. They cannot
cover the dimensions of what is in truth. They break, chop,
and impoverish it. An action is the perfection and publication of thought. A right action seems to fill the eye, and to
be related to all nature. "The wise man, in doing one thing,
does all; or, in the one thing he does rightly, he sees the
likeness of all which is done rightly."

Words and actions are not the attributes of brute nature.
They introduce us to the human form, of which all other
organizations appear to be degradations. When this appears
among so many that surround it, the spirit prefers it to all
others. It says, "From such as this have I drawn joy and

knowledge; in such as this have I found and beheld myself; I will speak to it; it can speak again; it can yield me thought already formed and alive." In fact, the eye—the mind—is always accompanied by these forms, male and female; and these are incomparably the richest informations of the power and order that lie at the heart of things. Unfortunately every one of them bears the marks as of some injury; is marred and superficially defective. Nevertheless, far different from the deaf and dumb nature around them, these all rest like fountain-pipes on the unfathomed sea of thought and virtue whereto they alone, of all organizations, are the entrances.

It were a pleasant inquiry to follow into detail their ministry to our education, but where would it stop? We are associated in adolescent and adult life with some friends, who, like skies and waters, are coextensive with our idea; who, answering each to a certain affection of the soul, satisfy our desire on that side; whom we lack power to put at such focal distance from us, that we can mend or even analyze them. We cannot choose but love them. When much intercourse with a friend has supplied us with a standard of excellence, and has increased our respect for the resources of God who thus sends a real person to outgo our ideal; when he has, moreover, become an object of thought, and, whilst his character retains all its unconscious effect, is converted in the mind into solid and sweet wisdom—it is a sign to us that his office is closing, and he is commonly withdrawn from our sight in a short time.   [W, I, 36–46]

BRAHMA

If the red slayer think he slays,
  Or if the slain think he is slain,
They know not well the subtle ways
  I keep, and pass, and turn again.

Far or forgot to me is near;
  Shadow and sunlight are the same;
The vanished gods to me appear;
  And one to me are shame and fame.

They reckon ill who leave me out;
  When me they fly, I am the wings;
I am the doubter and the doubt,
  And I the hymn the Brahmin sings.

The strong gods pine for my abode.
  And pine in vain the sacred Seven;
But thou, meek lover of the good!
  Find me, and turn thy back on heaven.

[W, IX, 195]

We are symbols and inhabit symbols; workmen, work, and tools, words and things, birth and death, all are emblems; but we sympathize with the symbols, and being infatuated with the economical uses of things, we do not know that they are thoughts. The poet, by an ulterior intellectual perception, gives them a power which makes their old use forgotten, and puts eyes and a tongue into every dumb and inanimate object. He perceives the independence of the thought on the symbol, the stability of the thought, the accidency and fugacity of the symbol.   [W, III, 20]

HAMATREYA

Bulkeley, Hunt, Willard, Hosmer, Meriam, Flint,
Possessed the land which rendered to their toil
Hay, corn, roots, hemp, flax, apples, wool and wood.
Each of these landlords walked amidst his farm,
Saying, " 'Tis mine, my children's and my name's.
How sweet the west wind sounds in my own trees!
How graceful climb those shadows on my hill!
I fancy these pure waters and the flags
Know me, as does my dog: we sympathize;
And, I affirm, my actions smack of the soil."

Where are these men? Asleep beneath their grounds:
And strangers, fond as they, their furrows plough.
Earth laughs in flowers, to see her boastful boys
Earth-proud, proud of the earth which is not theirs;
Who steer the plough, but cannot steer their feet
Clear of the grave.

They added ridge to valley, brook to pond,
And sighed for all that bounded their domain;
"This suits me for a pasture; that's my park;
We must have clay, lime, gravel, granite-ledge,
And misty lowland, where to go for peat.
The land is well—lies fairly to the south.
'Tis good, when you have crossed the sea and back,
To find the sitfast acres where you left them."

Ah! the hot owner sees not Death, who adds
Him to his land, a lump of mold the more.
Hear what the Earth says:

Earth-Song

"Mine and yours;
Mine, not yours.
Earth endures;
Stars abide—
Shine down in the old sea;
Old are the shores;
But where are old men?
I who have seen much,
Such have I never seen.

"The lawyer's deed
Ran sure,
In tail,
To them, and to their heirs
Who shall succeed,
Without fail,
Forevermore.

"Here is the land,
Shaggy with wood,
With its old valley,
Mound and flood.
But the heritors?—

Fled like the flood's foam.
The lawyer, and the laws,
And the kingdom,
Clean swept herefrom.

"They called me theirs,
Who so controlled me;
Yet every one
Wished to stay, and is gone,
How am I theirs,
If they cannot hold me,
But I hold them?"

When I heard the Earth-song
I was no longer brave;
My avarice cooled
Like lust in the chill of the grave.
[W, IX, 35–37]

A moment is a concentrated eternity. All that ever was is
now. Nature teaches all this herself, the spines of the shell,
the layers of the tree, the colors of the blossom, the veins
of the marble.   [J, IV, 117]

*Nature is the symbol of spirit, a hieroglyphic the poet
reads, and Emerson analyzes the thread of analogy that
makes a unity of variety. The genius locates the "central
identity," the cosmos in the microcosmos; imagination con-
verts "every thing into every other thing." And all men
delight in metaphor.*

Thought makes everything fit for use. The vocabulary of an
omniscient man would embrace words and images excluded
from polite conversation. What would be base, or even
obscene, to the obscene, becomes illustrious, spoken in a
new connection of thought.   [W, III, 17]

A happy symbol is a sort of evidence that your thought is
just. I had rather have a good symbol of my thought, or a
good analogy, than the suffrage of Kant or Plato. If you
agree with me, or if Locke or Montesquieu agree, I may yet
be wrong; but if the elm-tree thinks the same thing, if run-

ning water, if burning coal, if crystals, if alkalies, in their
several fashions say what I say, it must be true.
[W, VIII, 15]

The act of imagination is ever attended by pure delight.
It infuses a certain volatility and intoxication into all Nature. It has a flute which sets the atoms of our frame in a
dance. Our indeterminate size is a delicious secret which it
reveals to us. The mountains begin to dislimn, and float in
the air. In the presence and conversation of a true poet,
teeming with images to express his enlarging thought, his
person, his form, grows larger to our fascinated eyes. And
thus begins that deification which all nations have made of
their heroes in every kind—saints, poets, lawgivers and
warriors.   [W, VIII, 18–19]

The universe is a more amazing puzzle than ever, as you
glance along this bewildering series of animated forms—
the hazy butterflies, the carved shells, the birds, beasts,
fishes, insects, snakes, and the upheaving principle of life
everywhere incipient, in the very rock aping organized
forms. Not a form so grotesque, so savage, nor so beautiful
but is an expression of some property inherent in man the
observer—an occult relation between the very scorpions and
man. I feel the centipede in me—cayman, carp, eagle, and
fox. I am moved by strange sympathies; I say continually
"I will be a naturalist."   [J, III, 163]

The truth takes flesh in forms that can express it; and thus
in history an idea always overhangs, like the moon, and
rules the tide which rises simultaneously in all the souls of
a generation.   [W, X, 132]

Whoever discredits analogy and requires heaps of facts before any theories can be attempted, has no poetic power,
and nothing original or beautiful will be produced by him.
Locke is as surely the influx of decomposition and of prose,
as Bacon and the Platonists of growth. The Platonic is the
poetic tendency; the so-called scientific is the negative and
poisonous. 'Tis quite certain that Spenser, Burns, Byron

and Wordsworth will be Platonists, and that the dull men will be Lockists. [W, V, 239]

We are natural believers. Truth, or the connection between cause and effect, alone interests us. We are persuaded that a thread runs through all things: all worlds are strung on it, as beads; and men, and events, and life, come to us only because of that thread: they pass and repass only that we may know the direction and continuity of that line. A book or statement which goes to show that there is no line, but random and chaos, a calamity out of nothing, a prosperity and no account of it, a hero born from a fool, a fool from a hero—dispirits us. Seen or unseen, we believe the tie exists. Talent makes counterfeit ties; genius finds the real ones. [W, IV, 170]

. . . [Swedenborg] fastens each natural object to a theologic notion—a horse signifies carnal understanding; a tree, perception; the moon, faith; a cat means this; an ostrich that; an artichoke this other—and poorly tethers every symbol to a several ecclesiastic sense. The slippery Proteus is not so easily caught. In nature, each individual symbol plays innumerable parts, as each particle of matter circulates in turn through every system. The central identity enables any one symbol to express successively all the qualities and shades of real being. In the transmission of the heavenly waters, every hose fits every hydrant. Nature avenges herself speedily on the hard pedantry that would chain her waves. She is no literalist. Every thing must be taken genially, and we must be at the top of our condition to understand any thing rightly. [W, IV, 121]

The world globes itself in a drop of dew. The microscope cannot find the animalcule which is less perfect for being little. Eyes, ears, taste, smell, motion, resistance, appetite, and organs of reproduction that take hold on eternity—all find room to consist in the small creature. So do we put our life into every act. The true doctrine of omnipresence is that God reappears with all his parts in every moss and cobweb. The value of the universe contrives to throw itself into every point. If the good is there, so is the evil; if the affinity, so the repulsion; if the force, so the limitation.

[W, II, 101–102]

. . . [Plato] said, Culture; he said, Nature; and he failed not to add, "There is also the divine." There is no thought in any mind but it quickly tends to convert itself into a power and organizes a huge instrumentality of means. Plato, lover of limits, loved the illimitable, saw the enlargement and nobility which come from truth itself and good itself, and attempted as if on the part of the human intellect, once for all to do it adequate homage—homage fit for the immense soul to receive, and yet homage becoming the intellect to render. He said then, "Our faculties run out into infinity, and return to us thence. We can define but a little way; but here is a fact which will not be skipped, and which to shut our eyes upon is suicide. All things are in a scale; and, begin where we will, ascend and ascend. All things are symbolical; and what we call results are beginnings."

[W, IV, 67–68]

When the act of reflection takes place in the mind, when we look at ourselves in the light of thought, we discover that our life is embosomed in beauty. Behind us, as we go, all things assume pleasing forms, as clouds do far off. Not only things familiar and stale, but even the tragic and terrible are comely as they take their place in the pictures of memory. The river-bank, the weed at the water-side, the old house, the foolish person, however neglected in the passing, have a grace in the past. Even the corpse that has lain in the chambers has added a solemn ornament to the house. The soul will not know either deformity or pain. If in the hours of clear reason we should speak the severest truth, we should say that we had never made a sacrifice. In these hours the mind seems so great that nothing can be taken from us that seems much. All loss, all pain, is particular; the universe remains to the heart unhurt. Neither vexations nor calamities abate our trust. No man ever stated his griefs as lightly as he might. [W, II, 131]

Things are pretty, graceful, rich, elegant, handsome, but, until they speak to the imagination, not yet beautiful. This is the reason why beauty is still escaping out of all analysis. It is not yet possessed, it cannot be handled. Proclus says, "It swims on the light of forms." It is properly not in the form, but in the mind. It instantly deserts possession, and flies to an object in the horizon. If I could put my hand on the North Star, would it be as beautiful? The sea is lovely, but when we bathe in it the beauty forsakes all the near water. For the imagination and senses cannot be gratified at the same time. Wordsworth rightly speaks of "a light that never was on sea or land," meaning that it was supplied by the observer; and the Welsh bard warns his countrywomen, that

"Half of their charms with Cadwallon shall die."

The new virtue which constitutes a thing beautiful is a certain cosmical quality, or a power to suggest relation to the whole world, and so lift the object out of a pitiful individuality. [W, VI, 302–303]

The feat of the imagination is in showing the convertibility of every thing into every other thing. Facts which had never before left their stark common sense suddenly figure as Eleusinian mysteries. My boots and chair and candlestick are fairies in disguise, meteors and constellations. All the facts in nature are nouns of the intellect, and make the grammar of the eternal language. Every word has a double, treble or centuple use and meaning. What! has my stove and pepper-pot a false bottom? I cry you mercy, good shoe-box! I did not know you were a jewel-case. Chaff and dust begin to sparkle, and are clothed about with immortality. And there is a joy in perceiving the representative or symbolic character of a fact, which no bare fact or event can ever give. There are no days in life so memorable as those which vibrated to some stroke of the imagination.

[W, VI, 304]

The trivial experience of every day is always verifying some old prediction to us and converting into things the words and signs which we had heard and seen without heed. A lady with whom I was riding in the forest said to me that the woods always seemed to her *to wait,* as if the genii who inhabit them suspended their deeds until the wayfarer had passed onward; a thought which poetry has celebrated in the dance of the fairies, which breaks off on the approach of human feet. The man who has seen the rising moon break out of the clouds at midnight, has been present like an archangel at the creation of light and of the world. I remember one summer day in the fields my companion pointed out to me a broad cloud, which might extend a quarter of a mile parallel to the horizon, quite accurately in the form of a cherub as painted over churches—a round block in the centre, which it was easy to animate with eyes and mouth, supported on either side by wide-stretched symmetrical wings. What appears once in the atmosphere may appear often, and it was undoubtedly the archetype of that familiar ornament. I have seen in the sky a chain of summer lightning which at once showed to me that the Greeks drew from nature when they painted the thunderbolt in the hand of Jove. I have seen a snow-drift along the sides of the stone wall which obviously gave the idea of the common architectural scroll to abut a tower.   [W, II, 18–19]

This power of imagination, the making of some familiar object, as fire or rain, or a bucket, or shovel do new duty as an exponent of some truth or general law, bewitches and delights men. It is a taking of dead sticks, and clothing about with immortality; it is music out of creaking and scouring. All opaque things are transparent, and the light of heaven struggles through.   [J, IX, 277–278]

To see the meaning that plays over the face of the universe is to be free, and he who has once recognized these divine forms has become "the channel through which heaven flows to earth." The world holds no enchantment for the partial man, but he who has rested "upon the bosom of God" can read eternity in the commonplace.

The revelation of Thought takes man out of servitude into freedom. We rightly say of ourselves, we were born and afterward we were born again, and many times. We have successive experiences so important that the new forgets the old, and hence the mythology of the seven or the nine heavens. The day of days, the great day of the feast of life, is that in which the inward eye opens to the Unity in things, to the omnipresence of law—sees that what is must be and ought to be, or is the best. This beatitude dips from on high down on us and we see. It is not in us so much as we are in it. If the air come to our lungs, we breathe and live; if not, we die. If the light come to our eyes, we see; else not. And if truth come to our mind we suddenly expand to its dimensions, as if we grew to worlds. We are as lawgivers; we speak for Nature; we prophesy and divine.

[W, VI, 25]

When I converse with a profound mind, or if at any time being alone I have good thoughts, I do not at once arrive at satisfactions, as when, being thirsty, I drink water, or go to the fire, being cold; no! but I am at first apprised of my vicinity to a new and excellent region of life. By persisting to read or to think, this region gives further sign of itself, as it were in flashes of light, in sudden discoveries of its profound beauty and repose, as if the clouds that covered it parted at intervals and showed the approaching traveller the inland mountains, with the tranquil eternal meadows spread at their base, whereon flocks graze and shepherds pipe and dance. But every insight from this realm of thought is felt as initial, and promises a sequel. I do not make it; I arrive there, and behold what was there already. I make! Oh no! I clap my hands in infantine joy and amazement before the first opening to me of this august magnificence, old with the love and homage of innumerable ages, young with the life of life, the sunbright Mecca of the desert. And what a future it opens! I feel a new heart beating with the love of the new beauty. I am ready to die out of nature and be born again into this new yet unapproachable America I have found in the West:

"Since neither now nor yesterday began
These thoughts, which have been ever, nor yet can
A man be found who their first entrance knew."

If I have described life as a flux of moods, I must now add
that there is that in us which changes not and which
ranks all sensations and states of mind. The consciousness
in each man is a sliding scale, which identifies him now with
the First Cause, and now with the flesh of his body; life
above life, in infinite degrees. The sentiment from which it
sprung determines the dignity of any deed, and the question
ever is, not what you have done or forborne, but at whose
command you have done or forborne it.   [W, III, 71–72]

The vain traveller attempts to embellish his life by quoting
my lord and the prince and the countess, who thus said or
did to *him*. The ambitious vulgar show you their spoons
and brooches and rings, and preserve their cards and compliments. The more cultivated, in their account of their own
experience, cull out the pleasing, poetic circumstance—the
visit to Rome, the man of genius they saw, the brilliant
friend they know; still further on perhaps the gorgeous
landscape, the mountain lights, the mountain thoughts they
enjoyed yesterday—and so seek to throw a romantic color
over their life. But the soul that ascends to worship the
great God is plain and true; has no rose-color, no fine
friends, no chivalry, no adventures; does not want admiration; dwells in the hour that now is, in the earnest experience of the common day—by reason of the present moment and the mere trifle having become porous to thought
and bibulous of the sea of light.   [W, II, 290]

As a plant upon the earth, so a man rests upon the bosom
of God; he is nourished by unfailing fountains, and draws
at his need inexhaustible power. Who can set bounds to
the possibilities of man? Once inhale the upper air, being
admitted to behold the absolute natures of justice and
truth, and we learn that man has access to the entire mind
of the Creator, is himself the creator in the finite. This view,

which admonishes me where the sources of wisdom and power lie, and points to virtue as to

"The golden key
Which opes the palace of eternity,"

carries upon its face the highest certificate of truth, because it animates me to create my own world through the purification of my soul.

The world proceeds from the same spirit as the body of man. It is a remoter and inferior incarnation of God, a projection of God in the unconscious. But it differs from the body in one important respect. It is not, like that, now subjected to the human will. Its serene order is inviolable by us. It is, therefore, to us, the present expositor of the divine mind. It is a fixed point whereby we may measure our departure. As we degenerate, the contrast between us and our house is more evident. We are as much strangers in nature as we are aliens from God. We do not understand the notes of birds. The fox and the deer run away from us; the bear and tiger rend us. We do not know the uses of more than a few plants, as corn and the apple, the potato and the vine. Is not the landscape, every glimpse of which hath a grandeur, a face of him? Yet this may show us what discord is between man and nature, for you cannot freely admire a noble landscape if laborers are digging in the field hard by. The poet finds something ridiculous in his delight until he is out of the sight of men.   [W, I, 64–65]

I conceive a man as always spoken to from behind, and unable to turn his head and see the speaker. In all the millions who have heard the voice, none ever saw the face. As children in their play run behind each other, and seize one by the ears and make him walk before them, so is the spirit of our unseen pilot. That well-known voice speaks in all languages, governs all men, and none ever caught a glimpse of its form. If the man will exactly obey it, it will adopt him, so that he shall not any longer separate it from himself in his thought; he shall seem to be it, he shall be it. If he listen with insatiable ears, richer and greater wisdom is taught him; the sound swells to a ravishing music, he is

borne away as with a flood, he becomes careless of his food
and of his house, he is the fool of ideas, and leads a heavenly life. But if his eye is set on the things to be done, and
not on the truth that is still taught, and for the sake of which
the things are to be done, then the voice grows faint, and
at last is but a humming in his ears. His health and greatness consist in his being the channel through which heaven
flows to earth, in short, in the fulness in which an ecstatical
state takes place in him. It is pitiful to be an artist, when by
forbearing to be artists we might be vessels filled with the
divine overflowings, enriched by the circulations of omniscience and omnipresence. Are there not moments in the
history of heaven when the human race was not counted by
individuals, but was only the Influenced, was God in distribution, God rushing into multiform benefit? It is sublime
to receive, sublime to love, but this lust of imparting as from
us, this desire to be loved, the wish to be recognized as individuals—is finite, comes of a lower strain.

[W, I, 209–210]

Upborne and surrounded as we are by this all-creating
nature, soft and fluid as a cloud or the air, why should we
be such hard pedants, and magnify a few forms? Why
should we make account of time, or of magnitude, or of
figure? The soul knows them not, and genius, obeying its
law, knows how to play with them as a young child plays
with graybeards and in churches. Genius studies the casual
thought, and far back in the womb of things sees the rays
parting from one orb, that diverge, ere they fall, by infinite
diameters. Genius watches the monad through all his masks
as he performs the metempsychosis of nature. Genius detects through the fly, through the caterpillar, through the
grub, through the egg, the constant individual; through
countless individuals the fixed species; through many species
the genus; through all genera the steadfast type; through
all the kingdoms of organized life the eternal unity. Nature
is a mutable cloud which is always and never the same. She
casts the same thought into troops of forms, as a poet makes
twenty fables with one moral. Through the bruteness and
toughness of matter, a subtle spirit bends all things to its

own will. The adamant streams into soft but precise form before it, and whilst I look at it its outline and texture are changed again. Nothing is so fleeting as form; yet never does it quite deny itself. [W, II, 12–15]

Man is explicable by nothing less than all his history. Without hurry, without rest, the human spirit goes forth from the beginning to embody every faculty, every thought, every emotion which belongs to it, in appropriate events. But the thought is always prior to the fact; all the facts of history preëxist in the mind as laws. Each law in turn is made by circumstances predominant, and the limits of nature give power to but one at a time. A man is the whole encyclopædia of facts. The creation of a thousand forests is in one acorn, and Egypt, Greece, Rome, Gaul, Britain, America lie folded already in the first man. Epoch after epoch, camp, kingdom, empire, republic, democracy, are merely the application of his manifold spirit to the manifold world.

This human mind wrote history, and this must read it. The Sphinx must solve her own riddle. If the whole of history is in one man, it is all to be explained from individual experience. There is a relation between the hours of our life and the centuries of time. As the air I breathe is drawn from the great repositories of nature, as the light on my book is yielded by a star a hundred millions of miles distant, as the poise of my body depends on the equilibrium of centrifugal and centripetal forces, so the hours should be instructed by the ages and the ages explained by the hours. Of the universal mind each individual man is one more incarnation. All its properties consist in him. Each new fact in his private experience flashes a light on what great bodies of men have done, and the crises of his life refer to national crises. Every revolution was first a thought in one man's mind, and when the same thought occurs to another man, it is the key to that era. Every reform was once a private opinion, and when it shall be a private opinion again it will solve the problem of the age. The fact narrated must correspond to something in me to be credible or intelligible. We, as we read, must become Greeks, Romans, Turks, priest and king, martyr and executioner; must fasten these images to some reality in our secret experience, or we shall learn nothing rightly. What befell Asdrubal or Cæsar Borgia is as much an illustration of the mind's powers and depravations as what has befallen us. Each new law and political movement has a meaning for you. Stand before each of its tablets and say, "Under this mask did my Proteus nature hide itself." This remedies the defect of our too great nearness to ourselves. This throws our actions into perspective —and as crabs, goats, scorpions, the balance and the waterpot lose their meanness when hung as signs in the zodiac, so I can see my own vices without heat in the distant persons of Solomon, Alcibiades, and Catiline. [W, II, 4–5]

A work of art is an abstract or epitome of the world. It is the result or expression of nature, in miniature. For although the works of nature are innumerable and all different, the result or the expression of them all is similar and single. Nature is a sea of forms radically alike and even unique. A leaf, a sunbeam, a landscape, the ocean, make an analogous impression on the mind. What is common to them all—that perfectness and harmony, is beauty. The standard of beauty is the entire circuit of natural forms— the totality of nature; which the Italians expressed by defining beauty "il più nell' uno." Nothing is quite beautiful alone; nothing but is beautiful in the whole. A single object is only so far beautiful as it suggests this universal grace. The poet, the painter, the sculptor, the musician, the architect, seek each to concentrate this radiance of the world on one point, and each in his several work to satisfy the love of beauty which stimulates him to produce. Thus is Art a nature passed through the alembic of man. Thus in art does Nature work through the will of a man filled with the beauty of her first works.

The world thus exists to the soul to satisfy the desire of beauty. This element I call an ultimate end. No reason can be asked or given why the soul seeks beauty. Beauty, in its largest and profoundest sense, is one expression for the universe. God is the all-fair. Truth, and goodness, and beauty, are but different faces of the same All. But beauty in nature is not ultimate. It is the herald of inward and eternal beauty, and is not alone a solid and satisfactory good. It must stand as a part, and not as yet the last or highest expression of the final cause of Nature.　[W, I, 23–24]

Superstitious persons we see with respect, because their whole existence is not bounded by their hats and their shoes, but they walk attended by pictures of the imagination, to which they pay homage. You cannot impoverish man by taking away these objects above him without ruin.
　　　　　　　　　　　　　　　　　　[W, X, 206]

These grand rhymes or returns in nature—the dear, best-known face startling us at every turn, under a mask so un-expected that we think it the face of a stranger, and carry-ing up the semblance into divine forms. . . .　[W, IV, 110]

I cannot see without awe that no man thinks alone and no man acts alone, but the divine assessors who came up with him into life—now under one disguise, now under another, like a police in citizens' clothes—walk with him, step for step, through all the kingdom of time.　[W, VI, 226]

A man can only speak so long as he does not feel his speech to be partial and inadequate. It is partial, but he does not see it to be so whilst he utters it. As soon as he is released from the instinctive and particular and sees its partiality, he shuts his mouth in disgust. For no man can write any-thing who does not think that what he writes is for the time the history of the world; or do anything well who does not esteem his work to be of importance. My work may be of none, but I must not think it of none, or I shall not do it with impunity.　[W, III, 189]

Nothing interests us which is stark or bounded, but only what streams with life, what is in act or endeavor to reach somewhat beyond. The pleasure a palace or a temple gives the eye is, that an order and method has been communi-cated to stones, so that they speak and geometrize, become tender or sublime with expression. Beauty is the moment of transition, as if the form were just ready to flow into other forms. Any fixedness, heaping or concentration on one feature—a long nose, a sharp chin, a hump-back—is the reverse of the flowing, and therefore deformed. Beautiful as is the symmetry of any form, if the form can move we seek a more excellent symmetry. The interruption of equilibrium stimulates the eye to desire the restoration of symmetry, and to watch the steps through which it is attained. This is the charm of running water, sea waves, the flight of birds and the locomotion of animals. This is the theory of dancing, to recover continually in changes the lost equilibrium, not by abrupt and angular but by gradual and curving movements. . . . This fact suggests the reason of all mistakes and offence in our own modes. It is necessary in music, when you strike a discord, to let down the ear by an intermediate note or two to the accord again; and many a good experiment, born of good sense and destined to succeed, fails only because it is offensively sudden. . . . To this streaming or flowing belongs the beauty that all circular movement has; as the circulation of waters, the circulation of the blood, the periodical motion of planets, the annual wave of vegetation, the action and reaction of nature; and if we follow it out, this demand in our thought for an ever onward action is the argument for the immortality.   [W, VI, 292–294, *passim*]

The possibility of interpretation lies in the identity of the observer with the observed. Each material thing has its celestial side; has its translation, through humanity, into the spiritual and necessary sphere where it plays a part as indestructible as any other. And to these, their ends, all things continually ascend. The gases gather to the solid firmament: the chemic lump arrives at the plant, and grows; arrives at the quadruped, and walks; arrives at the man, and thinks. But also the constituency determines the vote of the representative. He is not only representative, but participant. Like can only be known by like. The reason why he knows about them is that he is of them; he has just come out of nature, or from being a part of that thing. . . . Man, made of the dust of the world, does not forget his origin; and all that is yet inanimate will one day speak and reason. Unpublished nature will have its whole secret told. . . .

Thus we sit by the fire and take hold on the poles of the earth.   [W, IV, 11–12]

Truth is such a fly-away, such a slyboots, so untransportable and unbarrelable a commodity, that it is as bad to catch as light. Shut the shutters never so quick to keep all the light in, it is all in vain; it is gone before you can cry, Hold. And so it happens with our philosophy. Translate, collate, distil all the systems, it steads you nothing; for truth will not be compelled in any mechanical manner.
[W, I, 171]

How wild and mysterious our position as individuals to the Universe; here is always a certain amount of truth lodged as intrinsic foundation in the depths of the soul, a certain perception of absolute being, as justice, love, and the like, natures which must be the God of God, and this is our capital stock, this is our centripetal force. We can never quite doubt, we can never be adrift, we can never be nothing, because of this Holy of Holies, out of sight of which we cannot go. Then, on the other side, all is to seek. We understand nothing; our ignorance is abysmal, the overhanging immensity staggers us, whither we go, what we do, who we are, we cannot even so much as guess. We stagger and grope.   [J, IV, 215]

Where do we find ourselves? In a series of which we do not know the extremes, and believe that it has none. We wake and find ourselves on a stair; there are stairs below us, which we seem to have ascended; there are stairs above us, many a one, which go upward and out of sight. But the Genius which according to the old belief stands at the door by which we enter, and gives us the lethe to drink, that we may tell no tales, mixed the cup too strongly, and we cannot shake off the lethargy now at noonday. Sleep lingers all our lifetime about our eyes, as night hovers all day in the boughs of the fir-tree. All things swim and glitter. Our life is not so much threatened as our perception. Ghostlike we glide through nature, and should not know our place again. Did our birth fall in some fit of indigence and frugality in nature, that she was so sparing of her fire and so liberal of her earth that it appears to us that we lack the affirmative principle, and though we have health and reason, yet we have no superfluity of spirit for new creation? We have enough to live and bring the year about, but not an ounce to impart or to invest. Ah that our Genius were a little more of a genius! We are like millers on the lower levels of a stream, when the factories above them have exhausted the water. We too fancy that the upper people must have raised their dams.   [W, III, 45–46]

The old fable covers a doctrine ever new and sublime; that there is One Man—present to all particular men only partially, or through one faculty; and that you must take the whole society to find the whole man. Man is not a farmer, or a professor, or an engineer, but he is all. Man is priest, and scholar, and statesman, and producer, and soldier. In the *divided* or social state these functions are parcelled out to individuals, each of whom aims to do his stint of the joint work, whilst each other performs his. The fable implies that the individual, to possess himself, must sometimes return from his own labor to embrace all the other laborers. But, unfortunately, this original unit, this fountain of power, has been so distributed to multitudes, has been so minutely subdivided and peddled out, that it is spilled into drops, and cannot be gathered. The state of society is one in which the members have suffered amputation from the trunk, and strut about so many walking monsters—a good finger, a neck, a stomach, an elbow, but never a man.

[W, I, 82–83]

The genius of humanity is the right point of view of history. The qualities abide; the men who exhibit them have now more, now less, and pass away; the qualities remain on another brow. No experience is more familiar. Once you saw phœnixes: they are gone; the world is not therefore disenchanted. The vessels on which you read sacred emblems turn out to be common pottery; but the sense of the pictures is sacred, and you may still read them transferred to the walls of the world.   [W, IV, 33–34]

The mind that grows could not predict the times, the means, the mode of that spontaneity. God enters by a private door into every individual. Long prior to the age of reflection is the thinking of the mind. Out of darkness it came insensibly into the marvellous light of today. In the period of infancy it accepted and disposed of all impressions from the surrounding creation after its own way. Whatever any mind doth or saith is after a law, and this native law remains over it after it has come to reflection or conscious thought. In the most worn, pedantic, introverted self-tormentor's life, the greatest part is incalculable by him, unforeseen, unimaginable, and must be, until he can take himself up by his own ears. What am I? What has my will done to make me that I am? Nothing. I have been floated into this thought, this hour, this connection of events, by secret currents of might and mind, and my ingenuity and wilfulness have not thwarted, have not aided to an appreciable degree.

Our spontaneous action is always the best. You cannot with your best deliberation and heed come so close to any question as your spontaneous glance shall bring you, whilst you rise from your bed, or walk abroad in the morning after meditating the matter before sleep on the previous night. Our thinking is a pious reception. Our truth of thought is therefore vitiated as much by too violent direction given by our will, as by too great negligence. We do not determine what we will think. We only open our senses, clear away as we can all obstruction from the fact, and suffer the intellect to see. We have little control over our thoughts. We are the prisoners of ideas. They catch us up for moments into their heaven and so fully engage us that we take no thought for the morrow, gaze like children, without an effort to make them our own. By and by we fall out of that rapture, bethink us where we have been, what we have seen, and repeat as truly as we can what we have beheld. As far as we can recall these ecstasies we carry away in the ineffaceable memory the result, and all men and all the ages confirm it. It is called truth. But the moment we cease to report and attempt to correct and contrive, it is not truth.

[W, II, 327–329]

*"Thoughts let us into realities," disclose the disparity
between ideals and institutions. "Every man beholds his
human condition with a degree of melancholy." But it is
when we see there can be no anarchy in Nature, that all
things cohere and shame us out of our idolatries.*

The event of death is always astounding; our philosophy
never reaches, never possesses it; we are always at the
beginning of our catechism; always the definition is yet to
be made. What is death?

I see nothing to help beyond observing what the mind's
habit is in regard to that crisis. Simply I have nothing to
do with it. It is nothing to me. After I have made my will
and set my house in order, I shall do in the immediate expectation of death the same things I should do without it.

But more difficult is it to know the death of another.
Mrs. Ripley says that her little Sophia told the mantua-
maker this morning "that in Heaven she was going to ask
Dod to let her sit by mother all the time," and if this little
darling should die, Mrs. R. thinks she could not live. So
with the expectation of the death of persons who are con-
veniently situated, who have all they desire, and to whom
death is fearful, she looks in vain for a consolation. In us
there ought to be a remedy. There ought to be, there can be
nothing to which the soul is called, to which the soul is not
equal. And I suppose that the roots of my relation to every
individual are in my own constitution, and not less the
causes of his disappearance from me.

Why should we lie so? A question is asked of the Understanding which lies in the province of the Reason, and we
foolishly try to make an answer. Our constructiveness over-
powers our love of truth. How noble is it when the mourner
looks for comfort in your face to give only sympathy and
confession; confession that it is a great grief, and the greater
because the apprehension of its nature still loiters. Who set
you up for Professor of omniscience and *cicerone* to the
Universe? Why teach? Learn rather. [J, IV, 343–345]

Every man beholds his human condition with a degree of
melancholy. As a ship aground is battered by the waves,

so man, imprisoned in mortal life, lies open to the mercy of coming events. But a truth, separated by the intellect, is no longer a subject of destiny. We behold it as a god upraised above care and fear. And so any fact in our life, or any record of our fancies or reflections, disentangled from the web of our unconsciousness, becomes an object impersonal and immortal. It is the past restored, but embalmed. A better art than that of Egypt has taken fear and corruption out of it. It is eviscerated of care. It is offered for science. What is addressed to us for contemplation does not threaten us but makes us intellectual beings.   [W, II, 327]

The toper finds, without asking, the road to the tavern, but the poet does not know the pitcher that holds his nectar. Every youth should know the way to prophecy as surely as the miller understands how to let on the water or the engineer the steam. A rush of thoughts is the only conceivable prosperity that can come to us. Fine clothes, equipages, villa, park, social consideration, cannot cover up real poverty and insignificance, from my own eyes or from others like mine.

Thoughts let us into realities. Neither miracle nor magic nor any religious tradition, not the immortality of the private soul is incredible, after we have experienced an insight, a thought. I think it comes to some men but once in their life, sometimes a religious impulse, sometimes an intellectual insight. But what we want is consecutiveness. 'Tis with us a flash of light, then a long darkness, then a flash again. The separation of our days by sleep almost destroys identity. Could we but turn these fugitive sparkles into an astronomy of Copernican worlds! With most men, scarce a link of memory holds yesterday and today together. Their house and trade and families serve them as ropes to give a coarse continuity. But they have forgotten the thoughts of yesterday; they say today what occurs to them, and something else tomorrow. This insecurity of possession, this quick ebb of power—as if life were a thunder-storm wherein you can see by a flash the horizon, and then cannot see your hand—tantalizes us. We cannot make the inspiration consecutive. A glimpse, a point of view that by

its brightness excludes the purview is granted, but no pano-
rama. A fuller inspiration should cause the point to flow
and become a line, should bend the line and complete the
circle. Today the electric machine will not work, no spark
will pass; then presently the world is all a cat's back, all
sparkle and shock. Sometimes there is no sea-fire, and again
the sea is aglow to the horizon. Sometimes the Æolian harp
is dumb all day in the window, and again it is garrulous and
tells all the secrets of the world. In June the morning is
noisy with birds; in August they are already getting old and
silent.   [W, VIII, 272–274]

There is no joke so true and deep in actual life as when
some pure idealist goes up and down among the institutions
of society, attended by a man who knows the world, and
who, sympathizing with the philosopher's scrutiny, sympathizes also with the confusion and indignation of the detected, skulking institutions. His perception of disparity,
his eye wandering perpetually from the rule to the crooked,
lying, thieving fact, makes the eyes run over with laughter.
    This is the radical joke of life and then of literature. The
presence of the ideal of right and of truth in all action
makes the yawning delinquencies of practice remorseful to
the conscience, tragic to the interest, but droll to the intellect. The activity of our sympathies may for a time hinder
our perceiving the fact intellectually, and so deriving mirth
from it; but all falsehoods, all vices seen at sufficient distance, seen from the point where our moral sympathies do
not interfere, become ludicrous. The comedy is in the intellect's perception of discrepancy. And whilst the presence
of the ideal discover the difference, the comedy is enhanced
whenever that ideal is embodied visibly in a man. Thus
Falstaff, in Shakespeare, is a character of the broadest comedy, giving himself unreservedly to his senses, coolly ig-
noring the Reason, whilst he invokes its name, pretending
to patriotism and to parental virtues, not with any intent
to deceive, but only to make the fun perfect by enjoying
the confusion betwixt Reason and the negation of Reason—
in other words, the rank rascaldom he is calling by its name.
Prince Hal stands by, as the acute understanding, who sees

the Right, and sympathizes with it, and in the heyday of
youth feels also the full attractions of pleasure, and is thus
eminently qualified to enjoy the joke. At the same time he
is to that degree under the Reason that it does not amuse
him as much as it amuses another spectator.

[W, VIII, 159–161]

It is a problem of metaphysics to define the province of
Fancy and Imagination. The words are often used, and
the things confounded. Imagination respects the cause. It
is the vision of an inspired soul reading arguments and
affirmations in all Nature of that which it is driven to say.
But as soon as this soul is released a little from its passion,
and at leisure plays with the resemblances and types, for
amusement, and not for its moral end, we call its action
Fancy. Lear, mad with his affliction, thinks every man who
suffers must have the like cause with his own. "What, have
his daughters brought him to this pass?" But when, his
attention being diverted, his mind rests from this thought,
he becomes fanciful with Tom, playing with the superficial
resemblances of objects. Bunyan, in pain for his soul, wrote
Pilgrim's Progress; Quarles, after he was quite cool, wrote
Emblems.

Imagination is central; fancy, superficial. Fancy relates
to surface, in which a great part of life lies. The lover is
rightly said to fancy the hair, eyes, complexion of the maid.
Fancy is a wilful, imagination a spontaneous act; fancy, a
play as with dolls and puppets which we choose to call men
and women; imagination, a perception and affirming of a
real relation between a thought and some material fact.
Fancy amuses; imagination expands and exalts us. Imagination uses an organic classification. Fancy joins by accidental
resemblance, surprises and amuses the idle, but is silent in
the presence of great passion and action. Fancy aggregates;
imagination animates. Fancy is related to color; imagination, to form. Fancy paints; imagination sculptures.

[W, VIII, 28–29]

Succession, division, parts, particles—-this is the condition, this the tragedy of man. All things cohere and unite.

Man studies the parts, strives to tear the part from its connexion, to magnify it, and make it a whole. He sides with the part against other parts; and fights for parts, fights for lies, and his whole mind becomes an *inflamed part*, an amputated member, a wound, an offence. Meantime within him is the soul of the whole, the wise silence, the Universal Beauty to which every part and particle is equally related, the eternal one. Speech is the sign of partiality, difference, ignorance, and the more perfect the understanding between men, the less need of words. And when I know all, I shall cease to commènd any part. An ignorant man thinks the divine wisdom is conspicuously shown in some fact or creature: a wise man sees that every fact contains the same. I should think Water the best invention, if I were not acquainted with Fire and Earth and Air. But as we advance, every proposition, every action, every feeling, runs out into the infinite. If we go to affirm anything we are checked in our speech by the need of recognizing all other things, until speech presently becomes rambling, general, indefinite, and merely tautology. The only speech will at last be action, such as Confucius describes the speech of God.

[J, V, 83–84]

Let it suffice that in the light of these two facts, namely, that the mind is One, and that nature is its correlative, history is to be read and written.

Thus in all ways does the soul concentrate and reproduce its treasures for each pupil. He too shall pass through the whole cycle of experience. He shall collect into a focus the rays of nature. History no longer shall be a dull book. It shall walk incarnate in every just and wise man. You shall not tell me by languages and titles a catalogue of the volumes you have read. You shall make me feel what periods you have lived. . . .

Is there somewhat overweening in this claim? Then I reject all I have written, for what is the use of pretending to know what we know not? But it is the fault of our rhetoric that we cannot strongly state one fact without seeming to belie some other. I hold our actual knowledge very cheap. Hear the rats in the wall, see the lizard on the fence, the fungus under foot, the lichen on the log. What do I know sympathetically, morally, of either of these worlds of life? As old as the Caucasian man—perhaps older—these creatures have kept their counsel beside him, and there is no record of any word or sign that has passed from one to the other. What connection do the books show between the fifty or sixty chemical elements and the historical eras? Nay, what does history yet record of the metaphysical annals of man? What light does it shed on those mysteries which we hide under the names Death and Immortality? Yet every history should be written in a wisdom which divined the range of our affinities and looked at facts as symbols. I am ashamed to see what a shallow village tale our so-called History is. How many times we must say Rome, and Paris, and Constantinople! [W, II, 38–40, *passim*]

The gods deal very strictly with us, make out quarter-bills, an exact specie payment, allow no partnerships, no stock companies, no arrangements, but hold us personally liable to the last cent. Ah, say I, I cannot do this and that, my cranberry field, my burned woodlot, the rubbish lumber about the summer house, my grass, my crop, my trees —can I not have some partner; can't we organize our new Society of poets and lovers, and have somebody with talent for business to look after these things, some deacons of trees and grass and cranberries, and leave me to letters and philosophy?

But the nettled gods say, No, go to the devil with your arrangements. You, you, you personally, you alone, are to answer body and soul for your things. Leases and covenants are to be punctually signed and sealed. Arithmetic and the practical study of cause and effect in the laws of Indian corn and rye meal is as useful as betting is in England to teach accuracy of statement, or duelling in France or Ireland to make men speak the truth. [J, VII, 496–497]

It is very unhappy, but too late to be helped, the discovery we have made that we exist. That discovery is called the Fall of Man. Ever afterwards we suspect our instruments. We have learned that we do not see directly, but mediately, and that we have no means of correcting these colored and distorting lenses which we are, or of computing the amount of their errors. Perhaps these subject-lenses have a creative power; perhaps there are no objects. Once we lived in what we saw; now, the rapaciousness of this new power, which threatens to absorb all things, engages us. Nature, art, persons, letters, religions, objects, successively tumble in, and God is but one of its ideas. Nature and literature are subjective phenomena; every evil and every good thing is a shadow which we cast. The street is full of humiliations to the proud. As the fop contrived to dress his bailiffs in his livery and make them wait on his guests at table, so the chagrins which the bad heart gives off as bubbles, at once take form as ladies and gentlemen in the street, shopmen or bar-keepers in hotels, and threaten or insult whatever is threatenable and insultable in us. 'Tis the same with our idolatries. People forget that it is the eye which makes the horizon, and the rounding mind's eye which makes this or that man a type or representative of humanity, with the name of hero or saint. Jesus, the "providential man," is a good man on whom many people are agreed that these optical laws shall take effect. By love on one part and by forbearance to press objection on the other part, it is for a time settled that we will look at him in the center of the horizon, and ascribe to him the properties that will attach to any man so seen. But the longest love or aversion has a speedy term. The great and crescive self, rooted in absolute nature, supplants all relative existence and ruins the kingdom of mortal friendship and love. Marriage (in what is called the spiritual world) is impossible, because of the inequality between every subject and every object. The subject is the receiver of Godhead, and at every comparison must feel his being enhanced by that cryptic might. Though not in energy, yet by presence, this magazine of substance cannot be otherwise than felt; nor can any force of intellect attribute to the object the proper deity which sleeps or wakes forever in every subject. Never can love make consciousness and ascription equal in force. There will be the same gulf between every me and thee as between the original and the picture. The universe is the bride of the soul. All private sympathy is partial. Two human beings are like globes, which can touch only in a point, and whilst they remain in contact all other points of each of the spheres are inert; their turn must also come, and the longer a particular union lasts the more energy of appetency the parts not in union acquire.

Life will be imaged, but cannot be divided nor doubled. Any invasion of its unity would be chaos. The soul is not twin-born but the only begotten, and though revealing itself as child in time, child in appearance, is of a fatal and universal power, admitting no co-life. Every day, every act betrays the ill-concealed deity. We believe in ourselves as we do not believe in others. We permit all things to ourselves, and that which we call sin in others is experiment for us. It is an instance of our faith in ourselves that men never speak of crime as lightly as they think; or every man thinks a latitude safe for himself which is nowise to be indulged to another. The act looks very differently on the inside and on the outside; in its quality and in its consequences. Murder in the murderer is no such ruinous thought as poets and romancers will have it; it does not unsettle him or fright him from his ordinary notice of trifles; it is an act quite easy to be contemplated; but in its sequel it turns out to be a horrible jangle and confounding of all relations. Especially the crimes that spring from love seem right and fair from the actor's point of view, but when acted are found destructive of society. No man at last believes that he can be lost, or that the crime in him is as black as in the felon. Because the intellect qualifies in our own case the moral judgments. For there is no crime to the intellect. That is antinomian or hypernomian, and judges law as well as fact. "It is worse than a crime, it is a blunder," said Napoleon, speaking the language of the intellect. To it, the world is a problem in mathematics or the science of quantity, and it leaves out praise and blame and all weak emotions. All stealing is comparative. If you come to absolutes, pray who does not steal? Saints are sad, because they behold sin (even when they speculate) from the point of view of the conscience, and not of the intellect; a confusion of thought. Sin, seen from the thought, is a diminution, or *less;* seen from the conscience or will, it is pravity or *bad*. The intellect names it shade, absence of light, and no essence. The conscience must feel it as essence, essential evil. This it is not; it has an objective existence, but no subjective.

[W, III, 75–79]

The ruin or the blank that we see when we look at nature, is in our own eye. The axis of vision is not coincident with the axis of things, and so they appear not transparent but opaque. The reason why the world lacks unity, and lies broken and in heaps, is because man is disunited with himself. He cannot be a naturalist until he satisfies all the demands of the spirit. Love is as much its demand as perception. Indeed, neither can be perfect without the other. In the uttermost meaning of the words, thought is devout, and devotion is thought. Deep calls unto deep. But in actual life, the marriage is not celebrated. There are innocent men who worship God after the tradition of their fathers, but their sense of duty has not yet extended to the use of all their faculties. And there are patient naturalists, but they freeze their subject under the wintry light of the understanding. Is not prayer also a study of truth—a sally of the soul into the unfound infinite? No man ever prayed heartily without learning something. But when a faithful thinker, resolute to detach every object from personal relations and see it in the light of thought, shall, at the same time, kindle science with the fire of the holiest affections, then will God go forth anew into the creation.

It will not need, when the mind is prepared for study, to search for objects. The invariable mark of wisdom is to see the miraculous in the common. What is a day? What is a year? What is summer? What is woman? What is a child? What is sleep? To our blindness, these things seem unaffecting. We make fables to hide the baldness of the fact and conform it, as we say, to the higher law of the mind. But when the fact is seen under the light of an idea, the gaudy fable fades and shrivels. We behold the real higher law. To the wise, therefore, a fact is true poetry, and the most beautiful of fables. These wonders are brought to our own door. You also are a man. Man and woman and their

social life, poverty, labor, sleep, fear, fortune, are known to
you. Learn that none of these things is superficial, but that
each phenomenon has its roots in the faculties and affections of the mind. Whilst the abstract question occupies
your intellect, nature brings it in the concrete to be solved
by your hands. It were a wise inquiry for the closet, to
compare, point by point, especially at remarkable crises in
life, our daily history with the rise and progress of ideas in
the mind.

So shall we come to look at the world with new eyes. It
shall answer the endless inquiry of the intellect—What is
truth? and of the affections—What is good? by yielding
itself passive to the educated Will. Then shall come to pass
what my poet said: "Nature is not fixed but fluid. Spirit
alters, moulds, makes it. The immobility or bruteness of
nature is the absence of spirit; to pure spirit it is fluid, it
is volatile, it is obedient. Every spirit builds itself a house,
and beyond its house a world, and beyond its world a
heaven. Know then that the world exists for you. For you
is the phenomenon perfect. What we are, that only can
we see. All that Adam had, all that Cæsar could, you have
and can do. Adam called his house, heaven and earth; Cæsar
called his house, Rome; you perhaps call yours, a cobbler's
trade; a hundred acres of ploughed land; or a scholar's garret.
Yet line for line and point for point your dominion is as great
as theirs, though without fine names. Build therefore your
own world. As fast as you conform your life to the pure idea
in your mind, that will unfold its great proportions. A correspondent revolution in things will attend the influx of the
spirit. So fast will disagreeable appearances, swine, spiders,
snakes, pests, mad-houses, prisons, enemies, vanish; they are
temporary and shall be no more seen. The sordor and filths of
nature, the sun shall dry up and the wind exhale. As when
the summer comes from the south the snow-banks melt and
the face of the earth becomes green before it, so shall the
advancing spirit create its ornaments along its path, and
carry with it the beauty it visits and the song which en-
chants it; it shall draw beautiful faces, warm hearts, wise
discourse, and heroic acts, around its way, until evil is no
more seen. The kingdom of man over nature, which com-

eth not with observation—a dominion such as now is beyond his dream of God—he shall enter without more wonder than the blind man feels who is gradually restored to sight." [W, I, 73–77]

One would think from the talk of men that riches and poverty were a great matter; and our civilization mainly respects it. But the Indians say that they do not think the white man, with his brow of care, always toiling, afraid of heat and cold, and keeping within doors, has any advantage of them. The permanent interest of every man is never to be in a false position, but to have the weight of nature to back him in all that he does. Riches and poverty are a thick or thin costume; and our life—the life of all of us—identical. For we transcend the circumstance continually and taste the real quality of existence; as in our employments, which only differ in the manifestations but express the same laws; or in our thoughts, which wear no silks and taste no ice-creams. We see God face to face every hour, and know the savor of nature. . . .

There is no chance and no anarchy in the universe. All is system and gradation. Every god is there sitting in his sphere. The young mortal enters the hall of the firmament; there is he alone with them alone, they pouring on him benedictions and gifts, and beckoning him up to their thrones. On the instant, and incessantly, fall snow-storms of illusions. He fancies himself in a vast crowd which sways this way and that and whose movement and doings he must obey: he fancies himself poor, orphaned, insignificant. The mad crowd drives hither and thither, now furiously commanding this thing to be done, now that. What is he that he should resist their will, and think or act for himself? Every moment new changes and new showers of deceptions to baffle and distract him. And when, by and by, for an instant, the air clears and the cloud lifts a little, there are the gods still sitting around him on their thrones—they alone with him alone. [W, VI, 323–325]

I shall . . . conclude . . . with some traditions of man and nature, which a certain poet sang to me; and which, as they have always been in the world, and perhaps reappear to every bard, may be both history and prophecy.

"The foundations of man are not in matter, but in spirit. But the element of spirit is eternity. To it, therefore, the longest series of events, the oldest chronologies are young and recent. In the cycle of the universal man, from whom the known individuals proceed, centuries are points, and all history is but the epoch of one degradation.

"We distrust and deny inwardly our sympathy with nature. We own and disown our relation to it, by turns. We are like Nebuchadnezzar, dethroned, bereft of reason, and eating grass like an ox. But who can set limits to the remedial force of spirit?

"A man is a god in ruins. When men are innocent, life shall be longer, and shall pass into the immortal as gently as we awake from dreams. Now, the world would be insane and rabid, if these disorganizations should last for hundreds of years. It is kept in check by death and infancy. Infancy is the perpetual Messiah, which comes into the arms of fallen men, and pleads with them to return to paradise.

"Man is the dwarf of himself. Once he was permeated and dissolved by spirit. He filled nature with his overflowing currents. Out from him sprang the sun and moon; from man the sun, from woman the moon. The laws of his mind, the periods of his actions externized themselves into day and night, into the year and the seasons. But, having made for himself this huge shell, his waters retired; he no longer fills the veins and veinlets; he is shrunk to a drop. He sees that the structure still fits him, but fits him colossally. Say, rather, once it fitted him, now it corresponds to him from far and on high. He adores timidly his own work. Now is man the follower of the sun, and woman the follower of the moon. Yet sometimes he starts in his slumber, and wonders at himself and his house, and muses strangely at the resemblance betwixt him and it. He perceives that if his law is still paramount, if still he have elemental power, if his word is sterling yet in nature, it is not conscious power, it is not inferior but superior to his will. It is instinct." Thus my Orphic poet sang.   [W, I, 70–72]

On the brink of the waters of life and truth, we are miserably dying. The inaccessibleness of every thought but that we are in, is wonderful. What if you come near to it; you are as remote when you are nearest as when you are farthest. Every thought is also a prison; every heaven is also a prison. Therefore we love the poet, the inventor, who in any form, whether in an ode or in an action or in looks and behavior, has yielded us a new thought. He unlocks our chains and admits us to a new scene.   [W, III, 33]

Emerson reflects on the infinitude of the self, divinely equipped yet slow to realize its gifts. Every man is a latent artist.

A man should think much of himself because he is a necessary being: a link was wanting between two craving parts of Nature and he was hurled into being as the bridge, over that yawning need. . . .   [J, V, 512]

. . . men are not made like boxes, a hundred or thousand to order, and all exactly alike, of known dimension, and all their properties known; but no, they come into nature through a nine months' astonishment, and of a character, each one, incalculable, and of extravagant possibilities. Out of darkness and out of the awful Cause they come to be caught up into this vision of a seeing, partaking, acting and suffering life, not foreknown, not fore-estimable, but slowly or speedily they unfold new, unknown, mighty traits: not boxes, but these machines are alive, agitated, fearing, sorrowing.   [J, V, 132]

It is the largest part of a man that is not inventoried. He has many enumerable parts: he is social, professional, political, sectarian, literary, and is this or that set and corporation. But after the most exhausting census has been made, there remains as much more which no tongue can tell. And this remainder is that which interests. This is that which the strong genius works upon; the region of destiny, of aspiration, of the unknown. Ah, they have a secret persuasion that as little as they pass for in the world, they are immensely rich in expectancy and power. Nobody has ever yet dispossessed this adhesive self to arrive at any glimpse or guess of the awful life that lurks under it.

Far the best part, I repeat, of every mind is not that which he knows, but that which hovers in gleams, suggestions, tantalizing, unpossessed, before him. His firm recorded knowledge soon loses all interest for him. But this dancing chorus of thoughts and hopes is the quarry of his future, is his possibility, and teaches him that his man's life is of a ridiculous brevity and meanness, but that it is his first age and trial only of his young wings, but that vast revolutions, migrations, and gyres on gyres in the celestial societies invite him.   [J, VII, 137–138]

A man is furnished with this superb case of instruments, the senses, and perceptive and executive faculties, and they betray him every day. He transfers his allegiance from Instinct and God to this adroit little committee. A man is an exaggerator. In every conversation see how the main end is still lost sight of by all but the best, and with slight apology or none, a digression made to a creaking door or a buzzing fly. What heavenly eloquence could hold the ear of an audience if a child cried! A man with a truth to express is caught by the beauty of his own words and ends with being a rhymester or critic. And Genius is sacrificed to talent every day.   [J, VI, 121]

I know not how it is that we need an interpreter, but the great majority of men seem to be minors, who have not yet come into possession of their own, or mutes, who cannot report the conversation they have had with nature. There is no man who does not anticipate a supersensual utility in the sun and stars, earth and water. These stand and wait to render him a peculiar service. But there is some obstruction or some excess of phlegm in our constitution, which does not suffer them to yield the due effect. Too feeble fall the impressions of nature on us to make us artists. Every touch should thrill. Every man should be so much an artist that he could report in conversation what had befallen him. Yet, in our experience, the rays or appulses have sufficient force to arrive at the senses, but not enough to reach the quick and compel the reproduction of themselves in speech. The poet is the person in whom these powers are in balance, the man without impediment, who sees and handles that which others dream of, traverses the whole scale of experience, and is representative of man, in virtue of being the largest power to receive and to impart. . . .

The sign and credentials of the poet are that he announces that which no man foretold. He is the true and only doctor; he knows and tells; he is the only teller of news, for he was present and privy to the appearance which he describes. He is a beholder of ideas and an utterer of the necessary and casual. For we do not speak now of men of poetical talents, or of industry and skill in metre, but of the true poet. [W, III, 5–6, 8–9, *passim*]

The poet is the explorer of the super-sensible regions, "exquisitely vital and sympathetic." He sees the unity in dissimilarity, regards the world as emblematic, encompasses all subjects, finds nothing unpoetic. The whole earth is his "park and manor," and his message is one of "joy and exultation."

. . . the quality of the imagination is to flow, and not to freeze. The poet did not stop at the color or the form, but read their meaning; neither may he rest in this meaning, but he makes the same objects exponents of his new thought. Here is the difference betwixt the poet and the mystic, that the last nails a symbol to one sense, which was a true sense for a moment, but soon becomes old and false. For all symbols are fluxional; all language is vehicular and transitive, and is good, as ferries and horses are, for conveyance, not as farms and houses are, for homestead. Mysticism consists in the mistake of an accidental and individual symbol for an universal one. [W, III, 34]

Transcendency. In a cotillon some persons dance and others await their turn when the music and the figure come to them. In the dance of God there is not one of the chorus but can and will begin to spin, monumental as he now looks, whenever the music and figure reach his place and duty. O celestial Bacchus! drive them mad—this multitude of vagabonds, hungry for eloquence, hungry for poetry, starving for symbols, perishing for want of electricity to vitalize this too much pasture, and in the long delay indemnifying themselves with the false wine of alcohol, of politics or of money.

Every man may be, and at some time a man is, lifted to a platform whence he looks beyond sense to moral and spiritual truth, and in that mood deals sovereignly with matter, and strings worlds like beads upon his thought. The success with which this is done can alone determine how genuine is the inspiration. The poet is rare because he must be exquisitely vital and sympathetic, and, at the same time, immovably centred. In good society, nay, among the angels in heaven, is not everything spoken in fine parable, and not so servilely as it befell to the sense? All is symbolized. Facts are not foreign, as they seem, but related. Wait a little and we see the return of the remote hyperbolic curve. The solid men complain that the idealist leaves out the fundamental facts; the poet complains that the solid men leave out the sky. To every plant there are two powers; one shoots down as rootlet, and one upward as tree. You must have eyes of science to see in the seed its nodes; you must have the vivacity of the poet to perceive in the thought its futurities. The poet is representative—whole man, diamond-merchant, symbolizer, emancipator; in him the world projects a scribe's hand and writes the adequate genesis. The nature of things is flowing, a metamorphosis. The free spirit sympathizes not only with the actual form, but with the power or possible forms; but for obvious municipal or parietal uses God has given us a bias or a rest on today's forms. Hence the shudder of joy with which in each clear moment we recognize the metamorphosis, because it is always a conquest, a surprise from the heart of things.

[W, VIII, 70–71]

The poet contemplates the central identity, sees it undulate and roll this way and that, with divine flowings, through remotest things; and, following it, can detect essential resemblances in natures never before compared. He can class them so audaciously because he is sensible of the sweep of the celestial stream, from which nothing is exempt. His own body is a fleeing apparition—his personality as fugitive as the trope he employs. In certain hours we can almost pass our hand through our own body. [W, VIII, 21]

I know there is entertainment and room for talent in the artist's selection of ancient or remote subjects; as when the poet goes to India, or to Rome, or to Persia, for his fable. But I believe nobody knows better than he that herein he consults his ease rather than his strength or his desire. He is very well convinced that the great moments of life are those in which his own house, his own body, the tritest and nearest ways and words and things have been illuminated into prophets and teachers. What else is it to be a poet? What are his garland and singing-robes? What but a sensibility so keen that the scent of an elder-blow, or the timber-yard and corporation-works of a nest of pismires is event enough for him—all emblems and personal appeals to him. His wreath and robe is to do what he enjoys; emancipation from other men's questions, and glad study of his own; escape from the gossip and routine of society, and the allowed right and practice of making better. He does not give his hand, but in sign of giving his heart; he is not affable with all, but silent, uncommitted or in love, as his heart leads him. There is no subject that does not belong to him—politics, economy, manufactures and stock-brokerage, as much as sunsets and souls; only, these things, placed in their true order, are poetry; displaced, or put in kitchen order, they are unpoetic. [W, VIII, 36–37]

In dreams we are true poets; we create the persons of the drama; we give them appropriate figures, faces, costume; they are perfect in their organs, attitude, manners: moreover they speak after their own characters, not ours—they speak to us, and we listen with surprise to what they say.

Indeed, I doubt if the best poet has yet written any five-act
play that can compare in thoroughness of invention with
this unwritten play in fifty acts, composed by the dullest
snorer on the floor of the watch-house.

[W, VIII, 44–45]

Apollo kept the flocks of Admetus, said the poets. When
the gods come among men, they are not known. Jesus was
not; Socrates and Shakespeare were not. Antæus was suffocated by the gripe of Hercules, but every time he touched
his mother-earth his strength was renewed. Man is the
broken giant, and in all his weakness both his body and his
mind are invigorated by habits of conversation with nature.
The power of music, the power of poetry, to unfix and as
it were clap wings to solid nature, interprets the riddle of
Orpheus. The philosophical perception of identity through
endless mutations of form makes him know the Proteus.
What else am I who laughed or wept yesterday, who slept
last night like a corpse, and this morning stood and ran?
And what see I on any side but the transmigrations of
Proteus? I can symbolize my thought by using the name of
any creature, of any fact, because every creature is man
agent or patient. Tantalus is but a name for you and me.
Tantalus means the impossibility of drinking the waters of
thought which are always gleaming and waving within sight
of the soul. The transmigration of souls is no fable. I would
it were; but men and women are only half human. Every
animal of the barn-yard, the field and the forest, of the
earth and of the waters that are under the earth, has contrived to get a footing and to leave the print of its features
and form in some one or other of these upright, heaven-
facing speakers. Ah! brother, stop the ebb of thy soul—
ebbing downward into the forms into whose habits thou
hast now for many years slid. As near and proper to us is
also that old fable of the Sphinx, who was said to sit in the
road-side and put riddles to every passenger. If the man
could not answer, she swallowed him alive. If he could
solve the riddle, the Sphinx was slain. What is our life but
an endless flight of winged facts or events? In splendid variety these changes come, all putting questions to the hu-

man spirit. Those men who cannot answer by a superior wisdom these facts or questions of time, serve them. Facts encumber them, tyrannize over them, and make the men of routine, the men of *sense,* in whom a literal obedience to facts has extinguished every spark of that light by which man is truly man. But if the man is true to his better instincts or sentiments, and refuses the dominion of facts, as one that comes of a higher race; remains fast by the soul and sees the principle, then the facts fall aptly and supple into their places; they know their master, and the meanest of them glorifies him.   [W, II, 31–33]

Jesus Christ belonged to the true race of prophets. He saw with open eye the mystery of the soul. Drawn by its severe harmony, ravished with its beauty, he lived in it, and had his being there. Alone in all history he estimated the greatness of man. One man was true to what is in you and me. He saw that God incarnates himself in man, and evermore goes forth anew to take possession of his World. He said, in this jubilee of sublime emotion, "I am divine. Through me, God acts; through me, speaks. Would you see God, see me; or see thee, when thou also thinkest as I now think." But what a distortion did his doctrine and memory suffer in the same, in the next, and the following ages! There is no doctrine of the Reason which will bear to be taught by the Understanding. The understanding caught this high chant from the poet's lips, and said, in the next age, "This was Jehovah come down out of heaven. I will kill you, if you say he was a man." The idioms of his language and the figures of his rhetoric have usurped the place of his truth; and churches are not built on his principles, but on his tropes. Christianity became a Mythus, as the poetic teaching of Greece and of Egypt, before. He spoke of miracles; for he felt that man's life was a miracle, and all that man doth, and he knew that this daily miracle shines as the character ascends. But the word Miracle, as pronounced by Christian churches, gives a false impression; it is Monster. It is not one with the blowing clover and the falling rain.

He felt respect for Moses and the prophets, but no unfit

tenderness at postponing their initial revelations to the hour and the man that now is; to the eternal revelation in the heart. Thus was he a true man. Having seen that the law in us is commanding, he would not suffer it to be commanded. Boldly, with hand, and heart, and life, he declared it was God. Thus is he, as I think, the only soul in history who has appreciated the worth of man.   [W, I, 128–130]

Doubt not, O poet, but persist. Say "It is in me, and shall out." Stand there, balked and dumb, stuttering and stammering, hissed and hooted, stand and strive, until at last rage draw out of thee that *dream*-power which every night shows thee is thine own; a power transcending all limit and privacy, and by virtue of which a man is the conductor of the whole river of electricity. Nothing walks, or creeps, or grows, or exists, which must not in turn arise and walk before him as exponent of his meaning. Comes he to that power, his genius is no longer exhaustible. All the creatures by pairs and by tribes pour into his mind as into a Noah's ark, to come forth again to people a new world. This is like the stock of air for our respiration or for the combustion of our fireplace; not a measure of gallons, but the entire atmosphere if wanted. And therefore the rich poets, as Homer, Chaucer, Shakespeare, and Raphael, have obviously no limits to their works except the limits of their lifetime, and resemble a mirror carried through the street, ready to render an image of every created thing.

O poet! a new nobility is conferred in groves and pastures, and not in castles or by the sword-blade any longer. The conditions are hard, but equal. Thou shalt leave the world, and know the muse only. Thou shalt not know any longer the times, customs, graces, politics, or opinions of men, but shalt take all from the muse. For the time of towns is tolled from the world by funereal chimes, but in nature the universal hours are counted by succeeding tribes of animals and plants, and by growth of joy on joy. God wills also that thou abdicate a manifold and duplex life, and that thou be content that others speak for thee. Others shall be thy gentlemen and shall represent all courtesy and worldly life for thee; others shall do the great and resounding actions also. Thou shalt lie close hid with nature, and canst not be afforded to the Capitol or the Exchange. The world is full of renunciations and apprenticeships, and this is thine; thou must pass for a fool and a churl for a long season. This is the screen and sheath in which Pan has protected his well-beloved flower, and thou shalt be known only to thine own, and they shall console thee with tenderest love. And thou shalt not be able to rehearse the names of thy friends in thy verse, for an old shame before the holy ideal. And this is the reward; that the ideal shall be real to thee, and the impressions of the actual world shall fall like summer rain, copious, but not troublesome to thy invulnerable essence. Thou shalt have the whole land for thy park and manor, the sea for thy bath and navigation, without tax and without envy; the woods and the rivers thou shalt own, and thou shalt possess that wherein others are only tenants and boarders. Thou true land-lord! sea-lord! air-lord! Wherever snow falls or water flows or birds fly, wherever day and night meet in twilight, wherever the blue heaven is hung by clouds or sown with stars, wherever are forms with transparent boundaries, wherever are outlets into celestial space, wherever is danger, and awe, and love —there is Beauty, plenteous as rain, shed for thee, and though thou shouldst walk the world over, thou shalt not be able to find a condition inopportune or ignoble.

[W, III, 40–42]

Skepticism esteems ignorance organic and irremovable, believes in the existence of pure malignity, believes in a poor decayed God who does what he can to keep down the nuisances, and to keep the world going for our day. It believes the actual to be necessary; it argues habitually from the exception instead of the rule; and, if it went to the legitimate extreme, the earth would smell with suicide.

[J, VI, 116]

There is a principle which is the basis of things, which all speech aims to say, and all action to evolve, a simple, quiet, undescribed, undescribable presence, dwelling very peacefully in us, our rightful lord: we are not to do, but to let do; not to work, but to be worked upon; and to this homage there is a consent of all thoughtful and just men in all ages and conditions. To this sentiment belong vast and sudden enlargements of power. 'Tis remarkable that our faith in ecstasy consists with total inexperience of it.

[W, VI, 213]

The doctrine of this Supreme Presence is a cry of joy and exultation. Who shall dare think he has come late into nature, or has missed anything excellent in the past, who seeth the admirable stars of possibility, and the yet untouched continent of hope glittering with all its mountains in the vast West? I praise with wonder this great reality, which seems to drown all things in the deluge of its light.

[W, I, 222–223]

Chapter Four

Friendship, Sex and Other
Subtle Antagonisms

*We come now to the comic and even farcical side of Trans-
cendentalism—the attempt to control friendship and sex
on the level of high principle. "We are armed all over with
subtle antagonisms, which, as soon as we meet, begin to
play, and translate all poetry into stale prose. Almost all
people descend to meet." The impossibility of intimacy between so many solitary and even mystical sages was under-
standable; the effort to impose upon the social and passional
world the same exalted consistency which these people knew
in the private world of their contemplations was comic,
when it was not pathetic. For to believe that people "descend to meet," while undoubtedly true, also shows a profound ignorance of the essential lawlessness of social dialogue, of friendship, as opposed to the sometimes abnormal
control exercised in private. It represents a valuation of
consistency over the truth of experience.*

*Yet this absurd or fanatical note is more in Thoreau's
style than in Emerson's. And the really humorous side of
Transcendentalism appears only in Emerson—by design
—for only he was social enough, witty and perceptive
enough, to measure his disability for friendship and love,
where Thoreau tended to condemn society altogether, and
Alcott to be oblivious to it. Emerson is not unconsciously
funny when he talks about having "to descend to meet";
in other passages, he comments freely on himself, aware of
his freezing shyness, his need to push people away. But need*

it be emphasized that it was he, almost alone among the Transcendentalists, who had to put people off at all? That it was precisely his attraction, his humor, his awareness that enforced the tension with which he had to reject certain people—among them passionate bluestockings like Margaret Fuller?

Nor is this the whole story. Almost every student of Emerson's life has remarked on the curious doubleness of his nature—the deep instinct to privacy and even to secrecy that contrasts with his long public life as a lecturer and national oracle. Emerson was a man who rejected intimacy and passion on principle—understandably, since not many men have been able to love the spirit as he did and to seek satisfaction from men at the same time. But he also guarded himself from any kind of hurt, he protected his feeling and his freedom to work, precisely because his sensitivity to people, his very acute general comprehension, did not always seem to fit his style and habit of life—or his life-long experience of solitude. We forget nowadays how physically isolated these people were. Thoreau said in his Journal that Concord was so empty, one could see from a mile off a chicken running across the street. Modern mass life has so involved people in each other's lives that they distrust solitude on principle precisely as Emerson distrusted society on principle. But it should not be forgotten that if Emerson's distrust is sometimes priggish and often consciously arch, his essential passion is that forgotten side of love which reserves the highest reach of it for God, not for man; for the incommunicable because "it is too fine for speech."

I spoke of friendship, but my friends and I are fishes in our habit. As for taking Thoreau's arm, I should as soon take the arm of an elm tree.   [J, VII, 498]

Solitude is impracticable, and society fatal. We must keep our head in the one and our hands in the other. The conditions are met, if we keep our independence, yet do not lose our sympathy. These wonderful horses need to be driven by fine hands.   [W, VII, 15]

. . . I wish my house to be a college, open as the air to all
to whom I spiritually belong, and who belong to me. But
it is not open to others, or for other purposes. I do not
wish that it should be a confectioner's shop wherein eaters
and drinkers may get strawberries and champagne. I do
not wish that it should be a playground or house of entertainment for boys. They do well to play; I like that they
should, but not with me, or in these precincts. . . .

[J, V, 239]

We are armed all over with subtle antagonisms, which, as
soon as we meet, begin to play, and translate all poetry into
stale prose. Almost all people descend to meet. All association must be a compromise, and, what is worst, the very
flower and aroma of the flower of each of the beautiful natures disappears as they approach each other. What a perpetual disappointment is actual society, even of the virtuous and gifted! After interviews have been compassed with
long foresight we must be tormented presently by baffled
blows, by sudden, unseasonable apathies, by epilepsies of
wit and of animal spirits, in the heyday of friendship and
thought. Our faculties do not play us true, and both parties are relieved by solitude.

I ought to be equal to every relation. It makes no difference how many friends I have and what content I can
find in conversing with each, if there be one to whom I am
not equal. If I have shrunk unequal from one contest, the
joy I find in all the rest becomes mean and cowardly. I
should hate myself, if then I made my other friends my
asylum. [W, II, 199–200]

Every man alone is sincere. At the entrance of a second person, hypocrisy begins. We parry and fend the approach
of our fellow-man by compliments, by gossip, by amuse-
ments, by affairs. We cover up our thought from him under a
hundred folds. I knew a man who under a certain religious
frenzy cast off this drapery, and omitting all compliment
and commonplace, spoke to the conscience of every person he encountered, and that with great insight and beauty.
At first he was resisted, and all men agreed he was mad.
But persisting—as indeed he could not help doing—for

some time in this course, he attained to the advantage of bringing every man of his acquaintance into true relations with him. No man would think of speaking falsely with him, or of putting him off with any chat of markets or reading-rooms. But every man was constrained by so much sincerity to the like plain-dealing, and what love of nature, what poetry, what symbol of truth he had, he did certainly show him. But to most of us society shows not its face and eye, but its side and its back. To stand in true relations with men in a false age is worth a fit of insanity, is it not?

[W, II, 202–203]

[*To Margaret Fuller*] None knows better than I—more's the pity—the gloomy inhospitality of the man, the want of power to meet and unite with even those whom he loves in his "flinty way." What amends can he make to his guests, he asked himself long since. Only to anticipate and thus if possible mitigate their disgust & suspicion at the discovery, by apprising them beforehand that this outside of wax covered an inside of stone. Ice has its uses when deception is not thought of and we are not looking for bread. Being made by chemistry & not by cooks its composition is unerring, and it has a universal value *as ice,* not as glass or gelatine. Would you know more of his history?—Diffident, shy, proud, having settled it long ago in his mind that he & society must always be nothing to each other—he received with astonishment the kind regards of such as coming from the opposite quarter of the heavens he now calls his friends —with surprise and when he dared to believe them, with delight. Can one be glad of an affection which he knows not how to return? I am. Humbly grateful for every expression of tenderness—which makes the day sweet and inspires unlimited hopes . . . Yet I did not deceive myself with thinking that the old bars would suddenly fall. No, I knew that if I would cherish my dear romance, I must treat it gently, forbear it long—worship, not use it—and so at last by piety I might be tempered & annealed to bear contact & conversation as well mixed natures should. Therefore, my friend, treat me always as a mute, not ungrateful though now incommunicable.   [L, II, 350–351]

[*To Caroline Sturgis*] . . . that which set me on this writing was the talk with Margaret F. [Fuller] last Friday who taxed me on both your parts with a certain inhospitality of soul inasmuch as you were both willing to be my friends in the full & sacred sense & I remained apart, critical, & after many interviews still a stranger. I count & weigh, but do not love.—I heard the charge, I own, with great humility & sadness. I confess to the fact of cold & imperfect inter-course, but not to the impeachment of my will, and not to the deficiency of my affection. If I count & weigh, I love also. [L, II, 325]

[*To Caroline Sturgis*] I hate every thing frugal and cow-ardly in friendship. *That,* at least should be brave and gen-erous. When we fear the withdrawal of love from ourselves by the new relations which our companions must form, it is mere infidelity. We believe in our eyes and not in the Cre-ator. . . . But we are wiser with the next sun, and know that a true and *native* friend is only the extension of our own being and perceiving into other skies and societies, there learning wisdom, there discerning spirits, and attracting our own for us, as truly as we had done hitherto in our strait enclosure. I wish you to go out an adventurous missionary, into all the nations of happy souls, and by all whom you can greatly, and by any whom you can wholly love, I see that I too must be immeasurably enriched. [L, II, 326]

Ah, my brave giant, you can never understand the silences and forbearances of such as are not giants. To those to whom we owe affection, let us be dumb until we are strong, though we should never be strong. I hate mumped and measled lovers. I hate cramp in all men—most in myself.
[E–C, II, 231]

GIVE ALL TO LOVE

> Give all to love;
> Obey thy heart;
> Friends, kindred, days,
> Estate, good-fame,

Plans, credit and the Muse,
Nothing refuse.

'Tis a brave master;
Let it have scope:
Follow it utterly,
Hope beyond hope:
High and more high
It dives into noon,
With wing unspent,
Untold intent;
But it is a god,
Knows its own path
And the outlets of the sky.

It was never for the mean;
It requireth courage stout.
Souls above doubt,
Valor unbending,
It will reward,
They shall return
More than they were,
And ever ascending.

Leave all for love;
Yet, hear me, yet,
One word more thy heart behoved,
One pulse more of firm endeavor,
Keep thee today,
Tomorrow, forever,
Free as an Arab
Of thy beloved.

Cling with life to the maid;
But when the surprise,
First vague shadow of surmise
Flits across her bosom young,
Of a joy apart from thee,
Free be she, fancy-free;
Nor thou detain her vesture's hem,
Nor the palest rose she flung
From her summer diadem.

> Though thou loved her as thyself,
> As a self of purer clay,
> Though her parting dims the day,
> Stealing grace from all alive;
> Heartily know,
> When half-gods go,
> The gods arrive.
>
>   [W, IX, 90–92]

I decline invitations to evening parties chiefly because, besides the time spent, commonly ill, in the party, the hours preceding and succeeding the visit are lost for any solid use, as I am put out of tune for writing or reading. That makes my objection to many employments that seem trifles to a bystander, as packing a trunk, or any small handiwork, or correcting proof-sheets, that they put me out of tune.

                    [J, V, 23]

The continual effort to raise himself above himself, to work a pitch above his last height, betrays itself in a man's relations. We thirst for approbation, yet cannot forgive the approver. The sweet of nature is love; yet if I have a friend I am tormented by my imperfections. The love of me accuses the other party. If he were high enough to slight me, then could I love him, and rise by my affection to new heights. A man's growth is seen in the successive choirs of his friends. For every friend whom he loses for truth, he gains a better. I thought as I walked in the woods and mused on my friends, why should I play with them this game of idolatry? I know and see too well, when not voluntarily blind, the speedy limits of persons called high and worthy. Rich, noble and great they are by the liberality of our speech, but truth is sad. O blessed Spirit, whom I forsake for these, they are not thou! Every personal consideration that we allow costs us heavenly state. We sell the thrones of angels for a short and turbulent pleasure.

                    [W, II, 307]

I saw yesterday, Sunday, whilst at dinner, my neighbor Hosmer creeping into my barn. At once it occurred, "Well,

men are lonely, to be sure, and here is this able, social,
intellectual farmer under this grim day, as grimly, sidling
into my barn, in the hope of some talk with me, showing
me how to husband my cornstalks. Forlorn enough!"

[J, VIII, 261]

In discourse with a friend, our thought, hitherto wrapped
in our consciousness, detaches itself, and allows itself to be
seen as a thought, in a manner as new and entertaining to
us as to our companions. For a provocation of thought, we
use ourselves and use each other. Some perceptions—I think
the best—are granted to the single soul; they come from
the depth and go to the depth and are the permanent and
controlling ones. Others it takes two to find. We must be
warmed by the fire of sympathy, to be brought into the
right conditions and angles of vision. Conversation; for
intellectual activity is contagious. We are emulous. If the
tone of the companion is higher than ours, we delight in
rising to it. 'Tis a historic observation that a writer must
find an audience up to his thought, or he will no longer care
to impart it, but will sink to their level or be silent.

[W, VIII, 292–293]

Let us feel if we will the absolute insulation of man. We
are sure that we have all in us. We go to Europe, or we
pursue persons, or we read books, in the instinctive faith
that these will call it out and reveal us to ourselves. Beggars
all. The persons are such as we; the Europe, an old faded
garment of dead persons; the books, their ghosts. Let us
drop this idolatry. Let us give over this mendicancy. Let us
even bid our dearest friends farewell, and defy them, saying "Who are you? Unhand me: I will be dependent no
more." Ah! seest thou not, O brother, that thus we part only
to meet again on a higher platform, and only be more each
other's because we are more our own? A friend is Janus-
faced; he looks to the past and the future. He is the child
of all my foregoing hours, the prophet of those to come, and
the harbinger of a greater friend.

I do then with my friends as I do with my books. I would
have them where I can find them, but I seldom use them.

We must have society on our own terms, and admit or exclude it on the slightest cause. I cannot afford to speak much with my friend. If he is great he makes me so great that I cannot descend to converse. In the great days, presentiments hover before me in the firmament. I ought then to dedicate myself to them. I go in that I may seize them, I go out that I may seize them. I fear only that I may lose them receding into the sky in which now they are only a patch of brighter light. Then, though I prize my friends, I cannot afford to talk with them and study their visions, lest I lose my own. It would indeed give me a certain household joy to quit this lofty seeking, this spiritual astronomy or search of stars, and come down to warm sympathies with you; but then I know well I shall mourn always the vanishing of my mighty gods. [W, II, 214–215]

What difference in the hospitality of minds! Some are actually hostile, and imprison me as in a hole. A blockhead makes a blockhead of me; whilst for my Oriental friend here, I have always claimed for him, that nothing could be so expansive as his element is.

My friends begin to value each other, now that Alcott is to go; and Ellery declares, "that he never saw that man without being cheered," and Henry says, "He is the best natured man I ever met. The rats and mice make their nests in him." [J, VII, 551–552]

We are always out-generaled by tacticians, choked off by the previous question or by insidious assistance, or by sly amendments, or by false friends. [J, VIII, 230]

I prefer a tendency to stateliness to an excess of fellowship. Let the incommunicable objects of nature and the metaphysical isolation of man teach us independence. Let us not be too much acquainted. I would have a man enter his house through a hall filled with heroic and sacred sculptures, that he might not want the hint of tranquillity and self-poise. We should meet each morning as from foreign countries, and, spending the day together, should depart at night, as into foreign countries. In all things I would have the island of a man inviolate. Let us sit apart as the gods, talking from peak to peak all round Olympus. No degree of affection need invade this religion. This is myrrh and rosemary to keep the other sweet. Lovers should guard their strangeness. If they forgive too much, all slides into confusion and meanness. It is easy to push this deference to a Chinese etiquette; but coolness and absence of heat and haste indicate fine qualities. A gentleman makes no noise; a lady is serene. Proportionate is our disgust at those invaders who fill a studious house with blast and running, to secure some paltry convenience. Not less I dislike a low sympathy of each with his neighbor's needs. Must we have a good understanding with one another's palates? as foolish people who have lived long together know when each wants salt or sugar. I pray my companion, if he wishes for bread, to ask me for bread, and if he wishes for sassafras or arsenic, to ask me for them, and not to hold out his plate as if I knew already. Every natural function can be dignified by deliberation and privacy. Let us leave hurry to slaves. The compliments and ceremonies of our breeding should recall, however remotely, the grandeur of our destiny.

[W, X, 136–138]

Jones Very is like the rain plentiful. He does not love individuals: he is annoyed by edge. He likes only community; and he likes the lowness also, if it be community. I like sharp slats. Strength is wonderful.   [J, VII, 120]

I can well hear a stranger converse on mysteries of love and romance of character; can easily become interested in his private love and fortunes; but as soon as I learn that he eats cucumbers, or hates parsnip, values his luncheon, and eats his dinner over again in his talk, I can never thenceforward hear that man talk of sentiment.

[J, VI, 527–528]

I finish this morning transcribing my old essay on Love, but I see well its inadequateness. I, cold because I am hot— cold at the surface only as a sort of guard and compensation for the fluid tenderness of the core—have much more

experience than I have written there, more than I will,
more than I can write. In silence we must wrap much of our
life, because it is too fine for speech, because also we cannot explain it to others, and because somewhat we cannot
yet understand. We do not live as angels, eager to introduce
each other to new perfections in our brothers and sisters,
and frankly avowing our delight in each new trait of character, in the magic of each new eyebeam, but that which
passes for love in the world gets official, and instead of em-
bracing, hates all the divine traits that dare to appear in
other persons. A better and holier society will mend this
selfish cowardice, and we shall have brave ties of affection,
not petrified by law, not dated or ordained by law to last
for one year, for five years, or for life; but drawing their
date, like all friendship, from itself only. [J, V, 411–412]

It is the necessity of my nature to shed all influences.
Who can come near to Kehama? Neither the rain, neither
the warm ray of love, nor the touch of human hand. It
seemed, as I mused in the street in Boston on the unpro-
pitious effect of the town on my humor, that there needs a
certain deliberation and tenacity in the entertainment of a
thought—a certain longanimity to make that confidence
and stability which can meet the demand others make on
us. I am too quick-eyed and unstable. My thoughts are too
short, as they say my sentences are. I step along from stone
to stone over the Lethe which gurgles around my path, but
the odds are that my companion encounters me just as I
leave one stone and before my foot has well reached the
other, and down I tumble into Lethe water. But the man of
long wind, the man who receives his thought with a certain
phlegmatic entertainment and unites himself to it for the
time, as a sailor to his boat, has a better principle of poise
and is not easily moved from the perpendicular.

[J, V, 355–356]

*Chary of deep personal commitments and jealous of his
privacy, Emerson still loves to engage in the "magnetic experiment" and "game" of conversation.*

In conversation the game is, to say something new with old words, and you shall observe a man of the people picking his way along, step by step, using every time an old boulder, yet never setting his foot on an old place

[J, VIII, 21]

Put any company of people together with freedom for conversation, and a rapid self-distribution takes place into sets and pairs. The best are accused of exclusiveness. It would be more true to say they separate as oil from water, as children from old people, without love or hatred in the matter, each seeking his like; and any interference with the affinities would produce constraint and suffocation. All conversation is a magnetic experiment. I know that my friend can talk eloquently; you know that he cannot articulate a sentence: we have seen him in different company. Assort your party, or invite none. Put Stubbs and Coleridge, Quintilian and Aunt Miriam, into pairs, and you make them all wretched. 'Tis an extempore Sing-Sing built in a parlor. Leave them to seek their own mates, and they will be as merry as sparrows. [W, VII, 14]

Let Nature bear the expense. The attitude, the tone, is all. Let our eyes not look away, but meet. Let us not look east and west for materials of conversation, but rest in presence and unity. A just feeling will fast enough supply fuel for discourse, if speaking be more grateful than silence. When people come to see us, we foolishly prattle, lest we be inhospitable. But things said for conversation are chalk eggs. Don't *say* things. What you *are* stands over you the while, and thunders so that I cannot hear what you say to the contrary. A lady of my acquaintance said, "I don't care so much for what they say as I do for what makes them say it." [W, VIII, 96]

. . . what a seneschal and detective is laughter! It seems to require several generations of education to train a squeaking or a shouting habit out of a man. Sometimes, when in almost all expressions the Choctaw and the slave have been worked out of him, a coarse nature still betrays itself in his contemptible squeals of joy. It is necessary for the purification of drawing-rooms that these entertaining explosions should be under strict control.   [W, VIII, 86–87]

We cannot forgive you that worst want of tact which incapacitates you from discriminating between what is to be disputed, and what is to be reverenced or cherished in your friend's communications. The babe of a Choctaw, the cub of a lion, may be strangled by a boy: and the ablest genius, if he trust you with his yet unripe fancies, casts himself helpless on your compassion. Life and death are in your hands, let his power and renown be what they may. There is no part then to be taken but to throw yourself as much as possible into the neutral state of mind and entertain his thought as far as you can; and where you cannot, be satisfied that you cannot, without criticism. It is, though you can kill it, the babe of a Choctaw, the cub of a lion, and will yet approve its sinewy stock.   [J, VI, 388–389]

Henry Thoreau sturdily pushes his economy into houses and thinks it the false mark of the gentleman that he is to pay much for his food. He ought to pay little for his food. Ice—he must have ice! And it is true, that, for each artificial want that can be invented and added to the ponderous expense, there is new clapping of hands of newspaper editors and the donkey public. To put one more rock to be lifted betwixt a man and his true ends. If Socrates were here, we could go and talk with him; but Longfellow, we cannot go and talk with; there is a palace and servants, and a row of bottles of different colored wines, and wine glasses, and fine coats.   [J, VIII, 396–397]

Henry Thoreau's idea of the men he meets is, that they are his old thoughts walking. It is all affectation to make much of them, as if he did not long since know them thoroughly.   [J, VIII, 294]

There is a superlative temperament which has no medium range, but swiftly oscillates from the freezing to the boiling point, and which affects the manners of those who share it with a certain desperation. Their aspect is grimace. They go tearing, convulsed through life—wailing, praying, exclaiming, swearing. We talk, sometimes, with people whose conversation would lead you to suppose that they had lived in a museum, where all the objects were monsters and extremes. Their good people are phœnixes; their naughty are like the prophet's figs. They use the superlative of grammar: "most perfect," "most exquisite," "most horrible." Like the French, they are enchanted, they are desolate, because you have got or have not got a shoe-string or a wafer you happen to want—not perceiving that superlatives are diminutives, and weaken; that the positive is the sinew of speech, the superlative the fat. If the talker lose a tooth, he thinks the universal thaw and dissolution of things has come. Controvert his opinion and he cries "Persecution!" and reckons himself with Saint Barnabas, who was sawn in two.

Especially we note this tendency to extremes in the pleasant excitement of horror-mongers. Is there something so delicious in disasters and pain? Bad news is always exaggerated, and we may challenge Providence to send a fact so tragical that we cannot contrive to make it a little worse in our gossip.

All this comes of poverty. We are unskilful definers. From want of skill to convey quality, we hope to move admiration by quantity. Language should aim to describe the fact. It is not enough to suggest it and magnify it. Sharper sight would indicate the true line. 'Tis very wearisome, this straining talk, these experiences all exquisite, intense and tremendous—"The best I ever saw"; "I never in my life!" One wishes these terms gazetted and forbidden. Every favorite is not a cherub, nor every cat a griffin, nor each unpleasing person a dark, diabolical intriguer; nor agonies, excruciations nor ecstasies our daily bread.

[W, X, 163–165]

Whip. My stories did not make them laugh, my facts did not quite fit the case, my arguments did not hit the white. Is it so? Then warm yourself, old fellow, with hot mince-pie and half a pint of port wine, and they will fit like a glove, and hit like a bullet.   [J, VII, 268]

A sensible man does not brag, avoids introducing the names of his creditable companions, omits himself as habitually as another man obtrudes himself in the discourse, and is content with putting his fact or theme simply on its ground. You shall not tell me that your commercial house, your partners or yourself are of importance; you shall not tell me that you have learned to know men; you shall make me feel that; your saying so unsays it. You shall not enumerate your brilliant acquaintances, nor tell me by their titles what books you have read. I am to infer that you keep good company by your better information and manners, and to infer your reading from the wealth and accuracy of your conversation.   [W, VIII, 304]

Now society in towns is infested by persons who, seeing that the sentiments please, counterfeit the expression of them. These we call sentimentalists—talkers who mistake the description for the thing, saying for having. They have, they tell you, an intense love of Nature; poetry—O, they adore poetry—and roses, and the moon, and the cavalry regiment, and the governor; they love liberty, "dear liberty!" they worship virtue, "dear virtue!" Yes, they adopt whatever merit is in good repute, and almost make it hateful with their praise. The warmer their expressions, the colder we feel; we shiver with cold. A little experience acquaints us with the unconvertibility of the sentimentalist, the soul that is lost by mimicking soul. Cure the drunkard, heal the insane, mollify the homicide, civilize the Pawnee, but what lessons can be devised for the debauchee of sentiment? Was ever one converted? The innocence and ignorance of the patient is the first difficulty; he believes his disease is blooming health. A rough realist or a phalanx of realists would be prescribed; but that is like proposing to mend your bad road with diamonds. Then poverty, famine, war, imprisonment, might be tried. Another cure would be to fight fire with fire, to match a sentimentalist with a sentimentalist. I think each might begin to suspect that something is wrong. [W, VIII, 105–106]

Emerson speculates on the fate and condition of woman in a man's world, "desired for her sex," ridden by private devils, yet needing only love to right her estate.

Woman hides her form from the eyes of men in our world: they cannot, she rightly thinks, be trusted. In a right state the love of one, which each man carried in his heart, should protect all women from his eyes as by an impenetrable veil of indifference. The love of one should make him indifferent to all others, or rather their protector and saintly friend, as if for her sake. But now there is in the eyes of all men a certain evil light, a vague desire which attaches them to the forms of many women, whilst their affections fasten on some one. Their natural eye is not fixed into coincidence with their spiritual eye. [J, VI, 73]

Nature wishes that woman should attract man, yet she often cunningly moulds into her face a little sarcasm, which seems to say, "Yes, I am willing to attract, but to attract a little better kind of man than any I yet behold." [W, VI, 296]

Love is necessary to the righting the estate of woman in this world. Otherwise nature itself seems to be in conspiracy against her dignity and welfare; for the cultivated, high-thoughted, beauty-loving, saintly woman finds herself unconsciously desired for her sex, and even enhancing the appetite of her savage pursuers by these fine ornaments she has piously laid on herself. She finds with indignation that she is herself a snare, and was made such. I do not wonder at her occasional protest, violent protest against nature, in fleeing to nunneries, and taking black veils. Love rights all this deep wrong. [J, VII, 534]

In every woman's conversation and total influence, mild or acid, lurks the *conventional devil.* [J, VI, 390]

Almost every woman described to you by a woman presents a tragic idea, and not an idea of well-being. One most deserving person whom I commiserated last night with my friends, has such peculiar and unfortunate habits of conversation that she can say nothing agreeable to me. Say what she will—rare and accomplished person that she is—I hear her never, but only *wait* until she is done. I think with a profound pity of her family. Were she my sister, I should sail for Australasia and put the earth's diameter between us.

[J, V, 25–26]

The Beatitude of Conversation. I am afraid books do stand in our way; for the best heads are writers, and when they meet and fall into profound conversation, they never quite lose all respects of their own economy and pour out the divinest wine, but each is a little wary, a little checked, by the thought of the rare helps this hour might afford him to some page which he has written. Each is apt to become abstracted and lose the remark of the other through too much attention to his own. Yet I have no book and no pleasure in life comparable to this.

Here I come down to the shore of the Sea and dip my hands in its miraculous waves. Here I am assured of the eternity, and can spare all omens, all prophecies, all religions, for I see and know that which they obscurely announce. I seem rich with earth and air and heaven; but the next morning I have lost my keys.

To escape this economy of writers, women would be better friends; but they have the drawback of the perplexities of sex.   [J, VII, 529–530]

She poured a stream of amber over the endless store of private anecdotes, of bosom histories which her wonderful persuasion drew out of all to her. When I heard that a trunk of her correspondence had been found and opened, I felt what a panic would strike all her friends, for it was as if a clever reporter had got underneath a confessional and agreed to report all that transpired there in Wall Street.

[J, VIII, 117]

Chapter Five

Our Abused Age

When it came to politics, Emerson had at first somewhat the same trouble that he had with friendship: his theory left no room for anything except the ideal. But unlike friendship (and sex, and love), which idealists can seem to neglect or to suppress, politics calls up ·tremendously dynamic response in people whose ideal has been flouted. And it is a sign of Emerson's remarkably adaptive and sinewy intelligence, as well of the persuasive power over his countrymen to which he aspired, that the young Emerson whose great early works came out of his absorption in religious and philosophical questions should have developed into the testy, downright, inspired critic of American slavery, American imperialism, American superficiality, American brag. Yet no one who even now finds himself in sympathy with Emerson's essential liberalism should overlook the fact that Emerson's political criticisms proceed from an exalted, an almost apocalyptic vision of the United States. At the same time, Emerson's religious conception of life made him look down on reformers as doctrinaires and literalists, as well as busybodies. His own need for seclusion and independence made him unhappy with any collective or utopian arrangement.

Emerson's observations on politics are full of sharp edges, inconsistencies, romantic visions. They are unified by his quiet perception that politics does come down very often to politicians, that a mass age—such as his was already tending to be—is an age of superstition and ignorance, and that

*the idealist in politics has to contend not only with a larger
residue of sin and contrariness in people than he will consciously admit to, but with his own natural impatience of
politics and all that disordered passion and selfish interest
which politics exemplifies. It is to Emerson's eternal credit
that, although it almost killed him to look at the great beast
of the "public," he supported the people, and could always
tell it apart from the "masses." He recognized "a good deal
of character in our abused age." At the same time he mar-
veled at the belief in human reconstruction when the recon-
structors were themselves so often "pale, withered people
with gold-filled teeth, ghastly, and with minds in the same
dilapidated condition." Nowhere in his characteristic subtle
realism, his feeling for balance, his sense of reality, so clear,
so admirable, as in his struggle to reconcile his vision of the
United States with the actualities of life in a period when
"things are in the saddle and ride mankind."*

*Inevitably, some of Emerson's pronouncements on man
in general and on political issues in particular (like the Civil
War) must now strike us as cold-blooded and abstract. But
when one remembers that Emerson's doctrine is essentially
personalist, it is a mark of his human sympathy—as well as
of his keenness as an observer—that he should have written in his Journal one of the best running accounts of the
tense years before the Civil War that anyone has given us.
After all, the man who commented so brilliantly—and ex-
plosively—on Webster and proslavery apologists, so wasp-
ishly on Lincoln, did believe, to the end, that "surely nobody would be a charlatan who could afford to be sincere."
It is remarkable that there was so much political light—as
well as heat—from a man so unprepared to believe in
politics at all.*

The reputations of the nineteenth century will one day be
quoted to prove its barbarism. [W, IV, 31]

The office of America is to liberate, to abolish kingcraft,
priestcraft, caste, monopoly, to pull down the gallows, to
burn up the bloody statute-book, to take in the immigrant,

to open the doors of the sea and the fields of the earth . . .
[J, X, 195]

Man is the most composite of all creatures. . . . Well, as in
the old burning of the Temple at Corinth, by the melting
and intermixture of silver and gold and other metals a new
compound more precious than any, called the Corinthian
brass, was formed; so in this continent—asylum of all nations—the energy of Irish, Germans, Swedes, Poles, and
Cossacks, and all the European tribes—of the Africans, and
of the Polynesians—will construct a new race, a new religion, a new state, a new literature, which will be as vigorous as the new Europe which came out of the smelting-pot
of the Dark Ages, or that which earlier emerged from the
Pelasgic and Etruscan barbarism. *La Nature aime les croise-
ments.* [J, VII, 115–116]

America. The irresistible convictions of men are sometimes as well expressed by braggart lips, or in jeers, that
sound blasphemous—and that word "manifest destiny,"
which is profanely used, signifies the sense all men have of
the prodigious energy and opportunity lying idle here. The
poor Prussian or Austrian or Italian, escaping hereto, discovers that he has been handcuffed and fettered and fast-
tied all his lifetime, with monopolies and duties at every
toll-gate on his little cart of corn, or wine, or straw, or on
his cow, or ox, or donkey; and padlocked lips, padlocked
mind, no country, no education, no vote—but passports,
police, monks, and foreign soldiers. [J, X, 106–107]

In the republic must always happen what happened here,
that the steamboats and stages and hotels vote one way and
the nation votes the other: and it seems to every meeting of
readers and writers as if it were intolerable that Broad Street
Paddies and bar-room politicians, the sots and loafers and
all manner of ragged and unclean and foul-mouthed persons without a dollar in their pocket should control the
property of the country and make the lawgiver and the law.
But is that any more than their share whilst you hold property selfishly? They are opposed to you: yes, but first you
are opposed to them: they, to be sure, malevolently, men-

acingly, with songs and rowdies and mobs; you cunningly, plausibly, and well-bred; you cheat and they strike; you sleep and eat at their expense; they vote and threaten and sometimes throw stones, at yours.   [J, VI, 99–100]

Cant. We only use different names; he calls it attar of rose, and I call it bilgewater.

The English and the Americans cant sadly. They cover over their greediness with a pretended zeal for religion or patriotism, and strew sugar on a bottled spider.

[J, VIII, 477]

Emerson finds fault with a drowsy education that ignores the realities of tariffs and caucuses and "the western clearing." Hence the effeminacy and sloth in American intellectual life, and the raucous vulgarity of the masses. "In America the geography is sublime, but the men are not."

Our young scholars read newspapers, smoke, and sleep in the afternoons. Goethe, Gibbon, Bentley might provoke them to industry. Undoubtedly the reason why our men are not learned, why G——, for instance, is not, is because the genius or the age does not tend that way. This old learning of Bentley and Gibbon was the natural fruit of the Traditional age in philosophy and religion. Ours is the Revolutionary age, when man is coming back to Consciousness, and from afar this mind begets a disrelish for lexicons. Alcott, therefore, and Very, who have this spirit in great exaltation, abhor books. But at least it behooves those who reject the new ideas, the sticklers of tradition, to be learned. But they are not.   [J, V, 214]

We are very careful of young pear trees and defend them from their enemies, from fire, blight, suckers, grass, slugs, pear-worm, but we let our young men, in whose youth and flower all inferior kinds have their flowering and completion, grow up in heaps and by chance, take the rough and tumble, as we say (which is the skepticism of Education), exposed to their borers, caterpillars, canker-worms, bugs, moping, sloth, seduction, wine, fear, hatred.

[J, VII, 500]

. . . let us honestly state the facts. Our America has a bad name for superficialness. Great men, great nations, have not been boasters and buffoons, but perceivers of the terror of life, and have manned themselves to face it.

[W, VI, 5]

I was at Cambridge yesterday to see Everett inaugurated. His political brothers came as if to bring him to the convent door, and to grace with a sort of bitter courtesy his taking of the cowl. It is like the marriage of a girl; not until the wedding and the departure with her husband, does it appear that she has actually and finally changed homes and connections and social caste. [J, VII, 166]

We have yet had no genius in America, with tyrannous eye, which knew the value of our incomparable materials, and saw, in the barbarism and materialism of the times, another carnival of the same gods whose picture he so much admires in Homer; then in the Middle Age; then in Calvinism. Banks and tariffs, the newspaper and caucus, Methodism and Unitarianism, are flat and dull to dull people, but rest on the same foundations of wonder as the town of Troy and the temple of Delphi, and are as swiftly passing away. Our log-rolling, our stumps and their politics, our fisheries, our Negroes and Indians, our boats and our repudiations, the wrath of rogues and the pusillanimity of honest men, the northern trade, the southern planting, the western clearing, Oregon and Texas, are yet unsung. Yet America is a poem in our eyes; its ample geography dazzles the imagination, and it will not wait long for metres. [W, III, 37–38]

Ours is the age of the omnibus, of the third person plural, of Tammany Hall. Is it that Nature has only so much vital force, and must dilute it if it is to be multiplied into millions? The beautiful is never plentiful. [W, XI, 538]

Alas for America, as I must so often say, the ungirt, the diffuse, the profuse, procumbent—one wide ground juniper, out of which no cedar, no oak will rear up a mast to the clouds! It all runs to leaves, to suckers, to tendrils, to miscellany. The air is loaded with poppy, with imbecility, with dispersion and sloth.

Eager, solicitous, hungry, rabid, busy-bodied America attempting many things, vain, ambitious to feel thy own existence, and convince others of thy talent, by attempting and hastily accomplishing much; yes, catch thy breath and correct thyself, and failing here, prosper out there; speed and fever are never greatness; but reliance and serenity and waiting.

America is formless, has no terrible and no beautiful condensation. Genius, always anthropomorphist, runs every idea into a fable, constructs, finishes, as the plastic Italian cannot build a post or a pump-handle but it terminates in a human head. [J, VII, 286–287]

I do not think very respectfully of the designs or the doings of the people who went to California in 1849. It was a rush and a scramble of needy adventurers, and, in the western country, a general jail delivery of all the rowdies of the rivers. Some of them went with honest purposes, some with very bad ones, and all of them with the very commonplace wish to find a short way to wealth. But nature watches over all, and turns this malfeasance to good. California gets peopled and subdued, civilized in this immoral way, and on this fiction a real prosperity is rooted and grown. 'Tis a decoy-duck; 'tis tubs thrown to amuse the whale; but real ducks, and whales that yield oil, are caught. . . .

In America the geography is sublime, but the men are not: the inventions are excellent, but the inventors one is sometimes ashamed of. The agencies by which events so grand as the opening of California, of Texas, of Oregon, and the junction of the two oceans, are effected, are paltry— coarse selfishness, fraud and conspiracy; and most of the great results of history are brought about by discreditable means. [W, VI, 255–256]

He discovers decay and aimlessness, simulations and fear
in his society, but also revolution and ferment. These are
not "dead times," and the host of silent heroes and heroines
presage a hidden vitality.

Yesterday I read Dickens's *American Notes*. It answers its
end very well, which plainly was to make a readable book,
nothing more. Truth is not his object for a single instant, but
merely to make good points in a lively sequence, and he
proceeds very well. As an account of America it is not to
be considered for a moment: it is too short, and too narrow,
too superficial, and too ignorant, too slight, and too fabulous, and the man totally unequal to the work. A very lively
rattle on that nuisance, a sea voyage, is the first chapter;
and a pretty fair example of the historical truth of the whole
book. We can hear throughout every page the dialogue between the author and his publisher—"Mr. Dickens, the
book must be entertaining—that is the essential point.
Truth? Damn truth! I tell you, it must be entertaining." As
a picture of American manners nothing can be falser. No
such conversations ever occur in this country in real life, as
he relates. He has picked up and noted with eagerness each
odd local phrase that he met with, and, when he had a story
to relate, has joined them together, so that the result is the
broadest caricature; and the scene might as truly have been
laid in Wales or in England as in the States. Monstrous
exaggeration is an easy secret of romance. But Americans
who, like some of us Massachusetts people, are not fond of
spitting, will go from Maine to New Orleans, and meet no
more annoyance than we should in Britain or France. So
with "yes," so with "fixings," so with soap and towels; and
all the other trivialities which this trifler detected in travelling over half the world. The book makes but a poor apology for its author, who certainly appears in no dignified or
enviable position. . . . [J, VI, 312–313]

Every glance at society—pale, withered people with gold-
filled teeth, ghastly, and with minds in the same dilapidated
condition, drugged with books for want of wisdom—sug-

gests at once the German thought of the progressive god, who has got thus far with his experiment, but will get out yet a triumphant and faultless race. [J, VIII, 120]

The physiognomy and phrenology of today are rash and mechanical systems enough, but they rest on everlasting foundations. We are sure that the sacred form of man is not seen in these whimsical, pitiful and sinister masks (masks which we wear and which we meet), these bloated and shrivelled bodies, bald heads, bead eyes, short winds, puny and precarious healths and early deaths. We live ruins amidst ruins. [W, VII, 108]

I feel the reasonableness of what the lawyer or merchant or laborer has to allege against readers and thinkers, until I look at each of their wretched industries, and find them without end or aim. [J, IX, 155]

Fear for ages has boded and mowed and gibbered over government and property. That obscene bird is not there for nothing. He indicates great wrongs which must be revised.
[W, II, 112]

A good deal of character in our abused age. The rights of woman, the antislavery-, temperance-, peace-, health-, and money-movements; female speakers, mobs and martyrs, the paradoxes, the antagonism of old and new, the anomalous church, the daring mysticism and the plain prose, the uneasy relation of domestics, the struggling toward better household arrangements—all indicate life at the heart, not yet justly organized at the surface. [J, IV, 465]

"These Men." In Massachusetts a number of young and adult persons are at this moment the subject of a revolution. They are not organized into any conspiracy: they do not vote, or print, or meet together. They do not know each other's faces or names. They are united only in a common love of truth and love of its work. They are of all conditions and natures. They are, some of them, mean in attire, and some mean in station, and some mean in body, having

inherited from their parents faces and forms scrawled with traits of every vice. Not in churches, or in courts, or in large assemblies; not in solemn holidays, where men were met in festal dress, have these pledged themselves to new life, but in lonely and obscure places, in servitude, in solitude, in solitary compunctions and shames and fears, in disappointments, in diseases, trudging beside the team in the dusty road, or drudging, a hireling in other men's cornfields, schoolmasters who teach a few children rudiments for a pittance, ministers of small parishes of the obscurer sects, lone women in dependent condition, matrons and young maidens, rich and poor, beautiful and hard-favored, without conceit or proclamation of any kind, have silently given in their several adherence to a new hope.

[J, V, 259–260]

Is it not better to live in Revolution than to live in dead times? Are we not little and low out of good nature now, when, if our companions were noble, or the crisis fit for heroes, we should be great also? [J, V, 34]

I see many generals without a command, besides Henry.
[J, IX, 427]

It is proposed to form a very large society to devise and execute means for propping in some secure and permanent manner this planet. It has long filled the minds of the benevolent and anxious part of the community with lively emotion, the consideration of the exposed state of the globe; the danger of its falling and being swamped in absolute space; the danger of its being drawn too near the sun and roasting the race of mankind, and the daily danger of its being overturned, and, if a stage-coach overset costs valuable lives, what will not ensue on the upset of this omnibus? It has been thought that by a strenuous and very extensive concert aided by a committee of masterbuilders and blacksmiths, a system of booms and chains might be set around the exterior surface and that it might be underpinned in such a manner as to enable the aged and women and children to sleep and eat with greater security henceforward.

It is true that there is not a perfect unanimity on this subject at present, and it is much to be regretted.

[J, V, 230–231]

For those who would prop up the planet by forming socialist communities, Emerson has friendly words and gentle satire, but he sees the chief value of Brook Farm as a happy experiment in group living. The economic and political import he discards as negligible. He recognizes the freakishness of fanatical reformers yet any expression of true individuality exhilarates him.

The society at Brook Farm existed, I think, about six or seven years, and then broke up, the Farm was sold, and I believe all the partners came out with pecuniary loss. Some of them had spent on it the accumulations of years. I suppose they all, at the moment, regarded it as a failure. I do not think they can so regard it now, but probably as an important chapter in their experience which has been of lifelong value. What knowledge of themselves and of each other, what various practical wisdom, what personal power, what studies of character, what accumulated culture many of the members owed to it! What mutual measure they took of each other! It was a close union, like that in a ship's cabin, of clergymen, young collegians, merchants, mechanics, farmers' sons and daughters, with men and women of rare opportunities and delicate culture, yet assembled there by a sentiment which all shared, some of them hotly shared, of the honesty of a life of labor and of the beauty of a life of humanity. The yeoman saw refined manners in persons who were his friends; and the lady or the romantic scholar saw the continuous strength and faculty in people who would have disgusted them but that these powers were now spent in the direction of their own theory of life.

[W, X, 368–369]

The Founders of Brook Farm should have this praise, that they made what all people try to make, an agreeable place to live in. All comers, even the most fastidious, found it the pleasantest of residences. It is certain that freedom from household routine, variety of character and talent, variety of work, variety of means of thought and instruction, art, music, poetry, reading, masquerade, did not permit sluggishness or despondency; broke up routine. There is agreement in the testimony that it was, to most of the associates, education; to many, the most important period of their life, the birth of valued friendships, their first acquaintance with the riches of conversation, their training in behavior. The art of letter-writing, it is said, was immensely cultivated. Letters were always flying not only from house to house, but from room to room. It was a perpetual picnic, a French Revolution in small, an Age of Reason in a patty-pan.

In the American social communities, the gossip found such vent and sway as to become despotic. The institutions were whispering-galleries, in which the adored Saxon privacy was lost. Married women I believe uniformly decided against the community. It was to them like the brassy and lacquered life in hotels. The common school was well enough, but to the common nursery they had grave objections. Eggs might be hatched in ovens, but the hen on her own account much preferred the old way. A hen without her chickens was but half a hen.

Of course every visitor found that there was a cosmic side to this Paradise of shepherds and shepherdesses. There was a stove in every chamber, and everyone might burn as much wood as he or she would saw. The ladies took cold on washing-day; so it was ordained that the gentlemen-shepherds should wring and hang out clothes; which they punctually did. And it would sometimes occur that when they danced in the evening, clothespins dropped plentifully from their pockets. The country members naturally were surprised to observe that one man ploughed all day and one looked out of the window all day, and perhaps drew his picture, and both received at night the same wages. One would meet also some modest pride in their advanced condition, signified by a frequent phrase, "Before we came out of civilization."

The question which occurs to you had occurred much

earlier to Fourier: "How in this charming Elysium is the dirty work to be done?" And long ago Fourier had exclaimed, "Ah! I have it," and jumped with joy. "Don't you see," he cried, "that nothing so delights the young Caucasian child as dirt? See the mud-pies that all children will make if you will let them. See how much more joy they find in pouring their pudding on the table-cloth than into their beautiful mouths. The children from six to eight, organized into companies with flags and uniforms, shall do this last function of civilization." [W, X, 364–367]

[*To Elizabeth Hoar*] The experiment of Brook Farm is just so far valuable that it has shown the possibility & eminent convenience of living in good neighborhood, and that part of the institution may be borrowed & the rest left. I can think of nothing so certain to stop the perpetual leakage of the continent—letting all the best people flow off continually in the direction of Europe—than to make them fond of home by concentrating good neighborhoods. Is not the universal rule for the prevention of rovers & bad husbands, to make their own house pleasant to them. Every week I hear of some conspicuous American who is embarking for France or Germany, and every such departure is a virtual postponement of the traveller's own work & endeavor.

[L, III, 203]

If a man should consider the nicety of the passage of a piece of bread down his throat, he would starve. At Education Farm the noblest theory of life sat on the noblest figures of young men and maidens, quite powerless and melancholy. It would not rake or pitch a ton of hay; it would not rub down a horse; and the men and maidens it left pale and hungry. A political orator wittily compared our party promises to western roads, which opened stately enough, with planted trees on either side to tempt the traveller, but soon became narrow and narrower and ended in a squirrel-track and ran up a tree. So does culture with us; it ends in headache. Unspeakably sad and barren does life look to those who a few months ago were dazzled with the splendor of the promise of the times. [W, III, 58–59]

Many a reformer perishes in his removal of rubbish; and
that makes the offensiveness of the class. They are partial;
they are not equal to the work they pretend. They lose their
way; in the assault on the kingdom of darkness they expend
all their energy on some accidental evil, and lose their sanity
and power of benefit. It is of little moment that one or two
or twenty errors of our social system be corrected, but of
much that the man be in his senses.

The criticism and attack on institutions, which we have
witnessed, has made one thing plain, that society gains nothing whilst a man, not himself renovated, attempts to reno-
vate things around him: he has become tediously good in
some particular but negligent or narrow in the rest; and
hypocrisy and vanity are often the disgusting result.

[W, III, 261]

There is of course to every theory a tendency to run to
an extreme, and to forget the imitations. In our free institutions, where every man is at liberty to choose his home and
his trade, and all possible modes of working, gaining are
open to him, fortunes are easily made by thousands, as in
no other country. Then property proves too much for the
man, and the men of science, art, intellect, are pretty sure
to degenerate into selfish housekeepers, dependent on wine,
coffee, furnace-heat, gas-light and fine furniture. Then instantly, things swing the other way, and we suddenly find
that civilization crowed too soon; that what we bragged as
triumphs were treacheries: that we have opened the wrong
door and let the enemy into the castle; that civilization was
a mistake; that nothing is so vulgar as a great warehouse of
rooms full of furniture and trumpery; that, in the circumstances, the best wisdom were an auction or a fire. Since the
foxes and the birds have the right of it, with a warm hole to
keep out the weather, and no more—a pent-house to fend
the sun and rain is the house which lays no tax on the
owner's time and thoughts, and which he can leave, when
the sun is warm, and defy the robber. This was Thoreau's
doctrine, who said that the Fourierists had a sense of duty
which led them to devote themselves to their second-best.
And Thoreau gave in flesh and blood and pertinacious

Saxon belief the purest ethics. He was more real and prac-
tically believing in them than any of his company, and forti-
fied you at all times with an affirmative experience which
refused to be set aside. Thoreau was in his own person a
practical answer, almost a refutation, to the theories of the
socialists. He required no Phalanx, no Government, no society, almost no memory. He lived extempore from hour to
hour, like the birds and the angels; brought every day a new
proposition, as revolutionary as that of yesterday, but different: the only man of leisure in his town; and his independence made all others look like slaves. He was a good Abbot
Samson, and carried a counsel in his breast. "Again and
again I congratulate myself on my so-called poverty, I
could not overstate this advantage." "What you call bareness
and poverty, is to me simplicity. God could not be unkind
to me if he should try. I love best to have each thing in its
season only, and enjoy doing without it at all other times.
It is the greatest of all advantages to enjoy no advantage at
all. I have never got over my surprise that I should have
been born into the most estimable place in all the world,
and in the very nick of time too." There's an optimist for
you. [W, X, 355–357]

Here came on Sunday morning (14th) [1838] Edward
Palmer and departed today, a gentle, faithful, sensible,
well-balanced man for an enthusiast. He has renounced,
since a year ago last April, the use of money. When he
travels, he stops at night at a house and asks if it would
give them any satisfaction to lodge a traveller without
money or price. If they do not give him a hospitable answer, he goes on, but generally finds the country people
free and willing. When he goes away, he gives them his
papers or tracts. He has sometimes found it necessary to go
twenty-four hours without food, and all night without
lodging. Once he found a wagon with a good buffalo under
a shed, and had a very good nap. By the seashore he finds
it difficult to travel, as they are inhospitable. He presents
his views with great gentleness; and is not troubled if he
cannot show the way in which the destruction of money is
to be brought about; he feels no responsibility to show or

know the details. It is enough for him that he is sure it must
fall, and that he clears himself of the institution altogether.
[J, V, 86–87]

Pillsbury, whom I heard last night, is the very gift from New
Hampshire which we have long expected, a tough oak stick
of a man not to be silenced or insulted or intimidated by a
mob, because he is more mob than they; he mobs the mob.
John Knox is come at last, on whom neither money nor
politeness nor hard words nor rotten eggs nor kicks and
brickbats make the slightest impression. He is fit to meet
the bar-room wits and bullies; he is a wit and a bully himself and something more; he is a graduate of the plough and
the cedar swamp and the snowbank, and has nothing new
to learn of labor or poverty or the rough of farming. His
hard head, too, had gone through in boyhood all the drill
of Calvinism, with text and mortification, so that he stands
in the New England assembly a purer bit of New England
than any, and flings his sarcasms right and left, sparing no
name or person or party or presence. [J, VII, 201–202]

Although Emerson finds American radicalism "destruc-
tive" and "aimless," a butt for his sarcasm, he reserves his
heavier scorn for the custom-bound conservatives, luxury-
loving, old, timid. If the radical is passionate and voracious,
the conservative is tame and fearful and dull. Yet conserva-
tism stands for the inevitable, and the old radical regards
the new seceder as "damnable as the pope himself."

The spirit of our American radicalism is destructive and
aimless: it is not loving; it has no ulterior and divine ends,
but is destructive only out of hatred and selfishness. On the
other side, the conservative party, composed of the most
moderate, able and cultivated part of the population, is
timid, and merely defensive of property. It vindicates no
right, it aspires to no real good, it brands no crime, it proposes no generous policy; it does not build, nor write, nor
cherish the arts, nor foster religion, nor establish schools,
nor encourage science, nor emancipate the slave, nor be-

friend the poor, or the Indian, or the immigrant. From neither party, when in power, has the world any benefit to expect in science, art, or humanity, at all commensurate with
the resources of the nation.   [W, III, 210]

For the *Dial* and its sins, I have no defence to set up. We
write as we can, and we know very little about it. If the
direction of these speculations is to be deplored, it is yet a
fact for literary history, that all the bright boys and girls in
New England, quite ignorant of each other, take the world
so, and come and make confession to fathers and mothers—
the boys that they do not wish to go into trade, the girls that
they do not like morning calls and evening parties. They are
all religious, but hate the churches; they reject all the ways
of living of other men, but have none to offer in their stead.
Perhaps, one of these days, a great Yankee shall come, who
will easily do the unknown deed.   [E–C, II, 14–15]

What is good that is said or written now lies nearer to men's
business and bosoms than of old. What is good goes now to
all. What was good a century ago is written under the manifest belief that it was as safe from the eye of the common
people as from the Tartars. The Universal Man is now as
real an existence as the Devil was then. Prester John no
more shall be heard of. Tamerlane and the Buccaneers vanish before Texas, Oregon territory, the Reform Bill, the
abolition of slavery and of capital punishment, questions of
education, and the Reading of Reviews; and in these all
men take part. The human race have got possession, and it
is all questions that pertain to their interest, outward or inward, that are now discussed, and many words leap out
alive from bar-rooms, Lyceums, Committee Rooms, that
escape out of doors and fill the world with their thunder.
When I spoke or speak of the democratic element, I do
not mean that ill thing, vain and loud, which writes lying
newspapers, spouts at caucuses, and sells its lies for gold, but
that spirit of love for the general good whose name this assumes. There is nothing of the true democratic element in
what is called Democracy; it must fall, being wholly commercial. I beg I may not be understood to praise anything

which the soul in you does not honor, however grateful may be names to your ear and your pocket.   [J, IV, 94–95]

I think the best argument of the conservative is this bad one: that he is convinced that the angry democrat, who wishes him to divide his park and chateau with him, will, on entering into the possession, instantly become conservative, and hold the property and spend it as selfishly as himself. For a better man, I might dare to renounce my estate; for a worse man, or for as bad a man as I, why should I? All the history of man with unbroken sequence of examples establishes this inference. Yet it is very low and degrading ground to stand upon. We must never reason from history, but plant ourselves on the ideal.   [J, VI, 522–523]

Is not every man sometimes a radical in politics? Men are conservatives when they are least vigorous, or when they are most luxurious. They are conservatives after dinner, or before taking their rest; when they are sick, or aged. In the morning, or when their intellect or their conscience has been aroused; when they hear music, or when they read poetry, they are radicals.   [W, III, 272]

In describing the two parties into which modern society divides itself—the democrat and the conservative—I said, Bonaparte represents the democrat, or the party of men of business, against the stationary or conservative party. I omitted then to say, what is material to the statement, namely that these two parties differ only as young and old. The democrat is a young conservative; the conservative is an old democrat. The aristocrat is the democrat ripe and gone to seed—because both parties stand on the one ground of the supreme value of property, which one endeavors to get, and the other to keep. Bonaparte may be said to represent the whole history of this party, its youth and its age; yes, and with poetic justice its fate, in his own. The counter-revolution, the counter-party, still waits for its organ and representative, in a lover and a man of truly public and universal aims.

Here was an experiment, under the most favorable conditions of the powers of intellect without conscience. Never was such a leader so endowed and so weaponed; never leader found such aids and followers. And what was the result of this vast talent and power, of these immense armies, burned cities, squandered treasures, immolated millions of men, of this demoralized Europe? It came to no result. All passed away like the smoke of his artillery, and left no trace. He left France smaller, poorer, feebler, than he found it; and the whole contest for freedom was to be begun again. The attempt was in principle suicidal. France served him with life and limb and estate, as long as it could identify its interest with him; but when men saw that after victory was another war; after the destruction of armies, new conscriptions; and they who had toiled so desperately were never nearer to the reward—they could not spend what they had earned, nor repose on their down-beds, nor strut in their chateaux—they deserted him. Men found that his absorbing egotism was deadly to all other men. It resembled the torpedo, which inflicts a succession of shocks on anyone who takes hold of it, producing spasms which contract the muscles of the hand, so that the man cannot open his fingers; and the animal inflicts new and more violent shocks, until he paralyzes and kills his victim. So this exorbitant egotist narrowed, impoverished and absorbed the power and existence of those who served him; and the universal cry of France and of Europe in 1814 was, "Enough of him"; *"Assez de Bonaparte."*

It was not Bonaparte's fault. He did all that in him lay to live and thrive without moral principle. It was the nature of things, the eternal law of man and of the world which baulked and ruined him; and the result, in a million experiments, will be the same. Every experiment, by multitudes or by individuals, that has a sensual and selfish aim, will fail. The pacific Fourier will be as inefficient as the pernicious Napoleon. As long as our civilization is essentially one of property, of fences, of exclusiveness, it will be mocked by delusions. Our riches will leave us sick; there will be bitterness in our laughter, and our wine will burn our mouth. Only that good profits which we can taste with all doors open, and which serves all men.

[W, IV, 256–258]

A good deal of our politics is physiological. Now and then a man of wealth in the heyday of youth adopts the tenet of broadest freedom. In England there is always some man of wealth and large connection, planting himself, during all his years of health, on the side of progress, who, as soon as he begins to die, checks his forward play, calls in his troops and becomes conservative. All conservatives are such from personal defects. They have been effeminated by position or nature, born halt and blind, through luxury of their parents, and can only, like invalids, act on the defensive. But strong natures, backwoodsmen, New Hampshire giants, Napoleons, Burkes, Broughams, Websters, Kossuths, are inevitable patriots, until their life ebbs and their defects and gout, palsy and money, warp them. [W, VI, 13]

. . . now the governments generally of the world, are cities and governments of the rich; and the masses are not men, but *poor men,* that is, men who would be rich; this is the ridicule of the class, that they arrive with pains and sweat and fury nowhere; when all is done, it is for nothing. They are like one who has interrupted the conversation of a company to make his speech, and now has forgotten what he went to say. The appearance strikes the eye everywhere of an aimless society, of aimless nations.

[W, III, 191–192]

All the universe over, there is but one thing, this old Two-Face, creator-creature, mind-matter, right-wrong, of which any proposition may be affirmed or denied. Very fitly therefore I assert that every man is a partialist; that nature secures him as an instrument by self-conceit, preventing the tendencies to religion and science; and now further assert, that, each man's genius being nearly affectionately explored, he is justified in his individuality, as his nature is found to be immense; and now I add that every man is a universalist also, and, as our earth, whilst it spins on its own axis, spins all the time around the sun through the celestial spaces, so the least of its rational children, the most dedicated to his private affair, works out, though as it were under a disguise, the universal problem. We fancy men are individuals; so are pumpkins; but every pumpkin in the field goes through every point of pumpkin history. The rabid democrat, as soon as he is senator and rich man, has ripened beyond possibility of sincere radicalism, and unless he can resist the sun, he must be conservative the remainder of his days. Lord Eldon said in his old age that "if he were to begin life again, he would be damned but he would begin as agitator." [W, III, 245–246]

Conservatism stands on this, that a man cannot jump out of his skin; and well for him that he cannot, for his skin is the world; and the stars of heaven do hold him there: in the folly of men glitters the wisdom of God. [J, VI, 317]

You are too historical by half. I show you a grievance, and you proceed to inquire, not if it is mischievous, but if it is old. I point the redress, and you inquire about a constitutional precedent for the redress. That which only requires perception—mischiefs that are rank and intolerable, which only need to be seen, to be hated and attacked, with you are ground for argument, and you are already preparing to defend them. The reliance on simple perception constitutes genius and heroism; and that is the religion before us. [J, IX, 151]

It is not the proposition, but the tone that signifies. Is it a man that speaks, or the mimic of a man? Universal Whiggery is tame and weak. Every proclamation, dinner-speech, report of victory, or protest against the government it publishes betrays its thin and watery blood. It is never serene nor angry nor formidable, neither cool nor red hot. Instead of having its own aims passionately in view, it cants about the policy of a Washington and a Jefferson. It speaks to expectation, and not the torrent of its wishes and needs, waits for its antagonist to speak that it may have something to oppose, and, failing that, having nothing to say, is happy to hurrah. What business have Washington or Jefferson in this age? . . . They lived in the greenness and timidity of the political experiment. The kitten's eyes were not yet opened. They shocked their contemporaries with their daring wisdom: have you not something which would have shocked *them?* If not, be silent, for others have.

Passion, appetite, seem to have self-reliance and reality; but Whiggery is a great fear.   [J, VI, 88]

"Dulness of the age." What age was not dull? When were not the majority wicked? or what progress was ever made by society? Society is always flat and foolish. The only progress ever known was of the individual. A great wit is, at any time, great solitude.   [J, IV, 85]

The two parties which divide the state, the party of Conservatism and that of Innovation, are very old, and have disputed the possession of the world ever since it was made. This quarrel is the subject of civil history. The conservative partly established the reverend hierarchies and monarchies of the most ancient world. The battle of patrician and plebeian, of parent state and colony, of old usage and accommodation to new facts, of the rich and the poor, reappears in all countries and times. The war rages not only in battlefields, in national councils and ecclesiastical synods, but agitates every man's bosom with opposing advantages every hour. On rolls the old world meantime, and now one, now the other gets the day, and still the fight renews itself as if for the first time, under new names and hot personalities.

Such an irreconcilable antagonism of course must have a correspondent depth of seat in the human constitution. It is the opposition of Past and Future, of Memory and Hope, of the Understanding and the Reason. It is the primal antagonism, the appearance in trifles of the two poles of nature. . . .

There is always a certain meanness in the argument of conservatism, joined with a certain superiority in its fact. It affirms because it holds. Its fingers clutch the fact, and it will not open its eyes to see a better fact. The castle which conservatism is set to defend is the actual state of things, good and bad. The project of innovation is the best possible state of things. Of course conservatism always has the worst of the argument, is always apologizing, pleading a necessity, pleading that to change would be to deteriorate: it must saddle itself with the mountainous load of the violence and vice of society, must deny the possibility of good, deny ideas, and suspect and stone the prophet; whilst innovation is always in the right, triumphant, attacking, and sure of final success. Conservatism stands on man's confessed limitations, reform on his indisputable infinitude; conservatism on circumstance, liberalism on power; one goes to make an adroit member of the social frame, the other to postpone all things to the man himself; conservatism is debonair and social, reform is individual and imperious. We are reformers in spring and summer, in autumn and winter we stand by the old; reformers in the morning, conservers at night. Reform is affirmative, conservatism negative; conservatism goes for comfort, reform for truth. Conservatism is more candid to behold another's worth; reform more disposed to maintain and increase its own. Conservatism makes no poetry, breathes no prayer, has no invention; it is all memory. Reform has no gratitude, no prudence, no husbandry. It makes a great difference to your figure and to your thought whether your foot is advancing or receding. Conservatism never puts the foot forward; in the hour when it does that, it is not establishment, but reform. Conservatism tends to universal seeming and treachery, believes in a negative fate; believes that men's temper governs them; that for me it avails not to trust in principles, they will fail me, I must bend a little; it distrusts nature; it thinks there is a general law without a particular application—law for all that does not include anyone. Reform in its antagonism inclines to asinine resistance, to kick with hoofs; it runs to egotism and bloated self-conceit; it runs to a bodiless pretension, to unnatural refining and elevation which ends in hypocrisy and sensual reaction.

That which is best about conservatism, that which, though it cannot be expressed in detail, inspires reverence in all, is the Inevitable. There is the question not only what the conservative says for himself, but, why must he say it? What insurmountable fact binds him to that side? Here is the fact which men call Fate, and fate in dread degrees, fate behind fate, not to be disposed of by the consideration that the Conscience commands this or that, but necessitating the question whether the faculties of man will play him true in resisting the facts of universal experience? . . .

We have all a certain intellection or presentiment of reform existing in the mind, which does not yet descend into the character, and those who throw themselves blindly on this lose themselves. Whatever they attempt in that direction, fails, and reacts suicidally on the actor himself. This is the penalty of having transcended nature. For the existing world is not a dream, and cannot with impunity be treated as a dream; neither is it a disease; but it is the ground on which you stand, it is the mother of whom you were born. Reform converses with possibilities, perchance with impossibilities; but here is sacred fact. This also was true, or it could not be: it had life in it, or it could not have existed; it has life in it, or it could not continue. Your schemes may be feasible, or may not be, but this has the endorsement of nature and a long friendship and cohabitation with the powers of nature. This will stand until a better cast of the dice is made. The contest between the Future and the Past is one between Divinity entering and Divinity departing. You are welcome to try your experiments, and, if you can, to displace the actual order by that ideal republic you announce, for nothing but God will expel God. But plainly the burden of proof must lie with the projector. We hold to this, until you can demonstrate something better. . . .

You who quarrel with the arrangements of society, and are willing to embroil all, and risk the indisputable good that exists, for the chance of better, live, move, and have your being in this, and your deeds contradict your words every day. For as you cannot jump from the ground without using the resistance of the ground, nor put out the boat to sea without shoving from the shore, nor attain liberty without rejecting obligation, so you are under the necessity of using the Actual order of things, in order to disuse it; to live by it, whilst you wish to take away its life. The past has baked your loaf, and in the strength of its bread you would break up the oven. But you are betrayed by your own nature. You also are conservatives. However men please to style themselves, I see no other than a conservative party. You are not only identical with us in your needs, but also in your methods and aims. You quarrel with my conservatism, but it is to build up one of your own; it will have a new beginning, but the same course and end, the same trials, the same passions; among the lovers of the new I observe that there is a jealousy of the newest, and that the seceder from the seceder is as damnable as the pope himself. . . . The boldness of the hope men entertain transcends all former experience. It calms and cheers them with the picture of a simple and equal life of truth and piety. And this hope flowered on what tree? It was not imported from the stock of some celestial plant, but grew here on the wild crab of conservatism. It is much that this old and vituperated system of things has borne so fair a child. It predicts that amidst a planet peopled with conservatives, one Reformer may yet be born.   [W, I, 295–326, *passim*]

O D E

Inscribed to W. H. Channing

Though loath to grieve
The evil time's sole patriot,
I cannot leave
My honied thought
For the priest's cant,
Or statesman's rant.

If I refuse
My study for their politique,
Which at the best is trick,
The angry Muse
Puts confusion in my brain.

But who is he that prates
Of the culture of mankind,
Of better arts and life?
Go, blindworm, go,
Behold the famous States
Harrying Mexico
With rifle and with knife!

Or who, with accent bolder,
Dare praise the freedom-loving mountaineer?

I found by thee, O rushing Contoocook!
And in thy valleys, Agiochook!
The jackals of the Negro-holder.

The God who made New Hampshire
Taunted the lofty land
With little men;
Small bat and wren
House in the oak:
If earth-fire cleave
The upheaved land, and bury the folk,
The southern crocodile would grieve.
Virtue palters; Right is hence;
Freedom praised, but hid;
Funeral eloquence
Rattles the coffin-lid.

What boots thy zeal,
O glowing friend,
That would indignant rend
The northland from the south?
Wherefore? to what good end?
Boston Bay and Bunker Hill
Would serve things still;
Things are of the snake.

The horseman serves the horse,
The neatherd serves the neat,
The merchant serves the purse,
The eater serves his meat;
'Tis the day of the chattel,
Web to weave, and corn to grind;
Things are in the saddle,
And ride mankind.

There are two laws discrete,
Not reconciled,
Law for man, and law for thing;
The last builds town and fleet,
But it runs wild,
And doth the man unking.

'Tis fit the forest fall,
The steep be graded,
The mountain tunnelled,
The sand shaded,
The orchard planted,
The glebe tilled,
The prairie granted,
The steamer built.

Let man serve law for man;
Live for friendship, live for love,
For truth's and harmony's behoof;
The state may follow how it can,
As Olympus follows Jove.

Yet do not I implore
The wrinkled shopman to my sounding woods,
Nor bid the unwilling senator
Ask votes of thrushes in the solitudes.
Everyone to his chosen work;
Foolish hands may mix and mar;
Wise and sure the issues are.
Round they roll till dark is light,
Sex to sex, and even to odd;
The over-god
Who marries Right to Might,
Who peoples, unpeoples,
He who exterminates
Races by stronger races,
Black by white faces,
Knows to bring honey
Out of the lion;
Grafts gentlest scion
On pirate and Turk.

The Cossack eats Poland,
Like stolen fruit;
Her last noble is ruined,
Her last poet mute:
Straight, into double band
The victors divide;

Half for freedom strike and stand;
The astonished Muse finds thousands at her side.
[W, IX, 76–79]

*"Good men must not obey the laws too well" nor need
a man, who is a state in himself, do more than succor occasionally the government, a "poor cow who does well by
you." The "less government we have the better—the fewer
laws, and the less confided power."*

The State is a poor, good beast who means the best: it
means friendly. A poor cow who does well by you—do not
grudge it its hay. It cannot eat bread, as you can; let it
have without grudge a little grass for its four stomachs. It
will not stint to yield you milk from its teat. You, who are
a man walking cleanly on two feet, will not pick a quarrel
with a poor cow. Take this handful of clover and welcome.
But if you go to hook me when I walk in the fields, then,
poor cow, I will cut your throat.   [J, VII, 220–221]

The power of love, as the basis of a State, has never been
tried. We must not imagine that all things are lapsing into
confusion if every tender protestant be not compelled to
bear his part in certain social conventions; nor doubt that
roads can be built, letters carried, and the fruit of labor
secured, when the government of force is at an end. Are
our methods now so excellent that all competition is hopeless? could not a nation of friends even devise better ways?
On the other hand, let not the most conservative and timid
fear anything from a premature surrender of the bayonet
and the system of force. For, according to the order of
nature, which is quite superior to our will, it stands thus;
there will always be a government of force where men are
selfish; and when they are pure enough to abjure the code
of force they will be wise enough to see how these public
ends of the post-office, of the highway, of commerce and
the exchange of property, of museums and libraries, of institutions of art and science can be answered.
[W, III, 219–220]

We are haunted by a conscience of this right to grandeur of character, and are false to it. But each of us has some talent, can do somewhat useful, or graceful, or formidable, or amusing, or lucrative. That we do, as an apology to others and to ourselves for not reaching the mark of a good and equal life. But it does not satisfy *us*, whilst we thrust it on the notice of our companions. It may throw dust in their eyes, but does not smooth our own brow, or give us the tranquillity of the strong when we walk abroad. We do penance as we go. Our talent is a sort of expiation, and we are constrained to reflect on our splendid moment with a certain humiliation, as somewhat too fine, and not as one act of many acts, a fair expression of our permanent energy. Most persons of ability meet in society with a kind of tacit appeal. Each seems to say, "I am not all here." Senators and presidents have climbed so high with pain enough, not because they think the place specially agreeable, but as an apology for real worth, and to vindicate their manhood in our eyes. This conspicuous chair is their compensation to themselves for being of a poor, cold, hard nature. They must do what they can. Like one class of forest animals, they have nothing but a prehensile tail; climb they must, or crawl. If a man found himself so rich-natured that he could enter into strict relations with the best persons and make life serene around him by the dignity and sweetness of his behavior, could he afford to circumvent the favor of the caucus and the press, and covet relations so hollow and pompous as those of a politician? Surely nobody would be a charlatan who could afford to be sincere.

[W, III, 217–218]

This is the history of governments—one man does something which is to bind another. A man who cannot be acquainted with me, taxes me; looking from afar at me ordains that a part of my labor shall go to this or that whimsical end—not as I, but as he happens to fancy. Behold the consequence. Of all debts men are least willing to pay the taxes. What a satire is this on government! Everywhere they think they get their money's worth, except for these.

Hence the less government we have the better—the fewer

laws, and the less confided power. The antidote to this abuse of formal government is the influence of private character, the growth of the Individual; the appearance of the principal to supersede the proxy; the appearance of the wise man; of whom the existing government is, it must be owned, but a shabby imitation. That which all things tend to educe; which freedom, cultivation, intercourse, revolutions, go to form and deliver, is character; that is the end of Nature, to reach unto this coronation of her king. To educate the wise man the State exists, and with the appearance of the wise man the State expires. The appearance of character makes the State unnecessary. The wise man is the State. He needs no army, fort, or navy—he loves men too well; no bribe, or feast, or palace, to draw friends to him; no vantage ground, no favorable circumstance. He needs no library, for he has not done thinking; no church, for he is a prophet; no statute-book, for he has the lawgiver; no money, for he is value; no road, for he is at home where he is; no experience, for the life of the creator shoots through him, and looks from his eyes. He has no personal friends, for he who has the spell to draw the prayer and the piety of all men unto him needs not husband and educate a few to share with him a select and poetic life. His relation to men is angelic; his memory is myrrh to them; his presence, frankincense and flowers.   [W, III, 215–216]

Every actual State is corrupt. Good men must not obey the laws too well. What satire on government can equal the severity of censure conveyed in the word *politic*, which now for ages has signified *cunning*, intimating that the State is a trick?   [W, III, 208]

Just as the timidity of the private man encourages the tyranny of the State, so his personal weaknesses and corruption lead to national catastrophe. "A certain personal virtue is essential to freedom." Slavery is the arsenic that poisons the body politic, and the hypocrisy of both North and South is the prelude to civil war.

All our political disasters grow as logically out of our attempts in the past to do without justice, as the sinking of some part of your house comes of defect in the foundation. One thing is plain; a certain personal virtue is essential to freedom; and it begins to be doubtful whether our corruption in this country has not gone a little over the mark of safety, so that when canvassed we shall be found to be made up of a majority of reckless self-seekers. The divine knowledge has ebbed out of us and we do not know enough to be free. [W, X, 86]

. . . if there be . . . a country where knowledge cannot be diffused without perils of mob law and statute law; where speech is not free; where the post-office is violated, mailbags opened and letters tampered with; where public debts and private debts outside of the State are repudiated; where liberty is attacked in the primary institution of social life; where the position of the white woman is injuriously affected by the outlawry of the black woman; where the arts, such as they have, are all imported, having no indigenous life; where the laborer is not secured in the earnings of his own hands; where suffrage is not free or equal—that country is, in all these respects, not civil, but barbarous; and no advantages of soil, climate or coast can resist these suicidal mischiefs. [W, VII, 33–34]

Every reform is only a mask under cover of which a more terrible reform, which dares not yet name itself, advances. Slavery and anti-slavery is the question of property and no property, rent and anti-rent; and anti-slavery dare not yet say that every man must do his own work, or, at least, receive no interest for money. Yet that is at last the upshot. [J, VII, 205]

A gentleman may have many innocent propensities, but if he chances to have the habit of slipping arsenic into the soup of whatever person sits next him at table, he must expect some inconvenience. He may call it his "peculiar institution," a mere way of his; he never puts it in his own soup, only in the soup of his neighbor, and even only in some of his neighbors'; for example, he is partial to light hair, and only spices the dish of such as have black hair, and he may persuade his chaplain to find him a text, and be very indignant and patriotic and quarrelsome and moral-religious on the subject, and swear to die in defence of this old and strong habit he has contracted. [J, VI, 540–541]

This filthy enactment [The Fugitive Slave Law] was made in the nineteenth century, by people who could read and write. I will not obey it, by God. [J, VIII, 236]

Intense selfishness which we all share. Planter will not hesitate to eat his Negro, because he can. We eat him in milder fashion by pelting the Negro's friend. We cannot lash him with a whip, because we dare not. We lash him with our tongues. I like the Southerner the best; he deals roundly and does not cant. The Northerner is surrounded with churches and Sunday schools and is hypocritical. How gladly, how gladly, if he dared, he would seal the lips of these poor men and poor women who speak for him. I see a few persons in the church, who, I fancy, will soon look about them with some surprise to see what company they are keeping. [J, VI, 539]

The young Southerner comes here a spoiled child, with graceful manners, excellent self-command, very good to be spoiled more, but good for nothing else—a mere parader. He has conversed so much with rifles, horses and dogs that he has become himself a rifle, a horse and a dog, and in civil, educated company, where anything human is going forward, he is dumb and unhappy, like an Indian in a church. Treat them with great deference, as we often do, and they accept it all as their due without misgiving. Give them an inch, and they take a mile. They are mere bladders of conceit. Each snipper-snapper of them all undertakes to speak for the entire Southern States. "At the South, the reputation of Cambridge," etc., etc., which being interpreted, is, In my Negro village of Tuscaloosa, or Cheraw, or St. Marks, I supposed so and so. "We, at the South," forsooth. They are more civilized than the Seminoles, however, in my opinion; a little more. Their question respecting any man is like a Seminole's—How can he

fight? In this country, we ask, What can he do? His pug-
nacity is all they prize in man, dog, or turkey. The proper
way of treating them is not deference, but to say as Mr.
Ripley does, "Fiddle faddle," in answer to each solemn
remark about "The South." "It must be confessed," said
the young man, "that in Alabama, we are dead to everything, as respects politics." "Very true," replied Mr. Ripley, "leaving out the last clause." [J, IV, 312–313]

[*To Hermann Grimm*] We are cleaning up America in
these days to give you a better reception. You will have interested yourself to some extent, I am sure, in our perverse
politics. What shall I say to you of them? 'Tis a mortification that because a nation had no enemy, it should become
its own; and, because it has an immense future, it should
commit suicide! Sometimes I think it a war of manners.
The people are haughty, self-possessed, suave, and affect to
despise Northern manners as of the shop and compting-
room; whilst we find the planters picturesque, but frivolous
and brutal. Northern labor encroaches on the planters
daily, diminishing their political power, whilst their haughty
temper makes it impossible for them to play a second part.
The day came when they saw that the Government, which
their party had hitherto controlled, must now, through the
irresistible census, pass out of their hands. They decided
to secede . . . our Federal Government has now 300,000
men in the field. To us, before yet a battle has been fought,
it looks as if the disparity was immense, and that we possess all advantages—whatever may be the issue of the first
collisions. If we may be trusted, the war will be short—and
yet the parties must long remain in false position, or can
only come right by means of the universal repudiation of
its leaders by the South. [E–G, 61–62]

Here we read no books. The [Civil] War is our sole and
doleful instructor. All our bright young men go into it, to
be misused and sacrificed hitherto by incapable leaders.
One lesson they all learn—to hate slavery, *teterrima causa*.
But the issue does not yet appear. We must get ourselves
morally right. Nobody can help us. 'Tis of no account what
England or France may do. Unless backed by our profligate

parties, their action would be nugatory, and, if so backed, the worst. But even the war is better than the degrading and descending politics that preceded it for decades of years, and our legislation has made great strides, and if we can stave off that fury of trade which rushes to peace at the cost of replacing the South in the *status ante bellum,* we can, with something more of courage, leave the problem to another score of years—free labor to fight with the Beast, and see if bales and barrels and baskets cannot find out that they pass more commodiously and surely to their ports through free hands, than through barbarians.

[E–C, II, 280–281]

Why are people so sensitive about the reputation of General McClellan? There is always something rotten about a sensitive reputation. Besides, is not General McClellan an American citizen? And is it not the first attribute and distinction of an American to be abused and slandered as long as he is heard of?   [J, IX, 435–436]

I have always the belief that a trip across the sea would have abated your despair of us. The world is laid out here in large lots, and the swing of natural laws is shared by the population, as it is not—or not as much—in your feudal Europe. My countrymen do not content me, but they are susceptible of inspirations. In the war it was humanity that showed itself to advantage—the leaders were prompted and corrected by the intuitions of the people, they still demanding the more generous and decisive measure, and giving their sons and their estates as we had no example before. In this heat, they had sharper perceptions of policy, of the ways and means and the life of nations, and on every side we read or heard fate-words, in private letters, in railway cars, or in the journals. We were proud of the people and believed they would not go down from this height. But Peace came, and everyone ran back into his shop again, and can hardly be won to patriotism more, even to the point of chasing away the thieves that are stealing not only the public gold, but the newly won rights of the slave, and the new muzzles we had contrived to keep the planter from sucking his blood.   [E–C, II, 296–297]

Chapter Six

The Great Man

*"It is natural to believe in great men." It would seem to be
less natural today than it was, and there is probably no feature of Emerson's thought which can be so strange to us
today as the fact that it was overwhelmingly natural for*
him *to believe in great men. To begin with, he thought that
he was a great man—he would not have been able to write
with such certainty of anything if he had not believed this
of himself. Compared with Goethe, or even with his own
friend Carlyle, Emerson thought himself not* that *much a
great man. But these men were Europeans, and Europe, by
reason of its cultural tradition, naturally produced great
men (they virtually produced one another) while America,
by reason of both need and opportunity, had to summon up
men who believed in the possibility of being great.*

*Measuring himself against America, Emerson thought of
himself as a great man because, while he knew what he
lacked, he knew that he was the passionate creature of a
belief, whereas nothing was so obvious about most Americans as their intellectual tameness and conformity. As William Butler Yeats was to say: "Belief makes the mind abundant"; Emerson's sense of his intellectual passion made him
think of his country as something still to be created—and
of himself as one of its creators. This was his idea of the
great man: whether as artist, statesman or religious force,
he was the man whose inherent originality or firmness of*

belief moved and changed societies. It was, of course, the argument of Carlyle—as in a debased and over-colored way it was to be the argument of Wagner. But Emerson's faith in this argument was based on universal instances from the history of religion. It was as the founder of a new spiritual consciousness that Emerson conceived his role. He was to pass out new life to the people—and it was to be his own life that he passed out first.

This emphasis on leadership is probably easier for us to take today than is Emerson's calm faith that the powers of leadership stem from a natural superiority of insight and perception. His idea of the great man is simply that he is the best man, the most comprehensive man, the deepest-seeing man. Just as man bridges the gap between nature and spirit (between the world and God), so the great man fills the gap between "God and the mob." He is the greatest possible consciousness—the poet is the voice of the deepest and fullest consciousness that man possessed; the poet represents the original endowment of man. By means of this orphic power, the poet is the priest, the founder, the Gautama, who gives out the word, and in whose words—light and fleeting as they seem—belief rests.

In point of fact, Emerson, Lincoln, Whitman, Mark Twain, have influenced this country in the way that Emerson thought a great man could—if not in the direction that Emerson sought. But on a lower plane, it is also true that in the American situation, a belief in great men is necessary because equality can tyrannize over quality, and because of the danger that a citizen in a mass society runs of idolatrizing the "normal" and the mediocre as a way of identification and self-protection in a mass society. This is where Emerson's doctrine of the great man works with such superb astringency today. The same man who conceived it his purpose as a writer and lecturer to bring out "the infinitude of the private man," the natural superiority so often buried in men, gave his whole heart to superiority wherever it was found. For him the great man is not merely a leader but a discoverer, and he is virtually defining genius in science itself when he tells us that "with each new mind, a new secret of nature transpires." To understand was to

*change—it was the only means to change that Emerson saw.
One of the things he understood was that the power of insight is allied to a strength of belief, and it is no contradiction at all that the saintly Emerson, who not only believed
in great men but also understood them, said: Take "egotism out, and you would castrate the benefactors."*

Take egotism out, and you would castrate the benefactors.
Luther, Mirabeau, Napoleon, John Adams, Andrew Jackson; and our nearer eminent public servants—Greeley, The-
odore Parker, Ward Beecher, Horace Mann, Garrison
would lose their vigor.   [J, IX, 519]

I said to Alcott that I thought that the great man should
occupy the whole space between God and the mob. . . .
[J, IV, 149–150]

Genius consists in health, in plenipotence of that "top
of condition" which allows of not only exercise but frolic
of faculty. To coax and woo the strong Instinct to bestir
itself and work its miracle is the end of all wise endeavor.
[J, VII, 98]

The orator is he whom every man is seeking when he goes
into the courts, into the conventions, into any popular assembly—though often disappointed, yet never giving over
the hope. He finds himself perhaps in the Senate, when the
forest has cast out some wild, black-browed bantling to
show the same energy in the crowd of officials which he had
learned in driving cattle to the hills, or in scrambling
through thickets in a winter forest, or through the swamp
and river for his game. In the folds of his brow, in the
majesty of his mien, Nature has marked her son; and in
that artificial and perhaps unworthy place and company
shall remind you of the lessons taught him in earlier days
by the torrent in the gloom of the pine-woods, when he was
the companion of the mountain cattle, of jays and foxes,
and a hunter of the bear.   [W, VIII, 113–114]

It is natural to believe in great men. If the companions of our childhood should turn out to be heroes, and their condition regal it would not surprise us. All mythology opens with demigods, and the circumstance is high and poetic; that is, their genius is paramount. In the legends of the Gautama, the first men ate the earth and found it deliciously sweet. [W, IV, 3]

There is a moment in the history of every nation, when, proceeding out of this brute youth, the perceptive powers reach their ripeness and have not yet become microscopic: so that man, at that instant, extends across the entire scale, and, with his feet still planted on the immense forces of night, converses by his eyes and brain with solar and stellar creation. That is the moment of adult health, the culmination of power. [W, IV, 46]

Ellery Channing railed an hour in good set terms at the usurpation of the past, at the great hoaxes of the Homers and Shakespeares, hindering the books and the men of today of their just meed. Oh certainly; I assure him that oaks and horse-chestnuts are entirely obsolete, that the Horticultural Society are about to recommend the introduction of cabbages as a shade tree, so much more convenient and every way comprehensible; all grown from the seed upward to its most generous crumpled extremity within one's own short memory; past contradiction the ornament of the world, and then so good to eat, as acorns and horse-chestnuts are not. Shade trees for breakfast! Then this whole business of one man taking the praise of all or more than his share of the praise. As all are alike in nature and possibility, it is absurd that any should pretend to exhibit more reason or virtue than I do. A man of genius, did you say? A man of virtue? I tell you both are malformations, painful inflammations of the brain and of the liver and such shall be punishable in the new Commonwealth. And if any such appear they shall be dealt with as all reasonable Spartans and Indians do with lame and deformed infants, toss them into the river and the average of the race improved. Nothing that is not *ex tempore* shall now be tolerated: pyramids and cities shall give place to tents. The man, the skeleton and body, which many years have built up, shall go for nothing: his dinner, the mutton and rice he ate two hours ago, now fast flowing into chyle, that is all we consider; and the problem how to detach new dinner from old man—what we respect from what we scorn—deserves the study of the scientific. [J, VI, 422–423]

What is the function of great men? Their private insurrections encourage us, and we are heartened by the aura of divinity that surrounds them. They teach us "the qualities of primary nature—admit us to the constitution of things." Great men are the "rich possibilities" to which we all may aspire. They are the antidotes to the torpidity and imbecility of the mass.

Great men serve us as insurrections do in bad governments. The world would run into endless routine, and forms incrust forms, till the life was gone. But the perpetual supply of new genius shocks us with thrills of life, and recalls us to principles. [W, X, 102]

Great geniuses have the shortest biographies. Their cousins can tell you nothing about them. They lived in their writings, and so their house and street life was trivial and commonplace. If you would know their tastes and complexions, the most admiring of their readers most resembles them. Plato especially has no external biography. If he had lover, wife, or children, we hear nothing of them. He ground them all into paint. [W, IV, 43]

It seems as if the Deity dressed each soul which he sends into nature in certain virtues and powers not communicable to other men, and sending it to perform one more turn through the circle of beings, wrote, *"Not transferable"* and *"Good for this trip only,"* on these garments of the soul. There is somewhat deceptive about the intercourse of minds. The boundaries are invisible, but they are never crossed.

[W, IV, 28]

The imbecility of men is always inviting the impudence of power. It is the delight of vulgar talent to dazzle and to blind the beholder. But true genius seeks to defend us from itself. [W, IV, 18]

Life is a scale of degrees. Between rank and rank of our great men are wide intervals. Mankind have in all ages attached themselves to a few persons who either by the quality of that idea they embodied or by the largeness of their reception were entitled to the position of leaders and lawgivers. These teach us the qualities of primary nature—admit us to the constitution of things. We swim, day by day, on a river of delusions and are effectually amused with houses and towns in the air, of which the men about us are dupes. But life is a sincerity. In lucid intervals we say, "Let there be an entrance opened for me into realities; I have worn the fool's cap too long." We will know the meaning of our economies and politics. Give us the cipher, and if persons and things are scores of a celestial music, let us read off the strains. We have been cheated of our reason; yet there have been sane men, who enjoyed a rich and related existence. What they know, they know for us. With each new mind, a new secret of nature transpires; nor can the Bible be closed until the last great man is born.

[W, IV, 20]

I can do that by another which I cannot do alone. I can say to you what I cannot first say to myself. Other men are lenses through which we read our own minds. Each man seeks those of different quality from his own, and such as are good of their kind; that is, he seeks other men, and the *otherest*. The stronger the nature, the more it is reactive. Let us have the quality pure. A little genius let us leave alone. A main difference betwixt men is, whether they attend their own affair or not. Man is that noble endogenous plant which grows, like the palm, from within outward. His own affair, though impossible to others, he can open with celerity and in sport. It is easy to sugar to be sweet and to nitre to be salt. We take a great deal of pains to waylay and entrap that which of itself will fall into our hands. I count him a great man who inhabits a higher sphere of thought, into which other men rise with labor and difficulty; he has but to open his eyes to see things in a true light and in large relations, whilst they must make painful corrections and keep a vigilant eye on many sources of error. His service to us is of like sort. It costs a beautiful person no exertion to paint her image on our eyes; yet how splendid is that benefit! It costs no more for a wise soul to convey his quality to other men. And everyone can do his best thing easiest. *"Peu de moyens, beaucoup d'effet."* He is great who is what he is from nature, and who never reminds us of others.

But he must be related to us, and our life receive from him some promise of explanation. I cannot tell what I would know; but I have observed there are persons who, in their character and actions, answer questions which I have not skill to put. One man answers some question which none of his contemporaries put, and is isolated. The past and passing religions and philosophies answer some other question. Certain men affect us as rich possibilities, but helpless to themselves and to their times—the sport perhaps of some instinct that rules in the air—they do not speak to our want. But the great are near; we know them at sight. They satisfy expectation and fall into place.

[W, IV, 5–7]

Divine persons are character born, or, to borrow a phrase from Napoleon, they are victory organized. They are usually received with ill-will, because they are new and because they set a bound to the exaggeration that has been made of the personality of the last divine person. Nature never rhymes her children, nor makes two men alike.

[W, III, 108]

. . . the effect of every action is measured by the depth of the sentiment from which it proceeds. The great man knew not that he was great. It took a century or two for that fact to appear. What he did, he did because he must; it was the most natural thing in the world, and grew out of the circumstances of the moment. But now, every thing he

did, even to the lifting of his finger or the eating of bread,
looks large, all-related, and is called an institution.

These are the demonstrations in a few particulars of the
genius of nature; they show the direction of the stream. But
the stream is blood; every drop is alive.   [W, II, 155]

In the streets we grow cynical. The men we meet are coarse
and torpid. The finest wits have their sediment. What quantities of fribbles, paupers, invalids, epicures, antiquaries,
politicians, thieves and triflers of both sexes might be ad-
vantageously spared! Mankind divides itself into two classes
—benefactors and malefactors. The second class is vast, the
first a handful. A person seldom falls sick but the bystanders
are animated with a faint hope that he will die—quantities
of poor lives, of distressing invalids, of cases for a gun.
Franklin said, "Mankind are very superficial and dastardly:
they begin upon a thing, but, meeting with a difficulty, they
fly from it discouraged; but they have capacities, if they
would employ them." Shall we then judge a country by
the majority, or by the minority? By the minority, surely.
'Tis pedantry to estimate nations by the census, or by square
miles of land, or other than by their importance to the mind
of the time.

Leave this hypocritical prating about the masses. Masses
are rude, lame, unmade, pernicious in their demands and
influence, and need not to be flattered but to be schooled. I
wish not to concede anything to them, but to tame, drill,
divide and break them up, and draw individuals out of
them. The worst of charity is that the lives you are asked to
preserve are not worth preserving. Masses! the calamity is
the masses. I do not wish any mass at all, but honest men
only, lovely, sweet, accomplished women only, and no
shovel-handed, narrow-brained, gin-drinking million stock-
ingers or lazzaroni at all. If government knew how, I should
like to see it check, not multiply the population. When it
reaches its true law of action, every man that is born will
be hailed as essential. Away with this hurrah of masses, and
let us have the considerate vote of single men spoken on
their honor and their conscience. In old Egypt it was established law that the vote of a prophet be reckoned equal to a

hundred hands. I think it was much underestimated. "Clay and clay differ in dignity," as we discover by our preferences every day. What a vicious practice is this of our politicians at Washington pairing off! as if one man who votes wrong going away, could excuse you, who mean to vote right, for going away; or as if your presence did not tell in more ways than in your vote. Suppose the three hundred heroes at Thermopylæ had paired off with three hundred Persians; would it have been all the same to Greece, and to history? Napoleon was called by his men *Cent Mille*. Add honesty to him, and they might have called him Hundred Million.

Nature makes fifty poor melons for one that is good, and shakes down a tree full of gnarled, wormy, unripe crabs, before you can find a dozen dessert apples; and she scatters nations of naked Indians and nations of clothed Christians, with two or three good heads among them. Nature works very hard, and only hits the white once in a million throws. In mankind she is contented if she yields one master in a century. The more difficulty there is in creating good men, the more they are used when they come.

[W, VI, 248–250]

The key to the age may be this, or that, or the other, as the young orators describe; the key to all ages is—Imbecility; imbecility in the vast majority of men at all times, and even in heroes in all but certain eminent moments; victims of gravity, custom and fear. This gives force to the strong—that the multitude have no habit of self-reliance or original action.   [W, VI, 54]

I think we very slowly admit in another man a higher degree of moral sentiment than our own—a finer conscience, more impressionable or which marks minuter degrees; an ear to hear acuter notes of right and wrong than we can. I think we listen suspiciously and very slowly to any evidence to that point. But, once satisfied of such superiority, we set no limit to our expectation of his genius. For such persons are nearer to the secret of God than others; are bathed by sweeter waters; they hear notices, they see visions, where

others are vacant. We believe that holiness confers a certain
insight, because not by our private but by our public force
can we share and know the nature of things.

[W, VI, 216–217]

We consecrate a great deal of nonsense because it was allowed by great men. There is none without his foible. I
believe that if an angel should come to chant the chorus of
the moral law, he would eat too much gingerbread, or take
liberties with private letters, or do some precious atrocity.

[W, III, 227]

The natural offset of terror is ridicule. And we have noted
examples among our orators, who have on conspicuous occasions handled and controlled, and, best of all, converted
a malignant mob, by superior manhood, and by a wit which
disconcerted and at last delighted the ringleaders. What
can a poor truckman, who is hired to groan and to hiss, do,
when the orator shakes him into convulsions of laughter so
that he cannot throw his egg? If a good story will not answer, still milder remedies sometimes serve to disperse a
mob. Try sending round the contribution-box.

[W, VIII, 147–148]

The beautiful fables of the Greeks, being proper creations
of the imagination and not of the fancy, are universal veri-
ties. What a range of meanings and what perpetual perti-
nence has the story of Prometheus! Beside its primary value
as the first chapter of the history of Europe (the mythology
thinly veiling authentic facts, the invention of the mechanic
arts and the migration of colonies) it gives the history of
religion, with some closeness to the faith of later ages.
Prometheus is the Jesus of the old mythology. He is the
friend of man; stands between the unjust "justice" of the
Eternal Father and the race of mortals, and readily suffers
all things on their account. But where it departs from the
Calvinistic Christianity and exhibits him as the defier of
Jove, it represents a state of mind which readily appears
wherever the doctrine of Theism is taught in a crude objective form, and which seems the self-defence of man against

this untruth, namely a discontent with the believed fact that a God exists, and a feeling that the obligation of reverence is onerous. It would steal if it could the fire of the Creator, and live apart from him and independent of him.

[W, II, 30–31]

Emerson hails the thinkers and doers, Socrates and Plato, Humboldt, Goethe, Whitman—those men "nearer to the secret of God than others."

Socrates, a man of humble stem, but honest enough; of the commonest history; of a personal homeliness so remarkable as to be a cause of wit in others—the rather that his broad good nature and exquisite taste for a joke invited the sally, which was sure to be paid. The players personated him on the stage; the potters copied his ugly face on their stone jugs. He was a cool fellow, adding to his humor a perfect temper and a knowledge of his man, be he who he might whom he talked with, which laid the companion open to certain defeat in any debate—and in debate he immoderately delighted. The young men are prodigiously fond of him and invite him to their feasts, whither he goes for conversation. He can drink, too; has the strongest head in Athens; and after leaving the whole party under the table, goes away as if nothing had happened, to begin new dialogues with somebody that is sober. In short, he was what our country-people call *an old one*.

He affected a good many citizen-like tastes, was monstrously fond of Athens, hated trees, never willingly went beyond the walls, knew the old characters, valued the bores and philistines, thought every thing in Athens a little better than anything in any other place. He was plain as a Quaker in habit and speech, affected low phrases, and illustrations from cocks and quails, soup-pans and sycamore-spoons, grooms and farriers, and unnamable offices—especially if he talked with any superfine person. He had a Franklin-like wisdom. Thus he showed one who was afraid to go on foot to Olympia, that it was no more than his daily walk within doors, if continuously extended, would easily reach.

Plain old uncle as he was, with his great ears, an immense talker—the rumor ran that on one or two occasions, in the war with Bœotia, he had shown a determination which had covered the retreat of a troop; and there was some story that under cover of folly, he had, in the city government, when one day he chanced to hold a seat there, evinced a courage in opposing singly the popular voice, which had well-nigh ruined him. He is very poor; but then he is hardy as a soldier, and can live on a few olives; usually, in the strictest sense, on bread and water, except when entertained by his friends. His necessary expenses were exceedingly small, and no one could live as he did. He wore no under garment; his upper garment was the same for summer and winter, and he went barefooted; and it is said that to procure the pleasure, which he loves, of talking at his ease all day with the most elegant and cultivated young men, he will now and then return to his shop and carve statues, good or bad, for sale. However that be, it is certain that he had grown to delight in nothing else than this conversation; and that, under his hypocritical pretence of knowing nothing, he attacks and brings down all the fine speakers, all the fine philosophers of Athens, whether natives or strangers from Asia Minor and the islands. Nobody can refuse to talk with him, he is so honest and really curious to know; a man who was willingly confuted if he did not speak the truth, and who willingly confuted others asserting what was false; and not less pleased when confuted than when confuting; for he thought not any evil happened to men of such a magnitude as false opinion respecting the just and unjust. A pitiless disputant, who knows nothing, but the bounds of whose conquering intelligence no man had ever reached. . . .   [W, IV, 70–73]

It is singular that wherever we find a man higher by a whole head than any of his contemporaries, it is sure to come into doubt what are his real works. Thus Homer, Plato, Raffaelle, Shakespeare. For these men magnetize their contemporaries, so that their companions can do for them what they can never do for themselves; and the great

man does thus live in several bodies, and write, or paint or
act, by many hands; and after some time it is not easy to say
what is the authentic work of the master and what is only
of his school.

Plato, too, like every great man, consumed his own times.
What is a great man but one of great affinities, who takes
up into himself all arts, sciences, all knowables, as his food?
He can spare nothing; he can dispose of everything. What
is not good for virtue, is good for knowledge. Hence his
contemporaries tax him with plagiarism. But the inventor
only knows how to borrow; and society is glad to forget the
innumerable laborers who ministered to this architect, and
reserves all its gratitude for him. When we are praising
Plato, it seems we are praising quotations from Solon and
Sophron and Philolaus. Be it so. Every book is a quotation; and every house is a quotation out of all forests and
mines and stone quarries; and every man is a quotation
from all his ancestors.   [W, IV, 41–42]

Sir Philip Sidney, the darling of mankind, Ben Jonson tells
us, "was no pleasant man in countenance, his face being
spoiled with pimples, and of high blood, and long." Those
who have ruled human destinies like planets for thousands
of years, were not handsome men. If a man can raise a
small city to be a great kingdom, can make bread cheap,
can irrigate deserts, can join oceans by canals, can subdue
steam, can organize victory, can lead the opinions of mankind, can enlarge knowledge—'tis no matter whether his
nose is parallel to his spine, as it ought to be, or whether
he has a nose at all; whether his legs are straight, or whether
his legs are amputated: his deformities will come to be
reckoned ornamental and advantageous on the whole. This
is the triumph of expression, degrading beauty, charming
us with a power so fine and friendly and intoxicating that
it makes admired persons insipid, and the thought of passing
our lives with them insupportable. There are faces so fluid
with expression, so flushed and rippled by the play of
thought, that we can hardly find what the mere features
really are.   [W, VI, 300–301]

Cosmos. The wonderful Humboldt, with his extended centre, expanded wings, marches like an army, gathering all things as he goes. How he reaches from science to science, from law to law, tucking away moons and asteroids and solar systems, in the clauses and parentheses of his encyclopædiacal paragraphs! [J, VII, 100]

Paris and London and New York, the spirit of commerce, of money and material power, were also to have their prophet; and Bonaparte was qualified and sent.

Every one of the million readers of anecdotes or memoirs or lives of Napoleon, delights in the page, because he studies in it his own history. Napoleon is thorough modern, and, at the highest point of his fortunes, has the very spirit of the newspapers. He is no saint—to use his own word, "no capuchin," and he is no hero, in the high sense. The man in the street finds in him the qualities and powers of other men in the street. He finds him, like himself, by birth a citizen, who, by very intelligible merits, arrived at such a commanding position that he could indulge all those tastes which the common man possesses but is obliged to conceal and deny: good society, good books, fast travelling, dress, dinners, servants without number, personal weight, the execution of his ideas, the standing in the attitude of a benefactor to all persons about him, the refined enjoyments of pictures, statues, music, palaces and conventional honors —precisely what is agreeable to the heart of every man in the nineteenth century, this powerful man possessed. . . .

Indeed a man of Napoleon's stamp almost ceases to have a private speech and opinion. He is so largely receptive, and is so placed, that he comes to be a bureau for all the intelligence, wit and power of the age and country. He gains the battle; he makes the code; he makes the system of weights and measures; he levels the Alps; he builds the road. All distinguished engineers, savans, statists, report to him: so likewise do all good heads in every kind: he adopts the best measures, sets his stamp on them, and not these alone, but on every happy and memorable expression. Every sentence spoken by Napoleon and every line of his writing, deserves reading, as it is the sense of France.

Bonaparte was the idol of common men because he had in transcendent degree the qualities and powers of common men. There is a certain satisfaction in coming down to the lowest ground of politics, for we get rid of cant and hypocrisy. Bonaparte wrought, in common with that great class he represented, for power and wealth—but Bonaparte, specially, without any scruple as to the means. All the sentiments which embarrass men's pursuit of these objects, he set aside. The sentiments were for women and children.

[W, IV, 225–228, *passim*]

On Goethe's Faust　The wonder of the book is its superior intelligence. In the menstruum of this man's wit, the past and the present ages, and their religions, politics and modes of thinking, are dissolved into archetypes and ideas. What new mythologies sail through his head! The Greeks said that Alexander went as far as Chaos; Goethe went, only the other day, as far; and one step farther he hazarded, and brought himself safe back.

There is a heart-cheering freedom in his speculation. The immense horizon which journeys with us lends its majesty to trifles and to matters of convenience and necessity, as to solemn and festal performances. He was the soul of his century. If that was learned, and had become, by population, compact organization and drill of parts, one great Exploring Expedition, accumulating a glut of facts and fruits too fast for any hitherto-existing savans to classify— this man's mind had ample chambers for the distribution of all. He had a power to unite the detached atoms again by their own law. He has clothed our modern existence with poetry. Amid littleness and detail, he detected the Genius of life, the old cunning Proteus, nestling close beside us, and showed that the dulness and prose we ascribe to the age was only another of his masks:

"His very flight is presence in disguise:"

—that he had put off a gay uniform for a fatigue dress, and was not a whit less vivacious or rich in Liverpool or the Hague than once in Rome or Antioch. He sought him in public squares and main streets, in boulevards and hotels;

and, in the solidest kingdom of routine and the senses, he
showed the lurking dæmonic power; that, in actions of
routine, a thread of mythology and fable spins itself: and
this, by tracing the pedigree of every usage and practice,
every institution, utensil and means, home to its origin in
the structure of man. He had an extreme impatience of
conjecture and of rhetoric. "I have guesses enough of my
own; if a man write a book, let him set down only what he
knows." He writes in the plainest and lowest tone, omitting
a great deal more than he writes, and putting ever a thing
for a word. He has explained the distinction between the
antique and the modern spirit and art. He has defined art,
its scope and laws. He has said the best things about nature
that ever were said. He treats nature as the old philosophers,
as the seven wise masters did—and, with whatever loss of
French tabulation and dissection, poetry and humanity
remain to us; and they have some doctoral skill. Eyes are
better on the whole than telescopes or microscopes. He has
contributed a key to many parts of nature, through the rare
turn for unity and simplicity in his mind. Thus Goethe suggested the leading idea of modern botany, that a leaf or the
eye of a leaf is the unit of botany, and that every part of a
plant is only a transformed leaf to meet a new condition;
and, by varying the conditions, a leaf may be converted
into any other organ, and any other organ into a leaf. In
like manner, in osteology, he assumed that one vertebra
of the spine might be considered as the unit of the skeleton:
the head was only the uttermost vertebræ transformed.
"The plant goes from knot to knot, closing at last with the
flower and the seed. So the tape-worm, the caterpillar, goes
from knot to knot and closes with the head. Man and the
higher animals are built up through the vertebræ, the powers
being concentrated in the head." In optics again he rejected
the artificial theory of seven colors, and considered that
every color was the mixture of light and darkness in new
proportions. It is really of very little consequence what
topic he writes upon. He sees at every pore, and has a
certain gravitation towards truth. He will realize what you
say. He hates to be trifled with and to be made to say over
again some old wife's fable that has had possession of men's

faith these thousand years. He may as well see if it is true as another. He sifts it. I am here, he would say, to be the measure and judge of these things. Why should I take them on trust? And therefore what he says of religion, of passion, of marriage, of manners, of property, of paper-money, of periods of belief, of omens, of luck, or whatever else, refuses to be forgotten.

Take the most remarkable example that could occur of this tendency to verify every term in popular use. The Devil had played an important part in mythology in all times. Goethe would have no word that does not cover a thing. The same measure will still serve: "I have never heard of any crime which I might not have committed." So he flies at the throat of this imp. He shall be real; he shall be modern; he shall be European; he shall dress like a gentleman, and accept the manners, and walk in the streets, and be well initiated in the life of Vienna and of Heidelberg in 1820— or he shall not exist. Accordingly, he stripped him of mythologic gear, of horns, cloven foot, harpoon tail, brimstone and blue-fire, and instead of looking in books and pictures, looked for him in his own mind, in every shade of coldness, selfishness and unbelief that, in crowds or in solitude, darkens over the human thought—and found that the portrait gained reality and terror by every thing he added and by every thing he took away. He found that the essence of this hobgoblin which had hovered in shadow about the habitations of men ever since there were men, was pure intellect, applied—as always there is a tendency—to the service of the senses: and he flung into literature, in his Mephistopheles, the first organic figure that has been added for some ages, and which will remain as long as the Prometheus. [W, IV, 272–277]

[*To Walt Whitman*]

Concord, Massachusetts, 21 July, 1855

Dear Sir:—I am not blind to the worth of the wonderful gift of "Leaves Of Grass." I find it the most extraordinary piece of wit and wisdom that America has yet contributed. I am very happy in reading it, as great power makes us happy. It meets the demand I am always making of what seemed the sterile and stingy nature, as if too much handiwork, or too much lymph in temperament, were making our western wits fat and mean. I give you joy of your free and brave thought. I have great joy in it. I find incomparable things said incomparably well, as they must be. I find the courage of treatment which so delights us, and which large perception only can inspire.

I greet you at the beginning of a great career, which yet must have had a long foreground somewhere, for such a start. I rubbed my eyes a little, to see if this sunbeam were no illusion; but the solid sense of the book is a sober certainty.

It has the best merits, namely, of fortifying and encouraging.

I did not know until I last night saw the book advertised in a newspaper that I could trust the name as real and available for a post-office. I wish to see my benefactor, and have felt much like striking my tasks and visiting New York to pay you my respects.—RALPH WALDO EMERSON.

[U, 208]

Chapter Seven

Art and Artists

A born writer, Emerson was limited to highly intellectual forms, and his critical sympathies are equally limited. He is the artist of the pensée, *a partisan of intellectual wit. The novel—the great modern form—meant nothing to him, and his remarks about Dickens and even about so introverted a "romancer" as Hawthorne are interesting only because they reveal Emerson's incapacity to understand writers who worked with dramatic, not explicit, meanings. His involvement in the great tradition of poetic drama in English was naturally greater, but he had so exalted a conception of the "poet" as the genius of humanity that even Shakespeare seemed to him incomplete.*

But it is this insistence on the "poet" as the only possible type of the artist—in all fields—that makes Emerson so luminous and inspiring a critic. For the "poet" is that side of all of us which makes images and tropes and symbols, which we rediscover in ourselves when we trace a word back to the metaphor that it originally expressed. "Language is fossil poetry," Emerson wrote, "made up of images or tropes, which now, in their secondary use, have long ceased to remind us of their poetic origin." The "poet," the artist, is the one who recalls us to the buried associations of the words and symbols that we use, who recreates for us man's natural concern with symbol and myth. Emerson's idea of the "poet" is very close to us, and his conception of the myth as the recurrent past of human history is the conception behind a work like Joyce's Finnegans Wake. *It was this imaginative and very* large *conception of the poet that originally inspired Whitman and, when* Leaves of Grass *appeared, led Emerson to recognize Whitman's importance.*

But along with this theoretical conception, so important to the development of our classic American literature in the symbolist and "poetic" tradition, it must be remembered that Emerson is naturally one of the shrewdest critics who ever lived. A virtuoso of style himself, he responded instantly to those whose use of language was original— Thoreau, Carlyle, the young Henry James whose travel sketches he admired. And it is this extraordinarily developed sense of style as a writer's instrument, the means to his vision, that made Emerson the great pioneer of a "functional" American esthetic, in the line that begins with him and Thoreau and went on, in other arts, to Louis Sullivan and Frank Lloyd Wright. By recognizing that style is not a decoration or ornament, not something added to content, but the very frame in which a true artist or writer works— that without which he cannot, as an artist, speak at all— Emerson gave to his fellow American writers, too eager to borrow from other cultures, a lasting idea that art begins with a writer's personal discovery of the form and style necessary to him.

This has often been misinterpreted as a demand for an "American," a "new" style on a national basis. Emerson was too shrewd and practiced a writer to fall for any patriotic distortion of the laws of art. Just as he was the first great theoretician of an American art based on individual vision and technical function, so, as a diagnoser of American writers, he put his finger, time and again, on certain typical faults—the tendency to substitute the will for the deed; the "American" rhetoric of democratic slogans; above all, that failure to develop which F. Scott Fitzgerald characterized when he said that "there are no second acts in American lives." "I value men as they can complete their creation," wrote Emerson. It is one of the severest things that a critic can say in America.

Literature is the only art that is ashamed of itself. The poet should be delivered as much as may be from routine, to increase his chances. It is a game of luck that he plays, and he must be liberated and ready to use the opportunities. Every one of them has been a high gambler. [J, VI, 467]

The poet is the Namer or Language-maker, naming things sometimes after their appearance, sometimes after their essence, and giving to every one its own name and not another's, thereby rejoicing the intellect, which delights in detachment or boundary. The poets made all the words, and therefore language is the archives of history, and, if we must say it, a sort of tomb of the muses. For though the origin of most of our words is forgotten, each word was at first a stroke of genius, and obtained currency because for the moment it symbolized the world to the first speaker and to the hearer. The etymologist finds the deadest word to have been once a brilliant picture. Language is fossil poetry. As the limestone of the continent consists of infinite masses of the shells of animalcules, so language is made up of images or tropes, which now, in their secondary use, have long ceased to remind us of their poetic origin. But the poet names the thing because he sees it, or comes one step nearer to it than any other. This expression or naming is not art, but a second nature, grown out of the first, as a leaf out of a tree. [W, III, 21–22]

I believe the man and the writer should be one, and not diverse, as they say Bancroft, as we know Bulwer is. Wordsworth gives us the image of the true-hearted man, as Milton, Chaucer, Herbert do; not ruffled fine gentlemen who condescend to write, like Shaftesbury, Congreve, and, greater far, Walter Scott. Let not the author eat up the man, so that he shall be a balcony and no house. Let him not be turned into a dapper, clerical anatomy, to be assisted like a lady over a gutter or a stone wall. In meeting Milton, I feel that I should encounter a real man; but Coleridge is a writer, and Pope, Waller, Addison and Swift and Gibbon, though with attributes, are too modish. It is not man, but the fashionable wit they would be. Yet Swift has proper-

ties. Allston is respectable to me. Novalis, Schiller are only
voices, no men. Dr. Johnson was a man, though he lived
in unfavorable solitude and society of one sort, so that he
was an unleavened lump at least on which a genial unfolding had only begun. Humanity cannot be the attribute of
these people's writing; humanity, which smiles in Homer,
in Chaucer, in Shakespeare, in Milton, in Wordsworth.
Montaigne is a man.   [J, IV, 356–357]

Men are born to write. The gardener saves every slip and
seed and peach-stone: his vocation is to be a planter of
plants. Not less does the writer attend his affair. Whatever
he beholds or experiences, comes to him as a model and
sits for its picture. He counts it all nonsense that they say,
that some things are undescribable. He believes that all that
can be thought can be written, first or last; and he would
report the Holy Ghost, or attempt it. Nothing so broad, so
subtle, or so dear, but comes therefore commended to his
pen, and he will write. In his eyes, a man is the faculty of
reporting, and the universe is the possibility of being reported. In conversation, in calamity, he finds new materials;
as our German poet said, "Some god gave me the power
to paint what I suffer." He draws his rents from rage and
pain. By acting rashly, he buys the power of talking wisely.
Vexations and a tempest of passion only fill his sail; as the
good Luther writes, "When I am angry, I can pray well and
preach well": and, if we knew the genesis of fine strokes of
eloquence, they might recall the complaisance of Sultan
Amurath, who struck off some Persian heads, that his physician, Vesalius, might see the spasms in the muscles of
the neck.   [W, IV, 262–263]

Proverbs, like the sacred books of each nation, are the
sanctuary of the intuitions. That which the droning world,
chained to appearances, will not allow the realist to say in
his own words, it will suffer him to say in proverbs without
contradiction. And this law of laws, which the pulpit, the
senate and the college deny, is hourly preached in all markets and workshops by flights of proverbs, whose teaching

is as true and as omnipresent as that of birds and flies.

[W, II, 109]

The artists must be sacrificed to their art. Like bees, they must put their lives into the sting they give. What is a man good for without enthusiasm? and what is enthusiasm but this daring of ruin for its object? There are thoughts beyond the reaches of our souls; we are not the less drawn to them. The moth flies into the flame of the lamp; and Swedenborg must solve the problems that haunt him, though he be crazed or killed.   [W, VIII, 275]

The young scholar fancies it happiness enough to live with people who can give an inside to the world; without reflecting that they are prisoners, too, of their own thought, and cannot apply themselves to yours. The conditions of literary success are almost destructive of the best social power, as they do not leave that frolic liberty which only can encounter a companion on the best terms. It is probable you left some obscure comrade at a tavern, or in the farms, with right mother-wit and equality to life, when you crossed sea and land to play bo-peep with celebrated scribes. I have, however, found writers superior to their books, and I cling to my first belief that a strong head will dispose fast enough of these impediments and give one the satisfaction of reality, the sense of having been met, and a larger horizon.

[W, V, 4]

The old writers, such as Montaigne, Milton, Browne, when they had put down their thoughts, jumped into their book bodily themselves, so that we have all that is left of them in our shelves; there is not a pinch of dust beside.

[J, VII, 502–503]

It would be so easy to draw two pictures of the literary man, as of one possessed and led by muses, or as of one ridden by some dragon, or dire distemper. A mechanic is driven by his work all day, but it ends at night; it has an end. But the scholar's work has none. . . .   [J, VII, 107]

If I judge from my own experience I should unsay all my fine things, I fear, concerning the manual labor of literary men. They ought to be released from every species of public or private responsibility. To them the grasshopper is a burden. I guard my moods as anxiously as a miser his money; for company, business, my own household chares, untune and disqualify me for writing. I think then the writer ought not to be married; ought not to have a family. I think the Roman Church with its celibate clergy and its monastic cells was right. If he must marry, perhaps he should be regarded happiest who has a shrew for a wife, a sharp-tongued notable dame who can and will assume the total economy of the house, and, having some sense that her philosopher is best in his study, suffers him not to intermeddle with her thrift. [J, V, 517–518]

In reading Henry Thoreau's journal, I am very sensible of the vigor of his constitution. That oaken strength which I noted whenever he walked, or worked, or surveyed woodlots, the same unhesitating hand with which a field-laborer accosts a piece of work, which I should shun as a waste of strength, Henry shows in his literary task. He has muscle, and ventures on and performs feats which I am forced to decline. In reading him, I find the same thought, the same spirit that is in me, but he takes a step beyond, and illustrates by excellent images that which I should have conveyed in a sleepy generality. 'Tis as if I went into a gymnasium, and saw youths leap, climb, and swing with a force unapproachable—though their feats are only continuations of my initial grapplings and jumps. [J, IX, 522]

Certain localities, as mountain-tops, the sea-side,_ the shores of rivers and rapid brooks, natural parks of oak and pine, where the ground is smooth and unencumbered, are excitants of the muse. Every artist knows well some favorite retirement. And yet the experience of some good artists has taught them to prefer the smallest and plainest chamber, with one chair and table and with no outlook, to these picturesque liberties. William Blake said, "Natural objects always did and do weaken, deaden and obliterate imagination in me." And Sir Joshua Reynolds had no pleasure in Richmond; he used to say "the human face was his landscape." These indulgences are to be used with great caution. . . . What prudence again does every artist, every scholar need in the security of his easel or his desk! These must be remote from the work of the house, and from all knowledge of the feet that come and go therein. Allston, it is said, had two or three rooms in different parts of Boston, where he could not be found. For the delicate muses lose their head if their attention is once diverted. Perhaps if you were successful abroad in talking and dealing with men, you would not come back to your book-shelf and your task. When the spirit chooses you for its scribe to publish some commandment, it makes you odious to men and men odious to you, and you shall accept that loathsomeness with joy. The moth must fly to the lamp, and you must solve those questions though you die.   [W, VIII, 291–292]

From artists, Emerson passes to the nature of art, the perfect blending of the idea with the artistic vehicle which conveys it "as a jewel is carried in a case." Excrescence is vicious; veracity is economy. Here are hints and observations of a technical sort, but behind all of his injunctions is the imperative: that the artist writes from experience and that "Art requires a living soul."

In architecture the beauty is increased in the degree in which the material is safely diminished; as when you break up a prose wall, and leave all the strength in the poetry of columns. As soon as you read aloud, you will find what sentences drag. Blot them out, and read again, you will find the words that drag. 'Tis like a pebble inserted in a mosaic. Resolute blotting rids you of all those phrases that sound like something and mean nothing, with which scriptural forms play a large part. Never say, "I beg not to be misunderstood." It is only graceful in the case when you are afraid that what is called a better meaning will be taken, and you wish to insist on a worse; a man has a right to pass,

like Dean Swift, for a worse man than he is, but not for a
better.   [W, XII, 291]

THE SNOW-STORM

Announced by all the trumpets of the sky,
Arrives the snow, and, driving o'er the fields,
Seems nowhere to alight: the whited air
Hides hills and woods, the river, and the heaven,
And veils the farm-house at the garden's end.
The sled and traveller stopped, the courier's feet
Delayed, all friends shut out, the housemates sit
Around the radiant fireplace, enclosed
In a tumultuous privacy of storm.

Come see the north wind's masonry.
Out of an unseen quarry evermore
Furnished with tile, the fierce artificer
Curves his white bastions with projected roof
Round every windward stake, or tree, or door.
Speeding, the myriad-handed, his wild work
So fanciful, so savage, nought cares he
For number or proportion. Mockingly,
On coop or kennel he hangs Parian wreaths;
A swan-like form invests the hidden thorn;
Fills up the farmer's lane from wall to wall,

Maugre the farmer's sighs; and at the gate
A tapering turret overtops the work.
And when his hours are numbered, and the world
Is all his own, retiring, as he were not,
Leaves, when the sun appears, astonished Art
To mimic in slow structures, stone by stone,
Built in an age, the mad wind's night-work,
The frolic architecture of the snow.

                                    [W, IX, 41–42]

Beauty rides on a lion. Beauty rests on necessities. The line
of beauty is the result of perfect economy. The cell of the
bee is built at that angle which gives the most strength

with the least wax; the bone or the quill of the bird gives the most alar strength with the least weight. "It is the purgation of superfluities," said Michael Angelo. There is not a particle to spare in natural structures. There is a compelling reason in the uses of the plant for every novelty of color or form; and our art saves material by more skilful arrangement, and reaches beauty by taking every superfluous ounce that can be spared from a wall, and keeping all its strength in the poetry of columns.   [W, VI, 294]

Allston's pictures are Elysian; fair, serene, but unreal.

I extend the remark to all the American geniuses. Irving, Bryant, Greenough, Everett, Channing, even Webster in his recorded Eloquence, all lack nerve and dagger.

[J, V, 205]

Do they think the composition too highly wrought? A poem should be a blade of Damascus steel, made up a mass of knife-blades and nails, and parts every one of which has had its whole surface hammered and wrought before it was welded into the sword, to be wrought over anew.

[J, IV, 278]

Poetry will never be a simple means, as when history or philosophy is rhymed, or laureate odes on state occasions are written. Itself must be its own end, or it is nothing. The difference between poetry and stock poetry is this, that in the latter the rhythm is given and the sense adapted to it; while in the former the sense dictates the rhythm. I might even say that the rhyme is there in the theme, thought and image themselves. Ask the fact for the form. For a verse is not a vehicle to carry a sentence as a jewel is carried in a case: the verse must be alive, and inseparable from its contents, as the soul of man inspires and directs the body, and we measure the inspiration by the music. In reading prose, I am sensitive as soon as a sentence drags; but in poetry, as soon as one word drags. Ever as the thought mounts, the expression mounts. 'Tis cumulative also; the poem is made up of lines each of which fills the ear of the poet in its turn, so that mere synthesis produces a work quite superhuman.

[W, VIII, 54]

For it is not metres, but a metre-making argument that makes a poem—a thought so passionate and alive that like the spirit of a plant or an animal it has an architecture of its own, and adorns nature with a new thing. The thought and the form are equal in the order of time, but in the order of genesis the thought is prior to the form. The poet has a new thought; he has a whole new experience to unfold; he will tell us how it was with him, and all men will be the richer in his fortune. For the experience of each new age requires a new confession, and the world seems always waiting for its poet.   [W, III, 9–10]

Art requires a living soul. The dunces believe that, as it must, at any one moment, work in one direction, an automaton will do as well, or nearly; and they beseech the Artist to say in what direction. "In every direction," he replies, "in any direction, or in no direction, but it must be alive."
[J, VII, 33]

No object really interests us but man, and in man only his superiorities; and though we are aware of a perfect law in nature, it has fascination for us only through its relation to him, or as it is rooted in the mind.   [W, VI, 286]

Fitness is so inseparable an accompaniment of beauty that it has been taken for it. The most perfect form to answer an end is so far beautiful. We feel, in seeing a noble building, which rhymes well, as we do in hearing a perfect song, that it is spiritually organic; that is, had a necessity, in Nature, for being; was one of the possible forms in the Divine mind, and is now only discovered and executed by the artist, not arbitrarily composed by him.   [W, VII, 531]

Yet is it not ridiculous, this that we do in this languid idle trick that we have gradually fallen into of writing and writing without end? After a day of humiliation and stripes, if I can write it down, I am straightway relieved and can sleep well. After a day of joy, the beating heart is calmed again by the diary. If grace is given me by all angels and I pray, if then I can catch one ejaculation of humility or hope and set it down in syllables, devotion is at an end. *

[J, VI, 94]

The experience of writing letters is one of the keys to the *modus* of inspiration. When we have ceased for a long time to have any fulness of thoughts that once made a diary a joy as well as a necessity, and have come to believe that an image or a happy turn of expression is no longer at our command, in writing a letter to a friend we may find that we rise to thought and to a cordial power of expression that costs no effort, and it seems to us that this facility may be indefinitely applied and resumed. The wealth of the mind in this respect of seeing is like that of a looking-glass, which is never tired or worn by any multitude of objects which it reflects. You may carry it all round the world, it is ready and perfect as ever for new millions.   [W, VIII, 281–282]

Happy is he who looks only into his work to know if it will succeed, never into the times or the public opinion; and who writes from the love of imparting certain thoughts and not from the necessity of sale—who writes always to *the unknown friend.*   [J, VII, 440]

The first valuable power in a reasonable mind, one would say, was the power of plain statement, or the power to receive things as they befall, and to transfer the picture of them to another mind unaltered. 'Tis a good rule of rhetoric which Schlegel gives—"In good prose, every word is underscored"; which, I suppose, means, Never italicize.

Spartans, stoics, heroes, saints and gods use a short and positive speech. They are never off their centres. As soon as they swell and paint and find truth not enough for them, softening of the brain has already begun. It seems as if inflation were a disease incident to too much use of words, and the remedy lay in recourse to things. I am daily struck with the forcible understatement of people who have no literary habit. The low expression is strong and agreeable.

[W, X, 168–169]

Accuracy is essential to beauty. The very definition of the
intellect is Aristotle's: "that by which we know terms or
boundaries." Give a boy accurate perceptions. Teach him
the difference between the similar and the same. Make him
call things by their right names. Pardon in him no blunder.
Then he will give you solid satisfaction as long as he lives.

[W, X, 147]

There is under the seeming poverty of metres an infinite
variety, as every artist knows. A right ode (however nearly
it may adopt conventional metre, as the Spenserian, or the
heroic blank-verse, or one of the fixed lyric metres) will by
any sprightliness be at once lifted out of conventionality,
and will modify the metre. Every good poem that I know
I recall by its rhythm also. Rhyme is a pretty good measure
of the latitude and opulence of a writer. If unskilful, he is
at once detected by the poverty of his chimes. A small, well-
worn, sprucely brushed vocabulary serves him. Now try
Spenser, Marlowe, Chapman, and see how wide they fly for
weapons, and how rich and lavish their profusion. In their
rhythm is no manufacture, but a vortex, or musical tornado,
which, falling on words and the experience of a learned
mind, whirls these materials into the same grand order as
planets and moons obey, and seasons, and monsoons.

[W, VIII, 49–50]

Every writer is a skater, and must go partly where he would,
and partly where the skates carry him; or a sailor, who can
only land where sails can be blown. And yet it is to be
added that high poetry exceeds the fact, or Nature itself,
just as skates allow the good skater far more grace than his
best walking would show, or sails more than riding. The
poet writes from a real experience, the amateur feigns one.
Of course one draws the bow with his fingers and the other
with the strength of his body; one speaks with his lips and
the other with a chest voice. Talent amuses, but if your
verse has not a necessary and autobiographic basis, though
under whatever gay poetic veils, it shall not waste my time.

[W, VIII, 31]

If your subject do not appear to you the flower of the world at this moment, you have not rightly chosen it. No matter what it is, grand or gay, national or private, if it has a natural prominence to you, work away until you come to the heart of it: then it will, though it were a sparrow or a spider-web, as fully represent the central law and draw all tragic or joyful illustration, as if it were the book of Genesis or the book of Doom. The subject—we must so often say it—is indifferent. Any word, every word in language, every circumstance, becomes poetic in the hands of a higher thought.   [W, VIII, 34–35]

I require that the poem should impress me so that after I have shut the book it shall recall me to itself, or that passages should. And inestimable is the criticism of memory as a corrective to first impressions. We are dazzled at first by new words and brilliancy of color, which occupy the fancy and deceive the judgment. But all this is easily forgotten. Later, the thought, the happy image which expressed it and which was a true experience of the poet, recurs to mind, and sends me back in search of the book. And I wish that the poet should foresee this habit of readers, and omit all but the important passages. Shakespeare is made up of important passages, like Damascus steel made up of old nails. Homer has his own,

> "One omen is best, to fight for one's country";

and again,

> "They heal their griefs, for curable are the hearts
>   of the noble."

Write, that I may know you. Style betrays you, as your eyes do. We detect at once by it whether the writer has a firm grasp on his fact or thought—exists at the moment for that alone, or whether he has one eye apologizing, deprecatory, turned on his reader. In proportion always to his possession of his thought is his defiance of his readers. There is no choice of words for him who clearly sees the truth. That provides him with the best word.

[W, VIII, 32–33]

The Persians have epics and tales, but, for the most part, they affect short poems and epigrams. Gnomic verses, rules of life conveyed in a lively image, especially in an image addressed to the eye and contained in a single stanza, were always current in the East; and if the poem is long, it is only a string of unconnected verses. They use an inconsecutiveness quite alarming to Western logic. . . .

[W, VIII, 243]

Literary history and all history is a record of the power of minorities, and of minorities of one. Every book is written with a constant secret reference to the few intelligent persons whom the writer believes to exist in the million. The artist has always the masters in his eye, though he affect to flout them. Michel Angelo is thinking of Da Vinci, and Raffaelle is thinking of Michel Angelo.   [W, VIII, 219]

Before launching forth on the art of writing well, Emerson discusses at random particular writers whose strength or sensitiveness or subject matter provoke his admiration or criticism. His criteria for good writing: simplicity, vigor, nerve, audacity, compression, eloquence. He calls for words impregnated with everyday life, that bleed when they are cut, that describe exactly and not merely approximately. Dangers to good writing: fossil language, false delicacy, superfluity.

Tennyson is endowed precisely in points where Wordsworth wanted. There is no finer ear, nor more command of the keys of language. Color, like the dawn, flows over the horizon from his pencil, in waves so rich that we do not miss the central form. Through all his refinements, too, he has reached the public—a certificate of good sense and general power, since he who aspires to be the English poet must be as large as London, not in the same kind as London, but in his own kind. But he wants a subject, and climbs no mount of vision to bring its secrets to the people. He contents himself with describing the Englishman as he is, and proposes no better. There are all degrees in poetry and we must be thankful for every beautiful talent. But it is only a first success, when the ear is gained.

[W, V, 257–258]

There is a hygienic simpleness, rough vigor and closeness to the matter in hand even in the second and third class of [English] writers; and, I think, in the common style of the people, as one finds it in the citation of wills, letters and public documents; in proverbs and forms of speech. The more hearty and sturdy expression may indicate that the savageness of the Norseman was not all gone. Their dynamic brains hurled off their words as the revolving stone hurls off scraps of grit.   [W, V, 236]

A good writer, if he has indulged in a Roman roundness, makes haste to chasten and nerve his period by English monosyllables.   [W, V, 235]

His [Plato's] strength is like the momentum of a falling planet, and his discretion the return of its due and perfect curve—so excellent is his Greek love of boundary and his skill in definition.   [W, IV, 59]

Antique. Our admiration of the Antique is not admiration of the old, but of the natural. We admire the Greek in an American ploughboy often. . . .   [J, IV, 171–172]

Carlyle . . . has seen, as no other in our time, how inexhaustible a mine is the language of Conversation. He does not use the *written* dialect of the time, in which scholars, pamphleteers and the clergy write, nor the Parliamentary dialect, in which the lawyer, the statesman, and the better newspapers write, but draws strength and mother-wit out of a poetic use of the spoken vocabulary, so that his paragraphs are all a sort of splendid conversation.

[J, IV, 196–197]

Alcott wants a historical record of conversations holden by you and me and him. I say, how joyful rather is some

Montaigne's book which is full of fun, poetry, business, divinity, philosophy, anecdote, smut, which dealing of bone and marrow, of cornbarn and flour barrel, of wife, and friend, and valet, of things nearest and next, never names names, or gives you the glooms of a recent date or relation, but hangs there in the heaven of letters, unrelated, untimed, a joy and a sign, an autumnal star. [J, V, 39]

I still feel a little uneasiness about these novels. Why should these sorceries have a monopoly of our delicious emotions?—The novel still weakly uses the cheap resource of property married away instead of earned, and that is the chief conjuring-stick it has; for the instincts of man always attach to property, as he knows what accumulations of spiritual force go to the creation of that, and sobs and heart-beats and sudden self-sacrifice very easily result from the dealing with it. But the novel will find the way to our interiors, one day, and will not always be novel of costume merely. These stories are to stories of real life what the figures which represent the fashions of the month on the front page of the magazine are to portraits and inspired pictures.

Are you fond of drama? say the Gods. Said you so my fine fellow? Verily? Speak the truth a little, and truth on truth, to every man and woman; try that a few hours, and you shall have dramatic situations, assaults and batteries, and heroic alternatives to your heart's content.

[J, VII, 511–512]

I have read *Oliver Twist* in obedience to the opinions of so many intelligent people as have praised it. The author has an acute eye for costume; he sees the expression of dress, of form, of gait, of personal deformities; of furniture, of the outside and inside of houses; but his eye rests always on surfaces; he has no insight into character. For want of key to the moral powers the author is fain to strain all his stage trick of grimace, of bodily terror, of murder, and the most approved performances of Remorse. It all avails nothing, there is nothing memorable in the book except the *flash*, which is got at a police office, and the dancing of the mad-

man which strikes a momentary terror. Like Cooper and
Hawthorne he has no dramatic talent. The moment he attempts dialogue the improbability of life hardens to wood
and stone. And the book begins and ends without a poetic
ray, and so perishes in the reading.   [J, V, 261]

Hawthorne invites his readers too much into his study,
opens the process before them. As if the confectioner should
say to his customers, "Now, let us make the cake."
[J, VII, 188]

Detachment. I value men as they can complete their creation. One man can hurl from him a sentence which is
spheral, and at once and forever disengaged from the author. Another can say excellent things, if the sayer and the
circumstances are known and considered; but the sentences
need a running commentary, and are not yet independent
individuals that can go alone.   [J, VII, 518]

Gibbon has a strength rare with such finish. He built a
pyramid, and then enamelled it.   [J, VII, 100]

The maker of a sentence, like the other artist, launches out
into the infinite and builds a road into Chaos and old Night,
and is followed by those who hear him with something of
a wild, creative delight.   [J, III, 395]

Writing should be the settlement of dew on the leaf, of
stalactites on the wall of the grotto, the deposit of flesh
from the blood, of woody fibre in the tree from the sap.
[J, VII, 49]

Compression. There is a wide difference between compression and an elliptical style. The dense writer has yet
ample room and choice of phrase, and even a gamesome
mood often, between his noble words. There is no disagreeable contraction in his sentence any more than there is a
human face, where in a square space of a few inches is
found room for command and love and frolic and wisdom
and for the expression even of great amplitude of surface.
[J, V, 213]

Whenever I read Plutarch or look at a Greek vase I am inclined to accept the common opinion of the learned that the Greeks had cleaner wits than any other people in the Universe. But there is anything but Time in my idea of the antique. A clear and natural expression by word or deed is that which we mean when we love and praise the antique. In society I do not find it; in modern books seldom; but the moment I get into the pastures I find antiquity again. Once in the fields with the lowing cattle, the birds, the trees, the waters and satisfying outlines of the landscape, and I cannot tell whether this is Tempe, Thessaly and Enna, or Concord and Acton.　[J, V, 434]

I think, if I were professor of Rhetoric—teacher of the art of writing well to young men—I should use Dante for my textbook. Come hither, youth, and learn how the brook that flows at the bottom of your garden, or the farmer who ploughs the adjacent field, your father and mother, your debts and credits, and your web of habits are the very best basis of poetry, and the material which you must work up. Dante knew how to throw the weight of his body into each act, and is, like Byron, Burke, and Carlyle, the Rhetorician. I find him full of the *nobil volgare eloquenza;* that he knows "God damn," and can be rowdy if he please, and he does please. Yet is not Dante reason or illumination and that essence we were looking for, but only a new exhibition of the possibilities of genius? Here is an imagination that rivals in closeness and precision the senses. But we must prize him as we do a rainbow, we can appropriate nothing of him.
[J, VIII, 33–34]

The language of the street is always strong. What can describe the folly and emptiness of scolding like the word *jawing?* I feel too the force of the double negative, though clean contrary to our grammar rules. And I confess to some pleasure from the stinging rhetoric of a rattling oath in the mouth of truckmen and teamsters. How laconic and brisk it is by the side of a page of the *North American Review.* Cut these words and they would bleed; they are vascular and alive; they walk and run. Moreover they who speak them have this elegancy, that they do not trip in their speech. It is a shower of bullets, whilst Cambridge men and Yale men correct themselves and begin again at every half sentence. [J, V, 419–420]

Language is made up of the spoils of all actions, trades, arts, games, of men. Every word is a metaphor borrowed from some natural or mechanical, agricultural or nautical process. The poorest speaker is like the Indian dressed in a robe furnished by half a dozen animals. It is like our marble foot-slab made up of countless shells and exuviæ of a foreign world. [J, V, 213]

I told Hawthorne yesterday that I think every young man at some time inclines to make the experiment of a dare-God and dare-devil originality like that of Rabelais. He would jump on the top of the nearest fence and crow. He makes the experiment, but it proves like the flight of pig-lead into the air, which cannot cope with the poorest hen. Irresistible custom brings him plump down, and he finds himself, instead of odes, writing gazettes and leases. Yet there is imitation and model, or suggestion, to the very archangels, if we knew their history, and if we knew Rabelais's reading we should see the rill of the Rabelais river. Yet his hold of his place in Parnassus is as firm as Homer's. A jester, but his is the jest of the world, and not of Touchstone or Clown or Harlequin. His wit is universal, not accidental, and the anecdotes of the time, which made the first butt of the satire and which are lost, are of no importance, as the wit transcends any particular mark, and pierces to permanent relations and interests. His joke will fit any town or community of men.

The style at once decides the high quality of the man. It flows like the river Amazon, so rich, so plentiful, so transparent, and with such long reaches, that longanimity or longsightedness which belongs to the Platos. No sand without lime, no short, chippy, indigent epigrammatist or proverbialist with docked sentences, but an exhaustless affluence. [J, VI, 278–279]

... in the days of the Pilgrims and the Puritans, the preachers were the victims of the same faith with which they whipped and persecuted other men, and their sermons are strong, imaginative, fervid, and every word a cube of stone.

[J, VI, 193]

I think that language should aim to describe the fact, and not merely suggest it. If you, with these sketchers and *dilettanti,* give me some conscious, indeterminate compound word, it is like a daub of colór to hide the defects of your drawing. Sharper sight would see and indicate the true line. The poet both draws well, and colors at the same time.

[J, VI, 215]

All writing is by the grace of God. People do not deserve to have good writing, they are so pleased with bad. In these sentences that you show me, I can find no beauty, for I see death in every clause and every word. There is a fossil or a mummy character which pervades this book. The best sepulchres, the vastest catacombs, Thebes and Cairo, Pyramids, are sepulchres to me. I like gardens and nurseries. Give me initiative, spermatic, prophesying, man-making words.   [J, VI, 132–133]

But Dante still appears to me, as ever, an exceptional mind, a prodigy of imaginative function, executive rather than contemplative or wise. Undeniable force of a peculiar kind, a prodigy, but not like Shakespeare, or Socrates, or Goethe, a beneficent humanity. His fames and infamies are so capriciously distributed—what odd reasons for putting his men in inferno! The somnambulic genius of Dante is dream strengthened to the tenth power—dream so fierce that it grasps all the details of the phantom spectacle, and, in spite of itself, clutches and conveys them into the waking memory, and can recite what every other would forget. What pitiless minuteness of horrible details! He is a curiosity like the mastadon, but one would not desire such for friends and contemporaries, abnormal throughout like Swedenborg. But at a frightful cost these obtain their fame. Dante a man to put in a museum, but not in your house. Indeed I never read him, nor regret that I do not.   [J, X, 210]

It takes twenty years to get a good book read. For each reader is struck with a new passage and at first only with the shining and superficial ones, and by this very attention to these the rest are slighted. But with time the graver and deeper thoughts are observed and pondered. New readers come from time to time—their attention whetted by frequent and varied allusions to the book—until at last every passage has found its reader and commentator.

[J, X, 239–240]

Mediocre books. There are the sound stomachs and the sick; the farmer and the butcher minister to the sound, the physician and the confectioner to the sick. The well can look at the sun, and use all his light and heat; the sick only what is reflected and shaded. It is the same in literature. Strong minds ask principles, direct *aperçus,* and original forms. The sick public want what is secondary, conventional, and imitations of imitations. There is need of Shakespeare and Hegel, and also of Martin Tupper (if that is his name) and McCosh.   [J, X, 263]

Le terrible don de la familiarité remains important. A man's connections must be looked after. If he surpasses everybody in mother wit, yet is scholar like the rest, be sure he has got a mother or father or aunt or cousin who has the uncorrupted slang of the street, the pure mud, and which is inestimable to him as spice and alterative, and which delights you in his rhetoric, like the devil's tunes when put to slow time in church-music.

All Aunt Mary's language was happy, but inimitable as if caught from some dream.   [J, IX, 436]

The art of the writer is to speak his fact and have done. Let the reader find that he cannot afford to omit any line of your writing, because you have omitted every word that he can spare.

You are annoyed—are you?—that your fine friends do not read you. They are better friends than you knew, and have done you the rarest service. Now write so that they must. When it is a disgrace to them that they do not know

what you have said, you will hear the echo.
[J, IX, 436–437]

The superlative, so dreary in dull people, in the hands of wit gives a fillip or shock most agreeable to the drowsy attention, and hints at poetic power. [J, IX, 499]

Immortality. I notice that as soon as writers broach this question they begin to quote. I hate quotations. Tell me what you know. [J, VIII, 20]

Surfaces. Good writing sips the foam of the cup. There are infinite degrees of delicacy in the use of the hands; and good workmen are so distinguished from laborers; and good horsemen, from rude riders; and people of elegant manners, from the vulgar. In writing, it is always at the surface, and can chip off a scale, where a coarser hand and eye find only solid wall. [J, IX, 116]

Eloquence. What unreckoned elements the orator carries with him, for example, silence.
He performs as much or more with judicious pauses, as by his best stroke. [J, IX, 152]

Him we call an artist who shall play on an assembly of men as a master on the keys of the piano—who, seeing the people furious, shall soften and compose them, shall draw them, when he will, to laughter and to tears. Bring him to his audience, and be they who they may—coarse or refined, pleased or displeased, sulky or savage, with their opinions in the keeping of a confessor, or with their opinions in their banksafes—he will have them pleased and humored as he chooses; and they shall carry and execute that which he bids them. [W, VII, 65]

I learned that the rhyme is there in the theme, thought, and image, themselves. I learned that there is a beyond to every place—and the bird moving through the air by successive dartings taught me. [J, IX, 209]

In reading prose, I am sensible as soon as a sentence drags, but in reading poetry, as soon as one word drags.
[J, IX, 214]

It is very hard to go beyond your public. If they are satisfied with your poor performance, you will not easily make better. But if they know what is good and delight in it, you will aspire, and burn, and toil, till you achieve it.
[J, IX, 304–305]

In poetry, tone. I have been reading some of Lowell's new poems, in which he shows unexpected advance on himself, but perhaps most in technical skill and courage. It is in talent rather than in poetic tone, and rather expresses his wish, his ambition, than the uncontrollable interior impulse which is the authentic mark of a new poem, and which is unanalysable, and makes the merit of an ode of Collins, or Gray, or Wordsworth, or Herbert, or Byron—and which is felt in the pervading tone, rather than in brilliant parts or lines; as if the sound of a bell, or a certain cadence expressed in a low whistle or booming, or humming, to which the poet first timed his step, as he looked at the sunset, or thought, was the incipient form of the piece, and was regnant through the whole.   [J, X, 267]

Good writing. All writing should be selection in order to drop every dead word. Why do you not save out of your speech or thinking only the vital things—the spirited *mot* which amused or warmed you when you spoke it—because of its luck and newness? I have just been reading, in this careful book of a most intelligent and learned man, any number of flat conventional words and sentences. If a man would learn to read his own manuscript severely—becoming really a third person, and search only for what interested him, he would blot to purpose—and how every page would gain! Then all the words will be sprightly, and every sentence a surprise.   [J, X, 302–303]

The plain speaking of Plutarch, as of the ancient writers generally, coming from the habit of writing for one sex only, has a great gain for brevity, and, in our new tendencies of civilization, may tend to correct a false delicacy.

[W, X, 306]

The American artist who would carve a wood-god, and who was familiar with the forest in Maine, where enormous fallen pine trees "cumber the forest floor," where huge mosses depending from the trees and the mass of the timber give a savage and haggard strength to the grove, would produce a very different statue from the sculptor who only knew a European woodland—the tasteful Greek, for example. [J, IV, 289]

I saw in Boston Fanny Elssler in the ballet of *Nathalie*. She must show, I suppose, the whole compass of her instrument, and add to her softest graces of motion or "the wisdom of her feet," the feats of the rope-dancer and tumbler: and perhaps on the whole the beauty of the exhibition is enhanced by this that is strong and strange, as when she stands erect on the extremities of her toes or on one toe, or "performs the impossible" in attitude. But the chief beauty is in the extreme grace of her movement, the variety and nature of her attitude, the winning fun and spirit of all her little coquetries, the beautiful erectness of her body, and the freedom and determination which she can so easily assume, and, what struck me much, the air of perfect sympathy with the house, and that mixture of deference and conscious superiority which puts her in perfect spirits and equality to her part. When she courtesies, her sweet and slow and prolonged salaam which descends and still descends whilst the curtain falls until she seems to have invented new depths of grace and condescension—she earns well the profusion of bouquets of flowers which are hurled on to the stage. [J, VI, 89]

These are ascending stairs—a good voice, winning manners, plain speech, chastened, however, by the schools into correctness; but we must come to the main matter, of power of statement—knowing your fact; hug your fact. For the essential thing is heat, and heat comes of sincerity. Speak what you do know and believe; and are personally in it; and are answerable for every word. Eloquence is *the power to translate a truth into language perfectly intelligible to the person to whom you speak.* [W, VIII, 129–130]

Wit makes its own welcome, and levels all distinctions. No dignity, no learning, no force of character, can make any stand against good wit. It is like ice, on which no beauty of form, no majesty of carriage can plead any immunity—they must walk gingerly, according to the laws of ice, or down they must go, dignity and all. [W, VIII, 163]

Chapter Eight

American Places

The American writer is famous for his treatment of land-scape. Up to the end of the nineteenth century, many an American writer had good reason to wonder if he had any-thing to describe except landscape. The country itself was always new and still relatively unexplored, and when Emer-son, on one of his regular lecture tours, crossed the frozen Mississippi on foot, or—nearer home—peeped in on Nan-tucket or Cape Cod, he felt like an explorer.

But unlike Thoreau, whose subject was his spiritual rela-tionship to landscape, Emerson (by far the greater traveler) had an eye for regional human characteristics. As a constant lecturer, he got to know the country better than many other writers, and he knew himself for such a type of New Eng-land that he enjoyed recognizing everything that was not. Precisely because Emerson did not need anything more than Concord, because he could live in it and describe it as if it were all the world he needed, he had brilliant and in-stantaneous reactions to the America madly growing beyond Concord. It was all so strange! America itself felt strange to over-civilized and bookish people. It was this physical feel-ing of strangeness in a new country that Emerson caught especially well. He caught the disproportion of man to this country with the same chilling effect of loneliness that Mel-ville felt about Ishmael adrift on the ocean. "The stark nakedness of the country could not be exaggerated," he wrote of Nantucket. In winter, he found himself in little New England villages that were as "few & cold as the Tobolks & Irkutsks of Siberia, & I bethought myself as I stared into the white night whether I had not committed some misdemeanor against some Czar and while I dreamed of Maine was bound a thousand versts into arctic Asia." Henry James described Emerson abroad in his own country, "Mercury shivering in a mackintosh." And in one of the most haunting descriptions of what it felt like to be an American in those days, Emerson summed up the major theme of man's involvement with nature when he wrote that in America "lies nature sleeping, overgrowing, almost conscious, too much by half for man in the picture."

I hear the whistle of the locomotive in the woods. Wherever that music comes it has its sequel. It is the voice of the civility of the Nineteenth Century saying, "Here I am." It is interrogative: it is prophetic; and this Cassandra is believed: "Whew! Whew! Whew! How is real estate here in the swamp and wilderness? Ho for Boston! Whew! Whew! Down with that forest on the side of the hill. I want ten thousand chestnut sleepers. I want cedar posts, and hundreds of thousands of feet of boards. Up! my masters of oak and pine! You have waited long enough—a good part of a century in the wind and stupid sky. Ho for axes and saws, and away with me to Boston! Whew! Whew! I will plant a dozen houses on this pasture next moon, and a village anon; and I will sprinkle yonder square mile with white houses like the broken snowbanks that strow it in March."

[J, VI, 322–323]

Perhaps in the village we have manners to paint which the city life does not know. Here we have Mr. S., who is man enough to turn away the butcher who cheats in weight, and introduce another butcher into town. The other neighbors could not take such a step. Here is Mr. E., who, when the moderator of the Town-meeting is candidate for representative, and so stands in the centre of the box inspecting each vote and each voter, dares carry up a vote for the opposite candidate and put it in. There is the hero who will not subscribe to the flag-staff or the engine, though all say it is mean. There is the man who gives his dollar, but refuses to give his name, though all other contributors are set down. There is Mr. H., who never loses his spirits, though always in the minority, and, though "the people behave as bad as if they were drunk," he is just as determined in opposition and just as cheerful as ever. Here is Mr. C., who says "honor bright" and keeps it so. Here is Mr. S., who warmly assents to whatever proposition you please to make, and Mr. M., who roundly tells you he will have nothing to do with the thing. The high people in the village are timid; the low people are bold and nonchalant, negligent too of each other's opposition, for they see the amount of it and know its uttermost limits, which the more remote proprietor does not. Here, too, are not to be forgotten our two companies, the Light Infantry and the Artillery, who brought up, one the Brigade Band, and one the Brass Band from Boston, set the musicians side by side under the great tree on the Common, and let them play two tunes and jangle and drown each other, and presently got the companies into actual hustling and kicking.

To show the force that is in you, and (whether you are a philosopher and call it heroism, or are a farmer and call it pluck) you need not go beyond the tinman's shop or the first corner; nay, the first man you meet who bows to you may look you in the eye and call it out. Here is J. M., not so much a citizen as a part of nature, in perfect rapport with the trout in the stream, the bird in the wood or pond side, and the plant in the garden; whatsoever is early, or rare, or nocturnal; game, or agriculture, he knows; he being awake when others sleep and asleep when others wake. Snipe, pelican, or breed of hogs, or grafting or cutting, woodcraft, or bees.   [J, IV, 352–354]

What is more alive among works of art than our plain old wooden church, built a century and a quarter ago, with the ancient New England spire? I pass it at night, and stand and listen to the beats of the clock—like heartbeats; not sounding, as Elizabeth Hoar well observed, so much like tickings, as like a step. It is the step of Time. You catch the sound first by looking up at the clock-face, and then you see this wooden tower rising thus alone, but stable and aged, towards the midnight stars. It has affiance and privilege with them. Not less than the marble cathedral it had its origin in sublime aspirations, in the august religion of man. Not less than those stars to which it points, it began to be *in the soul.* [J, V, 24]

We have the finest climate in the world . . . in Massachusetts. If we have coarse days, and dogdays, and white days, and days that are like ice-blinks, we have also yellow days, and crystal days—days which are neither hot nor cold, but the perfection of temperature. New England has a good climate—yet, in choosing a farm, we like a southern exposure, whilst Massachusetts, it must be owned, is on the northern slope towards the Arctic circle and the Pole. Our climate is a series of surprises, and among our many prognostics of the weather, the only trustworthy one that I know is that, when it is warm, it is a sign that it is going to be cold. [W, XII, 139]

Climate has much to do with it—climate and race. Set a New Englander to describe any accident which happened in his presence. What hesitation and reserve in his narrative! He tells with difficulty some particulars, and gets as fast as he can to the result, and, though he cannot describe, hopes to suggest the whole scene. Now listen to a poor Irishwoman recounting some experience of hers. Her speech flows like a river—so unconsidered, so humorous, so pathetic, such justice done to all the parts! It is a true transubstantiation— the fact converted into speech, all warm and colored and alive, as it fell out. Our Southern people are almost all speakers, and have every advantage over the New England people, whose climate is so cold that 'tis said we do not like to open our mouths very wide. [W, VII, 68–69]

I read the fabulous magnificence of these Karuns and Jamschids and Kai Kans and Feriduns of Persia, all gold and talismans; then I walk by the newsboys with telegraph

despatches; by the Post Office; and Pedding's shop with
English steamers' journals; and pass the Maine Depot; and
take my own seat in the Fitchburg cars, and see every man
dropped at his estate, as we pass it; and see what tens of
thousands of powerful and armed men, science-armed,
society-armed men, sit at large in this ample land of ours,
obscure from their numbers and the extent of territory, and
muse on the power which each of these can lay hold of at
pleasure—these men who wear no star nor gold-laced hat;
you cannot tell if they be poor or rich—and I think how far
these chains of intercourse and travel go, what levers, what
pumps, what searchings, are applied to Nature for the benefit of the youngest of these exorbitant republicans, and I
say, What a Negrofine royalty is that of Jamschid and Solomon; what a real sovereignty of Nature does the Bostonian
possess!—caoutchouc, steam, ether, telegraph—what bells
they can ring! . . .   [J, VII, 314–315]

I go twice a week over Concord with Ellery, and, as we
sit on the steep park at Conantum, we still have the same
regret as oft before. Is all this beauty to perish? Shall none
remake this sun and wind, the sky-blue river, the river-blue
sky; the yellow meadow spotted with sacks and sheets of
cranberry-pickers; the red bushes; the iron-gray house with
just the color of the granite rock; the paths of the thicket,
in which the only engineers are the cattle grazing on yonder
hill; the wide, straggling wild orchard in which Nature has
deposited every possible flavor in the apples of different
trees? Whole zones and climates she has concentrated into
apples. We think of the old benefactors who have con-
quered these fields; of the old man Moore, who is just
dying in these days, who has absorbed such volumes of sunshine like a huge melon or pumpkin in the sun—who has
owned in every part of Concord a woodlot, until he could
not find the boundaries of these, and never saw their interiors. But we say, where is he who is to save the present
moment, and cause that this beauty be not lost? Shakespeare
saw no better heaven or earth, but had the power and need
to sing, and seized the dull ugly England, ugly to this, and
made it amicable and enviable to all reading men, and now

we are fooled into likening this to that; whilst, if one of us
had the chanting constitution, that land would no more be
heard of.

The journal of one of our walks would be literature
enough for a cockney—or for us, if we should be shut up
in our houses—and we make no record of them. The cranberry meadow yonder is that where Darius Hubbard picked
one hundred bushels in one season, worth two hundred dollars, and no labor whatever is bestowed on the crop, not so
much as to mow the grass or cut down the bushes. Much
more interesting is the woodlot, which yields its gentle rent
of six per cent without any care or thought where the owner
sleeps or travels, and fears no enemy but fire. But Ellery
declares that the Railroad has proved too strong for all our
farmers and has corrupted them like a war, or the incur-
sion of another race—has made them all amateurs, given
the young men an air their fathers never had; they look as
if they might be railroad agents any day. We shall never see
Cyrus Hubbard, or Ephraim Wheeler, or Grass-and-Oats,
or Oats-and-Grass, or Barrett or Hosmer, in the next generation. These old Saxons have the look of pine trees and
apple trees, and might be the sons got between the two;
conscientious laborers with a science born with them from
out the sap vessels of these savage sires.   [J, VII, 506–508]

For walking, you must have a broken country. In Illinois,
everybody rides. There is no good walk in that state. The
reason is, a square yard of it is as good as a hundred miles.
You can distinguish from the cows a horse feeding, at the distance of five miles, with a naked eye. Hence, you have the
monotony of Holland, and when you step out of the door
can see all that you will have seen when you come home. In
Massachusetts, our land is agreeably broken, and is perme-
able like a park, and not like some towns in the more broken
country of New Hampshire, built on three or four hills
having each one side at forty-five degrees and the other side
perpendicular: so that if you go a mile, you have only the
choice whether you will climb the hill on your way out or
on your way back. The more reason we have to be content
with the felicity of our slopes in Massachusetts, undulating,

rocky, broken and surprising, but without this alpine inconveniency. Twenty years ago in Northern Wisconsin the pinery was composed of trees so big, and so many of them, that it was impossible to walk in the country, and the traveller had nothing for it but to wade in the streams. One more inconveniency, I remember, they showed me in Illinois, that, in the bottom lands, the grass was fourteen feet high. We may well enumerate what compensating advantages we have over that country, for 'tis a commonplace, which I have frequently heard spoken in Illinois, that it was a manifest leading of the Divine Providence that the New England states should have been first settled, before the Western country was known, or they would never have been settled at all. [W, XII, 143–144]

The apple is our national fruit. In October, the country is covered with its ornamental harvests. The American sun paints itself in these glowing balls amid the green leaves, the social fruit, in which Nature has deposited every possible flavor; whole zones and climates she has concentrated into apples. I am afraid you do not understand values. Look over the fence at the farmer who stands there. He makes every cloud in the sky, and every beam of the sun, serve him. His trees are full of brandy. He saves every drop of sap, as if it were wine. A few years ago those trees were whipsticks. Now, every one of them is worth a hundred dollars. Observe their form; not a branch nor a twig is to spare. They look as if they were arms and fingers, holding out to you balls of fire and gold. One tree yields the rent of an acre of land. Yonder pear has every property which should belong to a tree. It is hardy, and almost immortal. It accepts every species of nourishment, and yet could live, like an Arab, on air and water. [W, XII, 145]

The houses in Acton seemed to be filled with fat old people who looked like old tomatoes; their faces crumpled into red collops, fatting and rotting at their ease.
[J, VIII, 42]

Chelmsford. I know well the town in which they lived; the landscape which they saw. I spent an autumn and winter among these hills and plains. I knew where the chestnut first spread its brown harvest on a frosty morning for the boys; where the apples covered the ground with white fruit. I saw the last fires that burned in the old limekiln. I knew the ripples of the Baptist Pond, and the woods that grew where the corn is now ripening.

Plain homely land, sandy fields which the Merrimack washes, but the sun and stars do not disdain to fill it with magnificence in June, and with sublime lights in autumn.

[J, IX, 235]

Last week I went to Salem. At the Lafayette Hotel where I lodged, every five or ten minutes the barkeepers came into the sitting-room to arrange their hair and collars at the looking-glass. So many joys has the kind God provided for us dear creatures.   [J, IV, 20]

Nation of Nantucket makes its own war and peace. Place of winds, bleak, shelterless, and, when it blows, a large part of the island is suspended in the air and comes into your face and eyes as if it was glad to see you. The moon comes here as if it was at home, but there is no shade.

[J, VII, 271–272]

[*To Ellen Emerson*]   This island is like a ship sixty miles out at sea: anything that comes from the mainland is highly valued. And papas that leave their homes, and wander here, you may be very sure are glad to hear from their daughters. This is a strange place, the island is fifteen miles long, but there are no woods and no trees upon it, and hardly any fence. As soon as you have walked out of the town or village of Nantucket (in which there are a few little gardens and a few trees) you come on a wide bare common stretching as far as you can see on every side, with nothing upon it but here & there a few nibbling sheep. And if you walk on till you have lost sight of the town, and a fog rises, which is very common here, you will have no guide to show you the way, no houses, no trees, no hills, no stones, so that it has many times happened here that people have been lost, & when they did not come back, the whole town came out &

hunted for them. All the people live by killing whales, which in old times used to swim about the island & the men went out in boats & killed them with harpoons; but now they go to the Pacific Ocean for them in great ships. But one day when the ship Essex was sailing there, a great sperm whale was seen coming with full speed towards the vessel: in a moment he struck the ship with terrible force, staving in some planks, and causing a leak: then he went off a little way, & came back swiftly, the water all white with his violent motion, & struck the ship a second frightful blow; the crew were obliged instantly to escape in boats, and the ship sunk in a few minutes. The Captain is now here.

[L, III, 398–399]

Went to Yarmouth Sunday, 5th; to Orleans Monday, 6th; to Nauset Light on the back side of Cape Cod. Collins, the keeper told us he found obstinate resistance on Cape Cod to the project of building a lighthouse on this coast, as it would injure the wrecking business. He had to go to Boston, and obtain the strong recommendation of the Port Society. From the high hill in the rear of Higgins's, in Orleans, I had a good view of the whole Cape and the sea on both sides. The Cape looks like one of the Newfoundland Banks just emerged, a huge tract of sand half-covered with poverty grass and beach grass, and for trees, abele and locust and plantations of pitch pine. Some good oak, and in Dennis and Brewster were lately good trees for ship lumber, and they still are well wooded on the east side. But the view I speak of looked like emaciated Orkneys—Mull, Islay, and so forth—made of salt dust, gravel, and fish bones. They say the wind makes the roads, and, as at Nantucket, a large part of the real estate was freely moving back and forth in the air. I heard much of the coming railroad which is about to reach Yarmouth and Hyannis, and they hope will come to Provincetown. I fancied the people were only waiting for the railroad to reach them in order to evacuate the country. For the stark nakedness of the country could not be exaggerated. But no; nothing was less true. They are all attached to what they call *the soil*. Mr. Collins had been as far as Indiana; but, he said, hill on hill—he felt stifled, and "longed for the Cape, where he could see out." And whilst I was fancying that they would gladly give away land to anybody that would come and live there, and be a neighbor: no, they said, all real estate had risen, all over the Cape, and you could not buy land at less than fifty dollars per acre. And, in Provincetown, a lot on the Front Street of forty feet square would cost five or six hundred dollars. . . .

Still, I saw at the Cape, as at Nantucket, they are a little tender about your good opinion: for if a gentleman at breakfast says he don't like Yarmouth, all real estate seems to them at once depreciated two or three per cent.

They are very careful to give you directions what road you shall take from town to town; but, as the country has the shape of a piece of tape, it is not easy to lose your way. For the same reason it behooves everybody who goes on to the Cape to behave well, as he must stop on his return at all the same houses, unless he takes the packet at Province-town for Boston, six hours in good weather, and a week in bad. [J, VIII, 399–401]

At Dartmouth College, last July, was a good sheriff-like gentleman with a loud voice, a pompous air, and a fine coat, whose aid, it seemed, the College annually called in, to mar-shal their procession. He was in his element; he commanded us all with such despotic condescension, as put all dignities and talents but his own quite aside. He marched before, the College followed him like a tame dog. [J, V, 216–217]

It is one of the signs of our time, the ill health of all people. All the young people are nearsighted in the towns.
[J, V, 225]

[*To Margaret Fuller*] What would you have, that you come thus into my mind? My trivial travelling anecdotes? None have I to tell, & yet I was upset in the sleigh stage yesterday in a snowbank in Berwick with six-insides, an accident which produced some slight wounds & some sud-den developments of character in the ladies who emerged successively (one of them cursing & swearing without stint)

from the bowels of the coach. We saw the great Shaker settlement in Alfred, but after that in many & many a mile
nothing but snow & stars & pinetrees: and in travelling it is
sometimes possible to have a superfluity of these fine objects. The villages were few & cold as the Tobolks & Irkutsks
of Siberia, & I bethought myself as I stared into the *white*
night whether I had not committed some misdemeanor
against some Czar and while I dreamed of Maine was
bound a thousand versts into arctic Asia.   [L, III, 104]

Yankeedom. The Yankee means to make moonlight
work, if he can; and he himself, after he has spent all the
business hours in Wall Street, takes his dinner at a French
boarding-house, that his soup and cutlet may not be quite
unprofitable, but he shall learn the language between the
mouthfuls. I rode in the stagecoach with a pedlar: "Mind
the half-cent," said my companion. "A man can about pay
his shop-rent by minding the half-cent."   [J, VII, 211]

On the way to Winchester, whither our host accompanied
us in the afternoon, my friends asked many questions respecting American landscapes, forests, houses—my house,
for example. It is not easy to answer these queries well.
There, I thought, in America, lies nature sleeping, overgrowing, almost conscious, too much by half for man in
the picture, and so giving a certain *tristesse,* like the rank
vegetation of swamps and forests seen at night, steeped in
dews and rains, which it loves; and on it man seems not
able to make much impression. There, in that great sloven
continent, in high Allegheny pastures, in the sea-wide sky-
skirted prairie, still sleeps and murmurs and hides the great
mother, long since driven away from the trim hedge-rows
and over-cultivated garden of England. And, in England,
I am quite too sensible of this. Everyone is on his good behavior and must be dressed for dinner at six. So I put off
my friends with very inadequate details, as best I could.
[W, V, 288–289]

*Preferring New England, picturesque without inconven-
iency, to the bogs and forests of the West, Emerson never-*

*theless ventures forth beyond the sacred precincts to New
York and beyond the Alleghenies. He confesses a yearning
to explore the vast hinterlands, and grows familiar with
prairies, rains, and thaws. Everywhere, however, among
Yankees, New Yorkers, and Westerners, he finds a common appetite for dollars.*

[*To Margaret Fuller*] I am sorry we come so quickly to
the kernel & through the kernel of Cambridge society, but I
think I do not know any part of our American life which
is so superficial: the Hoosiers, the speculators, the custom
house officers—to say nothing of the Fanatics, interest us
so much more. If I had a pocket-full of money, I think I
should go down the Ohio & up & down the Mississippi by
way of antidote to what small remains of the Orientalism
(so endemic in these parts) there may still be in me, to cast
out, I mean, the passion for Europe by the passion for
America. My Aunt said to me when I was young, "I respect in a rich man the order of Providence." We must presently learn that the rich man is not Europe but America;
and our reverence for Cambridge which is only a part of
our reverence for London must be transferred across the
Allegheny ridge.   [L, II, 394–395]

I am here [New York] on a visit to my brother, who is
a lawyer in this city, and lives at Staten Island, at a distance of half an hour's sail. The city has such immense
natural advantages and such capabilities of boundless
growth, and such varied and ever increasing accommoda-
tions and appliances for eye and ear, for memory and wit,
for locomotion and lavation, and all manner of delectation,
that I see that the poor fellows that live here do get some
compensation for the sale of their souls. And how they
multiply! They estimate the population today at 350,000,
and forty years ago, it is said, there were but 20,000. But I
always seem to suffer some loss of faith on entering cities.
They are great conspiracies; the parties are all maskers, who
have taken mutual oaths of silence not to betray each other's
secret and each to keep the other's madness in countenance.
[E–C, I, 269]

Since I last wrote to you [Carlyle], I found it needful,
if only for the household's sake, to set some new lectures
in order, and go to new congregations of men. I live so
much alone, shrinking almost cowardly from the contact
of worldly and public men, that I need more than others
to quit home sometimes, and roll with the river of travellers, and live in hotels. . . . Between my two speeches at
Baltimore, I went to Washington, thirty-seven miles, and
spent four days. The two poles of an enormous political
battery, galvanic coil on coil, self-increased by series on
series of plates from Mexico to Canada, and from the sea
westward to the Rocky Mountains, here meet and play, and
make the air electric and violent. Yet one feels how little,
more than how much, man is represented there. I think, in
the higher societies of the Universe, it will turn out that the
angels are molecules, as the devils were always Titans, since
the dulness of the world needs such mountainous demon-
stration, and the virtue is so modest and concentrating.

[E–C, II, 28–29]

[*To Lidian Emerson*] Well we got away from Cairo [Illi-
nois], its sailor shops, tenpin-alleys and faro-tables, still on
the green & almost transparent Ohio, which now seemed so
broad that the yellow line in front for which we were steer-
ing, looked hopelessly narrow; but yellow line widened as
we drew nigh, and, at last, we reached & crossed the per-
fectly-marked line of green on one side, & mud-hue on the
other, & entered the Mississippi. It is one of the great river
landscapes of the world, wide wide eddying waters, low
shores. The great river takes in the Ohio which had grown
so large, turns it all to its own mud color, & does not become perceptibly larger.

The great sweeps of the Mississippi, the number of its
large islands made & unmade in short periods, your distance
from either shore, and the unvarying character of the green
wilderness on either side from hour to hour, from day to
day—the loneliest river—no towns, no houses, no dents in
the forest, no boats almost—we met I believe but one steamboat in the first hundred miles—now & again then we
notice a flat wood boat lying under the shore, blow our

whistle, ring our bell, & near the land, then out of some log-shed appear black or white men, & hastily put out their boat, a large mud-scow, loaded with corded wood . . . Then there were planters travelling, one with his family of slaves (6 blacks); peaceable looking farmer-like men who when they stretch themselves in the pauses of conversation disclose the butts of their pistols in their breast-pockets.

[L, IV, 209–211]

[*To Lidian Emerson*] Here I am [Springfield, Illinois] in the deep mud of the prairie, misled, I fear, into this bog, not by a will of the wisp, such as shine in bogs, but by a young New Hampshire Editor, who overestimated the strength of both of us, & fancied I should glitter in the prairie & draw the prairie birds & waders. In the prairie, it rains, & thaws incessantly, & if we step off the short street, we go up to the shoulders, perhaps, in mud. My chamber is a cabin. My fellow boarders are legislators, but of Illinois, or the big bog. Two or three Governors or ex-Governors live in the house. But in the prairie, we are all new men, just come, & must not stand for trifles. 'Tis of no use then for me to magnify mine. But I cannot command daylight or solitude for study, or for more than a scrawl.

[L, IV, 342]

I went lately to St. Louis and saw the Mississippi again. The powers of the River, the insatiate craving for nations of men to reap and cure its harvests, the conditions it imposes—for it yields to no engineering—are interesting enough. The Prairie exists to yield the greatest possible quantity of adipocere. For corn makes pig, pig is the export of all the land, and you shall see the instant dependence of aristocracy and civility on the fat four-legs. Working-men, ability to do the work of the River, abounded. Nothing higher was to be thought of. America is incomplete. Room for us all, since it has not ended, nor given sign of ending, in bard or hero. 'Tis a wild democracy, the riot of mediocrities, and none of your selfish Italies and Englands, where an age sublimates into a genius, and the whole population is made into Paddies to feed his porcelain veins, by transfusion from their brick arteries. Our few fine persons are apt to die. Horatio Greenough, a sculptor, whose tongue was far cunninger in talk than his chisel to carve, and who inspired great hopes, died two months ago at forty-seven years. Nature has only so much vital force, and must dilute it, if it is to be multiplied into millions. "The beautiful is never plentiful." On the whole, I say to myself, that our conditions in America are not easier or less expensive than the European. [E–C, II, 218–219]

I went out Northwest to great countries which I had not visited before; rode one day, fault of broken railroads, in a sleigh, sixty-five miles through the snow, by Lake Michigan, (seeing how prairies and oak-openings look in winter), to reach Milwaukee; "the world there was done up in large lots," as a settler told me. The farmer, as he is now a colonist and has drawn from his local necessities great doses of energy, is interesting, and makes the heroic age for Wisconsin. He lives on venison and quails. I was made much of, as the only man of the pen within five hundred miles, and by rarity worth more than venison and quails.

Greeley of the *New York Tribune* is the right spiritual father of all this region; he prints and disperses one hundred and ten thousand newspapers in one day—multitudes of them in these very parts. He had preceded me, by a few days, and people had flocked together, coming thirty and forty miles to hear him speak; as was right, for he does all their thinking and theory for them, for two dollars a year. Other than Colonists, I saw no man. "There are no singing birds in the prairie," I truly heard. All the life of the land and water had distilled no thought. Younger and better, I had no doubt been tormented to read and speak their sense for them. Now I only gazed at them and their boundless land. [E–C, II, 233–235]

The engineer was goading his boilers with pitch-pine knots.

The traveller looked out of the car window; the fences passed languidly by; he could scan curiously every post. But very soon the jerk of every pulse of the engine was felt; the whistle of the engineer moaned short moans, as it swept across any highway. He gazed out over the fields; the fences were tormented; every rail and rider writhed and twisted past the window; tne snowbanks swam past like fishes; and the speed seemed to increase every moment. The near trees and bushes wove themselves into colored ribbons. The rocks, walls, the fields themselves streaming like a mill-race. The train tore on with jumps and jerks that tested the strength of oak and iron. The passengers seemed to suffer their speed. Meantime, the wind cried like a child, complained like a sawmill, whistled like a fife, mowed like an idiot, roared like the sea, and yelled like a demon. [J, IX, 260–261]

Ah, my poor countrymen! Yankees and Dollars have such inextricable association that the words ought to rhyme. In New York, in Boston, in Providence, you cannot pass two men in the street without the word escaping them in the very moment of encounter, "dollars," "two and a half per cent," "three per cent." [J, V, 379]

In New York lately, as in cities generally, one seems to lose all substance, and become surface in a world of surfaces. Everything is external, and I remember my hat and coat, and all my other surfaces, and nothing else. If suddenly a reasonable question is addressed to me, what refreshment and relief! I visited twice and parted with a most polite lady without giving her reason to believe that she had met any other in me than a worshipper of surfaces, like all Broadway. It stings me yet. [J, VI, 165]

I think Tennyson got his inspiration in gardens, and that in this country, where there are no gardens, his musky verses could not be written. The Villa d'Este is a memorable poem in my life. [J, V, 6]

Chapter Nine

England and Elsewhere

English Traits—*from which most of the selections in this chapter are taken—is one of Emerson's most brilliant achievements. Nothing that he wrote about America reveals so clearly his concern with what was lacking to his own country as this extraordinary portrait of English traditionalism, English self-confidence, English manners. Like the "international" novels of Henry James, Emerson's book is concerned with a dramatic contrast between the New World and the Old, and* English Traits *itself is almost a treatise on what James, in a famous passage, described was particularly lacking to the American—"No sovereign, no court, no personal loyalty, no aristocracy, no church, no clergy, no army, no diplomatic service, no country gentlemen, no palaces, no castles, nor manors, nor old country houses. . . ."*

All these items of tradition, and many more, Emerson found overwhelmingly present in England, and his book is extraordinary because it sustains, by the power of his imagery and the strength of his impressions alone, his belief in the gross vitality and general superiority of the English. Yet Emerson's portrait of them, though it pays the greatest compliment to his subject by the brilliance and the felt excitement of his book, is by no means uncritically admiring. And a great many of the things which he felt to be most actively present in English tradition—as opposed to

*the mere potentiality and abstractness of American life—
he described with irony and some distaste. For the overwhelming impression he had of England was of its animal
strength and wealth, its negligent materialism. Yet it is typical of the balance and subtlety of Emerson's own mind, and
of his realism as an observer, that, though he did not personally possess this robustness in himself, he recognized
these traits as those solidly laid down by centuries of tradition and by the experience of a national community. As
opposed to the America where nature lies "sleeping, overgrowing, almost conscious, too much by half for man in the
picture," England seemed to him brilliantly humanized;
men's actions were on a recognizable human scale and had
a meaningful effect. And speaking out of the solitudes and
tristesse of the relatively empty American continent, he
makes it clear how continuously excited—and amusing—
these solid traits are. For they belong to a race who are
"good lovers and good haters," who are known, who know
themselves, who act out of centuries of habit and tradition
—as opposed to the Americans for whom Emerson himself
was acting as a cultural critic and as a prophet of national
hopes that were as yet unformulated, except by a few like
himself. The English appeared to Emerson like so many
characters in a play, and when he writes about the English
conceit, the English impatience of art, the English fanaticism about good form, the English vulgarity, he is actually
writing a comedy of manners, of national manners, which
no American could have written about Americans for half
a century.*

A good Englishman shuts himself out of three fourths of
his mind and confines himself to one fourth.   [W, V, 252]

A horizon of brass of the diameter of his umbrella shuts
down around his senses. Squalid contentment with conventions, satire at the names of philosophy and religion, paro-
chial and shop-till politics, and idolatry of usage, betray
the ebb of life and spirit. As they trample on nationalities
to reproduce London and Londoners in Europe and Asia,

so they fear the hostility of ideas, of poetry, of religion—
ghosts which they cannot lay; and, having attempted to
domesticate and dress the Blessed Soul itself in English
broadcoth and gaiters, they are tormented with fear that
herein lurks a force that will sweep their system away.

[W, V, 254]

England. The dinner, the wine, the homes of England
look attractive to the traveller, but they are the poor utmost
that illiberal wealth can perform. Alas! the halls of England are musty, the land is full of coal-smoke and carpet-
smell: not a breath of mountain air dilates the languishing
lungs—and the Englishman gets his amends by weaving
his web very fine: he is bold and absolute in his narrow
circle; he is versed in all his routine, sure, and elegant;
his stories are good, his sentences solid, and all his statesmen, lawyers, men of letters, and poets, finished and solid
as the pavement.   [J, VIII, 73]

The English race are reputed morose. I do not know that
they have sadder brows than their neighbors of northern
climates. They are sad by comparison with the singing and
dancing nations: not sadder, but slow and staid, as finding
their joys at home. They, too, believe that where there is
no enjoyment of life there can be no vigor and art in speech
or thought; that your merry heart goes all the way, your sad
one tires in a mile. . . . The Englishman finds no relief from
reflection, except in reflection. When he wishes for amusement, he goes to work. His hilarity is like an attack of fever.
Religion, the theatre and the reading the books of his
country all feed and increase his natural melancholy. The
police does not interfere with public diversions. It thinks
itself bound in duty to respect the pleasures and rare gayety
of this inconsolable nation; and their well-known courage
is entirely attributable to their disgust of life. . . .

The reputation of taciturnity they have enjoyed for six or
seven hundred years; and a kind of pride in bad public
speaking is noted in the house of Commons, as if they were
willing to show that they did not live by their tongues, or
thought they spoke well enough if they had the tone of gen-

tlemen. In mixed company they shut their mouths. A York-shire mill-owner told me he had ridden more than once all the way from London to Leeds, in the first-class carriage, with the same persons, and no word exchanged. The club-houses were established to cultivate social habits, and it is rare that more than two eat together, and oftenest one eats alone. Was it then a stroke of humor in the serious Swe-denborg, or was it only his pitiless logic, that made him shut up the English souls in a heaven by themselves? . . .

They are good lovers, good haters, slow but obstinate ad-mirers, and in all things very much steeped in their temper-ament, like man hardly awaked from deep sleep, which they enjoy. Their habits and instincts cleave to nature. They are of the earth, earthy; and of the sea, as the sea-kinds, at-tached to it for what it yields them, and not from any senti-ment. They are full of coarse strength, rude exercise, butch-er's meat and sound sleep; and suspect any poetic insinua-tion or any hint for the conduct of life which reflects on this animal existence, as if somebody were fumbling at the um-bilical cord and might stop their supplies. They doubt a man's sound judgment if he does not eat with appetite, and shake their heads if he is particularly chaste. Take them as they come, you shall find in the common people a surly in-difference, sometimes gruffness and ill temper; and in minds of more power, magazines of inexhaustible war, challenging.

"The ruggedest hour that time and spite dare bring
To frown upon the enraged Northumberland."

They are headstrong believers and defenders of their opin-ion, and not less resolute in maintaining their whim and perversity. Hezekiah Woodward wrote a book against the Lord's Prayer. And one can believe that Burton, the Anato-mist of Melancholy, having predicted from the stars the hour of his death, slipped the knot himself round his own neck, not to falsify his horoscope.

Their looks bespeak an invincible stoutness: they have extreme difficulty to run away, and will die game. Welling-ton said of the young coxcombs of the Life-Guards, deli-cately brought up, "But the puppies fight well"; and Nel-son said of his sailors, "They really mind shot no more than peas." Of absolute stoutness no nation has more or better examples. They are good at storming redoubts, at boarding frigates, at dying in the last ditch, or any desperate service which has daylight and honor in it; but not, I think, at enduring the rack, or any passive obedience, like jumping off a castle-roof at the word of a czar. Being both vascular and highly organized, so as to be very sensible of pain; and intellectual, so as to see reason and glory in a matter. . . .

The young men have a rude health which runs into peccant humors. They drink brandy like water, cannot expend their quantities of waste strength on riding, hunting, swimming and fencing, and run into absurd frolics with the gravity of the Eumenides. They stoutly carry into every nook and corner of the earth their turbulent sense; leaving no lie uncontradicted; no pretension unexamined. They chew hasheesh; cut themselves with poisoned creases; swing their hammock in the boughs of the Bohon Upas; taste every poison; buy every secret; at Naples they put St. Januarius's blood in an alembic; they saw a hole into the head of the "winking Virgin," to know why she winks; measure with an English footrule every cell of the Inquisition, every Turkish caaba, every Holy of holies; translate and send to Bentley the arcanum bribed and bullied away from shuddering Brahmins; and measure their own strength by the terror they cause. These travellers are of every class, the best and the worst; and it may easily happen that those of rudest behavior are taken notice of and remembered. The Saxon melancholy in the vulgar rich and poor appears as gushes of ill-humor, which every check exasperates into sarcasm and vituperation. There are multitudes of rude young English who have the self-sufficiency and bluntness of their nation, and who, with their disdain of the rest of mankind and with this indigestion and choler, have made the English traveller a proverb for uncomfortable and offensive manners. It was no bad description of the Briton generically, what was said two hundred years ago of one particular Oxford scholar: "He was a very bold man, uttered anything that came into his mind, not only among his companions, but in public coffee-houses, and would

often speak his mind of particular persons then accidentally
present, without examining the company he was in; for
which he was often reprimanded and several times threatened to be kicked and beaten."

The common Englishman is prone to forget a cardinal
article in the bill of social rights, that every man has a right
to his own ears. No man can claim to usurp more than a
few cubic feet of the audibilities of a public room, or to
put upon the company with the loud statement of his
crotchets or personalities. . . .

A saving stupidity masks and protects their perception,
as the curtain of the eagle's eye. Our swifter Americans,
when they first deal with English, pronounce them stupid;
but, later, do them justice as people who wear well, or hide
their strength. To understand the power of performance that
is in their finest wits, in the patient Newton, or in the versatile transcendent poets, or in the Dugdales, Gibbons, Hal-
lams, Eldons and Peels, one should see how English day-
laborers hold out. High and low, they are of an unctuous
texture. There is an adipocere in their constitution, as if they
had oil also for their mental wheels and could perform vast
amounts of work without damaging themselves.

[W, V, 127–139, *passim*]

A strong common sense, which it is not easy to unseat or
disturb, marks the English mind for a thousand years: a
rude strength newly applied to thought, as of sailors and
soldiers who had lately learned to read. They have no fancy,
and never are surprised into a covert or witty word, such as
pleased the Athenians and Italians, and was convertible
into a fable not long after; but they delight in strong earthy
expression, not mistakable, coarsely true to the human
body, and, though spoken among princes, equally fit and
welcome to the mob. This homeliness, veracity and plain
style appear in the earliest extant works and in the latest.
It imports into songs and ballads the smell of the earth, the
breath of cattle, and, like a Dutch painter, seeks a household charm, though by pails and pans. They ask their constitutional utility in verse. The kail and herrings are never
out of sight. The poet nimbly recovers himself from every

sally of the imagination. The English muse loves the farm-yard, the lane and market. She says, with De Staël, "I tramp in the mire with wooden shoes, whenever they would force me into the clouds." For the Englishman has accurate perceptions; takes hold of things by the right end, and there is no slipperiness in his grasp. He loves the axe, the spade, the oar, the gun, the steam-pipe: he has built the engine he uses. He is materialist, economical, mercantile. He must be treated with sincerity and reality; with muffins, and not the promise of muffins; and prefers his hot chop, with perfect security and convenience in the eating of it, to the chances of the amplest and Frenchiest bill of fare, engraved on embossed paper. When he is intellectual, and a poet or a philosopher, he carries the same hard truth and the same keen machinery into the mental sphere. His mind must stand on a fact. He will not be baffled, or catch at clouds, but the mind must have a symbol palpable and resisting. What he relishes in Dante is the vise-like tenacity with which he holds a mental image before the eyes, as if it were a scutcheon painted on a shield. Byron "liked something craggy to break his mind upon." A taste for plain strong speech, what is called a biblical style, marks the English. It is in Alfred and the Saxon Chronicle and in the Sagas of the Northmen. Latimer was homely. Hobbes was perfect in the "noble vulgar speech." Donne, Bunyan, Milton, Taylor, Evelyn, Pepys, Hooker, Cotton and the translators wrote it. How realistic or materialistic in treatment of his subject is Swift. He describes his fictitious persons as if for the police. Defoe has no insecurity or choice. Hudibras has the same hard mentality—keeping the truth at once to the senses and to the intellect.

It is not less seen in poetry. Chaucer's hard painting of his Canterbury pilgrims satisfies the senses. Shakespeare, Spenser and Milton, in their loftiest ascents, have this national grip and exactitude of mind. This mental materialism makes the value of England transcendental genius; in these writers and in Herbert, Henry More, Donne and Sir Thomas Browne. The Saxon materialism and narrowness, exalted into the sphere of intellect, makes the very genius of Shakespeare and Milton. When it reaches the pure ele-

ment, it treads the clouds as securely as the adamant. Even
in its elevations materialistic, its poetry is common sense inspired; or iron raised to white heat.   [W, V, 232–234]

The English, abhorring change in all things, abhorring it
most in matters of religion, cling to the last rag of form,
and are dreadfully given to cant. The English (and I wish
it were confined to them, but 'tis a taint in the Anglo-Saxon
blood in both hemispheres)—the English and the Americans cant beyond all other nations. The French relinquish
all that industry to them. What is so odious as the polite
bows to God, in our books and newspapers?
[W, V, 228–229]

The power of the newspaper is familiar in America and
in accordance with our political system. In England, it
stands in antagonism with the feudal institutions, and it is
all the more beneficent succor against the secretive tendencies of a monarchy. The celebrated Lord Somers "knew
of no good law proposed and passed in his time, to which
the public papers had not directed his attention." There is
no corner and no night. A relentless inquisition drags every
secret to the day, turns the glare of this solar microscope
on every malfaisance, so as to make the public a more terrible spy than any foreigner; and no weakness can be taken
advantage of by an enemy, since the whole people are already forewarned. Thus England rids herself of those in-
crustations which have been the ruin of old states. Of
course, this inspection is feared. No antique privilege, no
comfortable monopoly, but sees surely that its days are
counted; the people are familiarized with the reason of reform, and, one by one, take away every argument of the
obstructives.   [W, V, 261]

The religion of England is part of good-breeding. When
you see on the continent the well-dressed Englishman come
into his ambassador's chapel and put his face for silent
prayer into his smooth-brushed hat, you cannot help feeling how much national pride prays with him, and the religion of a gentleman. So far is he from attaching any mean-

ing to the words, that he believes himself to have done almost the generous thing, and that it is very condescending in him to pray to God. A great duke said on the occasion of a victory, in the House of Lords, that he thought the Almighty God had not been well used by them, and that it would become their magnanimity, after so great successes, to take order that a proper acknowledgment be made. It is the church of the gentry, but it is not the church of the poor. The operatives do not own it, and gentlemen lately testified in the House of Commons that in their lives they never saw a poor man in a ragged coat inside a church.

The torpidity on the side of religion of the vigorous English understanding shows how much wit and folly can agree in one brain. Their religion is a quotation; their church is a doll; and any examination is interdicted with screams of terror. In good company you expect them to laugh at the fanaticism of the vulgar; but they do not; they are the vulgar.   [W, V, 220–221]

The logical English train a scholar as they train an engineer. Oxford is a Greek factory, as Wilton mills weave carpet and Sheffield grinds steel. They know the use of a tutor, as they know the use of a horse; and they draw the greatest amount of benefit out of both.   [W, V, 204]

But a man must keep an eye on his servants, if he would not have them rule him. Man is a shrewd inventor and is ever taking the hint of a new machine from his own structure, adapting some secret of his own anatomy in iron, wood and leather to some required function in the work of the world. But it is found that the machine unmans the user. What he gains in making cloth, he loses in general power. There should be temperance in making cloth, as well as in eating. A man should not be a silk-worm, nor a nation a tent of caterpillars. The robust rural Saxon degenerates in the mills to the Leicester stockinger, to the imbecile Manchester spinner—far on the way to be spiders and needles. The incessant repetition of the same hand-work dwarfs the man, robs him of his strength, wit and versatility, to make a pin-polisher, a buckle-maker, or any other specialty; and presently, in a change of industry, whole towns are sacrificed like ant-hills, when the fashion of shoe-strings supersedes buckles, when cotton takes the place of linen, or railways of turnpikes, or when commons are enclosed by landlords. Then society is admonished of the mischief of the division of labor, and that the best political economy is care and culture of men; for in these crises all are ruined except such as are proper individuals, capable of thought and of new choice and the application of their talent to new labor. Then again come in new calamities. England is aghast at the disclosure of her fraud in the adulteration of food, of drugs and of almost every fabric in her mills and shops; finding that milk will not nourish, nor sugar sweeten, nor bread satisfy, nor pepper bite the tongue, nor glue stick. In true England all is false and forged. This too is the reaction of machinery, but of the larger machinery of commerce. 'Tis not, I suppose, want of probity, so much as the tyranny of trade, which necessitates a perpetual competition of underselling, and that again a perpetual deterioration of the fabric.

[W, V, 166–168]

The creation of wealth in England in the last ninety years is a main fact in modern history. The wealth of London determines prices all over the globe. All things precious, or useful, or amusing, or intoxicating, are sucked into this commerce and floated to London. Some English private fortunes reach, and some exceed a million of dollars a year A hundred thousand palaces adorn the island. All that can feed the senses and passions, all that can succor the talent or arm the hands of the intelligent middle class, who never spare in what they buy for their own consumption; all that can aid science, gratify taste, or soothe comfort, is in open market. Whatever is excellent and beautiful in civil, rural, or ecclesiastic architecture, in fountain, garden, or grounds— the English noble crosses sea and land to see and to copy at home. The taste and science of thirty peaceful generations; the gardens which Evelyn planted; the temples and pleasure-houses which Inigo Jones and Christopher Wren built; the wood that Gibbons carved; the taste of foreign and domestic artists, Shenstone, Pope, Brown, Loudon, Paxton—are in the vast auction, and the hereditary principle heaps on the owner of today the benefit of ages of owners. The present possessors are to the full as absolute as any of their fathers in choosing and procuring what they like. This comfort and splendor, the breadth of lake and mountain, tillage, pasture and park, sumptuous castle and modern villa—all consist with perfect order. They have no revolutions; no horse-guards dictating to the crown; no Parisian *poissardes* and barricades; no mob: but drowsy habitude, daily dress-dinners, wine and ale and beer and gin and sleep.

With this power of creation and this passion for independence, property has reached an ideal perfection. It is felt and treated as the national life-blood. The laws are framed to give property the securest possible basis, and the provisions to lock and transmit it have exercised the cunningest heads in a profession which never admits a fool. The rights of property nothing but felony and treason can override. The house is a castle which the king cannot enter. The Bank is a strong box to which the king has no key. Whatever surly sweetness possession can give, is tasted in England to the dregs. Vested rights are awful things, and absolute possession gives the smallest freeholder identity of interest with the duke. High stone fences and padlocked garden-gates announce the absolute will of the owner to be alone. Every whim of exaggerated egotism is put into stone and iron, into silver and gold, with costly deliberation and detail.   [W, V, 162–164]

George of Cappadocia, born at Epiphania in Cilicia, was a low parasite who got a lucrative contract to supply the army with bacon. A rogue and informer, he got rich and was forced to run from justice. He saved his money, embraced Arianism, collected a library, and got promoted by a faction to the episcopal throne of Alexandria. When Julian came, A.D. 361, George was dragged to prison; the prison was burst open by the mob and George was lynched, as he deserved. And this precious knave became, in good time, Saint George of England, patron of chivalry, emblem of victory and civility and the pride of the best blood of the modern world.

Strange, that the solid truth-speaking Briton should derive from an impostor. Strange, that the New World should have no better luck—that broad America must wear the name of a thief. Amerigo Vespucci, the pickle-dealer at Seville, who went out, in 1499, a subaltern with Hojeda, and whose highest naval rank was boatswain's mate in an expedition that never sailed, managed in this lying world to supplant Columbus and baptize half the earth with his own dishonest name. Thus nobody can throw stones. We are equally badly off in our founders; and the false pickle-dealer is an offset to the false bacon-seller.   [W, V, 152]

I find the Englishman to be him of all men who stands firmest in his shoes. They have in themselves what they value in their horses—mettle and bottom. . . .

They require you to dare to be of your own opinion, and they hate the practical cowards who cannot in affairs answer directly yes or no. They dare to displease, nay, they will let you break all the commandments, if you do it natively and with spirit. You must be somebody; then you may do this or that, as you will.

Machinery has been applied to all work, and carried to such perfection that little is left for the men but to mind the engines and feed the furnaces. But the machines require punctual service, and as they never tire, they prove too much for their tenders. Mines, forges, mills, breweries, railroads, steam-pump, steam-plough, drill of regiments, drill of police, rule of court and shop-rule have operated to give a mechanical regularity to all the habit and action of men. A terrible machine has possessed itself of the ground, the air, the men and women, and hardly even thought is free. . . .

The Englishman speaks with all his body. His elocution is stomachic—as the American's is labial. The Englishman is very petulant and precise about his accommodation at inns and on the roads; a quiddle about his toast and his chop and every species of convenience, and loud and pungent in his expressions of impatience at any neglect. His vivacity betrays itself at all points, in his manners, in his respiration, and the inarticulate noises he makes in clearing the throat—all significant of burly strength. He has stamina; he can take the initiative in emergencies. He has that *aplomb* which results from a good adjustment of the moral and physical nature and the obedience of all the powers to the will; as if the axes of his eyes were united to his backbone, and only moved with the trunk.

This vigor appears in the incuriosity and stony neglect, each of every other. Each man walks, eats, drinks, shaves, dresses, gesticulates, and, in every manner acts and suffers without reference to the bystanders, in his own fashion, only careful not to interfere with them or annoy them; not that he is trained to neglect the eyes of his neighbors—he is really occupied with his own affair and does not think of them. Every man in this polished country consults only his convenience, as much as a solitary pioneer in Wisconsin. I know not where any personal eccentricity is so freely allowed, and no man gives himself any concern with it. An Englishman walks in a pouring rain, swinging his closed umbrella like a walking-stick; wears a wig, or a shawl, or a saddle, or stands on his head, and no remark is made. And as he has been doing this for several generations, it is now in the blood.

In short, every one of these islanders is an island himself, safe, tranquil, incommunicable. In a company of strangers you would think him deaf; his eyes never wander from his table and newspaper. He is never betrayed into any curiosity or unbecoming emotion. They have all been trained in one severe school of manners, and never put off the harness. He does not give his hand. He does not let you meet his eye. It is almost an affront to look a man in the face without being introduced. In mixed or in select companies they do not introduce persons; so that a presentation is a circumstance as valid as a contract. Introductions are sacraments. He withholds his name. At the hotel, he is hardly willing to whisper it to the clerk at the book-office. If he give you his private address on a card, it is like an avowal of friendship; and his bearing, on being introduced, is cold, even

though he is seeking your acquaintance and is studying
how he shall serve you. . . .

Born in a harsh and wet climate, which keeps him indoors
whenever he is at rest, and being of an affectionate and
loyal temper, he dearly loves his house. If he is rich, he
buys a demesne and builds a hall; if he is in middle condition, he spares no expense on his house. Without, it is all
planted; within, it is wainscoted, carved, curtained, hung
with pictures and filled with good furniture. 'Tis a passion
which survives all others, to deck and improve it. Hither he
brings all that is rare and costly, and with the national
tendency to sit fast in the same spot for many generations,
it comes to be, in the course of time, a museum of heir-
looms, gifts and trophies of the adventures and exploits of
the family. He is very fond of silver plate, and though he
have no gallery of portraits of his ancestors, he has of their
punch-bowls and porringers. Incredible amounts of plate
are found in good houses, and the poorest have some spoon
or saucepan, gift of a godmother, saved out of better times.

An English family consists of a few persons, who, from
youth to age, are found revolving within a few feet of each
other, as if tied by some invisible ligature, tense as that
cartilage which we have seen attaching the two Siamese. . . .

They keep their old customs, costumes, and pomps, their
wig and mace, sceptre and crown. The Middle Ages still
lurk in the streets of London. The Knights of the Bath take
oath to defend injured ladies; the gold-stick-in-waiting survives. They repeated the ceremonies of the eleventh century
in the coronation of the present Queen. A hereditary tenure
is natural to them. Offices, farms, trades and traditions descend so. Their leases run for a hundred and a thousand
years. . . .

The English power resides also in their dislike of change.
They have difficulty in bringing their reason to act, and on
all occasions use their memory first. As soon as they have
rid themselves of some grievance and settled the better practice, they make haste to fix it as a finality, and never wish
to hear of alteration more. . . .

A sea-shell should be the crest of England, not only because it represents a power built on the waves, but also the

hard finish of the men. The Englishman is finished like a cowry or a murex. After the spire and the spines are formed, or with the formation, a juice exudes and a hard enamel varnishes every part. The keeping of the proprieties is as indispensable as clean linen. No merit quite countervails the want of this whilst this sometimes stands in lieu of all. " 'Tis in bad taste," is the most formidable word an Englishman can pronounce. But this japan costs them dear. There is a prose in certain Englishmen which exceeds in wooden deadness all rivalry with other countrymen. There is a knell in the conceit and externality of their voice, which seems to say, *Leave all hope behind.* In this Gibraltar of propriety, mediocrity gets intrenched and consolidated and founded in adamant. An Englishman of fashion is like one of those souvenirs, bound in gold vellum, enriched with delicate engravings on thick hot-pressed paper, fit for the hands of ladies and princes, but with nothing in it worth reading or remembering. [W, V, 102–112, *passim*]

The bias of the nation is a passion for utility. They love the lever, the screw and pulley, the Flanders draught-horse, the waterfall, wind-mills, tide-mills; the sea and the wind to bear their freight ships. More than the diamond Koh-i-noor, which glitters among their crown jewels, they prize that dull pebble which is wiser than a man, whose poles turn themselves to the poles of the world, and whose axis is parallel to the axis of the world. Now, their toys are steam and galvanism. They are heavy at the fine arts, but adroit at the coarse; not good in jewelry or mosaics, but the best iron-masters, colliers, wool-combers and tanners in Europe. They apply themselves to agriculture, to draining, to resisting encroachments of sea, wind, travelling sands, cold and wet sub-soil; to fishery, to manufacture of indispensable staples—salt, plumbago, leather, wool, glass, pottery and brick—to bees and silkworms—and by their steady combinations they succeed. A manufacturer sits down to dinner in a suit of clothes which was wool on a sheep's back at sunrise. You dine with a gentleman on venison, pheasant, quail, pigeons, poultry, mushrooms and pine-apples, all the growth of his estate. They are neat husbands for ordering all their tools pertaining to house and field. All are well kept. There is no want and no waste. They study use and fitness in their building, in the order of their dwellings and in their dress. The Frenchman invented the ruffle; the Englishman added the shirt. [W, V, 83–84]

There is a necessity on them [The English] to be logical. They would hardly greet the good that did not logically fall—as if it excluded their own merit, or shook their understandings. They are jealous of minds that have much facility of association, from an instinctive fear that the seeing many relations to their thought might impair this serial continuity and lucrative concentration. They are impatient of genius, or of minds addicted to contemplation, and cannot conceal their contempt for sallies of thought, however lawful, whose steps they cannot count by their wonted rule. Neither do they reckon better a syllogism that ends in syllogism. For they have a supreme eye to facts, and theirs is a logic that brings salt to soup, hammer to nail, oar to boat; the logic of cooks, carpenters and chemists, following the sequence of nature, and one on which words make no impression. Their mind is not dazzled by its own means, but locked and bolted to results. They love men who, like Samuel Johnson, a doctor in the schools, would jump out of his syllogism the instant his major proposition was in danger, to save that at all hazards. Their practical vision is spacious, and they can hold many threads without entangling them. All the steps they orderly take; but with the high logic of never confounding the minor and major proposition; keeping their eye on their aim, in all the complicity and delay incident to the several series of means they employ. There is room in their minds for this and that—a science of degrees. In the courts the independence of the judges and the loyalty of the suitors are equally excellent. In parliament they have hit on that capital invention of freedom, a constitutional opposition. And when courts and parliament are both deaf, the plaintiff is not silenced. Calm, patient, his weapon of defence from year to year is the obstinate reproduction of the grievance, with calculations and estimates. But, meantime, he is drawing numbers and money to his opinion, resolved that if all remedy fails, right of revolution is at the bottom of his charter-box. They are bound to see their measure carried, and stick to it through ages of defeat. [W, V, 79–81]

The Normans came out of France into England worse men than they went into it one hundred and sixty years before. They had lost their own language and learned the Romance or barbarous Latin of the Gauls, and had acquired with the language, all the vices it had names for. The conquest has obtained in the chronicles the name of the "memory of sorrow." Twenty thousand thieves landed at Hastings. These founders of the House of Lords were greedy and ferocious dragons, sons of greedy and ferocious pirates. They were all alike, they took everything they could carry, they burned, harried, violated, tortured and killed, until everything English was brought to the verge of ruin. Such however is the illusion of antiquity and wealth, that decent and dignified men now existing boast their descent from these filthy thieves, who showed a far juster conviction of their own merits, by assuming for their types the swine, goat, jackal, leopard, wolf and snake, which they severally resembled. [W, V, 60–61]

The English derive their pedigree from such a range of nationalities that there needs sea-room and land-room to unfold the varieties of talent and character. Perhaps the ocean serves as a galvanic battery, to distribute acids at one pole and alkalies at the other. So England tends to accumulate her liberals in America, and her conservatives at London. The Scandinavians in her race still hear in every age the murmurs of their mother, the ocean; the Briton in the blood hugs the homestead still. [W, V, 52]

The English composite character betrays a mixed origin. Everything English is a fusion of distant and antagonistic elements. The language is mixed; the names of men are of different nations—three languages, three or four nations— the currents of thought are counter: contemplation and practical skill; active intellect and dead conservatism; world-wide enterprise and devoted use and wont; aggressive freedom and hospitable law with bitter class-legislation; a people scattered by their wars and affairs over the face of the whole earth, and homesick to a man; a country of extremes—dukes and chartists, Bishops of Durham and naked heathen colliers—nothing can be praised in it without damning exceptions, and nothing denounced without salvos of cordial praise. [W, V, 50–51]

I stayed in London till I had become acquainted with all the styles of face in the street, and till I had found the suburbs and then straggling houses on each end of the city. Then I took a cab, left my farewell cards, and came home.
[J, VII, 489]

Elsewhere . . .

I have been to the Sistine Chapel to see the Pope bless the palms, and hear his choir chaunt the Passion. The Cardinals came in, one after another, each wearing a purple robe, an ermine cape, and a small red cap to cover the tonsure. A priest attended each one, to adjust the robes of their eminences. As each cardinal entered the chapel, the rest rose. One or two were fine persons. Then came the Pope in scarlet robes and bishop's mitre. After he was seated, the cardinals went in turn to the throne and kneeled and kissed his hand. After this ceremony the attendants divested the cardinals of their robes and put on them a gorgeous cope of cloth-of-gold. When this was arranged, a sort of ornamental baton made of the dried palm leaf was brought to his Holiness and blessed, and each of the cardinals went again to the throne and received one of these from the hands of the Pope. They were supplied from a large pile at the side of the papal chair. After the cardinals, came other dignitaries, bishops, deans, canons—I know them not, but there was much etiquette, some kissing the hand only, and some the foot also of the Pope. Some received olive branches. Lastly several officers performed the same ceremony.

When this long procession of respect was over, and all the robed multitude had received their festal palms and olives, his Holiness was attended to a chair of state, and, being seated, was lifted up by his bearers, and, preceded by the long official array and by his chaunting choir, he rode out of the chapel.

It was hard to recognize in this ceremony the gentle Son of Man who sat upon an ass amidst the rejoicings of his fickle countrymen. Whether from age or from custom, I knew not, but the Pope's eyes were shut or nearly shut as he rode. After a few minutes he reëntered the chapel in like state, and soon after retired and left the sacred college of cardinals to hear the Passion chaunted by themselves. The chapel is that whose walls Michel Angelo adorned with his Last Judgment. But today I have not seen the picture well.

All this pomp is conventional. It is imposing to those who know the customs of courts, and of what wealth and of what rank these particular forms are the symbols. But to the eye of an Indian I am afraid it would be ridiculous. There is no true majesty in all this millinery and imbecility. . . .

I counted twenty-one cardinals present. Music at St. Peter's in the afternoon, and better still at Chiesa Nuova in the evening. Those mutilated wretches sing so well it is painful to hear them.   [J, III, 81–83]

. . . on the whole I am thankful for Paris, as I am for the discovery of ether and chloroform; I like to know that, if I should need an amputation, there is this balm; and if hard should come to hard, and I should be driven to seek some refuge of solitude and independency, why, here is Paris.
[J, VII, 472–473]

Germany. How impossible to find Germany! Our young men went to the Rhine to find the genius which had charmed them, and it was not there. They hunted it in

Heidelberg, in Göttingen, in Halle, in Berlin; no one knew where it was; from Vienna to the frontier, it was not found, and they very slowly and mournfully learned, that in the speaking it had escaped, and as it had charmed them in Boston, they must return and look for it there.

[J, VII, 532–533]

I find the French all soldiers, all speakers. The *aplomb* which these need, every Frenchman has; every *gamin* a certain trimness or trigness and a certain fancy cut like a dandy boat at a regatta. A certain ingenuity and verbal clearness of statement they require, and that satisfies them that they have a new and lucid and coherent statement, though it is artificial, and not an idea; verbally help, and not really. [J, VII, 452–453]

Life in the East is fierce, short, hazardous, and in extremes. Its elements are few and simple, not exhibiting the long range and undulation of European existence, but rapidly reaching the best and the worst. The rich feed on fruits and game—the poor, on a watermelon's peel. All or nothing is the genius of Oriental life. Favor of the sultan, or his displeasure, is a question of Fate. A war is undertaken for an epigram or a distich, as in Europe for a duchy. The prolific sun and the sudden and rank plenty which his heat engenders, make subsistence easy. On the other side, the desert, the simoon, the mirage, the lion and the plague endanger it, and life hangs on the contingency of a skin of water. [W, VIII, 238]

Chapter Ten

Portraits and Appraisals

*On every side of him, Emerson was a great reader of men.
With a philosophy so strongly personalist, with a central
belief in the importance of great men, and of course a very
strong belief in his own greatness, he also had a keen sense
of human character based on a profoundly individualistic
way of life in which, as in England, eccentricity seemed a
matter of course and in which many strong characters were
admired as types of the Yankee race.*

*But in addition to this, Emerson had a sense of irony,
an awareness of the distance between human pretense and
the actualities of character, such as is to be gained from
spending so much of one's life in churches and with church-
men. Emerson on this subject is deliciously dry. Writing of
his step-grandfather, the famous Dr. Ezra Ripley, he noted
that after praying for rain, the rains had come, and that
when he complimented Dr. Ripley, that great man looked
"modest." There is a downright and frequently down-east
quality about Emerson's portraits and appraisals of others.
He could never take his disciple Thoreau altogether seriously ("I am very familiar with all his thoughts—they are
my own quite originally drest"), he remembered to say that
Alcott (whom he was always praising) was a great man
even "if he cannot write well," and some of his notations
on conventional clergymen of the time sizzle with contempt.*

*These are the marks of a man who knew his own value
and limitations, and who was not easily deceived by others;
who in any portrait of an author, always saw the man; who
was a born artist, and therefore haunted by details, as when
he described Wordsworth striking a pose like a schoolboy's
when he recited his poems to Emerson. Yet, as one sees*

in Emerson's extraordinary portraits of Webster, he had a
particular gift for describing, in Americans, certain national
traits. As a new people, learning how to be a people, Amer-
icans naturally had a special cult of leadership, and their
leaders were often of a special pedantry. They reasoned too
much, for they had no tradition, no emotional foundation,
that they could trust. It is this ponderousness that Emerson
caught so unforgettably in his portraits of Webster. Few
writers in America have ever had such an eye for the local
character as Emerson did. This directness was his tradition,
and his tradition is itself summed up in his feeling for
character. No wonder, when his famous aunt, Mary Moody
Emerson, who helped to bring him up, "had an eye that
went through and through you like a needle."

The head of Washington hangs in my dining-room for a
few days past, and I cannot keep my eyes off of it. It has a
certain Appalachian strength, as if it were truly the first-
fruits of America, and expressed the Country. The heavy,
leaden eyes turn on you, as the eyes of an ox in a pasture.
And the mouth has a gravity and depth of quiet, as if this
MAN had absorbed all the serenity of America, and left
none for his restless, rickety, hysterical countrymen. Noble,
aristocratic head, with all kinds of elevation in it, that come
out by turns. Such majestical ironies, as he hears the day's
politics, at table. We imagine him hearing the letter of
General Cass, the letter of General Scott, the letter of Mr.
Pierce, the effronteries of Mr. Webster recited. This man
listens like a god to these low conspirators.   [J, VIII, 300]

I saw Webster on the street—but he was changed since I
saw him last—black as a thunder-cloud, and careworn; the
anxiety that withers this generation among the young and
thinking class had crept up also into the great lawyer's
chair, and too plainly, too plainly he was one of us. I did
not wonder that he depressed his eyes when he saw me,
and would not meet my face. The cankerworms have
crawled to the topmost bough of the wild elm and swing
down from that. No wonder the elm is a little uneasy.
[J, VI, 91–92]

Webster. Webster is very dear to the Yankees because he is a person of very commanding understanding with every talent for its adequate expression. The American, foreigners say, always reasons, and he is the most American of the Americans. They have no abandonment, but dearly love logic, as all their churches have so long witnessed. His external advantages are very rare and admirable; his noble and majestic frame, his breadth and projection of brows, his coal-black hair, his great cinderous eyes, his perfect self-possession, and the rich and well-modulated thunder of his voice (to which I used to listen, sometimes, abstracting myself from his sense merely for the luxury of such noble explosions of sound) distinguish him above all other men. In a million you would single him out. In England, he made the same impression by his personal advantages as at home, and was called the Great Western. In speech he has a great good sense—is always pertinent to time and place, and has an eye to the simple facts of nature—to the place where he is, to the hour of the day, to the sun in heaven, to his neighborhood, to the sea or to the mountains—but very sparingly notices these things, and clings closely to the business part of his speech with great gravity and faithfulness. "I do not inflame," he said on one occasion, "I do not exaggerate; I avoid all incendiary allusion." He trusts to his simple strength of statement—in which he excels all men—for the attention of his assembly. His statement is lucid throughout, and of equal strength. He has great fairness and deserves all his success in debate, for he always carries a point from his adversary by really taking superior ground, as in the Hayne debate. There are no puerilities, no tricks, no academical play in any of his speeches—they are all majestic men of business. Every one is a first-rate Yankee.

He has had a faithful apprenticeship to his position, for he was born in New Hampshire, a farmer's son, and his youth spent in those hardships and privations which add such edge to every simple pleasure and every liberalizing opportunity. The Almanac does not come unnoticed, but is read and committed to heart by the farmer's boys. And when it was announced to him by his father that he would send him to college he could not speak. The struggles— brothers and sisters in poor men's houses in New England are dear to each other, and the bringing up of a family involves many sacrifices, each for the other.

The faults that shade his character are not such as to hurt his popularity. He is very expensive, and always in debt; but this rather commends him, as he is known to be generous, and his countrymen make for him the apology of Themistocles, that to keep treasure undiminished is the virtue of a chest and not of a man. Then there is in him a large share of good nature and a sort of *bonhomie*. It is sometimes complained of him that he is a man of pleasure, and all his chosen friends are easy epicures and debauchees. But this is after Talleyrand's taste, who said of his foolish wife that he found nonsense very refreshing: so Webster, after he has been pumping his brains in the courts and the Senate, is, no doubt, heartily glad to get among cronies and gossips where he can stretch himself at his ease and drink his mulled wine. They also quote as his *three rules* of living: (1) Never to pay any debt that can by any possibility be avoided; (2) Never to do anything today that can be put off till tomorrow; (3) Never to do anything himself which he can get anybody else to do for him.

All is forgiven to a man of such surpassing intellect, and such prodigious powers of business which have so long been exerted. There is no malice in the man, but broad good humor and much enjoyment of the hour; so that Stetson said of him, "It is true that he sometimes commits crimes, but without any guilt."

A great man is always entitled to the most liberal interpretation, and the few anecdotes by which his opponents have most deeply stabbed at his reputation admit of explanation. I cannot but think, however, that his speech at Richmond was made to bear a meaning by his Southern backers which he did not intend, and I have never forgiven him that he did not say, Not so fast, good friends, I did not mean what you say.

He has misused the opportunity of making himself the darling of the American world in all coming time by abstaining from putting himself at the head of the Anti-slavery interest, by standing for New England and for man against the bullying and barbarism of the South.

I should say of him that he was not at all majestic, but the purest intellect that was ever applied to business. He is Intellect applied to affairs. He is the greatest of lawyers; but a very indifferent statesman for carrying his points. He carries points with the bench, but not with the caucus. No following has he, no troop of friends, but those whose intellect he fires. No sweaty mob will carry him on their shoulders. And yet all New England to the remotest farmhouse, or lumberers' camp in the woods of Maine, delights to tell and hear of anecdotes of his forensic eloquence. What he said at Salem, at the Knapp trial; and how in Boston he looked a witness out of court—once, he set his great eyes on him, and searched him through and through; then as the cause went on, and this prisoner's perjury was not yet called for, he looked round on him as if to see if he was safe and ready for the inquisition he was preparing to inflict on him. The witness felt for his hat, and edged towards the door; a third time he looked on him, and the witness could sit no longer, but seized his opportunity, fled out of court, and could nowhere be found, such was the terror of those eyes.   [J, VI, 341–346]

It seems to me the Quixotism of Criticism to quarrel with Webster because he has not this or that fine evangelical property. He is no saint, but the wild olive wood, ungrafted yet by grace, but according to his lights a very true and admirable man. His expensiveness seems to be necessary to him. Were he too prudent a Yankee it would be a sad deduction from his magnificence. I only wish he would never truckle; I do not care how much he spends.

[J, VI, 434]

There was Webster, the great cannon loaded to the lips: he told Cheney that if he should close by addressing the jury, he should blow the roof off. As it was, he did nothing but pound. Choate put in the nail and drove it; Webster came after and pounded. The natural grandeur of his face and manners always satisfies; easily great; there is no strut in his voice or behavior, as in the others. Yet he is all wasted; he seems like a great actor who is not supported on the boards; and Webster, like the actor, ought to go to London. Ah! if God had given to this Demosthenes a heart to lead New England, what a life and death and glory for him. Now he is a fine symbol and mantel ornament—costly enough to those who must keep it; for the great head aches, and the great trunk must be curiously fed and comforted.

[J, VII, 87–88]

Webster is a man by himself of the great mould, but he also underlies the American blight, and wants the power of the initiative, the affirmative talent, and remains, like the literary class, only a commentator, his great proportions only exposing his defect. America seems to have immense resources, land, men, milk, butter, cheese, timber, and iron, but it is a village littleness—village squabble and rapacity characterize its policy. It is a great strength on a basis of weakness.   [J, VII, 218]

I cannot tell you how glad I am that you have seen my brave Senator [Charles Sumner], and seen him as I see him. All my days I have wished that he should go to England, and never more than when I listened two or three times to debates in the House of Commons. We send out usually mean persons as public agents, mere partisans, for whom I can only hope that no man with eyes will meet them; and now those thirsty eyes, those portrait-eating, portrait-painting eyes of thine, those fatal perceptions, have fallen full on the great forehead which I followed about all my young days, from court-house to senate-chamber, from caucus to street. He has his own sins no doubt, is no saint, is a prodigal. He has drunk this rum of Party too so long, that his strong head is soaked, sometimes even like the soft sponges, but the "man's a man for a' that." Better, he is a great boy—as wilful, as nonchalant and good-humored. But you must hear him speak, not a show speech which he never does well, but *with cause* he can strike a stroke like a smith. I owe to him a hundred fine hours and two or three moments of Eloquence. His voice in a great house is admirable. I am sorry if you decided not to visit him. He loves a *man*, too. [E–C, I, 255–256]

You cannot refine Mr. Lincoln's taste, extend his horizon, or clear his judgment; he will not walk dignifiedly through the traditional part of the President of America, but will pop out his head at each railroad station and make a little speech, and get into an argument with Squire A. and Judge B. He will write letters to Horace Greeley, and any editor or reporter or saucy party committee that writes to him, and cheapen himself.

But this we must be ready for, and let the clown appear, and hug ourselves that we are well off, if we have got good nature, honest meaning, and fidelity to public interest, with bad manners—instead of an elegant *roué* and malignant self-seeker. [J, IX, 557]

I shall go far, and see many, before I find such an extraordinary insight as Alcott's. In his fine talk, last evening, he ran up and down the scale of powers, with as much ease and precision as a squirrel the wires of his cage, and is never dazzled by his means, or by any particular, and a fine heroic action or a poetic passage would make no impression on him, because he expects heroism and poetry in all. Ideal Purity, the poet, the artist, the man, must have. I have never seen any person who so fortifies the believer, so confutes the skeptic. And the almost uniform rejection of this man by men of parts, Carlyle and Browning inclusive, and by women of piety, might make one despair of society. If he came with a cannonade of acclaim from all nations, as the first wit on the planet, these masters would sustain the reputation: or if they could find him in a book a thousand years old, with a legend of miracles appended, there would be churches of disciples: but now they wish to know if his coat is out at the elbow, or whether somebody did not hear from somebody, that he had got a new hat, etc., etc. He has faults, no doubt, but I may safely know no more about them than he does; and some that are most severely imputed to him are only the omissions of a preoccupied mind. [J, IX, 38–39]

Mr. Alcott has been here with his Olympian dreams. He is a world-builder. Evermore he toils to solve the problem, whence is the world? The point at which he prefers to begin is the mystery of the Birth of a child. I tell him it is idle for him to affect to feel an interest in the compositions of anyone else. Particulars—particular thoughts, sentences, facts even—cannot interest him, except as for a moment they take their place as a ray from his orb. The Whole—Nature proceeding from himself—is what he studies. But he loses, like other sovereigns, great pleasures by reason of his grandeur. I go to Shakespeare, Goethe, Swift, even to Tennyson, submit myself to them, become merely an organ of hearing, and yield to the law of their being. I am paid for thus being nothing by an entire new mind, and thus, a Proteus, I enjoy the universe through the powers and organs of a hundred different men. But Alcott cannot delight in Shakespeare, cannot get near him. And so with all things. What is characteristic also, he cannot recall one word or part of his own conversation or of anyone's, let the expression be never so happy. He made here some majestic utterances, but so inspired me that even I forgot the words often.   [J, IV, 71–72]

A Bronson Alcott, who is a great man if he cannot write well, has come to Concord with his wife and three children and taken a cottage and an acre of ground to get his living by the help of God and his own spade. I see that some of the Education people in England have a school called "Alcott House" after my friend. At home here he is despised and rejected of men as much as was ever Pestalozzi. But the creature thinks and talks, and I am glad and proud of my neighbor.   [E–C, I, 285–286]

Bryant has learned where to hang his titles, namely, by tying his mind to autumn woods, winter mornings, rain, brooks, mountains, evening winds, and wood-birds. Who speaks of these is forced to remember Bryant. [He is] American. Never despaired of the Republic. Dared name a jay and a gentian, crows also. His poetry is sincere. I think of the young poets that they have seen pictures of moun-

tains, and sea-shores, but in his that he has seen mountains and has the staff in his hand.   [J, X, 76–77]

"True bard, but simple," I fear he has not escaped the
infirmity of fame, like the presidential malady, a virus once
in, not to be got out of the system: he has this, so cold and
majestic as he sits there—has this to a heat which has
brought to him the devotion of all the young men and
women who love poetry, and of all the old men and
women who once were young. 'Tis a perfect tyranny. Talk
of the shopmen who advertise their drugs or cosmetics on
the walls and on the palisades and huge rocks along the
railways—why, this man, more cunning by far, has contrived to levy on all American Nature and subsidized every
solitary forest and Monument Mountain in Berkshire or
the Katskills, every waterfowl, every partridge, every gentian and goldenrod, the prairies, the gardens of the desert,
the song of the stars, the Evening Wind—has bribed every
one of these to speak for him, so that there is scarcely a
feature of day and night in the country which does not—
whether we will or not—recall the name of Bryant. This
high-handed usurpation I charge him with, and on the top
of this, with persuading us and all mankind to hug our
fetters and rejoice in our subjugation.   [J, X, 81–82]

Dr. Charles Chauncy was, a hundred years ago, a man of
marked ability among the clergy of New England. But when
once going to preach the Thursday lecture in Boston (which
in those days people walked from Salem to hear), on going
up the pulpit-stairs he was informed that a little boy had
fallen into Frog Pond on the Common and was drowned,
and the doctor was requested to improve the sad occasion.
The doctor was much distressed, and in his prayer he hes-
itated, he tried to make soft approaches, he prayed for
Harvard College, he prayed for the schools, he implored
the Divine Being "to—to—to bless to them all the boy that
was this morning drowned in Frog Pond." Now this is not
want of talent or learning, but of manliness. The doctor,
no doubt, shut up in his closet and his theology, had lost
some natural relation to men, and quick application of his

thought to the course of events. I should add what is told of him—that he so disliked the "sensation" preaching of his time, that he had once prayed that "he might never be eloquent"; and, it appears, his prayer was granted.
[W, VIII, 127–128]

My aunt [Mary Moody Emerson] had an eye that went through and through you like a needle. "She was endowed," she said, "with the fatal gift of penetration." She disgusted everybody because she knew them too well.   [J, II, 525]

Elizabeth Peabody brought me yesterday Hawthorne's *Footprints on the Seashore* to read. I complained that there was no inside to it. Alcott and he together would make a man.   [J, IV, 479]

Nathaniel Hawthorne's reputation as a writer is a very pleasing fact, because his writing is not good for anything, and this is a tribute to the man.   [J, VI, 240]

Yesterday, May 23 [1864], we buried Hawthorne in Sleepy Hollow, in a pomp of sunshine and verdure, and gentle winds. James Freeman Clarke read the service in the church and at the grave. Longfellow, Lowell, Holmes, Agassiz, Hoar, Dwight, Whipple, Norton, Alcott, Hillard, Fields, Judge Thomas, and I attended the hearse as pall-bearers. Franklin Pierce was with the family. The church was copiously decorated with white flowers delicately arranged. The corpse was unwillingly shown—only a few moments to this company of his friends. But it was noble and serene in its aspect—nothing amiss—a calm and powerful head. A large company filled the church and the grounds of the cemetery. All was so bright and quiet that pain or mourning was hardly suggested, and Holmes said to me that it looked like a happy meeting.
Clarke in the church said that Hawthorne had done more justice than any other to the shades of life, shown a sympathy with the crime in our nature, and, like Jesus, was the friend of sinners.
I thought there was a tragic element in the event, that might be more fully rendered—in the painful solitude of

the man, which, I suppose, could not longer be endured, and he died of it.

I have found in his death a surprise and disappointment. I thought him a greater man than any of his works betray, that there was still a great deal of work in him, and that he might one day show a purer power. Moreover, I have felt sure of him in his neighborhood, and in his necessities of sympathy and intelligence—that I could well wait his time—his unwillingness and caprice—and might one day conquer a friendship. It would have been a happiness, doubtless to both of us, to have come into habits of unreserved intercourse. It was easy to talk with him—there were no barriers—only, he said so little, that I talked too much, and stopped only because, as he gave no indications, I feared to exceed. He showed no egotism or self-assertion, rather a humility, and, at one time, a fear that he had written himself out. One day, when I found him on the top of his hill, in the woods, he paced back the path to his house, and said, "This path is the only remembrance of me that will remain." Now it appears that I waited too long. Lately he had removed himself the more by the indignation his perverse politics and unfortunate friendship for that paltry Franklin Pierce awakened, though it rather moved pity for Hawthorne, and the assured belief that he would outlive it, and come right at last.   [J, X, 39–41]

Dr. Ripley prays for rain with great explicitness on Sunday, and on Monday the showers fell. When I spoke of the speed with which his prayers were answered, the good man looked modest. [J, V, 18]

Dr. Ripley died this morning. The fall of this oak of ninety years makes some sensation in the forest, old and doomed as it was. He has identified himself with the forms at least of the old church of the New England Puritans, his nature was eminently loyal, not in the least adventurous or democratical; and his whole being leaned backward on the departed, so that he seemed one of the rear-guard of this great camp and army which have filled the world with fame, and with him passes out of sight almost the last banner and guidon flag of a mighty epoch. For these Puritans, however in our last days they have declined into ritualists, solemnized the hey-day of their strength by the planting and the liberating of America.

Great, grim, earnest men, I belong by natural affinity to other thoughts and schools than yours, but my affection hovers respectfully about your retiring footprints, your unpainted churches, strict platforms, and sad offices; the iron-gray deacon and the wearisome prayer rich with the diction of ages.

Well, the new is only the seed of the old. What is this abolition and non-resistance and temperance but the continuation of Puritanism, though it operate inevitably the destruction of the church in which it grew, as the new is always making the old superfluous? . . . [J, VI, 52–53]

He [Ezra Ripley] was identified with the ideas and forms of the New England Church, which expired about the same time with him, so that he and his coevals seemed the rear guard of the great camp and army of the Puritans, which, however, in its last days declining into formalism, in the heyday of its strength had planted and liberated America. It was a pity that his old meeting-house should have been modernized in his time. I am sure all who remember both will associate his form with whatever was grave and droll in the old, cold, unpainted, uncarpeted, square-pewed meeting-house, with its four iron-gray deacons in their little box under the pulpit—with Watts's hymns, with long prayers, rich with the diction of ages; and not less with the report like musketry from the movable seats. He and his contemporaries, the old New England clergy, were believers in what is called a particular providence—certainly, as they held it, a very particular providence—following the narrowness of King David and the Jews, who thought the universe existed only or mainly for their church and congregation. . . .

He used to tell the story of one of his old friends, the minister of Sudbury, who, being at the Thursday lecture in Boston, heard the officiating clergyman praying for rain. As soon as the service was over, he went to the petitioner, and said, "You Boston ministers, as soon as a tulip wilts under your windows, go to church and pray for rain, until all Concord and Sudbury are under water." . . .

His partiality for ladies was always strong, and was by no means abated by time. He claimed privilege of years, was much addicted to kissing; spared neither maid, wife nor widow, and, as a lady thus favored remarked to me, "seemed as if he was going to make a meal of you." . . .

He had a foresight, when he opened his mouth, of all that he would say, and he marched straight to the conclusion. In debate, in the the vestry of the Lyceum, the structure of his sentences was admirable; so neat, so natural, so terse, his words fell like stones; and often, though quite unconscious of it, his speech was a satire on the loose, voluminous, draggle-tail periods of other speakers. He sat down when he had done. A man of anecdote, his talk in the parlor was chiefly narrative. We remember the remark of a gentleman who listened with much delight to his conversation at the time when the Doctor was preparing to go to Baltimore and Washington, that "a man who could tell a story so well was company for kings and John Quincy Adams." . . .

With a very limited acquaintance with books, his knowledge was an external experience, an Indian wisdom, the observation of such facts as country life for nearly a century could supply. He watched with interest the garden, the field, the orchard, the house and the barn, horse, cow, sheep and dog, and all the common objects that engage the thought of the farmer. He kept his eye on the horizon, and knew the weather like a sea-captain. The usual experiences of men, birth, marriage, sickness, death, burial; the common temptations; the common ambitions—he studied them all, and sympathized so well in these that he was excellent company and counsel to all, even the most humble and ignorant. With extraordinary states of mind, with states of enthusiasm or enlarged speculation, he had no sympathy, and pretended to none. He was sincere, and kept to his point, and his mark was never remote. His conversation was strictly personal and apt to the party and the occasion. An eminent skill he had in saying difficult and unspeakable things; in delivering to a man or a woman that which all their other friends had abstained from saying, in uncovering the bandage from a sore place, and applying the surgeon's knife with a truly surgical spirit. Was a man a sot, or a spendthrift, or too long time a bachelor, or suspected of some hidden crime, or had he quarrelled with his wife, or collared his father, or was there any cloud or suspicious circumstances in his behavior, the good pastor knew his way straight to that point, believing himself entitled to a full explanation, and whatever relief was to the conscience of both parties plain speech could effect was sure to be procured.

[W, X, 383–394]

I told Henry Thoreau that his freedom is in the form, but he does not disclose new matter. I am very familiar with all his thoughts—they are my own quite originally drest. But if the question be, what new ideas has he thrown into circulation, he has not yet told what that is which he was created to say. I said to him what I often feel, I only know three persons who seem to me fully to see this law of reciprocity or compensation—himself, Alcott, and myself: and 'tis odd that we should all be neighbors, for in the wide land or the wide earth I do not know another who seems to have it as deeply and originally as these three Gothamites.

[J, VI, 74]

Henry Thoreau sends me a paper with the old fault of unlimited contradiction. The trick of his rhetoric is soon learned: it consists in substituting for the obvious word and thought its diametrical antagonist. He praises wild mountains and winter forests for their domestic air; snow and ice for their warmth; villages and wood-choppers for their urbanity, and the wilderness for resembling Rome and Paris. With the constant inclination to dispraise cities and civilization, he yet can find no way to know woods and woodsmen except by paralleling them with towns and townsmen. Channing declared the piece is excellent: but it makes me nervous and wretched to read it, with all its merits.

[J, VI, 440–441]

Henry Thoreau's conversation consisted of a continual coining of the present moment into a sentence and offering it to me. I compared it to a boy, who, from the universal snow lying on the earth, gathers up a little in his hand, rolls it into a ball, and flings it at me. [J, VI, 515]

Water is the first gardener: he always plants grasses and flowers about his dwelling. There came Henry with music-book under his arm, to press flowers in; with telescope in his pocket, to see the birds, and microscope to count stamens; with a diary, jack-knife, and twine; in stout shoes, and strong grey trousers, ready to brave the shrub-oaks and smilax, and to climb the tree for a hawk's nest. His strong legs, when he wades, were no insignificant part of his armor. Two alders we have, and one of them is here on the northern border of its habitat. [J, IX, 45]

Henry Thoreau remains erect, calm, self-subsistent, before me, and I read him not only truly in his Journal, but he is not long out of mind when I walk, and, as today, row upon the pond. He chose wisely no doubt for himself to be the bachelor of thought and nature that he was—how near to the old monks in their ascetic religion! He had no talent for wealth, and knew how to be poor without the least hint of squalor or inelegance. Perhaps he fell—all of us do—into his way of living, without forecasting it much, but approved and confirmed it with later wisdom. [J, IX, 425]

If there is a little strut in the style of Henry, it is only from a vigor in excess of the size of his body. [J, IX, 427]

He [Thoreau] was a born protestant. He declined to give up his large ambition of knowledge and action for any narrow craft or profession, aiming at a much more comprehensive calling, the art of living well. If he slighted and defied the opinions of others, it was only that he was more intent to reconcile his practice with his own belief. Never idle or self-indulgent, he preferred, when he wanted money, earning it by some piece of manual labor agreeable to him, as building a boat or a fence, planting, grafting, surveying, or other short work, to any long engagements. With his hardy habits and few wants, his skill in woodcraft, and his powerful arithmetic, he was very competent to live in any part of the world. It would cost him less time to supply his wants than another. He was therefore secure of his leisure. . . .

He interrogated every custom, and wished to settle all his practice on an ideal foundation. He was a protestant *à outrance,* and few lives contain so many renunciations. He was bred to no profession; he never married; he lived alone; he never went to church; he never voted; he refused to pay a tax to the State; he ate no flesh, he drank no wine, he never knew the use of tobacco; and, though a naturalist, he used neither trap nor gun. He chose, wisely no doubt for himself, to be the bachelor of thought and Nature. He had no talent for wealth, and knew how to be poor without the least hint of squalor or inelegance. Perhaps he fell into his way of living without forecasting it much, but approved it with later wisdom. "I am often reminded," he wrote in his journal, "that if I had bestowed on me the wealth of Crœsus, my aims must be still the same, and my means essentially the same." He had no temptations to fight against—no appetites, no passions, no taste for elegant trifles. A fine house, dress, the manners and talk of highly cultivated people were all thrown away on him. He much preferred a good Indian, and considered these refinements as impediments to conversation, wishing to meet his companion on the simplest terms. He declined invitations to dinner-parties, because there each was in everyone's way, and he could not meet the individuals to any purpose. "They make their pride," he said, "in making their dinner cost much; I make my pride in making my dinner cost little." When asked at table what dish he preferred, he answered, "The nearest." He did not like the taste of wine, and never had a vice in his life. He said, "I have a faint recollection of pleasure derived from smoking dried lily-stems, before I was a man. I had commonly a supply of these. I have never smoked anything more noxious."

He chose to be rich by making his wants few, and supplying them himself. In his travels, he used to railroad only to get over so much country as was unimportant to the present purpose, walking hundreds of miles, avoiding taverns, buying a lodging in farmers' and fishermen's houses, as cheaper, and more agreeable to him, and because there he could better find the men and the information he wanted.

There was somewhat military in his nature, not to be subdued, always manly and able, but rarely tender, as if he did not feel himself except in opposition. He wanted a fallacy to expose, a blunder to pillory, I may say required a little sense of victory, a roll of the drum, to call his powers into full exercise. It cost him nothing to say No; indeed he found it much easier than to say Yes. It seemed as if his first instinct on hearing a proposition was to controvert it, so impatient was he of the limitations of our daily thought. This habit, of course, is a little chilling to the social affections; and though the companion would in the end acquit him of any malice or untruth, yet it mars conversation. Hence, no equal companion stood in affectionate relations with one so pure and guileless. "I love Henry," said one of his friends, "but I cannot like him; and as for taking his arm, I should as soon think of taking the arm of an elm tree."

Yet, hermit and stoic as he was, he was really fond of sympathy, and threw himself heartily and childlike into the company of young people whom he loved, and whom he delighted to entertain, as he only could, with the varied and endless anecdotes of his experiences by field and river: and he was always ready to lead a huckleberry-party or a search for chestnuts or grapes. Talking, one day, of a public discourse, Henry remarked, that whatever succeeded with the audience was bad. I said, "Who would not like to write something which all can read, like Robinson Crusoe? and who does not see with regret that his page is not solid with a right materialistic treatment, which delights everybody?" Henry objected, of course, and vaunted the better lectures which reached only a few persons. But, at supper, a young girl, understanding that he was to lecture at the Lyceum, sharply asked him, whether his lecture would be a nice, interesting story, such as she wished to hear, or whether it was one of those old philosophical things that she did not care about. Henry turned to her, and bethought himself, and, I saw, was trying to believe that he had matter that might fit her and her brother, who were to sit up and go to the lecture, if it was a good one for them.

He was a speaker and actor of the truth, born such, and was ever running into dramatic situations from this cause. In any circumstance it interested all by-standers to know what part Henry would take, and what he would say; and he did not disappoint expectation, but used an original judgment on each emergency. In 1845 he built himself a small framed house on the shores of Walden Pond, and lived there two years alone, a life of labor and study. This action was quite native and fit for him. No one who knew him would tax him with affectation. He was more unlike his neighbors in his thought than in his action. As soon as he had exhausted the advantages of that solitude, he abandoned it. In 1847, not approving some uses to which the public expenditure was applied, he refused to pay his town tax, and was put in jail. A friend paid the tax for him, and he was released. The like annoyance was threatened the next year. But, as his friends paid the tax, notwithstanding his protest, I believe he ceased to resist. No opposition or ridicule had any weight with him. He coldly and fully stated his opinion without affecting to believe that it was the opinion of the company. It was of no consequence if everyone present held the opposite opinion. . . .

He said he wanted every stride his legs made. The length of his walk uniformly made the length of his writing. If shut up in the house he did not write at all. . . .

His robust common sense, armed with stout hands, keen perceptions and strong will, cannot yet account for the superiority which shone in his simple and hidden life. I must add the cardinal fact, that there was an excellent wisdom in him, proper to a rare class of men, which showed him the material world as a means and symbol. This discovery, which sometimes yields to poets a certain casual and interrupted light, serving for the ornament of their writing, was in him an unsleeping insight; and whatever faults or obstructions of temperament might cloud it, he was not disobedient to the heavenly vision: In his youth, he said, one day, "The other world is all my art; my pencils will draw no other; my jack-knife will cut nothing else; I do not use it as a means." . . .

He understood the matter in hand at a glance, and saw

the limitations and poverty of those he talked with, so that nothing seemed concealed from such terrible eyes. I have repeatedly known young men of sensibility converted in a moment to the belief that this was the man they were in search of, the man of men, who could tell them all they should do. His own dealing with them was never affectionate, but superior, didactic, scorning their petty ways—very slowly conceding, or not conceding at all, the promise of his society at their houses, or even at his own. "Would he not walk with them?" "He did not know. There was nothing so important to him as his walk; he had no walks to throw away on company." . . .

He saw as with microscope, heard as with ear-trumpet, and his memory was a photographic register of all he saw and heard. And yet none knew better than he that it is not the fact that imports, but the impression or effect of the fact on your mind. Every fact lay in glory in his mind, a type of the order and beauty of the whole. . . .

His virtues, of course, sometimes ran into extremes. It was easy to trace the inexorable demand on all for exact truth that austerity which made this willing hermit more solitary even than he wished. Himself of a perfect probity, he required not less of others. He had a disgust at crime, and no worldly success would cover it. He detected paltering as readily in dignified and prosperous persons as in beggars, and with equal scorn. Such dangerous frankness was in his dealing that his admirers called him "that terrible Thoreau," as if he spoke when silent, and was still present when he had departed. I think the severity of his ideal interfered to deprive him of a healthy sufficiency of human society. . . .

Had his genius been only contemplative, he had been fitted to his life, but with his energy and practical ability he seemed born for great enterprise and for command; and I so much regret the loss of his rare powers of action, that I cannot help counting it a fault in him that he had no ambition. Wanting this, instead of engineering for all America, he was the captain of a huckleberry-party. Pounding beans is good to the end of pounding empires one of these days; but if, at the end of years, it is still only beans! . . .

He had many elegancies of his own, whilst he scoffed at conventional elegance. Thus, he could not bear to hear the sound of his own steps, the grit of gravel; and therefore never willingly walked in the road, but in the grass, on mountains and in woods. His senses were acute, and he remarked that by night every dwelling-house gives out bad air, like a slaughter-house. He liked the pure fragrance of melilot. He honored certain plants with special regard, and, over all, the pond-lily; then, the gentian, and the *Mikania scandens,* and "life-everlasting," and a bass-tree which he visited every year when it bloomed, in the middle of July. He thought the scent a more oracular inquisition than the sight—more oracular and trustworthy. The scent, of course, reveals what is concealed from the other senses. By it he detected earthiness. He delighted in echoes, and said they were almost the only kind of kindred voices that he heard. He loved Nature so well, was so happy in her solitude, that he became very jealous of cities and the sad work which their refinements and artifices made with man and his dwelling. The ax was always destroying his forest. "Thank God," he said, "they cannot cut down the clouds!" . . .

The scale on which his studies proceeded was so large as to require longevity, and we were the less prepared for his sudden disappearance. The country knows not yet, or in the least part, how great a son it has lost. It seems an injury that he should leave in the midst his broken task which none else can finish, a kind of indignity to so noble a soul that he should depart out of Nature before yet he has been really shown to his peers for what he is. But he, at least, is content. His soul was made for the noblest society; he had in a short life exhausted the capabilities of this world; wherever there is knowledge, wherever there is virtue, wherever there is beauty, he will find a home.   [W, X, 452–485, *passim*]

One book, last summer, came out in New York, a nondescript monster which yet had terrible eyes and buffalo strength, and was indisputably American—which I thought to send you; but the book throve so badly with the few to whom I showed it, and wanted good morals so much, that I never did. Yet I believe now àgain, I shall. It is called

Leaves of Grass—was written and printed by a journeyman printer in Brooklyn, New York, named Walter Whitman; and after you have looked into it, if you think, as you may, that it is only an auctioneer's inventory of a warehouse, you can light your pipe with it.   [E–C, II, 251]

Emerson turns his attention from Americans to Europeans, those with whom he conversed or those whose writings confirmed what he already instinctively knew to be true. He visits Carlyle, Coleridge, Landor and Wordsworth, and pays tribute to some of his "representative" men.

[*To Thomas Carlyle*]   I thought as I read this piece [*The Diamond Necklace*] that your strange genius was the instant fruit of your London. It is the aroma of Babylon. Such as the great metropolis, such is this style: so vast, enormous, related to all the world, and so endless in details. I think you see as pictures every street, church, parliament-house, barrack, baker's shop, mutton-stall, forge, wharf, and ship, and whatever stands, creeps, rolls, or swims thereabouts, and make all your own. Hence your encyclopediacal allusion to all knowables, and the virtues and vices of your panoramic pages. Well, it is your own; and it is English; and every word stands for somewhat; and it cheers and fortifies me. And what more can a man ask of his writing fellow-man? Why, all things; inasmuch as a good mind creates wants at every stroke.   [E–C, I, 119]

From Edinburgh I went to the Highlands. On my return I came from Glasgow to Dumfries, and being intent on delivering a letter which I had brought from Rome, inquired for Craigenputtock. It was a farm in Nithsdale, in the parish of Dunscore, sixteen miles distant. No public coach passed near it, so I took a private carriage from the inn. I found the house amid desolate heathery hills, where the lonely scholar nourished his mighty heart. Carlyle was a man from his youth, an author who did not need to hide from his readers, and as absolute a man of the world, unknown and exiled on that hill-farm, as if holding on his own terms what

is best in London. He was tall and gaunt, with a cliff-like
brow, self-possessed and holding his extraordinary powers
of conversation in easy command; clinging to his northern
accent with evident relish; full of lively anecdote and with
a streaming humor which floated everything he looked upon.
His talk playfully exalting the familiar objects, put the
companion at once into an acquaintance with his Lars and
Lemurs, and it was very pleasant to learn what was predes-
tined to be a pretty mythology. Few were the objects and
lonely the man; "not a person to speak to within sixteen
miles except the minister of Dunscore"; so that books inevitably made his topics.

He had names of his own for all the matters familiar to
his discourse. Blackwood's was the "sand magazine"; Fra-
ser's nearer approach to possibility of life was the "mud
magazine"; a piece of road near by, that marked some
failed enterprise, was the "grave of the last sixpence." When
too much praise of any genius annoyed him he professed
hugely to admire the talent shown by his pig. He had spent
much time and contrivance in confining the poor beast to
one enclosure in his pen, but pig, by great strokes of judgment, had found out how to let a board down, and had
foiled him. For all that he still thought man the most plastic
little fellow in the planet, and he liked Nero's death, *"Qualis
artifex pereo!"* better than most history. He worships a
man that will manifest any truth to him. At one time he had
inquired and read a good deal about America. Landor's
principle was mere rebellion; and *that* he feared was the
American principle. The best thing he knew of that country
was that in it a man can have meat for his labor. He had
read in Stewart's book that when he inquired in a New York
hotel for the Boots, he had been shown across the street and
had found Mungo in his own house dining on roast turkey.

We talked of books. Plato he does not read, and he disparaged Socrates; and, when pressed, persisted in making
Mirabeau a hero. Gibbon he called the "splendid bridge
from the old world to the new." His own reading had been
multifarious. Tristram Shandy was one of his first books
after Robinson Crusoe, and Robertson's America an early
favorite. Rousseau's Confessions had discovered to him

that he was not a dunce; and it was now ten years since he had learned German, by the advice of a man who told him he would find in that language what he wanted.

He took despairing or satirical views of literature at this moment; recounted the incredible sums paid in one year by the great booksellers for puffing. Hence it comes that no newspaper is trusted now, no books are bought, and the booksellers are on the eve of bankruptcy.

He still returned to English pauperism, the crowded country, the selfish abdication by public men of all that public persons should perform. Government should direct poor men what to do. Poor Irish folk come wandering over these moors. My dame makes it a rule to give to every son of Adam bread to eat, and supplies his wants to the next house. But here are thousands of acres which might give them all meat, and nobody to bid these poor Irish go to the moor and till it. They burned the stacks and so found a way to force the rich people to attend to them.

We went out to walk over long hills, and looked at Criffel, then without his cap, and down into Wordsworth's country. There we sat down and talked of the immortality of the soul. It was not Carlyle's fault that we talked on that topic, for he had the natural disinclination of every nimble spirit to bruise itself against walls, and did not like to place himself where no step can be taken. But he was honest and true, and cognizant of the subtile links that bind ages together, and saw how every event affects all the future. "Christ died on the tree; that built Dunscore kirk yonder; that brought you and me together. Time has only a relative existence."

He was already turning his eyes towards London with a scholar's appreciation. London is the heart of the world, he said, wonderful only from the mass of human beings. He liked the huge machine. Each keeps its own round. The baker's boy brings muffins to the window at a fixed hour every day, and that is all the Londoner knows or wishes to know on the subject. But it turned out good men. He named certain individuals, especially one man of letters, his friend, the best mind he knew, whom London had well served.

[W, V, 14–19]

I called him [Carlyle] a trip-hammer with "an Æolian attachment." He has, too, the strong religious tinge you sometimes find in burly people. That, and all his qualities, have a certain virulence, coupled though it be in his case with the utmost impatience of Christendom and Jewdom and all existing presentments of the good old story. He talks like a very unhappy man—profoundly solitary, displeased and hindered by all men and things about him, and, biding his time, meditating how to undermine and explode the whole world of nonsense which torments him.

[W, X, 489–490]

Nothing is useless. A superstition is a hamper or basket to carry useful lessons in.

I told Miss Peabody last night that Mr. Coleridge's churchmanship is thought to affect the value of his criticism, etc. I do not feel it. It is a harmless freak and sometimes occurs in a wrong place, as when he refuses to translate some alleged blasphemy in Wallenstein. Some men are affected with hemorrhage of the nose; it is of no danger, but unlucky when it befalls where it should not, as at a wedding or in the rostrum. But Coleridge's is perfectly separable. I know no such critic. Every opinion he expresses is a canon of criticism that should be writ in steel, and his italics are italics of the mind.   [J, IV, 152–153]

From London, on the 5th August [1833], I went to Highgate, and wrote a note to Mr. Coleridge, requesting leave to pay my respects to him. It was near noon. Mr. Coleridge sent a verbal message that he was in bed, but if I would call after one o'clock he would see me. I returned at one, and he appeared, a short, thick old man, with bright blue eyes and fine clear complexion, leaning on his cane. He took snuff freely, which presently soiled his cravat and neat black suit. He asked whether I knew Allston, and spoke warmly of his merits and doings when he knew him in Rome; what a master of the Titianesque he was, etc., etc. He spoke of Dr. Channing. It was an unspeakable misfortune that he should have turned out a Unitarian after all. On this he burst into a declamation on the folly and ignorance of Unitarian-

ism—its high unreasonableness; and taking up Bishop
Waterland's book, which lay on the table, he read with
vehemence two or three pages written by himself in the fly-
leaves—passages, too, which, I believe, are printed in the
Aids to Reflection. When he stopped to take breath, I interposed that "whilst I highly valued all his explanations, I was
bound to tell him that I was born and bred a Unitarian."
"Yes," he said, "I supposed so"; and continued as before.
It was a wonder that after so many ages of unquestioning
acquiescence in the doctrine of St. Paul—the doctrine of
the Trinity, which was also according to Philo Judæus the
doctrine of the Jews before Christ—this handful of Priest-
leians should take on themselves to deny it, etc., etc. He was
very sorry that Dr. Channing, a man to whom he looked up
—no, to say that he looked *up* to him would be to speak
falsely, but a man whom he looked *at* with so much interest—should embrace such views. When he saw Dr. Channing he had hinted to him that he was afraid he loved Christianity for what was lovely and excellent—he loved the good
in it, and not the true—"And I tell you, sir, that I have
known ten persons who loved the good, for one person who
loved the true; but it is a far greater virtue to love the true
for itself alone, than to love the good for itself alone." He
(Coleridge) knew all about Unitarianism perfectly well,
because he had once been a Unitarian and knew what
quackery it was. He had been called "the rising star of Unitarianism." He went on defining, or rather refining: "The
Trinitarian doctrine was realism; the idea of God was not
essential, but super-essential"; talked of *trinism* and *tetra-
kism* and much more, of which I only caught this, "that the
will was that by which a person is a person; because, if one
should push me in the street, and so I should force the man
next me into the kennel, I should at once exclaim, I did
not do it, sir, meaning it was not my will." And this also,
that "if you should insist on your faith here in England, and
I on mine, mine would be the hotter side of the fagot." . . .

I took advantage of a pause to say that he had many
readers of all religious opinion in America, and I proceeded
to inquire if the "extract" from the Independent's pamphlet,
in the third volume of the Friend, were a veritable quota-

tion. He replied that it was really taken from a pamphlet in
his possession entitled "A Protest of one of the Independ-
ents," or something to that effect. I told him how excellent
I thought it and how much I wished to see the entire work.
"Yes," he said, "the man was a chaos of truths, but lacked
the knowledge that God was a God of order. Yet the passage would no doubt strike you more in the quotation than
in the original, for I have filtered it."

When I rose to go, he said, "I do not know whether you
care about poetry, but I will repeat some verses I lately
made on my baptismal anniversary," and he recited with
strong emphasis, standing, ten or twelve lines beginning—

"Born unto God in Christ—"

He inquired where I had been travelling; and on learning
that I had been in Malta and Sicily, he compared one island
with the other, repeating what he had said to the Bishop of
London when he returned from that country, that Sicily was
an excellent school of political economy; for, in any town
there, it only needed to ask what the government enacted,
and reverse that, to know what ought to be done; it was the
most felicitously opposite legislation to anything good and
wise. There were only three things which the government
had brought into that garden of delights, namely, itch, pox
and famine. Whereas in Malta, the force of law and mind
was seen, in making that barren rock of semi-Saracen inhabitants the seat of population and plenty. Going out, he
showed me in the next apartment a picture of Allston's, and
told me that Montague, a picture-dealer, once came to see
him, and glancing towards this, said, "Well, you have got
a picture!" thinking it the work of an old master; afterwards, Montague, still talking with his back to the canvas,
put up his hand and touched it, and exclaimed, "By Heaven!
this picture is not ten years old"—so delicate and skilful was
that man's touch.

I was in his company for about an hour, but find it impossible to recall the largest part of his discourse, which
was often like so many printed paragraphs in his book—
perhaps the same—so readily did he fall into certain com-
monplaces. As I might have foreseen, the visit was rather

a spectacle than a conversation, of no use beyond the satisfaction of my curiosity. He was old and preoccupied, and could not bend to a new companion and think with him.

[W, V, 10–14]

Dr. Johnson was a man of no profound mind—full of English limitations, English politics, English Church, Oxford philosophy; yet, having a large heart, mother-wit and good sense which impatiently overleaped his customary bounds, his conversation as reported by Boswell has a lasting charm. Conversation is the vent of character as well as of thought; and Dr. Johnson impresses his company, not only by the point of the remark, but also, when the point fails, because *he* makes it. His obvious religion or superstition, his deep wish that they should think so or so, weighs with them—so rare is depth of feeling, or a constitutional value for a thought or opinion, among the light-minded men and women who make up society; and though they know that there is in the speaker a degree of shortcoming, of insincerity and of talking for victory, yet the existence of character, and habitual reverence for principles over talent or learning, is felt by the frivolous.　[W, VII, 236]

On the 15th May [1833] I dined with Mr. Landor. I found him noble and courteous, living in a cloud of pictures at his Villa Gherardesca, a fine house commanding a beautiful landscape. I had inferred from his books, or magnified from some anecdotes, an impression of Achillean wrath— an untamable petulance. I do not know whether the imputation were just or not, but certainly on this May day his courtesy veiled that haughty mind and he was the most patient and gentle of hosts. He praised the beautiful cyclamen which grows all about Florence; he admired Washington; talked of Wordsworth, Byron, Massinger, Beaumont and Fletcher. To be sure, he is decided in his opinions, likes to surprise, and is well content to impress, if possible, his English whim upon the immutable past. No great man ever had a great son, if Philip and Alexander be not an exception; and Philip he calls the greater man. In art, he loves the Greeks, and in sculpture, them only. He prefers the

Venus to everything else, and, after that, the head of Alexander, in the gallery here. He prefers John of Bologna to Michael Angelo; in painting, Raffaelle, and shares the growing taste for Perugino and the early masters. The Greek histories he thought the only good; and after them, Voltaire's. I could not make him praise Mackintosh, nor my more recent friends; Montaigne very cordially—and Charron also, which seemed undiscriminating. He thought Degerando indebted to "Lucas on Happiness" and "Lucas on Holiness"! He pestered me with Southey; but who is Southey? [W, V, 7–8]

. . . the defect of Plato in power is only that which results inevitably from his quality. He is intellectual in his aim; and therefore, in expression, literary. Mounting into heaven, diving into the pit, expounding the laws of the state, the passion of love, the remorse of crime, the hope of the parting soul—he is literary, and never otherwise. It is almost the sole deduction from the merit of Plato that his writings have not—what is no doubt incident to this regnancy of intellect in his work—the vital authority which the screams of prophets and the sermons of unlettered Arabs and Jews possess. There is an interval; and to cohesion, contact is necessary.

I know not what can be said in reply to this criticism but that we have come to a fact in the nature of things: an oak is not an orange. The qualities of sugar remain with sugar, and those of salt with salt.

In the second place, he has not a system. The dearest defenders and disciples are at fault. He attempted a theory of the universe, and his theory is not complete or self-evident. One man thinks he means this, and another that; he has said one thing in one place, and the reverse of it in another place. He is charged with having failed to make the transition from ideas to matter. Here is the world, sound as a nut, perfect, not the smallest piece of chaos left, never a stitch nor an end, not a mark of haste, or botching, or second thought; but the theory of the world is a thing of shreds and patches.

The longest wave is quickly lost in the sea. Plato would

willingly have a Platonism, a known and accurate expression for the world, and it should be accurate. It shall be the world passed through the mind of Plato—nothing less. Every atom shall have the Platonic tinge; every atom, every relation or quality you knew before, you shall know again and find here, but now ordered; not nature, but art. And you shall feel that Alexander indeed overran, with men and horses, some countries of the planet; but countries, and things of which countries are made, elements, planet itself, laws of planet and of men, have passed through this man as bread into his body, and become no longer bread, but body: so all this mammoth morsel has become Plato. He has clapped copyright on the world. This is the ambition of individualism. But the mouthful proves too large. *Boa constrictor* has good will to eat it, but he is foiled. He falls abroad in the attempt; and biting, gets strangled: the bitten world holds the biter fast by his own teeth. There he perishes: unconquered nature lives on and forgets him.

[W, IV, 75–77]

The jockey looks at the chest of the horse, the physician looks at the breast of the babe, to see if there is room enough for the free play of the lungs. Arteries, perspiration. Shakespeare sweats like a haymaker—all pores.

[J, VII, 280]

[*On Shakespeare*] . . . this man of men, he who gave to the science of mind a new and larger subject than had ever existed, and planted the standard of humanity some furloughs forward into Chaos. . . .   [W, IV, 218]

So far from Shakespeare's being the least known, he is the one person, in all modern history, known to us.

[W, IV, 209]

He [Shakespeare] was the master of the revel to mankind. Is it not as if one should have, through majestic powers of science, the comets given into his hand, or the planets and their moons, and should draw them from their orbits to glare with the municipal fireworks on a holiday, and adver-

tise in all towns, "Very superior pyrotechny this evening"?
[W, IV, 217]

[*On Swedenborg's theological works*]   Their immense and
sandy diffuseness is like the prairie or the desert, and their
incongruities are like the last deliration.   [W, IV, 123]

A colossal soul, he [Swedenborg] lies vast abroad on his
times, uncomprehended by them, and requires a long focal
distance to be seen. . . . His superb speculation, as from a
tower, over nature and arts, without ever losing sight of
the texture and sequence of things, almost realizes his own
picture, in the "Principia," of the original integrity of
man. . . . One of the missouriums and mastodons of literature, he is not to be measured by whole colleges of ordinary
scholars. His stalwart presence would flutter the gowns of
an university. Our books are false by being fragmentary:
their sentences are *bonmots,* and not parts of natural discourse; childish expressions of surprise or pleasure in nature; or, worse, owing a brief notoriety to their petulance,
or aversion from the order of nature—being some curiosity
or oddity, designedly not in harmony with nature and pur-
posely framed to excite surprise, as jugglers do by conceal-
ing their means. But Swedenborg is systematic and respec-
tive of the world in every sentence; all the means are orderly
given; his faculties work with astronomic punctuality, and
this admirable writing is pure from all pertness or egotism.
[W, IV, 102–103]

On the 28th [1833], August I went to Royal Mount, to
pay my respects to Mr. Wordsworth. His daughters called
in their father, a plain, elderly, white-haired man, not pre-
possessing, and disfigured by green goggles. He sat down,
and talked with great simplicity. He had just returned from
a journey. His health was good, but he had broken a tooth
by a fall, when walking with two lawyers, and had said
that he was glad it did not happen forty years ago; where-
upon they had praised his philosophy.
He had much to say of America, the more that it gave
occasion for his favorite topic—that society is being en-
lightened by a superficial tuition, out of all proportion to

its being restrained by moral culture. Schools do no good. Tuition is not education. He thinks more of the education of circumstances than of tuition. 'Tis not question whether there are offences of which the law takes cognizance, but whether there are offences of which the law does not take cognizance. Sin is what he fears—and how society is to escape without gravest mischiefs from this source. He has even said, what seemed a paradox, that they needed a civil war in America, to teach the necessity of knitting the social ties stronger. "There may be," he said, "in America some vulgarity in manner, but that's not important. That comes of the pioneer state of things. But I fear they are too much given to the making of money; and secondly, to politics; that they make political distinction the end and not the means. And I fear they lack a class of men of leisure—in short, of gentlemen—to give a tone of honor to the community. I am told that things are boasted of in the second class of society there, which, in England—God knows, are done in England every day, but would never be spoken of. In America I wish to know not how many churches or schools, but what newspapers? My friend Colonel Hamilton, at the foot of the hill, who was a year in America, assures me that the newspapers are atrocious, and accuse members of Congress of stealing spoons!" He was against taking off the tax on newspapers in England—which the reformers represent as a tax upon knowledge—for this reason, that they would be inundated with base prints. He said he talked on political aspects, for he wished to impress on me and all good Americans to cultivate the moral, the conservative, etc., etc., and never to call into action the physical strength of the people, as had just now been done in England in the Reform Bill—a thing prophesied by Delolme. He alluded once or twice to his conversation with Dr. Channing, who had recently visited him (laying his hand on a particular chair in which the Doctor had sat).

The conversation turned on books. Lucretius he esteems a far higher poet than Virgil; not in his system, which is nothing, but in his power of illustration. Faith is necessary to explain anything and to reconcile the foreknowledge of

God with human evil. Of Cousin (whose lectures we had
all been reading in Boston), he knew only the name.

I inquired if he had read Carlyle's critical articles and
translations. He said he thought him sometimes insane. He
proceeded to abuse Goethe's Wilhelm Meister heartily. It
was full of all manner of fornication. It was like the crossing
of flies in the air. He had never gone farther than the first
part; so disgusted was he that he threw the book across the
room. I deprecated this wrath, and said what I could for
the better parts of the book, and he courteously promised
to look at it again. Carlyle he said wrote most obscurely.
He was clever and deep, but he defied the sympathies of
everybody. Even Mr. Coleridge wrote more clearly, though
he had always wished Coleridge would write more to be
understood. He led me out into his garden, and showed me
the gravel walk in which thousands of his lines were composed. His eyes are much inflamed. This is no loss except
for reading, because he never writes prose, and of poetry he
carries even hundreds of lines in his head before writing
them. He had just returned from a visit to Staffa, and within
three days had made three sonnets on Fingal's Cave, and
was composing a fourth when he was called in to see me.
He said, "If you are interested in my verses perhaps you
will like to hear these lines." I gladly assented, and he recol-
lected himself for a few moments and then stood forth and
repeated, one after the other, the three entire sonnets with
great animation. I fancied the second and third more beautiful than his poems are wont to be. The third is addressed
to the flowers, which, he said, especially the ox-eye daisy,
are very abundant on the top of the rock. The second al-
ludes to the name of the cave, which is "Cave of Music";
the first to the circumstance of its being visited by the pro-
miscuous company of the steamboat.

This recitation was so unlooked for and surprising—he,
the old Wordsworth, standing apart, and reciting to me in
a garden-walk, like a school-boy declaiming—that I at first
was near to laugh; but recollecting myself, that I had come
thus far to see a poet and he was chanting poems to me. I
saw that he was right and I was wrong, and gladly gave my-

self up to hear. I told him how much the few printed extracts had quickened the desire to possess his unpublished poems. He replied he never was in haste to publish; partly because he corrected a good deal, and every alteration is ungraciously received after printing; but what he had written would be printed, whether he lived or died. I said Tintern Abbey appeared to be the favorite poem with the public, but more contemplative readers preferred the first books of the Excursion, and the Sonnets. He said, "Yes, they are better." He preferred such of his poems as touched the affections, to any others; for whatever is didactic—what theories of society, and so on—might perish quickly; but whatever combined a truth with an affection was κτῆμα ἐς ἀεί, good today and good forever. He cited the sonnet, On the feelings of a highminded Spaniard, which he preferred to any other (so I understood him), and the Two Voices; and quoted, with evident pleasure, the verses addressed To the Skylark. In this connection he said of the Newtonian theory that it might yet be superseded and forgotten; and Dalton's atomic theory.

When I prepared to depart he said he wished to show me what a common person in England could do, and he led me into the enclosure of his clerk, a young man to whom he had given this slip of ground, which was laid out, or its natural capabilities shown, with much taste. He then said he would show me a better way towards the inn; and he walked a good part of a mile, talking and ever and anon stopping short to impress the word or the verse, and finally parted from me with great kindness and returned across the fields.

Wordsworth honored himself by his simple adherence to truth, and was very willing not to shine; but he surprised by the hard limits of his thought. To judge from a single conversation, he made the impression of a narrow and very English mind; of one who paid for his rare elevation by general tameness and conformity. Off his own beat, his opinions were of no value. It is not very rare to find persons loving sympathy and ease, who expiate their departure from the common in one direction, by their conformity in every other. [W, V, 19–24]

Chapter Eleven

Himself

*Emerson knew himself with an exactness that is impressive
if not always inspiring. He knew himself as a good crafts-
man knows his tool—for in everything Emerson wrote, he
trusted to his personal impression; he listened to himself, he
obeyed himself, he virtually recorded himself, by being altogether in touch with himself. Freud's famous self-analysis
was in itself not a more remarkable communion with one's
unconscious than Emerson's lifelong notes on himself in his
Journal. In this habit Emerson was, of course, merely prac-
ticing the cardinal Romantic principle of trusting to his
own consciousness for his relation to the external world.
But the same precision of conscience which had made it
impossible for him to continue in the church made Emerson
precise about every vagary and oddity of himself. He knew
what he could do—and what he couldn't—in a fashion that
sometimes makes him seem more like a writing machine
than he actually was, so little—after his first struggles with
himself were over—did he ever try to do what did not come
easily and naturally.*

*In writing about himself, Emerson was correspondingly
dry, deprecating, humorous. He knew his instrument; he
knew, among many things, that he had no gift for sustained
thought or writing, that his genius came in moments and
was expressed in fragments, that he could think profoundly
but not systematically, and that all his success as a writer,
his special luster as an American, came from his steady gift
of "self-trust." All these traits and sidelights, all his*

strengths and weaknesses, Emerson described with calm de-
tachment. But on the emotional and passional side of him-
self, where he knew himself to be cold from the long habit
of self-protection, he was equally knowing but less frank.
And it is only in those rare moments when the emotional
vehemence of someone like Margaret Fuller provoked him
to give an explanation of himself, that one sees the compar-
atively suave surface of his writing ruffled by an emotion
that was essentially unexpected. *For the worst of Emerson,*
as well as the best, lies exactly in the readiness of what he
always knew and expected of himself, in smooth conversion
of his indispensable orphic gift into a steady flow of ideas.
We like him better when he is surprised, nettled, irritated—
and admits it. For egotism—which in the narrow sense of
the word was not one of Emerson's faults—is never so seri-
ous a blemish as being a little too much in control of one-
self, in using oneself altogether too confidently as an instru-
ment. But it has to be said that, in line with his philosophy,
with his extraordinary gift of openness to himself, Emerson
was quick to admit when he was surprised and even dis-
concerted. But it seems to have been only intense personal
affectation that could do this for him, and in this role it was
only women who ever did upset him.

I find myself often idle, vagrant, stupid and hollow. This is
somewhat appalling and, if I do not discipline myself with
diligent care, I shall suffer severely from remorse and the
sense of inferiority hereafter. All around me are industrious
and will be great, I am indolent and shall be insignificant.
Avert it, heaven! avert it, virtue! I need excitement.

[J, I, 70 (age 17)]

Milton describes himself in his letter to Diodati as enamored
of moral perfection. He did not love it more than I. That
which I cannot yet declare has been my angel from childhood until now. It has separated me from me. It has watered
my pillow, it has driven sleep from my bed. It has tortured
me for my guilt. It has inspired me with hope. It cannot be
defeated by my defeats. It cannot be questioned, though all

the martyrs apostatize. It is always the glory that shall be revealed; it is the "open secret" of the universe; and it is only the feebleness and dust of the observer that makes it future, the whole *is* now potentially in the bottom of his heart.   [J, III, 208–209]

. . . I know not why it is, but a letter is scarcely welcome to me. I expect to be lacerated by it, and if I come safe to the end of it, I feel like one escaped.   [J, IV, 63]

I cultivate ever my humanity. This I would always propitiate, and judge of a book as a peasant does, not as a book by pedantic and individual measures, but by number and weight, counting the things that are in it. My debt to Plato is a certain number of sentences: the like to Aristotle. A larger number, yet still a finite number, make the worth of Milton and Shakespeare to me. I would . . . run over what I have written, save the good sentences, and destroy the rest.
[J, IV, 23–24]

I occupy, or *improve,* as we Yankees say, two acres only of God's earth; on which is my house, my kitchen-garden, my orchard of thirty young trees, my empty barn. My house is now a very good one for comfort, and abounding in room. Besides my house, I have, I believe, $22,000, whose income in ordinary years is six per cent. I have no other tithe or glebe except the income of my winter lectures, which was last winter $800. Well, with this income, here at home, I am a rich man. I stay at home and go abroad at my own instance. I have food, warmth, leisure, books, friends. Go away from home, I am rich no longer. I never have a dollar to spend on a fancy. As no wise man, I suppose, ever was rich in the sense of *freedom to spend,* because of the inundation of claims, so neither am I, who am not wise. But at home, I am rich—rich enough for ten brothers. My wife Lidian is an incarnation of Christianity—I call her Asia—and keeps my philosophy from Antinomianism; my mother, whitest, mildest, most conservative of ladies, whose only exception to her universal preference for old things is her son; my boy, a piece of love and sunshine, well worth my watching from morning to night—these, and three domestic women, who cook and sew and run for us, make all my household. Here I sit and read and write, with very little system, and, as far as regards composition, with the most fragmentary result: paragraphs incompressible, each sentence an infinitely repellent particle. [E–C, I, 161–162]

I have urged you to pay us a visit in America, and in Concord. I have believed that you would come one day, and do believe it. But if, on your part, you have been generous and affectionate enough to your friends here—or curious enough concerning our society—to wish to come, I think you must postpone, for the present, the satisfaction of your friendship and your curiosity. At this moment I would not have you here, on any account. The publication of my *Address to the Divinity College* (copies of which I sent you) has been the occasion of an outcry in all our leading local newspapers against my "infidelity," "pantheism," and "atheism." The writers warn all and sundry against me, and against whatever is supposed to be related to my connection of opinion, &c.; against Transcendentalism, Goethe, and *Carlyle*. I am heartily sorry to see this last aspect of the storm in our washbowl. For, as Carlyle is nowise guilty, and has unpopularities of his own, I do not wish to embroil him in my parish differences. You were getting to be a great favorite with us all here, and are daily a greater with the American public, but just now, *in Boston,* where I am known as your editor, I fear you lose by the association. Now it is indispensable to your right influence here, that you should never come before our people here as one of a clique, but as a detached, that is, universally associated man; so I am happy, as I could not have thought, that you have not yielded yourself to my entreaties. Let us wait a little until this foolish clamor be overblown. My position is fortunately such as to put me quite out of the reach of any real inconvenience from the panic-strikers or the panic-struck; and, indeed, so far as this uneasiness is a necessary result of mere inaction of mind, it seems very clear to me that, if I live, my neighbors must look for a great many more shocks, and perhaps harder to bear. [E–C, I, 183–184]

Thanks for your too friendly and generous expectations from my wit.

Alas! my friend, I can do no such gay thing as you say. I do not belong to the poets, but only to a low department of literature, the reporters; suburban men.   [E–C, I, 238]

I am here at work now for a fortnight to spin some single cord out of my thousand and one strands of every color and texture that lie ravelled around me in old snarls. We need to be possessed with a mountainous conviction of the value of our advice to our contemporaries, if we will take such pains to find what that is. But no, it is the pleasure of the spinning that betrays poor spinners into the loss of so much good time. I shall work with the more diligence on this book to-be of mine, that you inform me again and again that my penny tracts are still extant; nay, that, beside friendly men, learned and poetic men read and even review them. I am like Scholasticus of the Greek Primer, who was ashamed to bring out so small a dead child before such grand people.
[E–C, I, 282–283]

I told him [R. M. Milnes] that if I should print more he would find me worse than ever with my rash, unwhipped generalization. For my journals, which I dot here at home day by day, are full of disjointed dreams, audacities, unsystematic irresponsible lampoons of systems, and all manner of rambling reveries, the poor drupes and berries I find in my basket after endless and aimless rambles in woods and pastures. I ask constantly of all men whether life may not be poetic as well as stupid?   [E–C, I, 288–289]

[*To the Reverend Henry Ware, Jr.*] It strikes me very oddly that good and wise men at Cambridge and Boston should think of raising me into an object of criticism. I have always been, from my very incapacity of methodical writing, "a chartered libertine," free to worship and free to rail; lucky when I could make myself understood, but never esteemed near enough to the institutions and mind of society to deserve the notice of the masters of literature and religion. I have appreciated fully the advantage of my position;

for I well know that there is no scholar less willing or less able to be a polemic. I could not give account of myself, if challenged. I could not possibly give you one of the "arguments" you cruelly hint at, on which any doctrine of mine stands. For I do not know what arguments mean in reference to any expression of a thought. I delight in telling what I think, but if you ask how I dare say so, or why it is so, I am the most helpless of mortal men. I do not even see that either of these questions admits of an answer. So that, in the present droll posture of my affairs, when I see myself suddenly raised into the importance of a heretic, I am very uneasy when I advert to the supposed duties of such a personage, who is expected to make good his thesis against all comers.

I certainly shall do no such thing. I shall read what you and other good men write, as I have always done—glad when you speak my thought, and skipping the page that has nothing for me. I shall go on, just as before, seeing whatever I can, and telling what I see; and, I suppose, with the same fortune that has hitherto attended me—the joy of finding that my abler and better brothers, who work with the sympathy of society, loving and beloved, do now and then unexpectedly confirm my perceptions, and find my nonsense is only their own thought in motley. [U, 198]

[*To Margaret Fuller*] I know but one solution to my nature & relations, which I find in the remembering the joy with which in my boyhood I caught the first hint of the Berkleian [sic] philosophy, and which I certainly never lost sight of afterwards. There is a foolish man who goes up & down the country giving lectures on Electricity—this one secret he has, to draw a spark out of every object, from desk, & lamp, & wooden log, & the farmer's blue frock, & by this he gets his living: for paupers & Negroes will pay to see this celestial emanation from their own basket & their own body. Well, I was not an electrician, but an Idealist. I could see that there was a cause behind every stump & clod, & by the help of some fine words could make every old wagon & woodpile & stone wall oscillate a little & threaten to dance; nay, give me fair field—& the Selectmen of Con-

cord & the Reverend Doctor Poundmedown himself began
to look unstable & vaporous. You saw me do my feat—it
fell in with your own studies—and you would give me gold
& pearls. Now there is this difference between the Electrician—Mr. Quimby—is his name?—(I never saw him)—
and the Idealist, namely, that the spark is to that philosopher
a toy, but the dance is to the Idealist terror & beauty, life &
light. It is & it ought to be; & yet sometimes there will be a
sinful empiric who loves exhibition too much. This Insight
is so precious to society that where the least glimmer of it
appears all men should befriend & protect it for its own
sake.   [L, II, 384–385]

As usual at this season of the year, I, incorrigible spout-
ing Yankee, am writing an oration to deliver to the boys in
one of our little country colleges, nine days hence. You will
say I do not deserve the aid of any Muse. O but if you knew
how natural it is to me to run to these places! Besides, I always am lured on by the hope of saying something which
shall stick by the good boys.   [E–C, I, 343]

I think I shall never be killed by my ambition. I behold my
failures and shortcomings there in writing, wherein it would
give me much joy to thrive, with an equanimity which my
worst enemy might be glad to see. And yet it is not that I
am occupied with better things. One could well leave to
others the record, who was absorbed in the life. But I have
done nothing. I think the branch of the "tree of life" which
headed to a bud in me, curtailed me somehow of a drop or
two of sap, and so dwarfed all my florets and drupes. Yet as
I tell you I am very easy in my mind, and never dream of
suicide. My whole philosophy—which is very real—teaches
acquiescence and optimism. Only when I see how much
work is to be done, what room for a poet—for any spiritual-
ist—in this great, intelligent, sensual, and avaricious America, I lament my fumbling fingers and stammering tongue.
[E–C, I, 341–342]

I think myself more a man than some men I know, inasmuch as I see myself to be open to the enjoyment of talents

and deeds of other men, as they are not. When a talent comes by, which I cannot appreciate and other men can, I instantly am inferior. With all my ears I cannot detect unity or plan in a strain of Beethoven. Here is a man who draws from it a frank delight. So much is he more a man than I.
[J, V, 19]

I have usually read that a man suffered more from one hard word than he enjoyed from ten good ones. My own experience does not confirm the saying. The censure (I either know or fancy) does not hit me; and the praise is very good. [J, V, 33–34]

Nearness and distinctness seem to be convertible. A noise, a jar, a rumble, is infinitely far off from my nature, though it be within a few inches of the tympanum, but a voice speaking the most intelligible of propositions is so near as to be already a part of myself. [J, V, 70]

I like my boy, with his endless, sweet soliloquies and iterations, and his utter inability to conceive why I should not leave all my nonsense business and writing, and come to tie up his toy horse, as if there was or could be any end to nature beyond his horse. And he is wiser than we when threatens his whole threat, "I will not love you."

Nature delights in punishing stupid people. The very strawberry vines are more than a match for them with all their appetites, and all their fumbling fingers. The little, defenceless vine coolly hides the best berry, now under this leaf, then under that, and keeps the treasure for yonder darling boy with the bright eyes when Booby is gone.
[J, V, 238–239]

When I was thirteen years old, my Uncle Samuel Ripley one day asked me, "How is it, Ralph, that all the boys dislike you and quarrel with you, whilst the grown people are fond of you?" Now am I thirty-six and the fact is reversed—the old people suspect and dislike me, and the young love me. [J, V, 270–271]

I closed last Wednesday, 12th instant, my course of lectures in Boston, on "The Present Age," which were read on ten consecutive Wednesday evenings (except Christmas evening).

I judge from the account rendered me by the sellers of tickets, added to an account of my own distribution of tickets to my friends, that the average audience at a lecture consisted of about 400 persons. 256 course tickets were sold and 305 evening tickets or passes. I distributed about 110 to 120 course tickets.

These lectures give me little pleasure. I have not done what I hoped when I said, I will try it once more. I have not once transcended the coldest self-possession. I said I will agitate others, being agitated myself, I dared to hope for extasy and eloquence. A new theatre, a new art, I said, is mine. Let us see if philosophy, if ethics, if chiromancy, if the discovery of the divine in the house and the barn, in all works and all plays, cannot make the cheek blush, the lip quiver, and the tear start. I will not waste myself. On the strength of Things I will be borne, and try if Folly, Custom, Convention, and Phlegm cannot be made to hear our sharp artillery. Alas! alas! I have not the recollection of one strong moment. A cold mechanical preparation for a delivery as decorous—fine things, pretty things, wise things—but no arrows, no axes, no nectar, no growling, no transpiercing, no loving, no enchantment. [J, V, 372–374]

In all my lectures, I have taught one doctrine, namely, the infinitude of the private man. This the people accept readily enough, and even with loud commendation, as long as I call the lecture Art, or Politics, or Literature, or the Household; but the moment I call it Religion, they are shocked, though it be only the application of the same truth which they receive everywhere else, to a new class of facts. [J, V, 380–381]

I submitted to what seemed a necessity of petty literary patriotism—I know not what else to call it—and took charge of our thankless little *Dial*, here, without subscribers enough to pay even a publisher, much less any laborer; it has no penny for editor or contributor, nothing but abuse in the newspapers, or, at best, silence; but it serves as a sort of portfolio, to carry about a few poems or sentences which would otherwise be transcribed and circulated; and always we are waiting when somebody shall come and make it good. But I took it, as I said, and it took me, and a great deal of good time, to a small purpose. I am ashamed to compute how many hours and days these chores consume for me. I had it fully in my heart to write at large leisure in noble mornings opened by dearest to the Morning Muse, a chapter on Poetry, for which all readings, all studies, are but preparation; but now it is July, and my chapter is in rudest beginnings. Yet when I go out of doors in the summer night, and see how high the stars are, I am persuaded that there is time enough, here or somewhere, for all that I must do; and the good world manifests very little impatience. [E–C, II, 2–3]

I doubt not your stricture on the book as sometimes unconnected and inconsecutive is just. Your words are very gentle. I should describe it much more harshly. My knowledge of the defects of these things I write is all but sufficient to hinder me from writing at all. I am only a sort of lieutenant here in the deplorable absence of captains, and write the laws ill as thinking it a better homage than universal silence. You Londoners know little of the dignities and duties of country lyceums. But of what you say now and heretofore respecting the remoteness of my writing and thinking from real life, though I hear substantially the same criticism made by my countrymen, I do not know what it means. If I can at any time express the law and the ideal right, that should satisfy me without measuring the divergence from it of the last act of Congress. And though I sometimes accept a popular call, and preach on Temperance or the Abolition of Slavery, as lately on the 1st of August, I am sure to feel, before I have done with it, what an intrusion it is into another sphere, and so much loss of virtue in my own. [E–C, II, 85]

[*To William Emerson*] I take to myself great praise for hiding my intellectual poverties by my diligence, to such a creditable extent, & not being cashiered long ago. Weak eyes, that will only serve a few hours daily; *no animal spirits,* an immense & fatal negative with our Anglican race. No Greek, no mathematics, no politics— How the deuce, man, do you contrive to live & talk with this nervous exigent race? Alas, I know not how they [have] borne with me so long—and the oddity & ridicule of it all, is—given me a literary reputation too, which I make dangerous drafts upon, every day I live. The will o' the wisp, the light invisible except in certain angles, & in all but impossible circumstances, seems to me how often the type & symbol of us all. We cannot overestimate or underestimate these strange goodfor-nothing immortal men that we are. [L, IV, 101–102]

I avoid the Stygian anniversaries at Cambridge, those hurrahs among the ghosts, those yellow, bald, toothless meetings in memory of red cheeks, black hair, and departed health. Most forcible Feeble made the oration that fits the occasion, that contains all the obituary eloquences. Bluebirds celebrate theirs. [J, VII, 60]

I observe that all the bookish men have a tendency to believe that they are unpopular. Parker gravely informs me by word and by letter that he is precisely the most unpopular of all men in New England. Alcott believes the same thing of himself, and I, no doubt, if they had not anticipated me in claiming this distinction, should have claimed it for myself. [J, VII, 502]

Like the New England soil, my talent is good only whilst
I work it. If I cease to task myself, I have no thoughts.
This is a poor sterile Yankeeism. What I admire and love
is the generous and spontaneous soil which flowers and
fruits at all seasons.   [J, VIII, 74]

The fate of my books is like the impression of my face. My
acquaintances, as long back as I can remember, have always
said, "Seems to me you look a little thinner than when I
saw you last."   [J, VIII, 88]

Call yourself preacher, pedler, lecturer, tinman, grocer,
scrivener, jobber, or whatever lowest name your business
admits, and leave your lovers to find the fine name.
[J, VIII, 146–147]

I found when I had finished my new lecture that it was a
very good house, only the architect had unfortunately
omitted the stairs.   [J, VIII, 167]

I, too, am an American and value practical ability. I delight in people who can do things, I prize talent—perhaps
no man more. But I think of the wind, and not of the
weathercocks.   [J, VIII, 473]

I am a natural reader, and only a writer in the absence
of natural writers. In a true time, I should never have written.   [J, IX, 181]

I have been writing and speaking what were once called
novelties, for twenty-five or thirty years, and have not now
one disciple. Why? Not that what I said was not true; not
that it has not found intelligent receivers; but because it did
not go from any wish in me to bring men to me, but to
themselves. I delight in driving them from me. What could
I do, if they came to me?—they would interrupt and encumber me. This is my boast that I have no school follower. I should account it a measure of the impurity of insight, if it did not create independence.   [J, IX, 188–189]

Beatitudes of Intellect. Am I not, one of these days, to write consecutively of the beatitude of intellect? It is too great for feeble souls, and they are over-excited. The wineglass shakes, and the wine is spilled. What then? The joy which will not let me sit in my chair, which brings me bolt upright to my feet, and sends me striding around my room, like a tiger in his cage, and I cannot have composure and concentration enough even to set down in English words the thought which thrills me—is not that joy a certificate of the elevation? What if I never write a book or a line? for a moment, the eyes of my eyes were opened, the affirmative experience remains, and consoles through all suffering.

> For art, for music, overthrilled,
> The wineglass shakes, the wine is spilled.
> [J, IX, 221]

When I sprained my foot I soon found it was all one as if I had sprained my head, if I must sit in my chair. Then I thought Nature had sprained her foot; and that King Lear had never sprained his, or he would have thought there were worse evils than unkind daughters. When I see a man unhappy, I ask, has a sprained foot brought him to this pass? [J, IX, 223–224]

My new book sells faster, it appears, than either of its foregoers. This is not for its merit, but only shows that old age is a good advertisement. Your name has been seen so often that your book must be worth buying. [J, X, 312]

I write laboriously after a law, which I see, and then lose, and then see again. And, I doubt not, though I see around me many men of superior talent, that my reader will do me the justice to feel that I am not contriving something to surprise or to tickle him, but am seriously striving to say that which is. [J, IX, 468]

Our moods do not believe in each other. Today I am full of thoughts and can write what I please. I see no reason why

I should not have the same thought, the same power of expression, tomorrow. What I write, whilst I write it, seems the most natural thing in the world; but yesterday I saw a dreary vacuity in this direction in which now I see so much; and a month hence, I doubt not, I shall wonder who he was that wrote so many continuous pages. Alas for this infirm faith, this will not strenuous, this vast ebb of a vast flow! I am God in nature; I am a weed by the wall.

[W, II, 306–307]

I only write by spasms, and these ever more rare—and daemons that have no ears. [E–C, II, 311]

The true preacher can be known by this, that he deals out to the people his life—life passed through the fire of thought. [W, X, 216]

Chapter Twelve

The Way Things Are

The most commonplace remark about Emerson is that he lacked a sense of evil. It would be more accurate to say that he deliberately omitted some of his perceptions from the public expression of his philosophy. Since Emerson saw himself as the spiritual catalyst and mentor who could save his generation from the pessimism of a wholly materialistic outlook, he deliberately emphasized in his lectures his conception of man as a creative agent rather than as a mere bystander or onlooker or victim in the universe. It was plainly part of his public strategy to support what he called "the party of hope" rather than the profound tendency, expressed by Herman Melville, to look on man as, at best, a doomed hero who never knew when he was beaten.

But the profoundly mystical bent of Emerson's mind, his sense of the individual soul's irresistible flight toward God, was combined with a highly developed Yankee shrewdness. He combined, with an artist's intuition about human beings, the New Englander's legendary canniness and directness. And on this side of his nature, confided mostly to his Journals but by no means invisible to the reader of his formal works, Emerson is one of the sharpest, most unrelenting, quietly balanced "realists" that we have.

To a writer with Emerson's essential religious bent, "realism," in the sense in which modern novelists have made it famous, is not merely impossible but undesirable. It was not in order to be a "realist," like Stendhal or Flaubert, that Emerson wrote. But with all the characteristic "rapture," the "flight," of the mystical mind, Emerson succeeds in showing the devil in man. For he is, after all, very much of a "naturalist," which is why he regards churches as unnecessary and is concerned with a wholly individual relation of man to the divine. His view of life is profoundly influenced by his sense of natural process, of the evolution of species, of the "fate" that is transmitted not merely by our immediate ancestors, but by man in his cumulative history. And it is as an evolutionist that Emerson can be so profoundly interesting to our generation. He is concerned not only with the obvious force that works in us as heredity ("How shall a man escape from his ancestors . . . draw off from his veins the black drop which he drew from his father's or his mother's life?") but with invisible force that works in us as unconsciousness. The remarkable prescience of the Romantic mind in its concern with the unconscious is shown in Emerson's awareness that there is an "invisible horse, which, if it became visible, all their seemingly mad plunging motions would be explained." As has often been shown in this book, Emerson worked by welcoming unconscious thoughts, moods, fancies. But by the same token, he realized, quite as much as we do in the Freudian age, that this "unconscious" was also full of "hydras and crocodiles." The difference between ourselves and Emerson, in this regard, is that he saw the unconscious largely as a storehouse of literary inspiration, not from a clinical standpoint. He believes that man's "id" is nothing without reconciliation to, and conversion by, the ego—the searching, humanistic, purposeful mind of man that was the first to reach into the unconscious, and of which it must be the master.

The existence of evil and malignant men does not depend on themselves or on men; it indicates the virulence that still remains uncured in the universe, uncured and corrupting, and hurling out these pestilent rats and tigers, and men rat-like and wolf-like. [J, VIII, 452]

Nature is a tropical swamp in sunshine, on whose purlieus we hear the song of summer birds, and see prismatic dew-drops—but her interiors are terrific, full of hydras and crocodiles. [W, X, 188]

There is a crack in everything God has made. It would seem there is always this vindictive circumstance stealing in at unawares even into the wild poesy in which the human fancy attempted to make bold holiday and to shake itself free of the old laws—this back-stroke, this kick of the gun, certifying that the law is fatal; that in nature nothing can be given, all things are sold. [W, II, 107]

Oh, yes, he may escape from shackles and dungeons, but how shall he get away from his temperament?—how from his hereditary sins and infusions?—how from the yellow humors through which he must ever see the blue sky and the sun and stars? Sixty centuries have squatted and stitched and hemmed to shape and finish for him that strait jacket which he must wear. [J, VII, 156]

How shall a man escape from his ancestors, or draw off from his veins the black drop which he drew from his father's or his mother's life? It often appears in a family as if all the qualities of the progenitors were potted in several jars—some ruling quality in each son or daughter of the house; and sometimes the unmixed temperament, the rank unmitigated elixir, the family vice is drawn off in a separate individual and the others are proportionally relieved. We sometimes see a change of expression in our companion and say his father or his mother comes to the windows of his eyes, and sometimes a remote relative. In different hours a man represents each of several of his ancestors, as if there were seven or eight of us rolled up in each man's skin—seven or eight ancestors at least, and they constitute the variety of notes for that new piece of music which his life is. At the corner of the street you read the possibility of each passenger in the facial angle, in the complexion, in the depth of his eye. His parentage determines it. Men are what their mothers made them. You may as well ask a loom which weaves huckabuck why it does not make cashmere, as expect poetry from this engineer, or a chemi-

cal discovery from that jobber. Ask the digger in the ditch to explain Newton's laws; the fine organs of his brain have been pinched by overwork and squalid poverty from father to son for a hundred years. When each comes forth from his mother's womb, the gate of gifts closes behind him.
[W, VI, 9–11]

By his machines man can dive and remain under water like a shark; can fly like a hawk in the air; can see atoms like a gnat; can see the system of the universe like Uriel, the angel of the sun; can carry whatever loads a ton of coal can lift; can knock down cities with his fist of gunpowder; can recover the history of his race by the medals which the deluge, and every creature, civil or savage or brute, has involuntarily dropped of its existence; and divine the future possibility of the planet and its inhabitants by his perception of laws of Nature. Ah! what a plastic little creature he is! so shifty, so adaptive! his body a chest of tools, and he making himself comfortable in every climate, in every condition.   [W, VIII, 140–141]

Emerson expatiates further on the crack in the universe. Aboriginal man lingers on in his modern counterpart, and the fierce and the loathsome are as perdurable as beauty. Let us admit that civilization is "onerous" and life full of frictions.

The aboriginal man, in geology and in the dim lights of Darwin's microscope, is not an engaging figure. We are very glad that he ate his fishes and snails and marrow-bones out of our sight and hearing, and that his doleful experiences were got through with so very long ago. They combed his mane, they pared his nails, cut off his tail, set him on end, sent him to school and made him pay taxes, before he could begin to write his sad story for the compassion or the repudiation of his descendants, who are all but unanimous to disown him. We must take him as we find him—pretty well on in his education, and, in all *our* knowledge of him, an interesting creature, with a will, an invention, an imagination, a conscience and an inextinguishable hope.

[W, VIII, 270]

. . . we see faces every day which have a good type but have been marred in the casting; a proof that we are all entitled to beauty, should have been beautiful if our ancestors had kept the laws—as every lily and every rose is well. But our bodies do not fit us, but caricature and satirize us.

[W, VI, 298]

I do not pity the misery of a man underplaced: that will right itself presently: but I pity the man overplaced. A certain quantity of power belongs to a certain quantity of faculty. Whoever wants more power than is the legitimate attraction of his faculty, is a politician, and must pay for that excess; must truckle for it. This is the whole game of society and the politics of the world.   [W, X, 47]

How Nature, to keep her balance true, invented a Cat. What phantasmagoria in these animals! Why is the snake so frightful, which is the line of beauty, and every resemblance to it pleases? See what disgust and horror of a rat, loathsome in its food, loathsome in its form, and a tail which is villainous, formidable by its ferocity; yet interposed between this horror and the gentler kinds is the cat, a beautiful horror, or a form of many bad qualities, but tempered and thus strangely inserted as an offset, check, and temperament, to that ugly horror. See then the squirrel strangely adorned with his tail, which is his saving grace in human eyes.   [J, VII, 544)

He has seen but half the universe who never has been shown the house of Pain. As the salt sea covers more than two thirds of the surface of the globe, so sorrow encroaches in man on felicity. The conversation of men is a mixture of regrets and apprehensions. I do not know but the prevalent hue of things to the eye of leisure is melancholy. In the dark hours, our existence seems to be a defensive war, a struggle against the encroaching All, which threatens

surely to engulf soon, and is impatient of our short re-
prieve.   [W, XII, 405]

Too much friction in life. The proverb teaches that there
is a pound of grindstone to a pound of cheese, but I think
there are always many pounds of grindstone to an ounce of
cheese. How much arrangement and combination and
drudgery to bring about a pleasant hour, to hear an eloquent argument, or a fine poetic reading, or a little superior conversation; what rattle and jingle; how many
miles must be ridden, how many woods and meadows, al-
der-borders and stone walls must be tediously passed!
[J, VII, 153]

The property proves too much for the man, and now all
the men of science, art, intellect, are pretty sure to degenerate into selfish housekeepers dependent on wine, coffee,
furnace, gaslight, and furniture. *Then* things swing the
other way, and we suddenly find that civilization crowed too
soon; that what we bragged as triumphs were treacheries;
that we have opened the wrong door, and let the enemy
into the castle; that civilization was a mistake; that nothing
is so vulgar as a great warehouse of rooms full of furniture
and trumpery; that, in the circumstances, the best wisdom
were an auction, or a fire; since the foxes and birds have the
right of it, with a warm hole to fend the weather, and no
more; that a pent-house, to fend the sun and wind and
rain, is the house which makes no tax on the owner's time
and thought, and which he can leave when the sun reaches
noon.   [J, IX, 27–28]

Cows are dull, sluggish creatures, but with a decided
talent in one direction—for extracting milk out of meadows
—mine have a genius for it—leaking cream, "larding the
lean earth as they walk along." Wasps, too, for making
paper. Then what soothing objects are the hens!   [J, X, 80]

Material greatness captivates the vulgar; and egotists live
in nervous exaggeration; as when a man sits under the
dentist, he fancies his teeth have some acres of extent.
[J, VIII, 324]

High Criticism. You must draw your rule from the genius of that which you do, and not from by-ends. Don't make a novel to establish a principle of political economy. You will spoil both. Don't set out to teach Theism from your Natural History, like Paley and Agassiz. You spoil both. [J, IX, 134]

It must be admitted, that civilization is onerous and expensive; hideous expense to keep it up—let it go, and be Indians again; but why Indians?—that is costly, too; the mud-turtle and trout life is easier and cheaper, and oyster, cheaper still. [J, IX, 42]

The belief of some of our friends in their duration suggests one of those musty householders who keep every broomstick and old grate, put in a box every old tooth that falls out of their heads, preserve the ancient frippery of their juvenile wardrobe, and they think God saves all the old souls which he has used up. What does he save them for? [J, VIII, 292–293]

Beauty. It is curious that we so peremptorily require beauty, and if it do not exist in anyone, we feel at liberty to insult over that subject, without end. Thus the poor Donkey is not handsome, and so is the gibe of all mankind in all ages, notwithstanding his eminent usefulness; whilst those handsome cats, the lion, leopard, tiger are allowed to tear and devour because handsome mischiefs, and are the badges of kings. [J, VIII, 126]

The world, the universe may be reeled off from any Idea, like a ball of yarn. Thus, if you please, it is all mechanical. The mental phenomena all admit very well of being solved so. . . . Or it is all electrical; or chemical; or moral. Suit yourself. [J, VII, 172]

The fine prints and pictures which the dentist hangs in his ante-room have a satirical air to the waiting patient.
[J, IV, 107]

A natural transition to the spectacle of old age, sickness and doubt. The disenchantment of old age and sharp consciousness of personal humiliation. Each man attends his private theater and confronts himself nakedly in his dreams. In dreams we are given the "wise and sometimes terrible hints."

Old Age. Sad spectacle that a man should live and be fed that he may fill a paragraph every year in the newspapers for his wonderful age, as we record the weight and girth of the Big Ox or Mammoth Girl. We do not count a man's years until he has nothing else to count.   [J, V, 405]

Old age brings along with its uglinesses the comfort that you will soon be out of it—which ought to be a substantial relief to such discontented pendulums as we are. To be out of the war, out of debt, out of the drouth, out of the blues, out of the dentist's hands, out of the second thoughts, mortifications and remorses that inflict such twinges and shooting pains—out of the next winter, and the high prices, and company below your ambition—surely these are soothing hints. And harbinger of this, what an alleviator is sleep, which muzzles all these dogs for me every day?
[W, VII, 449]

There are three wants which can never be satisfied: that of the traveller, who says, "Anywhere but here"; that of the rich who wants *something more;* and that of the sick who wants *something different.*   [J, VI, 112]

Alas! our Penetration increases as we grow older, and we are no longer deceived by great words when unrealized and unembodied. Say rather, we detect littleness in expressions and thoughts that once we should have taken and cited as proofs of strength.   [J, VII, 13]

There are people who have an appetite for grief, pleasure is not strong enough and they crave pain, mithridatic stomachs which must be fed on poisoned bread, natures so doomed that no prosperity can soothe their ragged and dishevelled desolation. They mis-hear and mis-behold, they suspect and dread. They handle every nettle and ivy in the hedge, and tread on every snake in the meadow.

[W, XII, 409–410]

We remember those things which we love and those things which we hate. The memory of all men is robust on the subject of a debt due to them, or of an insult inflicted on them. "They can remember," as Johnson said, "who kicked them last."   [W, XII, 105]

What would it avail me, if I could destroy my enemies? There would be as many tomorrow. That which I hate and fear is really in myself, and no knife is long enough to reach to its heart.   [W, X, 120]

The perception of the Comic is a tie of sympathy with other men, a pledge of sanity, and a protection from those perverse tendencies and gloomy insanities in which fine intellects sometimes lose themselves. A rogue alive to the ludicrous is still convertible. If that sense is lost, his fellow men can do little for him.   [W, VIII, 161–162]

I was about to add just now, in speaking of Morals as the foundation of nobility, that we do with that as our farmers, who carry all their best peaches and apples to market and feed their families with the refuse. We parade our nobilities in poems, instead of working them up into happiness. Then we must bring the day about with draff and prose.   [J, VIII, 15]

The merchant will not allow a book in the counting-house, suspects every taste and tendency but that for goods, has no conversation, no thought but cotton, qualities of cotton, and its advance or fall a penny or a farthing. What a cramping of the form in wooden cap, wooden belt, and wooden shoes, is this, and how should not the Negro be more a man than one of these victims?—the Negro, who, if low and imperfect in organization, is yet no wooden sink, but a wild cedar swamp, rich with all vegetation of grass and moss and confervæ and ferns and flags, with rains and sunshine; mists and moonlight, birds and insects filling its wilderness with life and promise. [J, VI, 66]

The chief fact in history of the world is the penury with which the stream of thought runs. In five hundred years millions and millions of men, and not a hundred lines of poetry; though almost all of them have some ear and apprehension for poetry, and not a few try to write. Poetical persons hum a verse, and go as far as half a quatrain— which they cannot complete. Exaggerating people talk of moments when their brain seemed bursting with the multitude of thoughts! I believe they were mistaken; there was no danger. Yet nothing but thought is precious, and we must respect in ourselves this possibility, and abide its time. Jones Very, who thought it an honor to wash his own face, seems to me less insane than men who hold themselves cheap. [J, VIII, 542–543]

Skeptic. Pure intellect is the pure devil when you have got off all the masks of Mephistopheles. It is a painful symbol to me that the index or forefinger is always the most soiled of all the fingers. [J, VI, 497]

Men go through the world each musing on a great fable, dramatically pictured and rehearsed before him. If you speak to the man, he turns his eyes from his own scene, and slower or faster endeavors to comprehend what you say. When you have done speaking, he returns to his private music. Men generally attempt early in life to make their brothers first, afterwards their wives, acquainted with what is going forward in their private theatre, but they soon desist from the attempt, or finding that they also have some farce, or perhaps some ear and heart-rending tragedy forward on their secret boards, on which they are intent, all parties acquiesce at last in a private box with the whole play performed before himself *solus.* [J, VII, 75]

Men ride on a thought, as if each bestrode an invisible horse, which, if it became visible, all their seemingly mad plunging motions would be explained. [J, VIII, 522]

A man finds out that there is somewhat in him that knows more than he does. Then he comes presently to the curious question, Who's who? which of these two is really me? the one that knows more, or the one that knows less? the little fellow or the big fellow? [J, IX, 190]

'Tis superfluous to think of the dreams of multitudes, the astonishment remains that one should dream; that we should resign so quietly this deifying Reason, and become the theatre of delirious shows, wherein time, space, persons, cities, animals, should dance before us in merry and mad confusion; a delicate creation outdoing the prime and flower of actual Nature, antic comedy alternating with horrid pictures. Sometimes the forgotten companions of childhood reappear:

> "They come, in dim procession led,
> The cold, the faithless, and the dead,
> As warm each hand, each brow as gay,
> As if they parted yesterday":

or we seem busied for hours and days in peregrinations over seas and lands, in earnest dialogues, strenuous actions for nothings and absurdities, cheated by spectral jokes and waking suddenly with ghastly laughter, to be rebuked by the cold, lonely, silent midnight, and to rake with confusion in memory among the gibbering nonsense to find the motive of this contemptible cachinnation. Dreams are jealous of being remembered; they dissipate instantly and angrily if you try to hold them. When newly awaked from lively dreams, we are so near them, still agitated by them, still in their sphere—give us one syllable, one feature, one hint, and we should repossess the whole; hours of this strange entertainment would come trooping back to us; but we cannot get our hand on the first link or fibre, and the whole is lost. There is a strange wilfulness in the speed with which it disperses and baffles our grasp.

A dislocation seems to be the foremost trait of dreams. A painful imperfection almost always attends them. The fairest forms, the most noble and excellent persons, are deformed by some pitiful and insane circumstance. The very landscape and scenery in a dream seem not to fit us, but like a coat or cloak of some other person to overlap and encumber the wearer; so is the ground, the road, the house, in dreams, too long or too short, and if it served no other purpose would show us how accurately Nature fits man awake.

There is one memory of waking and another of sleep. In our dreams the same scenes and fancies are many times associated, and that too, it would seem, for years. In sleep one shall travel certain roads in stage-coaches or gigs, which he recognizes as familiar, and has dreamed that ride a dozen times; or shall walk alone in familiar fields and meadows, which road or which meadow in waking hours he never looked upon. This feature of dreams deserves the more attention from its singular resemblance to that obscure yet startling experience which almost every person confesses in daylight, that particular passages of conversation and action have occurred to him in the same order before, whether dreaming or waking; a suspicion that they have been with precisely these persons in precisely this room, and heard precisely this dialogue, at some former hour, they know not when. . . .

Dreams have a poetic integrity and truth. This limbo and dust-hole of thought is presided over by a certain reason, too. Their extravagance from nature is yet within a higher nature. They seem to us to suggest an abundance and fluency of thought not familiar to the waking experience. They pique us by independence of us, yet we know ourselves in this mad crowd, and owe to dreams a kind of divination and wisdom. My dreams are not me; they are not Nature, or the Not-me: they are both. They have a double consciousness, at once sub- and ob-jective. We call the phantoms that rise, the creation of our fancy, but they act like mutineers, and fire on their commander; showing that every act, every thought, every cause, is bipolar, and in the act is contained the counteraction. If I strike, I am struck; if I chase, I am pursued.

Wise and sometimes terrible hints shall in them be thrown to the man out of a quite unknown intelligence. He shall be startled two or three times in his life by the justice as well as the significance of this phantasmagoria. Once or twice the conscious fetters shall seem to be unlocked, and a freer utterance attained. A prophetic character in all ages has haunted them. They are the maturation often of opinions not consciously carried out to statements, but whereof we already possessed the elements. Thus, when awake, I know the character of Rupert, but do not think what he may do. In dreams I see him engaged in certain actions which seem preposterous—out of all fitness. He is hostile, he is cruel, he is frightful, he is a poltroon. It turns out prophecy a year later. But it was already in my mind as character, and the sibyl dreams merely embodied it in fact. Why then should not symptoms, auguries, forebodings be, and, as one said, the moanings of the spirit? . . .

Sleep takes off the costume of circumstance, arms us with terrible freedom, so that every will rushes to a deed. A skilful man reads his dreams for his self-knowledge; yet not the details, but the quality. What part does he play in them—a cheerful, manly part, or a poor drivelling part? However monstrous and grotesque their apparitions, they have a substantial truth. . . .

The lovers of marvels, of what we call the occult and un-proved sciences, of mesmerism, of astrology, of coincidences, of intercourse, by writing or by rapping or by painting, with departed spirits, need not reproach us with incredulity because we are slow to accept their statement. It is not the incredibility of the fact, but a certain want of harmony between the action and the agents. We are used to vaster wonders than these that are alleged. In the hands of poets, of devout and simple minds, nothing in the line of their character and genius would surprise us. But we should look for the style of the great artist in it, look for completeness and harmony. Nature never works like a conjuror, to surprise, rarely by shocks, but by infinite graduation; so that we live embosomed in sounds we do not hear, scents we do not smell, spectacles we see not, and by in-

numerable impressions so softly laid on that though important we do not discover them until our attention is called
to them. . . .

Dreams retain the infirmities of our character. The good
genius may be there or not, our evil genius is sure to stay.
The Ego partial makes the dream; the Ego total the interpretation. Life is also a dream on the same terms. . . .

The history of man is a series of conspiracies to win
from Nature some advantage without paying for it. It is
curious to see what grand powers we have a hint of and are
mad to grasp, yet how slow Heaven is to trust us with such
edge-tools. "All that frees talent without increasing self-
command is noxious." Thus the fabled ring of Gyges, making the wearer invisible, which is represented in modern
fable by the telescope as used by Schlemil, is simply mischievous. A new or private language, used to serve only
low or political purposes; the transfusion of the blood; the
steam battery, so fatal as to put an end to war by the threat
of universal murder; the desired discovery of the guided
balloon, are of this kind. Tramps are troublesome enough
in the city and in the highways, but tramps flying through
the air and descending on the lonely traveller or the lonely
farmer's house or the bank-messenger in the country, can
well be spared. Men are not fit to be trusted with these talismans.

Before we acquire great power we must acquire wisdom
to use it well. Animal magnetism inspires the prudent and
moral with a certain terror; so the divination of contingent
events, and the alleged second-sight of the pseudo-spiritual-
ists. There are many things of which a wise man might wish
to be ignorant, and these are such. Shun them as you would
the secrets of the undertaker and the butcher. The best are
never demoniacal or magnetic; leave this limbo to the
Prince of the power of the air. The lowest angel is better.
It is the height of the animal; below the region of the divine. Power as such is not known to the angels. . . .

The fault of most men is that they are busybodies; do not
wait the simple movement of the soul, but interfere and
thwart the instructions of their own minds. . . .

Men who had never wondered at anything, who had

thought it the most natural thing in the world that they should exist in this orderly and replenished world, have been unable to suppress their amazement at the disclosures of the somnambulist. The peculiarity of the history of Animal Magnetism is that it drew in as inquirers and students a class of persons never on any other occasion known as students and inquirers. Of course the inquiry is pursued on low principles. Animal Magnetism peeps. It becomes in such hands a black art. The uses of the thing, the commodity, the power, at once come to mind and direct the course of inquiry. It seemed to open again that door which was open to the imagination of childhood—of magicians and fairies and lamps of Aladdin, the travelling cloak, the shoes of swiftness and the sword of sharpness that were to satisfy the uttermost wish of the senses without danger or a drop of sweat. But as Nature can never be outwitted, as in the Universe no man was ever known to get a cent's worth without paying in some form or other the cent, so this prodigious promiser ends always and always will, as sorcery and alchemy have done before, in very small and smoky performance.   [W, X, 3–25, *passim*]

How slowly, how slowly we learn that witchcraft and ghostcraft, palmistry and magic and all the other scattered superstitions, which, with so much police, boastful skepticism and scientific committees, we had finally dismissed to the moon as nonsense, are really no nonsense at all, but subtle and valid influences, always starting up, mowing, muttering in our path and shading our day. The things are real, only they have shed their skin, which with much insult we have gibbeted and buried. One person fastens an eye on us and the very graves of the memory render up their dead, the secrets that make us wretched either to keep or to betray must be betrayed; and another person fastens an eye on us, and we cannot speak a syllable, and the very bones of the body seem to lose their cartilages.

[W, X, 519]

Memory. It sometimes occurs that memory has a personality of its own, and volunteers or refuses its information at *its* will, not at mine. I ask myself, Is it not some old aunt who goes in and out of the house, and occasionally recites anecdotes of old times and persons, which I recognize as having heard before—and she being gone again, I search in vain for any trace of the anecdotes? [J, X, 286]

Mythology is no man's work; but, what we daily observe in regard to the *bon-mots* that circulate in society—that every talker helps a story in repeating it, until, at last, from the slenderest filament of fact a good fable is constructed— the same growth befalls mythology: The legend is tossed from believer to poet, from poet to believer, everybody adding a grace or dropping a fault or rounding the form, until it gets an ideal truth. [W, VIII, 181–182]

"Respect the child." This is Emerson's educational dictum. He reverences these precious foreigners and fears the paralyzing effects of a frozen system. Religion, too, has lost its savor—"the ministers take too much for granted."

I believe that our own experience instructs us that the secret of Education lies in respecting the pupil. It is not for you to choose what he shall know, what he shall do. It is chosen and foreordained, and he only holds the key to his own secret. By your tampering and thwarting and too much governing he may be hindered from his end and kept out of his own. Respect the child. Wait and see the new product of Nature. Nature loves analogies, but not repetitions. Respect the child. Be not too much his parent. Trespass not on his solitude. [W, X, 143]

How few thoughts! In a hundred years, millions of men and not a hundred lines of poetry, not a theory of philosophy that offers a solution of the great problems, not an art of education that fulfils the conditions. In this delay and vacancy of thought we must make the best amends we can by seeking the wisdom of others to fill the time.

[W, VIII, 179–180]

Children are all foreigners. We treat them as such. We cannot understand their speech or the mode of life, and so our Education is remote and accidental and not closely applied to the facts.   [J, V, 261–262]

It is ominous, a presumption of crime, that this word Education has so cold, so hopeless a sound. A treatise on education, a convention for education, a lecture, a system, affects us with slight paralysis and a certain yawning of the jaws.   [W, X, 133]

People live like these boys who watch for a sleigh-ride and mount on the first that passes, and when they meet another that they know, swing themselves on to that, and ride in another direction, until a third passes, and they change again; 'tis no matter where they go, as long as there is snow and company.   [J, IX, 200–201]

Riches. Neither will poverty suit every complexion. Socrates and Franklin may well go hungry and in plain clothes, if they like; but there are people who cannot afford this, but whose poverty of nature needs wealth of food and clothes to make them decent.   [J, VIII, 25]

The religion of one age is the literary entertainment of the next. We use in our idlest poetry and discourse the words Jove, Neptune, Mercury, as mere colors, and can hardly believe that they had to the lively Greek the anxious meaning which, in our towns, is given and received in churches when our religious names are used: and we read with surprise the horror of Athens when, one morning, the statues of Mercury in the temples were found broken, and the like consternation was in the city as if, in Boston, all the Orthodox churches should be burned in one night.
[W, X, 105]

It seems as if the present age of words should naturally be followed by an age of silence, when men shall speak only through facts, and so regain their health. We die of words. We are hanged, drawn and quartered by diction-

aries. We walk in the vale of shadows. It is an age of hob-
goblins. . . . When shall we attain to be real, and be born
into the new heaven and earth of nature and truth?

[J, V, 254]

A man signing himself George R——— (of Madison, Wis.)
and who seems to be drunk, writes me, that "the secret of
drunkenness is, that it insulates us in thought, whilst it
unites us in feeling."   [J, IX, 92–93]

Dr. Channing asked Dr. Hare, of Philadelphia, why he
did not go to church. "Because," answered the Doctor,
"the ministers take too much for granted."   [J, VIII, 351]

Vestiges of Creation. What is so ungodly as these polite
bows to God in English books? He is always mentioned in
the most respectful and deprecatory manner, "that august,"
"that almighty," "that adorable providence," etc., etc.

[J, VII, 51–52]

It is very funny to go in to a family where the father
and mother are devoted to the children. You flatter yourself
for an instant that you have secured your friend's ear, for
his countenance brightens; then you discover that he has
just caught the eye of his babe over your shoulder, and is
chirruping to him.   [J, VI, 348]

I like the sentiment of the poor woman who, coming from
a wretched garret in an inland manufacturing town for
the first time to the seashore, gazing at the ocean, said she
was "glad for once in her life to see something which there
was enough of."   [W, VIII, 138–139]

The superlative is as good as the positive, if it be alive.
If man loves the conditioned, he also loves the uncondi-
tioned. We don't wish to sin on the other side, and
to be purists, nor to check the invention of wit or the sally
of humor. 'Tis very different, this weak and wearisome lie,
from the stimulus to the fancy which is given by a romanc-
ing talker who does not mean to be exactly taken—like the

gallant skipper who complained to his owners that he had pumped the Atlantic Ocean three times through his ship on the passage, and 'twas common to strike seals and porpoises in the hold.   [W, X, 171–172]

Bishop Clark, of Rhode Island, told of a dispute in a vestry at Providence between two hot church-members. One said at last, "I should like to know who *you* are."— "Who I am!" cried the other,—"who I am! I am a humble Christian, you damned old heathen, you!"   [J, IX, 322]

The old school of Boston citizens whom I remember in my childhood had great vigor, great noisy bodies; I think a certain sternutatory vigor the like whereof I have not heard again. When Major B. or old Mr. T. H. took out their pocket handkerchiefs at church, it was plain they meant business; they would snort and roar through their noses, like the lowing of an ox, and make all ring again. Ah, it takes a Northender to do that!   [J, IX, 402]

Chapter Thirteen

The World in Brief

*Here are some particularly concentrated examples of that
aphoristic gift which is the* raison d'être *of this anthology.
To be able to present the world in brief, one must be able
to see it all in a single character and as evidence of a single
law. This is the secret of Emerson's genius for compression—he really sees the world as a unity, and he sees all of
it in every moment. "God works in moments"—and seeking
to read the self-same law that is recorded in each moment, the mystic, by force of extreme compression, becomes the wit.*

*Emerson's briefest sayings are witty in their intelligence,
in their impatience, in their independence—all attributes of
the same quality. But they are witty, too, as conversation,
which is so often provocation; he wishes to unsettle, to dazzle, to shock, to persuade—and he does. This is eminently
social writing, addressed to an audience for a particular
effect. His sayings often amuse by the very abruptness and
authority with which they are said. Let no one doubt that
Emerson, though "God-intoxicated," knew his own value,
too. The force with which he speaks always derives from
the pleasure he takes in his particular idiom: the epigram,
the* aperçu, *the stray thought. Many of these sentences cut
to the mark because Emerson felt that he had been visited
by them as laws. He surrendered instantly to them as truth
—which is why, in such arrow-quick sentences, we recognize, along with the familiar nobility of his mind, its light-
ness and ease.*

Nothing is old but the mind.   [W, VIII, 213]

The truth, the hope of any time, must always be sought in the minorities.   [W, VIII, 216]

I like the sayers of No better than the sayers of Yes.
[J, III, 122]

Of all wit's uses the main one
Is to live well with who has none.
[W, IX, 351]

That each should in his house abide,
Therefore was the world so wide.
[W, IX, 354]

This shining moment is an edifice
Which the Omnipotent cannot rebuild.
[W, IX, 350]

Life is in short cycles or periods; rapid rallies, as by a good night's sleep.   [J, IX, 515]

Every new writer is only a new crater of an old volcano.
[J, IX, 555–556]

All the thoughts of a turtle are turtle.   [J, VIII, 495]

Tennyson is a beautiful half of a poet.   [J, V, 57]

There are some men above grief and some men below it.
[J, V, 110]

It is strange, how simple a thing it is to be a man; so simple that almost all fail by overdoing it.   [J, IV, 55]

The grey past, the white future.   [J, IV, 78]

En peu d'heure
Dieu labeure.

God works in moments.   [J, IV, 82]

A wife, a babe, a brother, poverty, and a country, which the Greek had, I have.   [J, IV, 145]

Slavery is an institution for converting men into monkeys.
[J, IV, 200]

Your reading you may use in conversation, but your writing should stop with your own thought.   [J, VI, 41]

Bores are good too. They may help you to a good indignation, if not to a sympathy.   [W, III, 309]

People say law, but they mean wealth.   [J, VI, 86]

Scholars should not carry their memories to balls.
[J, VI, 113]

Balzac has two merits, talent and Paris.   [J, VI, 231]

It makes men very bad to talk good.   [J, VI, 337]

A man of genius is privileged only as far as he is a genius. His dulness is as insupportable as any other dulness. Only success will justify a departure and a license.
[J, VI, 358–359]

Every book is a quotation; and every house is a quotation out of all forests and mines and stone-quarries; and every man is a quotation from all his ancestors.   [W, VIII, 176]

People wish to be settled. It is only as far as they are un-settled that there is any hope for them.   [J, V, 401–402]

The late Dr. Gardiner, in a funeral sermon on some parish-ioner whose virtues did not readily come to mind, honestly said, "He was good at fires."   [W, X, 391]

The witchcraft of sleep divides with truth the empire of our lives.   [W, X, 3]

New actions are the only apologies and explanations of old ones which the noble can bear to offer or to receive.
[W, III, 102–103]

Money, which represents the prose of life, and which is hardly spoken of in parlors without an apology, is, in its effects and laws, as beautiful as roses.   [W, III, 231]

Each man too is a tyrant in tendency, because he would im-pose his idea on others; and their trick is their natural de-fence. Jesus would absorb the race; but Tom Paine or the coarsest blasphemer helps humanity by resisting this exu-berance of power.   [W, III, 239]

A great style of hero draws equally all classes, all the ex-tremes of society, till we say the very dogs believe in him.
[W, VIII, 318]

It [poetry] must be as new as foam and as old as the rock.
[W, VIII, 40]

To live without duties is obscene.   [W, X, 52]

We are born too late for the old and too early for the new faith.   [W, X, 217]

There is an oracle current in the world, that nations die by suicide. The sign of it is the decay of thought.

[W, X, 246]

See a political revolution dogging a book. See armies, institutions, literatures, appearing in the train of some wild Arabian's dream.   [W, X, 253]

He [Shakespeare] is all pulverized into proverbs, and dispersed into human discourse.   [J, VIII, 39]

Love is the bright foreigner, the foreign self.   [J, VIII, 43]

Dante's imagination is the nearest to hands and feet that we have seen.   [J, VIII, 45]

Intellect strips, affection clothes.   [J, VIII, 236]

The poet is the lover loving; the critic is the lover advised.

[J, VIII, 240]

I find that the Americans have no passions, they have appetites.   [J, VIII, 321]

Sin is when a man trifles with himself, and is untrue to his own constitution.   [J, IX, 20]

Everything is the cause of itself.   [J, IX, 20]

The classic unfolds: the romantic adds.   [J, IX, 25]

There is a sort of climate in every man's speech running from hot noon, when words flow like steam and perfume —to cold night, when they are frozen. [J, VII, 553]

I should say, that, in English, only those sentences stand, which are good both for the scholar and the cabman, Latin and Saxon; half and half; perfectly Latin and perfectly English. [J, VII, 561]

There is one other reason for dressing well than I have ever considered, namely, that dogs respect it, and will not attack you in good clothes. [J, VII, 318]

All conversation and writing is rhetoric, and the great secret is to know thoroughly, and not to be affected, and to have a steel spring. [J, VII, 361]

That immensity of condescension in a fat old lubber does not appear at Washington except in men very long distinguished. [J, X, 16]

'Tis bad when believers and unbelievers live in the same manner—I distrust the religion. [J, X, 43]

Nationality is often silly. Every nation believes that the Divine Providence has a sneaking kindness for it. [J, X, 195]

It is easy to read Plato, difficult to read his commentators.
[J, VII, 56]

If an American should wake up some morning and discover that his existence was unnecessary, he would think himself excessively ill-used, and would declare himself instantly against the government of the Universe.
[J, VII, 58]

Whiggism, a feast of shells, idolatrous of the forms of legislature; like a cat loving the house, not the inhabitant.
[J, VII, 99]

No wonder a writer is rare—It requires one inspiration, or transmutation of Nature into thought, to yield him the truth; another inspiration to write it.   [J, VII, 113]

Shakespeare's fault that the world appears so empty. He has educated you with his painted world, and this real one seems a huckster's shop.   [J, VII, 140]

What a pity that the mother and child cannot change states. The child is always awake, and the mother is always asleep.   [J, VII, 173]

A good scholar will find Aristophanes and Hafiz and Rabelais full of American history   [J, VII, 257]

You cannot make a cheap palace.   [J, IX, 89]

Miscellany is as bad as drunkenness.   [J, IX, 133]

The least mistake in sentiment takes all the beauty out of your clothes.   [J, IX, 266]

When our friends die, we not only lose them, but we lose a great deal of life which in the survivors was related to them.   [J, IX, 272]

I like dry light, and hard clouds, hard expressions, and hard manners.   [J, IX, 309]

Blessed are the unconscious. I wish the man to please himself; then he will please me.   [J, IX, 318]

Cannot we let people be themselves, and enjoy life in their own way? You are trying to make that man another *you*. One's enough. [J, IX, 355]

Why have only two or three ways of life, and not thousands? Every man is wanted, and no man is wanted much. [W, III, 240]

The capital defect of cold, arid natures is the want of animal spirits. They seem a power incredible, as if God should raise the dead. [W, VII, 12]

. . . the end of eloquence is—is it not?—to alter in a pair of hours, perhaps in a half hour's discourse, the convictions and habits of years. [W, VII, 64]

Indeed, a man's library is a sort of harem, and I observe that tender readers have a great pudency in showing their books to a stranger. [W, VII, 209]

It is impossible to extricate oneself from the questions in which your age is involved. You can no more keep out of politics than you can keep out of the frost. [J, IX, 369]

The human mind cannot be burned, nor bayonetted, nor wounded, nor missing. [J, IX, 429]

He tears into a book for a sentence as a woodpecker grubs into a tree for a worm. [J, IX, 538]

The worst thing I know of poverty is that if a man is dead, they call him *poor fellow*. [J, VII, 19]

God's ways are parabolic projections that do not return to themselves. [J, VII, 20]

The imaginative-practical. Imagination is suspected, the mechanical is despised; write the solid *and* the ethereal, for the divine. . . .   [J, VII, 31]

God builds his temple in the heart on the ruins of churches and religions.   [W, VI, 204]

Heaven always bears some proportion to earth.
[W, VI, 205]

The secret of heaven is kept from age to age.
[W, IV, 140]

[*On Swedenborg*]   A man should not tell me that he has walked among the angels; his proof is that his eloquence makes me one.   [W, IV, 142]

Iron cannot rust, nor beer sour, nor timber rot, nor calicos go out of fashion, nor money stocks depreciate, in the few swift moments in which the Yankee suffers any one of them to remain in his possession.   [W, II, 235]

I knew a man scared by the rustle of his own hat-band.
[J, IV, 262]

We fancy that men are individuals; but every pumpkin in the field goes through every point of pumpkin history. . . .
[J, VI, 495]

I am always environed by myself: what I am, all things reflect to me.   [J, VI, 503]

Be an opener of doors for such as come after thee, and do not try to make the universe a blind alley.   [J, VI, 525]

It is vain to bawl "constitution" and "patriotism"; these words repeated once too often have a most ironical hoarseness. [J, VI, 531]

In Maine they have not a summer, but a thaw.

[J, VI, 538]

Late in life we live by memory, and in our solstices or periods of stagnation; as the starved camel in the desert lives on his own humps. [W, XII, 94]

I wish there was no more good nature in the world; tomahawks are better. [J, VI, 373]

The poets, the great, have been illustrious wretches who have beggared the world which has beggared them.

[J, VI, 398]

It is for the novelist to make no character act absurdly, but only absurdly as seen by the others. . . . [J, VI, 410]

I respect cats, they seem to have so much else in their heads besides their mess. . . . I prefer a tendency to stateliness to an excess of fellowship. [J, VI, 439]

We love morals until they come to us with mountainous melancholy and grim overcharged rebuke: then we so gladly prefer intellect, the light-maker. [J, VI, 480]

I have no right of nomination in the choice of my friends. Sir, I should be happy to oblige you, but my friends must elect themselves. [J, V, 241]

Progress of the species! why the world is a treadmill.

[J, V, 230]

Reform. The past has baked my loaf, and in the strength of its bread I break up the old oven.   [J, V, 236]

Also I hate Early Poems.   [J, IV, 266]

Imagination is not good for anything unless there be enough.   [J, V, 437]

What is a man but Nature's final success in self-explication?
[J, V, 437]

An autobiography should be a book of answers from one individual to the many questions of the time.   [J, VII, 264]

Criticism should not be querulous and wasting, all knife and root-puller, but guiding, instructive, inspiring, a south wind, not an east wind.   [J, VII, 291]

I am always reminded, and now again by reading last night in Rousseau's *Confessions,* that it is not the events in one's life, but in the faculty of selecting and reporting them, that the interest lies.   [J, VII, 318]

I suppose you could never prove to the mind of the most ingenious mollusk that such a creature as a whale was possible.   [J, VII, 453]

Writing selects only the eminent experiences; Poetry, the supereminent.   [J, VII, 517]

Only write a dozen lines, and rest on your oars forever, you are dear and necessary to the human race and worth all the old trumpery Plutarchs and Platos and Bacons of the world.   [J, VII, 539]

Until history is interesting, it is not yet written.
[W, XII, 298]

The great always introduce us to facts; small men introduce us always to themselves. [W, XII, 314]

The great never with their own consent become a load on the minds they instruct. The more they draw us to them, the farther from them or more independent of them we are, because they have brought us to the knowledge of somewhat deeper than both them and us. [W, XII, 315]

Some men are above grief, and some below it. Few are capable of love. In phlegmatic natures calamity is unaffecting, in shallow natures it is rhetorical. [W, XII, 410]

The three practical rules, then, which I have to offer, are,— 1. Never read any book that is not a year old. 2. Never read any but famed books. 3. Never read any but what you like. . . . [W, VII, 196]

Next to the originator of a good sentence is the first quoter of it. Many will read the book before one thinks of quoting a passage. As soon as he has done this, that line will be quoted east and west. Then there are great ways of borrowing. Genius borrows nobly. When Shakespeare is charged with debts to his authors, Landor replies: "Yet he was more original than his originals. He breathed upon dead bodies and brought them into life." [W, VIII, 191]

We are too civil to books. For a few golden sentences we will turn over and actually read a volume of four or five hundred pages. Even the great books—"Come," say they, "we will give you the key to the world." Each poet, each philosopher says this, and we expect to go like a thunderbolt to the centre. . . . [J, V, 561]

Few know how to read. Women read to find a hero whom they can love; men, for amusement; editors, for something to crib; authors, for something that supports their view: and hardly one reads comprehensively and wisely.

[J, VIII, 277]

They say the insane like a master; so always does the human heart hunger after a leader, a master through truth.

[J, IV, 281]

The loves of flint and iron are naturally a little rougher than those of the nightingale and the rose. [J, VIII, 36]

Every scholar is surrounded by wiser men than he—if they cannot write as well. [W, VII, 244]

An actually existent fly is more important than a possibly existent angel. [*Emerson to Moncure D. Conway*]

The old artist said, *Pingo in eternitatem* [I paint for eternity]; this *eternitatem* for which I paint is not in past or future, but is the height of every living hour.

[*Emerson to Moncure D. Conway*]

LIFE CONSISTS IN WHAT A MAN
IS THINKING OF ALL DAY.

Chapter Fourteen

On Emerson

Few writers have ever aroused so much respect, and so much irritation, as did Emerson. Like so many great religious figures, he was so single and insurrectionary in his opinions, he worked so disturbingly and provokingly on men's hearts, that it was—it is—impossible to regard him as purely a literary figure with technical achievements to his credit. He assumed so much—so much, indeed, that the gratitude he aroused was overmatched by the quite violent revulsion he aroused in others.

In making up this section we have relied—not deliberately but inevitably—on the opinions of writers, for no other class of readers has responded to Emerson with so much intensity. From John Quincy Adams, no mean writer himself, to Whitman, whose career would not have been possible without Emerson, the record of opinions, arranged alphabetically, has its abundant humor because of the characteristic intensity with which writers respond to each other and the particular intensity with which they respond to Emerson. It is worth noting here, since even professional students of American literature are so rarely aware of Emerson's importance to great European writers like Nietzsche, how many first-rate figures Emerson has influenced—and provoked—from Herman Melville to D. H. Lawrence, from both Henry and William James to George Santayana. In this gallery of opinions, Emerson is seen in the company of his peers. Here he stands judged by those revolutionary and original figures in the history of modern literature who, whatever else they may think of him, have always known him as one of their own.

A young man named Ralph Waldo Emerson . . . after failing in the every-day vocations of a Unitarian preacher and schoolmaster, starts a new doctrine of transcendentalism, declares all the old revelations superannuated and worn out, and announces the approach of new revelations and prophecies. Garrison and the non-resistant abolitionists, Brownson and the Marat democrats, phrenology and animal magnetism, all come in, furnishing each some plausible rascality as an ingredient for the bubbling cauldron of religion and politics. *John Quincy Adams*

Say whatever may be said in praise or dispraise of him, this is the master-mind of our country and time. Match him who shall from England, Germany, France! Nor shall Hungary's and Italy's Kossuth and Mazzini abase his titles. Far less is the American theirs than they are his. . . . Continents and countries have their equipments, and what were ours with Emerson? Take him from the population, from the Lyceum and Library, smite this Orion from our Zodiac, and what of national splendor and ideal significance is fallen! Emerson is as necessary to our hemisphere as the day-star and the evening and morning maiden who feeds her urn at its beams. *Bronson Alcott*

We have not in Emerson a great poet, a great writer, a great philosophy-maker. His relation to us is not that of one of those personages; yet it is a relation of, I think, even superior importance. His relation to us is more like that of the Roman Emperor Marcus Aurelius . . . he is the friend and aider of those who would live in the spirit. Emerson is the same. . . .

One can scarcely overrate the importance of thus holding fast to happiness and hope. It gives to Emerson's work an invaluable virtue. As Wordsworth's poetry is, in my judgment, the most important work done in verse, in our language, during the present century, so Emerson's *Essays* are, I think, the most important work done in prose.

Matthew Arnold

I should never forget the Visitor, who years ago in the Desert descended on us, out of the clouds as it were, and made one day there look like enchantment for us, and left me weeping that it was only *one* day. When I think of America, it is of you—neither Harriet Martineau nor any one else succeeds in giving me a more extended idea of it. When I wish to see America it is still you, and those that are yours.

Jane Welsh Carlyle

My friend! you know not what you have done for me there. It was long decades of years that I had heard nothing but the infinite jangling and jabbering, and inarticulate twittering and screeching, and my soul had sunk down sorrowful, and said there is no articulate speaking then any more, and thou art solitary among stranger-creatures? and lo, out of the West comes a clear utterance, clearly recognizable as a *man's* voice, and I *have* a kinsman and a brother. . . .

You are a new era, my man, in your new huge country. . . . And if the Devil will be pleased to set all the Popularities *against* you and evermore against you—perhaps that is of all things the very kindest any *Angel* could do.

By the bye, I ought to say, the sentences are very *brief;* and did not, in my *sheet* reading, always entirely cohere for me. Pure genuine Saxon; strong and simple; of a clearness, of a beauty— But they did not, sometimes, rightly stick to their foregoers and their followers: the paragraph not as a beaten *ingot,* but as a beautiful square *bag of duck-shot* held together by canvas! *Thomas Carlyle*

The only thing we really admire is personal liberty. Those who fought for it and those who enjoyed it are our heroes. . . .

Emerson represents a protest against the tyranny of democracy. He is the most recent example of elemental hero-worship. His opinions are absolutely unqualified except by his temperament. He expresses a form of belief in the importance of the individual which is independent of any personal relations he has with the world. It is as if a man had been withdrawn from the earth and dedicated to condensing and embodying this eternal idea—the value of the individual soul—so vividly, so vitally, that his words could not die, yet in such illusive and abstract forms that by no chance and by no power could his creed be used for purposes of tyranny. . . .

There is an implication of a fundamental falsehood in every bit of Transcendentalism, including Emerson. That falsehood consists in the theory of the self-sufficiency of each individual, men and women alike. . . . If an inhabitant of another planet should visit the earth, he would receive, on the whole, a truer notion of human life by attending an Italian opera than he would by reading Emerson's volumes. He would learn from the Italian opera that there were two sexes; and this, after all, is probably the fact with which the education of such a stranger ought to begin. . . .

If a soul be taken and crushed by democracy till it utter a cry, that cry will be Emerson. *John Jay Chapman*

He is the first man I have seen. *George Eliot*

Emerson's greatness is preeminently that of a verbal artist. . . . The artist in him, the artist in words, was dominant— exiled from his verse to be the tyrant of his prose. Such a word-watcher, such a word-catcher, such a weigher-in-the-balance of niceties of rhythm and order, as well as of phrase, has seldom been. *H. W. Garrod*

Of all the writers of our day you seem to me to understand the genius of the time most profoundly, to anticipate our future most clearly.

You write so that everyone reading your words must think that you had thought of him alone. The love which you have for all mankind is felt so strongly that one thinks it impossible that you should not have thought of single preferred persons, among whom the reader counts himself. What a happiness for a country to possess such a man! When I think of America I think of you, and America appears to me as the first country of the world.

Hermann Grimm

. . . that everlasting rejector of all that is, and seeker for he knows not what. . . .   *Nathaniel Hawthorne*

Mr. Emerson is bounteous and gracious, but thin, dry, angular, in intercourse as in person.

Thomas Wentworth Higginson

. . . the only firebrand of my youth that burns to me as brightly as ever, is Emerson.

Justice Oliver Wendell Holmes, Jr.

I like Emerson to read, I guess.   *Edward Hopper*

It was his great fortune to have been mostly misunderstood, and to have reached the dense intelligence of his fellow-men after a whole lifetime of perfectly simple and lucid appeal, and his countenance expressed the patience and forbearance of a wise man content to bide his time. It would be hard to persuade people now that Emerson once represented to the popular mind all that was most hopelessly impossible, and that in a certain sort he was a national joke, the type of the incomprehensible, the byword of the poor paragrapher. He had perhaps disabused the community somewhat by presenting himself here and there as a lecturer, and talking face to face with men in terms which they could not refuse to find as clear as they were wise; he was more and more read, by certain persons, here and there; but we are still so far behind him in the reach of his far-thinking that it need not be matter of wonder that twenty years before his death he was the most misunderstood man in America. Yet in that twilight where he dwelt he loomed large upon the imagination; the minds that could not conceive him were still aware of his greatness. *William Dean Howells*

He did something better than any one else; he had a particular faculty, which has not been surpassed, for speaking to the soul in a voice of direction and authority. There have been many spiritual voices appealing, consoling, reassuring, exhorting, or even denouncing and terrifying, but none has had just that firmness and just that purity. It penetrates further, it seems to go back to the roots of our feelings, to where conduct and manhood begin. . . . *Henry James*

Oh, you man without a *handle!* Shall one never be able to help himself out of you, according to his needs, and be dependent only upon your fitful tippings-up?

I found, in fact, before I had been with him a week, that the immense superiority I ascribed to him was altogether personal or practical—by no means intellectual; that it came to him by birth or genius like a woman's beauty or charm of manners; that no other account was to be given of it in truth than that Emerson himself was an unsexed woman, a veritable fruit of almighty power in the sphere of our *nature*.

He was . . . fundamentally treacherous to civilization, without being at all aware himself of the fact. . . . He appeared to me utterly unconscious of himself as either good or evil. He had no conscience, in fact, and lived by perception, which is an altogether lower or less spiritual faculty. . . .

Incontestably the main thing about him, however . . . was that he unconsciously brought you face to face with the infinite in humanity. When I looked upon myself, or upon the ordinary rabble of ecclesiastics and politicians, everything in us seemed ridiculous. When I looked upon Emerson, these same undivine things were what gave *him* his manifest divine charm. *Henry James, Sr.*

Emerson himself was a real seer. He could perceive the full squalor of the individual fact, but he could also see the transfiguration. . . .

Be how it may, this is Emerson's revelation:—The point of any pen can be an epitome of reality; the commonest person's act, if genuinely actuated, can lay hold on eternity. This vision is the headspring of all his outpourings; and it is for this truth, given to no previous literary artist to express in such penetratingly persuasive tones, that posterity will reckon him a prophet, and, perhaps neglecting other pages, piously turn to those that convey this message. His life was one long conversation with the invisible divine, expressing itself through individuals and particulars:—"So nigh is grandeur to our dust, so near is God to man!"

William James

Well, Emerson is a great man still: or a great individual. And heroes are heroes still, though their banners may decay, and stink.

It is true that lilies may fester. And virtues likewise. The great Virtue of one age has a trick of smelling far worse than weeds in the next. . . .

When Emerson says: "I am surrounded by messengers of God who send me credentials day by day," then all right for him. But he cosily forgot that there are many messengers. He knew only a sort of smooth-shaven Gabriel. . . . There are other cherubim with outlandish names bringing very different messages than those Ralph Waldo got: Israfel, and even Mormon. And a whole bunch of others. But Emerson had a stone-deaf ear for all except a nicely aureoled Gabriel *qui n'avait pas de quoi.*

Emerson listened to one sort of message and only one. To all the rest he was blank. Ashtaroth and Ammon are gods as well, and hand out their own credentials. But Ralph Waldo wasn't having any. They could never ring *him* up. He was only connected on the Ideal phone. "We are all aiming to be idealists," says Emerson, "and covet the society of those who make us so, as the sweet singer, the orator, the ideal painter."

Well, we're pretty sick of the ideal painters and the up-lifting singers. As a matter of fact we have worked the ideal bit of our nature to death, and we shall go crazy if we can't start working from some other bit. Idealism now is a sick nerve, and the more you rub on it the worse you feel after-wards. . . .

Emerson believes in having the courage to treat all men as equals. It takes some courage *not* to treat them so now.

"Shall I not treat all men as gods?" he cries.

If you like, Waldo, but we've got to pay for it, when you've made them *feel* that they are gods. A hundred million American godlets is rather much for the world to deal with.

The fact of the matter is, all those gorgeous inrushes of exaltation and spiritual energy which made Emerson a great man, now make us sick. They are with us a drug habit. . . .

I like Emerson's real courage. I like his wild and genuine belief in the Oversoul and the inrushes he got from it. But it is a museum-interest. Or else it is a taste of the old drug to the old spiritual drug-fiend in me.

We've got to have a different sort of sardonic courage. And the sort of credentials we are due to receive from the god in the shadow would have been real bones out of hell-broth to Ralph Waldo. . . .   *D. H. Lawrence*

We used to walk in from the country to the Masonic Tem-ple (I think it was), through the crisp winter night, and listen to that thrilling voice of his, so charged with subtle meaning and subtle music, as shipwrecked men on a raft to the hail of a ship that came with unhoped-for food and rescue. Cynics might say what they liked. Did our own imaginations transfigure dry remainder-biscuit into am-brosia? At any rate, he brought us *life,* which, on the whole, is no bad thing. Was it all transcendentalism? magic-lantern pictures on mist? . . . it was not so. The delight and the benefit were that he put us in communication with a larger style of thought, sharpened our wits with a more pungent phrase, gave us ravishing glimpses of an ideal under the dry husk of our New England; made us conscious of the supreme and everlasting originality of whatever bit of soul might be in any of us. . . . And who that saw the audience will ever forget it, where every one still capable of fire, or longing to renew in himself the half-forgotten sense of it, was gathered? . . .

Emerson's oration was more disjointed than usual, even with *him*. It began nowhere and ended everywhere, and yet, as always with that divine man, it left you feeling that something beautiful had passed that way—something more beautiful than anything else, like the rising and setting of stars. Every possible criticism might have been made on it but one—that it was not noble. There was a tone in it that awakened all elevating associations. He boggled, he lost his place, he had to put on his glasses; but it was as if a creature from some fairer world had lost his way in our fogs, and it was *our* fault, not his. It was chaotic, but it was all such stuff as stars are made of, and you couldn't help feeling that, if you waited awhile, all that was nebulous would be whirled into planets, and would assume the mathematical gravity of system. All through it I felt something in me that cried, "Ha, ha, to the sound of the trumpets!"

James Russell Lowell

Nay, I do not oscillate in Emerson's rainbow, but prefer rather to hang myself in mine own halter than swing in any other man's swing. Yet I think Emerson is more than a brilliant fellow. Be his stuff begged, borrowed, or stolen, or of his own domestic manufacture he is an uncommon man. Swear he is a humbug—then is he no common humbug. . . . There is a something about every man elevated above mediocrity, which is, for the most part, instinctively perceptible. This I see in Mr. Emerson. And, frankly, for the sake of the argument, let us call him a fool;— Then had I rather be a fool than a wise man.— I love all men who *dive*. . . .

I could readily see in Emerson, notwithstanding his merit, a gaping flaw. It was, the insinuation, that had he lived in those days when the world was made, he might have offered some valuable suggestions. *Herman Melville*

There have been four very singular and truly poetical men in this century who have arrived at a mastership of prose, for which otherwise this century is not suited, owing to lack of poetry. . . . Not to take Goethe into account, for he is reasonably claimed by the century that produced him, I look only on Giacomo Leopardi, Prosper Mérimée, Ralph Waldo Emerson, and Walter Savage Landor . . . as worthy to be called masters of prose. *Friedrich Nietzsche*

Little more than a respectful imitation of Carlyle.

Mr. Ralph Waldo Emerson belongs to a class of gentlemen with whom we have no patience whatever—the mystic for mysticism's sake. *Edgar Allan Poe*

A full philosophy, full persuasion, a critique of American life, Emerson never offered. His communications were broken, lyrical, rhapsodic; his writing and speech had the air of improvisation. Even his poetry has the same strange air of incompletion: it is that of a born lyrist struggling with a strange language in a new country of the mind, and unable to find an unpremeditated freedom.

Emotion had a large part in Emerson's writing, but it was seldom a personal emotion, most often the revelation of some common happy mood. "I read with joy some of the auspicious signs of the coming days." He followed the form of the native monologue, in which the first person had been steadily used, the personal revelation of fact or feeling consistently avoided, which had moved toward the generic, including the many experiences rather than the one. . . . In Emerson the interior voice was heard unmistakably in reverie or soliloquy. He has often been linked with the Puritan divines by way of the pulpit, but these men attempted to unroll the voice of God; their own part was impersonal. In Emerson the personal inner voice spoke; and this belonged not to the realm of introspection cultivated by the Puritan, but to that other realm of the plain Yankee, who consciously listened to his own mind, whose deliberate speech had room for undertones and further meanings.

Constance Rourke

Reality eluded him. He was far from being, like a Plato or an Aristotle, past master in the art and the science of life. But his mind was endowed with unusual plasticity, with unusual spontaneity and liberty of movement—it was a fairyland of thoughts and fancies. He was like a young god making experiments in creation: he blotched the work, and always began on a new and better plan. Every day he said, "Let there be light," and every day the light was new. His sun, like that of Heraclitus, was different every morning.

George Santayana

His mind is like a rag-picker's basket, full of all manner of trash. His books are valuable, however, for the very reason they are of no earthly account. They illustrate the utter worthlessness of the philosophy of free society. Egoism, or rather Manism (if we may coin a word), propounded in short scraps, tags, and shreds of sentences may do very well for a people who have no settled opinions in politics, religion or morals, and have lived for forty years on pure fanaticisms. We of the South require something better than this no-system. Your fragmentary philosopher, of the *Emerson* stamp, who disturbs the beliefs of common folk, without again composing or attempting to compose them with a higher and purer faith, is a curse to society. Such a man ought to be subject to the mild punishment of perpetual confinement, with plenty of pens, ink and paper. Burn his writings as fast as they come from his table, and bury the writer quietly in the back yard of the prison as soon as he is dead. If in early life, the speculative lobes of his brain had been eaten out with nitric acid, *Emerson* would have made a better poet than any New England has yet given us. As it is, he is a moral nuisance. He ought to be abated by act of Congress and his works suppressed.

Southern Literary Messenger, April, 1861

Well, I suppose there's a great many things that Mr. Emerson knows that I couldn't understand; but I *know* that there's a damn sight of things that I know that he don't know anything about. *Samuel Staples [Concord neighbor: sometime bar-tender, clerk, constable and jailer, deputy-sheriff, representative to the General Court, auctioneer, real-estate agent and gentleman-farmer]*

It is as character and not as accomplishment or education, that he holds his own in all comparisons with his contemporaries, the fine, crystallized mind, the keen, clear-faceted thinker and seer. I loved more Agassiz and Lowell, but we shall have many a Lowell and Agassiz before we see Emerson's like again. Attainments will be greater, and discovery and accomplishments will surpass themselves as we go on, but to *be,* as Emerson was, is absolute and complete existence. *W. J. Stillman*

If Emerson went to hell the devil would not know what do do with him. *Edward Thompson Taylor ["Father Taylor"]*

P.M.—Talked, or tried to talk, with R. W. E. Lost my time —nay, almost my identity. He, assuming a false opposition where there was no difference of opinion, talked to the wind—told me what I knew—and I lost my time trying to imagine myself somebody else to oppose him.
         Henry David Thoreau [Journal, May 24, 1853]

. . . his central doctrine is that of submission to emotion, which for the pantheist is a kind of divine instigation: an inadmissible doctrine, for it eliminates at a stroke both choice and the values that serve as a basis for choice, it substitutes for a doctrine of values a doctrine of equivalence, thus rendering man an automaton and paralyzing all genuine action, so that Emerson's acceptable acts of expression are accidental poems or epigrams drawing their only nutriment from the fringe or from beyond the fringe of his doctrine. . . . his doctrine abandoned the last connection with Christianity and the last support for personal dignity,

and the difference, though it does not appear in his life as a man, is already apparent in the whimsical facility of feeling to be discerned equally in his prose and in his verse. . . .
Yvor Winters

His quality, his meaning has the quality of the light of day, which startles nobody. You cannot put your finger upon it yet there is nothing more palpable, nothing more wonderful, nothing more vital and refreshing. There are some things in the expression of this philosoph, this poet, that are full mates of the best, the perennial masters, and will so stand in fame and the centuries. America in the future, in her long train of poets and writers, while knowing more vehement and luxuriant ones, will, I think, acknowledge nothing nearer [than] this man, the actual beginner of the whole procession—and certainly nothing purer, cleaner, sweeter, more canny, none, after all, more thoroughly her own and native. The most exquisite taste and caution are in him, always saving his feet from passing beyond the limits, for he is transcendental of limits, and you see underneath the rest a secret proclivity, American maybe, to dare and violate and make escapades. *Walt Whitman*

Biographical Sketch

Ralph Waldo Emerson was born in Boston, May 25, 1803. His father, William Emerson, a clergyman, died in 1811, and Ralph grew up under the tutelage of his mother and his strong-willed and gifted aunt, Mary Moody Emerson. Between 1813 and 1817, he attended the Boston Latin School. After four years at Harvard (1817-1821), Emerson taught school and studied at the Harvard Divinity School (1821-1828). A short trip to Florida in the winter of 1826-1827 for reasons of health marked his first venture outside the precincts of New England.

In the early spring of 1829, Emerson became pastor of a Boston church and in the fall of that year married Ellen Louisa Tucker. Her death in February, 1831, hurt him cruelly although outwardly he remained tranquil. In 1832, he gave up his pastorate and made the first of his three trips to Europe. His meeting with Thomas Carlyle occurred in August, 1833. After his return to America, he married Lydia Jackson ("my Lydian Queen") who bore him a son, Waldo, in October, 1836. It was in this year, too, that he published "Nature," his first transcendental manifesto. His *Essays, First Series* appeared in 1841, and between 1842 (the year his son, Waldo, died) and 1844, he edited the *Dial,* the organ of the Transcendentalists. In the succeeding years he published *Essays, Second Series* (1844), *Poems* (1847), *Nature, Addresses and Lectures* (1849), *Representative Men* (1850), *English Traits* (1856), *Conduct of Life* (1860), *Society and Solitude* (1870), and *Letters and Social Aims* (1875).

As a lecturer and essayist, Emerson divided his time largely between Concord and Boston, but he managed to visit various parts of New England and his lecture tours took him to New York and finally beyond the Alleghenies to the states of the old Northwest. By nature retiring and reluctant to participate actively in the political and social conflicts of the day, his convictions forced him to speak out against slavery and to protest against those forces and institutions which in his eyes threatened the sanctity of the individual. But he much preferred to confine his social life to the company of his chosen intimates—men or women like Henry David Thoreau (his neighbor and disciple), Amos Bronson Alcott (whose enraptured conversation he found so stimulating), William Ellery Channing (a favorite walking companion), Margaret Fuller (a formidable intellectual and passionate woman whom Emerson admired enormously) and her protegé, Caroline Sturgis. In the post Civil War years, Emerson gradually retired into his private mental solitude although from time to time he addressed himself to the world. In April, 1882, this "austerely genial" man died in Concord.

Bibliography

The writing on Emerson is vast and various, but the following selected list may prove helpful for readers who are curious about his life and ideas. Ralph R. Rusk's *The Life of Ralph Waldo Emerson* (Scribners, 1949), the most authoritative and detailed of the many Emerson biographies, successfully challenges the stereotype of the "Concord seer" which Emerson's commentators have unquestionably accepted for so many years. A more incisively critical study of Emerson's mind is Stephen E. Whicher's *Freedom and Fate. An Inner Life of Ralph Waldo Emerson* (University of Pennsylvania Press, 1953). *Emerson Handbook* by Frederick Ives Carpenter contains succinct summaries of Emerson's life, ideas, and influence. Significant explanations of Emersonian esthetic doctrines may be found in F. O. Matthiessen, *American Renaissance: Art and Expression in the Age of Emerson and Whitman* (Oxford, 1941); Vivian C. Hopkins, *Spires of Form. A Study of Emerson's Aesthetic Theory* (Harvard University Press, 1951); and Sherman Paul, *Emerson's Angle of Vision* (Harvard University Press, 1952). Perry G. E. Miller's anthology of Emerson's Transcendental contemporaries, *The Transcendentalists* (Harvard University Press, 1950) provides an illuminating background for Emerson's thought and influence. John Jay Chapman's remarkable essay, "Emerson," originally published in 1898, is included together with documents on the relation between Emerson and Whitman in Edmund Wilson's *The Shock of Recognition* (Universal Library, Volume I).

Index

Accuracy, beauty of, 240
Action
  affirmation through, 143
  raw material of thought, 24
  rewards of, 25
  spontaneous, 138
  superiority of, to thought,
    118
Acton, Massachusetts, 260
Adam, 148
Adams, John, 213
Adams, John Quincy, on Emerson, 370
Addison, Joseph, 34, 231
Address to the Divinity College, 326
Admetus, 156
Affection
  formality in, 170
  intellect compared, 360
  See also Friendship *and* Love
Agassiz, Louis, 299, 343
Age
  conservatism of, 195–96
  humiliation of, 344
  pains of, 48
  rewards of, 55
Age of Revolution
  advantages of, 60, 186
  characterized by hatred of
    books, 181
Alcott, Bronson, 169, 213,
  243–44, 299, 303, 333
  as hater of books, 181

characterized, 296–97
  on Emerson, 370
Alexander the Great, 316
Ambition
  Emerson's lack of, 329
  Thoreau's lack of, criticized,
    308
America
  democratic benefits of, 58–
    59
  greatness and failure of,
    180–210
  lack of genius in, 267–68
  materialism of, 269
  native culture of, 89
  need for poets of, 329
  office of, 179–80
  Webster as typical of, 295
American Notes (Dickens), 184
Amerigo Vespucci, 281
Amurath, Sultan, 232
Analogy, value of, 123
Ancient subjects, poets' use of,
  155
Animal Magnetism, 351
Antaeus, 156
Antiquity, 243, 246
Apollo, 156
Appearances
  as governors of men, 66
  character revealed by, 68
  stripped by proverbs, 232–
    33
Apples, 260

Man (cont.)
Jesus's appreciation of, 157–58
many-sided duties of, 144
office of, 357
oneness of, 78, 142–43
position of, in creation, 136–37
power of, 90
power of, derived from God, 129–30
power of, within himself, 99
relation of, to nature, 67, 106, 123, 136, 366
self-consciousness of, 69
woman's attractiveness to, 176
"Manifest destiny" for America, true meaning of, 180
Mann, Horace, 213
Manners, character revealed by, 97–98
Marlowe, Christopher, 240
Marvell, Andrew, 94
Massinger, Philip, 316
Materialism
criticized, 342
falseness of, 190–91
pointlessness of, 182
value of, to English literature, 275–77
Maturity, trials and rewards of, 48
Mediocrity
in books, 249
of the English, 284
Melancholy, in English race, 272–73
Melville, Herman, on Emerson, 377–78
Memory
independence of, 351–52
of poetry, 24
Mephistopheles, 225–27
Merchants
aimlessness of, 185
poverty of, 345–46
Michaelangelo, 118, 237, 242, 288, 317
Milnes, R. M., 327

Milton, John, 95, 99, 231, 232, 233, 324, 325
Mind
as creator of beauty, 126
as symbolized in nature, 110–12
effect of convention on, 65
exploring the, 75
isolation of, 215
nature as inspiring the, 37–38
oneness of, 143
unknowability of, 152
Mirabeau, Honoré, 213, 311
Miracles, 157
Mississippi River, 266–67
Mob
advantages of, over intellectuals, 68
as characteristic of the age, 65
orators as leading, 220
stupidity of, 87
Montaigne, Michel, 232, 233, 244, 317
Montesquieu, Charles de Secondat, 122
Moral judgment, 219–20
Moral perfection, 324–25
Moral principle
failure caused by lack of, 195
importance of, 96
intellect as limiting, 146
nature as demonstrating, 116
Moses, 99
Music, 118
Musketaquit River, 28
Mystic and poet, 153
Myths, 220, 352

Nantucket, 261–62
Napoleon. *See* Bonaparte
Nations
best moments of, 214
evaluation of, 218
Nature
as archetype of art, 126–27
as correlative of mind, 143
as field of the scholar, 78–80